ROMAN LAW & COMMON LAW

Roman Law & Common Law

A Comparison in Outline

by

THE LATE

W. W. BUCKLAND

and

ARNOLD D. McNAIR, K.C., LL.D.

Fellow of Gonville and Caius College

Second Edition Revised by

F. H. LAWSON, D.C.L.

*Professor of Comparative Law, Fellow of
Brasenose College, Oxford*

CAMBRIDGE

AT THE UNIVERSITY PRESS

1952

PUBLISHED BY
THE SYNDICS OF THE CAMBRIDGE UNIVERSITY PRESS
London Office: Bentley House, N.W. 1
American Branch: New York

Agents for Canada, India, and Pakistan: Macmillan

First edition   1936
Second edition 1952

Printed in Great Britain at the University Press, Cambridge
(Brooke Crutchley, University Printer)

CONTENTS

PREFACE

It will be convenient to state what this book is and what
it is not. It is far from being a comprehensive statement
of Roman law and common law comparatively treated. It
is rather a comparison of some of the leading rules and
institutions of the two systems. One of us many years ago
produced a small book entitled *Equity in Roman Law*,[1]
the aim of which was to show the way in which the Roman
lawyer worked. The institutions with which he dealt were
subordinated to the way in which he worked on them, and
an attempt was made to show that, working on institutions
often very differently shaped, he handled them in ways
very similar to those of English lawyers and reached
results, especially in the field covered by modern English
equity, astonishingly like theirs. In this book, on the
other hand, it is the rules and institutions themselves that
are compared. These are no doubt to some extent the
work of the lawyers, but that is not true of the most basic
notions: these were formed in their essentials long before
there was such a thing as the professional study of law.
They may be regarded as given, as not being the lawyers'
work but the materials on which they worked, moulded
however into the form in which we know them from the
sources by many generations of lawyers and, no doubt,
politicians.

Least of all does this book attempt to estimate the influence of Roman law upon English law, as has been done
by the late Lord Justice Scrutton in his Yorke Prize
Essay, by Dr Oliver in *Cambridge Legal Essays* and by
Professor Mackintosh in his *Roman Law in Modern Prac-*

---

[1] By W. W. Buckland, published in 1911 by the University of London
Press, which has been kind enough to allow us to use parts of the book in the
preparation of this volume.

tice. Our interest lies not in the borrowing by England from Rome but in examining the independent approach of the two peoples and their lawyers to the same facts of human life, sometimes with widely different, sometimes with substantially identical, results. For our belief is that one of the main juridical features of this century must be a big advance in the comparative study of law; and one of the obstacles to that advance is the difficulty which the Continental lawyer deriving much of his mode of thought from the Roman law, and the Anglo-Saxon lawyer with his independent heritage, have in understanding one another.

It will be seen that this book assumes in its readers a greater knowledge of the common law than of Roman law and in consequence deals more lightly with the former and cites no authority for many of the more familiar rules. The expression 'common law' in its title is used in the sense in which a 'common law' country is contrasted with a country which has 'received' the civil law. At the same time it so happens, and largely because of the earlier publication of *Equity in Roman Law*, that the English rules and institutions described in this book come more from the common law than from equity. Finally it must be noted that the subject is the common law as understood in England. In its adaptation to the conditions of what are now the United States of America it has diverged in some respects from the original pattern. With these divergencies it was impossible to deal.

Those who are acquainted with the work of the two authors will have little difficulty in assigning responsibility for the contents of this book. But, though the original scheme and most of the preliminary work are due to the senior partner, every chapter is in fact the result of collaboration.

Cambridge 1936

PREFACE TO THE SECOND EDITION

It was originally intended that I should merely take the place, so far as I could hope to do so, of the late Professor Buckland in the partnership which produced this book; but Sir Arnold McNair soon found that his other duties made too great demands on his time, and asked me to undertake the full task of preparing a new edition. In the end therefore, although Sir Arnold has from time to time given me help for which I am most grateful, the responsibility for this edition is entirely mine.

I have tried not to change the general character of the book; but I have not merely brought it up to date, by taking account of alterations in English law or of the constantly changing views held on Roman law. Indeed little has needed to be done in either direction, for the statements on Roman law were for the most part uncontroversial, and the parts of English law chosen for comparison were seldom such as undergo serious changes in a short space of time. Moreover, the book was never intended to be a compendium of Roman and Common law, and a display of learning was far from the thoughts of either author. On the other hand, they did intend a comparison, and it was obvious to me from the start that the comparison must be brought up to date. What was not so obvious was how far I should incorporate in the book the conclusions to which I had myself come during the last fifteen years. I had little difficulty in deciding to include additional comparisons which had not occurred to the authors, but which they might well have made had their attention been directed to the points in question, or had the state of English law at the time been such as to make comparison worth while. An example will be found in the section on soldiers' wills, and another, of a slightly different kind, in the section dealing with the relation between the general law of contract and the law of the particular contracts. All such alterations and additions have been made without emphasis, and the reader who wishes to detect them must look for differences of style or have recourse to the last edition.

On a number of points I was led to take a different view from that of the authors; and while not feeling at liberty to substitute my own statement for theirs, I could not withhold it in justice to the reader or myself. I have adopted the compromise of letting the original text stand, sometimes with minor alterations of an uncontroversial character, and adding to it an excursus of my own. Perhaps this edition may exhibit unduly my peculiar interests; I can only plead that no comparative lawyer can be armed at all points, and that it is better to follow one's bent than to strive for a shallow evenness of treatment. If my interests do not always coincide with those of the original authors, I have at any rate not excluded anything of theirs, and the result is, I hope, merely an added richness.

Above all, I have not tried to make the book more systematic than it was. I do not see how a comparison between two laws can be systematic, and I think Buckland would have agreed with one of the profoundest remarks in Holmes's letters to Pollock:[1] 'A man's system is forgotten: only his *aperçus* remain.'

F.H.L.

I must take this opportunity of expressing to Professor Lawson the gratitude of Professor Buckland's daughter and myself for the combination of skill, care and learning which he has brought to the preparation of this new edition. I am confident that it will be a source of deep satisfaction to Professor Buckland's friends to learn that we succeeded in inducing Professor Lawson to undertake this task.

A.D. M^cN.

[1] *The Pollock-Holmes Letters*, ii. 52.

INTRODUCTION

As stated in the Preface, the purpose of this book is a comparison of some of the leading rules and institutions of Roman law and English law. This is in no way new. Apart from earlier work, Professor Pringsheim, some years ago, dealt with the matter at Cambridge.[1] Professor Schulz's *Principles of Roman Law* contains much on the topic.[2] But these writers are mainly concerned with striking resemblances which they find. Dean Roscoe Pound, however, in his brilliant *Spirit of the Common Law*, is concerned to point out differences between the Roman conceptions and ours. In fact, however, his comparison is in the main not between the common law and the law of the Romans but between the common law and the law of the Civilians.[3] The central notion of the developed Romanist system, he says, is to secure and effectuate the will. The Romanist thinks in terms of willed transactions, the common lawyer in terms of legal relations. But this 'Willenstheorie' is not Roman. It was developed by the nineteenth-century Pandectists,[4] under the influence of Kant, who makes it clear that he is not dealing with any actual system of law. For the view that the Romanist thinks in terms of willed transactions rather than of relations Dean Pound gives terminological evidence, but it would not be difficult to find evidence of the same character for the contrary proposition. The point need not be pressed, for Dean Pound is well aware of the distinction between the ancient and

[1] See *Cambridge Law Journal*, v. p. 347.

[2] It is dealt with in some contributions to the Congresso Internazionale di Diritto Romano, Bologna, 1933.

[3] Much the same is true of Lord Macmillan's stimulating lecture, *Two Ways of Thinking*, 1934, Cambridge.

[4] Adumbrated in the seventeenth and eighteenth centuries, but everything exists before it is born.

the modern Roman law.[1] It may be a paradox, but it seems to be the truth that there is more affinity between the Roman jurist and the common lawyer than there is between the Roman jurist and his modern civilian successor. Both the common lawyer and the Roman jurist avoid generalisations and, so far as possible, definitions. Their method is intensely casuistic. They proceed from case to case, being more anxious to establish a good working set of rules, even at the risk of some logical incoherence which may, sooner or later, create a difficulty, than to set up anything like a logical system. That is not the method of the Pandectist. For him the law is a set of rules to be deduced from a group of primary principles, the statement of which constitutes the 'Allgemeiner Teil' of his structure. It is true that he has to make concessions to popular needs and that the superstructure is not quite so securely based on these fundamental principles as might have been expected. But the point of interest is that his method is not that of the Roman or of the common lawyer.

In spite of this affinity of the Roman jurist and the common lawyer the two systems present a number of outstanding differences, which are discussed in some detail in the succeeding chapters. The notion of the family is entirely different. For the Romans it is a civil conception. Strangers in blood could become members of the family by adoption from the earliest times. With us it may be called a natural conception, resting on marriage and the blood tie. For though we have recently introduced into our law what we call adoption, it was until still more recently adoption only in name and had no effect in the law of succession. The clear-cut Roman conception of *dominium* and the sharp distinction between possession and ownership are not found in our system. Indeed the fact that wrongful withholding of another person's property is regarded by our Courts as an attack on the 'right of

[1] See, e.g., his *Interpretations of Legal History*, pp. 35, 55.

possession' and handled as a tort, with the result that in some branches of the law certain cases of possession are called 'special property', might almost lead an incautious observer to think that our common law had managed to dispense with the notion of property.

The Roman law gives us a conception of *hereditas* as an entity, almost a person. It 'sustinet personam defuncti'. The rights and obligations of the deceased person vest in it, and it in turn transmits them to the *heres*, who in turn is a universal successor. How far these notions are 'classical' need not be here considered: they are plain in the sources. Our law knows nothing of *hereditas* as an entity, or of the *heres* as universal successor, though the executor or administrator under the property legislation of 1945 bears a superficial resemblance to him. The primary function of the Roman Will is the appointment of a successor: that of our Will is to regulate the devolution of property. But a large degree of freedom of testation is a feature of both systems. Both peoples exhibit the same dislike of intestacy and the same desire to do what one likes with one's own after death. Our power of post-mortem disposition disappeared as regards land for some centuries, but the instinct of the people reasserted itself by means of the Use, and later the power of testamentary disposition was extended to such property by legislation. In both systems testators have much power in controlling the destination of their property, in spite of restrictions dictated by public policy and imposed either by legislation or by judicial decision. In Roman law this power was very small at first, suddenly and immensely expanded under Augustus by means of the *fideicommissum*, restricted in the following centuries, but not brought back to its original limits, immensely expanded again by Justinian, and finally subjected by him to a slight restriction. It is to be noted that both the great expansions were due to imperial intervention and it is quite probable that neither of them was really intended by its author. The matter has little to do with juridical ways of thinking.

To the Roman lawyer limitation of actions was one thing and acquisition of ownership by lapse of time quite another. We are not so logical. We seem to have stumbled into the latter as a by-product of the former, and for no apparent reason have confined this mode of acquiring ownership to certain interests in land, easements and the like. In other cases where limitation of actions has seemed to be inadequate, we have chosen to make lapse of time extinguish title rather than transfer it from one person to another. Our present periods for the limitation of actions are much shorter than those eventually reached by the Romans, who seem to have attached more importance to the right of the individual and less to the principle 'interest reipublicae ut sit finis litium' than we do, an attitude which also accounts for their lack of any system of bankruptcy: till a man had paid his debt in full, he owed it. In many cases, till the fifth century there was no prescription, and even then the period (thirty years) was extremely long.

Again, in regard to contracts our law comes much nearer to a general theory of contract than the Roman law did. We have a law of contract, while theirs was a law of contracts. In the Roman law no agreement was a contract unless the law made it binding. In our law every agreement purporting to affect legal relations is a contract unless the law for some reason, such as illegality or lack of consideration, rejects it. In the main we can say that our particular contracts are special varieties of a general type, whereas in Roman law the process was the reverse and most of the particular contracts had entirely independent origins and histories. We owe much to *assumpsit*. The Romans had no such general conception of the *prima facie* enforceability of an undertaking.

This is not the place, and we are not competent, to enter into the controversy between Sir Frederick Pollock on the one hand and Sir John Salmond on the other upon the question whether our law of civil wrongs is 'based on the principle that (1) all injuries done to another person are torts, unless there be some justification recognised by law; or on the principle that (2) there is a definite number of torts outside which liability in tort does not exist'.[1] Although the movement of opinion in favour of the former principle seems to have recently been checked, there can be no doubt that the encroaching power of the tort of negligence tends to impart generality into large parts of the law of torts; to that extent the common law presents another contrast to the Roman law. The latter recognised a definite number of categories of liability, increasing in the course of its history, but no general principle of liability for wrongful acts and omissions (for the famous 'alterum non laedere' is moral rather than legal), though *iniuria* and *dolus* exhibit in a minor degree the fecundity of our 'fertile mother of actions', Trespass. There are other points of contrast and comparison. Delictal liability is more primitive, more criminal, than our liability in tort, and closer to the idea of vengeance. Although the action of trespass emerged from the semi-criminal appeal of felony and both it and its progeny for a long time carried the marks of their criminal ancestry, our law of tort is now mainly compensatory in its object, while delict remained definitely penal. If we turn to specific delicts and torts, there is one noticeable difference. The rule that fraud causing loss was an actionable wrong appeared early in Roman law, in what may perhaps be reckoned as corresponding to the Year Book age; but in our law it did not appear, at least as a general rubric in common law courts, till relatively modern times. The same thing may perhaps

---

[1] In the words of Professor Winfield's lucid summary of the controversy in chapter iii of his *Province of the Law of Tort*. He adopts Sir Frederick Pollock's view, and Dr Stallybrass was moving in that direction. But see Glanville Williams in *Cambridge Law Journal*, 1939, pp. 111–135.

be said of negligence as a tort, for negligence causing
damage was a delict in Rome from very early times, while
with us its specific emergence is late. But this is probably
only apparent, as the majority of negligent acts causing
damage would probably have been remediable either by
Trespass or by Case.

In another respect there seems to be a marked difference
in the evolution of the two systems. In all systems of law,
at all stages except the most primitive, there is a constant
conflict between two methods of interpretation, the strict
and the 'equitable', sometimes expressed as being between
verba and *voluntas*, which is not quite the same. There is
both in Roman and in English law a steady tendency towards the triumph of the 'equitable' doctrine. But in our
system equity has passed from the vague to the precise,
'from a sort of arbitrary fairness into a legal system of
ameliorated law'.[1] In Roman law, though equity did not
first appear in, and was very far indeed from being confined to, the Praetor's Edict, a great part of it very early
took form in the Edict as a set of strict concrete rules administered by the same Courts as dealt with the ordinary
law; that is, it was of much the same nature as our modern
equity since the Judicature Acts,[2] though it came into
existence by what was practically legislation. There had,
however, always been equitable interpretations quite independent of the Edict. The Edict became fixed early in the
second century, but juristic *interpretatio* went on and was
applied to edictal rules as to all others. However, as time
went on, and the great jurists were succeeded by men of a
much lower calibre, and the influence of an oriental en-
vironment made itself felt, equitable notions became laxer

[1] A. V. Dicey: see *Cambridge Law Journal*, iv (1932), p. 303.
[2] The state of things was not unlike that in our early law when there
were no equity courts, but the common law courts held themselves free to
apply equitable principles. See Hazeltine, 'Early History of English
Equity', in *Essays in Legal History*, ed. Vinogradoff, 1913.

and less clearly conceived, and the fairness and justice which were the ideal of the classical lawyer tend to be replaced by a *benignitas* which has no stable measure. From clearness and precision Roman equity passed to indeterminate vagueness. It is like the history of Gothic architecture. Our equity passed into the stiffness and rigidity of the Perpendicular style: Roman equity passed into the weak indecisiveness of the Flamboyant.

The law of a nation expresses, in the long run, the character of the nation, and similarity of legal method corresponds to similarity in other aspects of social life. Both races seem to have had special gifts both for administering and for being administered. Both races have been given to action, rather than reflexion. Both made not only laws, but roads, and not only made laws, but in the main obeyed them, all rather in contrast with the Greeks, but not, it seems, with the Babylonians and Assyrians; indeed gifts and habits of this kind are necessary for any great and durable empire. Both have had a keen eye to practical needs, with rather inadequate theory. Both have had a profound respect for the plighted word, evidenced by their early acceptance of consensual executory contracts, which the Greeks do not seem to have reached at all, and by the rarity of any requirement of writing, unlike the practice of the Greeks. Both were in their earlier stages intensely individualistic, with a clear conception of *meum* and *tuum*, but perhaps no very exact analysis of the notion. Both systems reveal a high degree of inventiveness and capacity for adaptation. The Roman Will with its free *institutio heredis* was a thing unknown to the other Mediterranean systems. Our Trust, which in the words of Maitland[1] 'perhaps forms the most distinctive achievement of English lawyers', is an instrument of great utility and flexibility. In both systems, in the most formative period, express legislation played a minor part.

[1] *Equity*, p. 23.

For in Rome legislation by *Comitia* and Senate accounts for but little of the private law, and even the Edict, important as it was, did little after the fall of the Republic. In both, expansion and improvement were gradual, 'from precedent to precedent', though the precedents were not established in the same way. In both, it seems to be true, as Maine puts it for the Roman law,[1] that 'substantive law has the look of being gradually secreted in the interstices of procedure'. In both, in the later stages (*absit omen*) the earlier freedom of contract was checked by a great mass of restrictive legislation, so that the progress of society 'from status to contract' was interrupted.

It seems to follow from what has been said that the English lawyer, proud of his almost unique success in Western Europe in averting a reception of Roman law, has been inclined to exaggerate the differences between himself and his Roman brother. While the fundamental conceptions upon which the Roman law was built show but little similarity to the corresponding notions of the common law, which is not surprising, since one is of a Germanic stock and the other of a Mediterranean, the practical rules of the two systems show an astonishing amount of similarity. It is reasonable to attribute this to a certain similarity in the habits, the morale, the 'Anschauungen' of the two nations, though this has been obscured by the subsequent developments of Roman law in the countries which it invaded and which now form the home of the only serious rival to the English common law.

[1] *Early Law and Custom,* p. 389.

ABBREVIATIONS

(The last edition is referred to unless otherwise stated)

Holdsworth = Holdsworth, *History of English Law* (12 volumes).

P. and M. = Pollock and Maitland, *History of English Law*.

Hailsham = Halsbury, *Laws of England*, second edition edited by Lord Hailsham.

Buckland,
Text-book = Buckland, *Text-book of Roman Law*.

H.L.R. = *Harvard Law Review*.

L.Q.R. = *Law Quarterly Review*.

B.G.B. = Bürgerliches Gesetzbuch (German Civil Code).

C.C. = Code Civil (French Civil Code).

C.Com. = Code de Commerce (French Commercial Code).

ROMAN AND COMMON LAW

A COMPARISON IN OUTLINE

CHAPTER I. THE SOURCES

1. LEGISLATION

With us legislation has always been in form the act of the
King, though for many centuries the co-operation of the
two Houses of Parliament has been necessary and, for two
centuries, the Royal veto has not been exercised so far as the
English law is concerned. But, in Rome, the legislative
power shifted in much more striking ways. During the
Republic it was in the hands of Assemblies of the people,
not representative bodies such as our House of Commons,
but bodies in which all male citizens sat and voted. There
were several such Assemblies and we need not here
consider the vexed questions of their relations to each
other and their respective competences.[1] The different
Assemblies were grouped in different ways and while the
voting within each group was by head, this decided only
the vote of the group, which was the effective vote in the
Assembly. As might have been expected the legislative
power was at first in the hands of the Assembly (*comitia
centuriata*) in which the grouping was such that an over-
whelming preponderance was given to the wealthy and
noble, but passed ultimately to the Tribual Assembly,
arranged on democratic lines. But the machinery was
very different from that by which an Act of Parliament
is produced. There was no such thing as a 'Private Member's Bill': every measure had to be proposed by the

[1] Jolowicz, *Historical Introduction to Roman Law*, ch. v.

presiding officer, himself an elected 'magistrate', i.e. a high officer of State. There could be no amendments: the measure must be passed or rejected as it stood. Even the presiding magistrate had not a free hand in early times; no measure could become law without 'auctoritas patrum', the approval of a body which seems to have consisted of the patrician members of the Senate. And, till the bad times at the close of the Republic, all measures were previously considered by the Senate and submitted to the Assembly in a form which the Senate had approved.[1] The Senate was not elective; vacancies were filled by nomination, at first by the Consul, later by the Censor, for the time being.

By the end of the Republic, when the Empire had become a vast area, popular Assemblies of the old type had become impracticable, and, early in the Empire, by no act of legislation, but by the Emperor's influence, legislation passed to the Senate, which was now substantially nominated by him. Its enactments (*senatusconsulta*) show a gradual transition from instructions to the magistrates, which had always been within the province of the Senate, to direct legislation. Here, too, the measures were proposed by the presiding magistrate, who was the Emperor or his nominee, so that the Senate had very little independence. And when in the second century the Emperor claimed to legislate directly, *senatusconsulta* soon ceased to be utilised: thenceforward the Emperor was the sole legislator. Thus the evolution of legislative power was from popular legislation to legislation by the Head of the State, exactly the opposite course to that which it has hitherto taken with us, though it must be admitted that to-day the tendency is for very few bills to become law which are not prepared by the government and then submitted to the legislature.

In addition to these methods, there existed in the later centuries of the Republic and in the first century of the

---

[1] Jolowicz, *cit.* pp. 30, 31.

Empire a method of legislation to which the common law has no real parallel. The administration was in the hands of annually elected magistrates, and the more important of these, Consuls, Praetors, Aediles, had the *ius edicendi*, i.e. the power of issuing proclamations of the principles they intended to follow. For the most part these seem to have been no more than declarations of policy, but that of the Praetor became a great deal more. The Praetor Urbanus had charge of the administration of justice. All ordinary litigation came before him in the first instance and the issue was framed under his supervision, though the actual trial was before a *iudex*, who was not a professional lawyer, but a mere private citizen of the wealthier class, aided by professed lawyers. At some time in the second century B.C., a statute, the *l. Aebutia*, authorised a more elastic system than the *legis actio* hitherto in force.[1] The new method, by *formulae*, needed explanation, and the Praetor's Edict at once assumed great importance as the agency by which this was given. The power of moulding the procedure and the forms of action carried with it, inevitably, much power over the law itself, though there is no reason to suppose this was originally contemplated. However this may be— it may have been only a tolerated usurpation of power— the Praetor began to give actions where the civil law had given none and defences which the civil law had not recognised, in such a way as to create a great mass of law. The Edict was valid only for the year, but in fact it was renewed from year to year by the successive Praetors, with only such changes as experience suggested. It was thus a convenient mode of experimental legislation. A good rule survived: a bad one was dropped or modified. The tendencies of change were of course in the direction of equity and thus it is common to speak of praetorian law as the Roman Equity. And, apart from the general equitable

---

[1] It is probable that the formula was in use for some purposes before this enactment. (Jolowicz, *cit*. pp. 223 *sqq*.)

trend of his innovations, the Praetor, like the Chancellor, respects the earlier law: he does not set aside the civil law, but he circumvents it.

Herein is another similarity. The fundamental notions, the general scheme of the Roman law, must be looked for in the civil law, a set of principles gradually evolved and refined by a jurisprudence extending over many centuries, with little interference by a legislative body. The Edict is a collection of ordinances issued by the Praetor, by virtue of his *imperium*, which, while formally respecting the civil law (for the Praetor cannot alter this) practically modifies its working at a number of points where conditions called for such modification. The Edict can hardly be said to express any general principle: even in its latest form as *ordinatum* by Julian, it remained a set of sporadic rules (it has been called 'chaotic'[1]), a mere appendage to the civil law. All this may be said equally well of our Equity, except that in the nineteenth century it became much more systematised than ever the Roman Edict was. On this it is enough to cite a few words of Maitland:[2]

> Equity was not a self-sufficient system, at every point it presupposed the existence of Common Law. Common Law was a self-sufficient system.... If the legislature had passed a short act saying 'Equity is hereby abolished', we might still have got on fairly well; in some respects our law would have been barbarous... but still the great elementary rights... would have been decently protected.... On the other hand had the legislature said 'Common Law is hereby abolished', this decree... would have meant anarchy. At every point equity presupposed the existence of common law.... It [equity] is a collection of appendixes between which there is no very close connexion.

All this might have been said, *mutatis mutandis*, of the Praetor's Edict.

It would be hard to find a better description of the functions of English Equity than Papinian's words (D. 1. 1. 7. 1): 'ius praetorium est quod praetores introduxerunt adiuvandi vel supplendi vel corrigendi iuris

---

[1] Biondi, *Prospettive Romanistiche*, p. 40.
[2] *Equity*, p. 19.

civilis gratia propter utilitatem publicam'. And, just as the personality of the Praetor seems to have exercised a considerable influence on the Edict during his term of office, at any rate in early times, so we may say that the personality of the Chancellor, for a long time the sole, and until the nineteenth century the dominant, judge in Equity, was a powerful factor in the development of Equity.

Some of the Edict, however, has nothing particularly equitable about it, and a great part of the Roman equitable development owes nothing to the Edict. And the Edict differs from Equity in many ways. It was not administered by a separate tribunal, like the Chancellor's Court, or by a Court acting in special capacity, like the Exchequer. It did not acquire a special ethos through being handled by a separate Bar. A praetorian action was formulated before the Praetor and tried by a *iudex*, like a civil action. And the fields are very different. The Praetor never developed the Trust concept, which is probably the most important product of Equity, and he revolutionised the law of succession not only under wills, but in intestacy, which the Chancellor never touched. There is for the Praetor no question of the principle that 'Equity acts *in personam*': he creates both actions *in rem* and actions *in personam*. There is nothing corresponding to the writ of Subpoena. He has means of putting pressure on parties, but he applies them in civil actions as much as in praetorian. And the rules are not established, as those of Equity are, by a gradual crystallisation out of a series of cases, but by definite acts of legislation, though it is legislation of a peculiar kind. In fact the Edict is much more like a series of reforming statutes than it is like Equity as conceived in common law countries. Most law reform is equitable in some sense.

One further parallel between the Praetor and the Chancellor may be drawn. Just as the Praetor introduced by his Edict new actions, so, in the early years of our writ system, and before the growth of parliamentary power in the thirteenth and fourteenth centuries, the Chancellor, by reason of his control, as the head of the royal secretariat, over the issue of original writs, had a quasi-legislative power of developing the common law. To quote Pollock and Maitland:[1] 'A new form of action might be easily created. A few words said by the chancellor to his clerks: "such writs as this are for the future to be issued as of course"— would be as effective as the most solemn legislation.'[2]

2. CASE LAW

The Romans had, in principle, no case law: the decision of one Court did not make a precedent binding if the point arose again. This was inevitable. In a system in which the *iudex* was not a lawyer, but a private citizen, little more than an arbitrator, it would be impossible for his judgements to bind. It is true that he usually acted with legal advisers, but this would not suffice, for to make the decisions binding on others would be to give legislative power, within limits, to indeterminate groups of irresponsible advisers.[3] This does not indeed apply with the same force in the later Roman law, when, in principle, cases were tried to decision by the magistrate himself, who was often a distinguished lawyer; and when they were, as they might be, delegated for trial, the *iudex datus* was normally a lawyer chosen from those practising in the Court.[4] But it is not surprising that no such innovation was made as to give their judgements force as precedents. The later Emperors were autocrats, not likely to allow to the lawyers what was in effect legislative power.

[1] i. p. 171.
[2] See also Holdsworth, i. pp. 397, 398: 'writ, remedy and right are correlative terms'.
[3] On the *consilium* of the *iudex*, Wenger, *Römisches Zivilprozessrecht*, pp. 29, 194. It is quite possible that some of the advice so given found its way into the writings of the jurists, and so acquired authority.
[4] Bethmann-Hollweg, *Civilprozess*, iii. pp. 121 *sqq.*

It is sometimes said, and it is literally true, that decisions by the Emperor constituted an exception. His *decreta* were binding precedents, at least if they were meant to be such.[1] This however is not really the introduction of a new idea into the law. The Emperor was a legislator with a free hand and he could lay down the law in any way he thought fit. Whether he decided a point in a general enactment or in the course of the hearing of a case, what he said was law. Our books too contain cases which definitely break with pre-existing law and introduce absolutely new principles,[2] but in general, each decision is only a step forward on a way already marked out. However, the *decreta* of the Emperor are under no such limitation. We have remains of some collections of *decreta*[3] from which it is plain that the Emperor often establishes what he thinks a salutary rule without reference to its relation to the earlier law.[4] In fact, the usual mode of statement puts the emphasis wrongly. We ought not to say that decisions were binding if they were by the Emperor, but that what the Emperor laid down was law even if it was merely in a decision.

It is, however, clear that though decisions were not binding precedents, a current of decisions in the same sense did in fact influence judges.[5] But this is a very different matter. It is no more than evidence of general expert opinion regarding the law on the point. It is exactly what happens, e.g., in France, where our doctrine of 'case law' is rejected and called 'la superstition du cas', but the

---

[1] G. 1. 5; D. 1. 4. 1. 1; Buckland, *Text-book*, p. 18.

[2] E.g. restraint on anticipation, see *Parkes* v. *White* (1805), 11 Vesey 209, 211; *Jackson* v. *Hobhouse* (1817), 2 Mer. at p. 487; see Hart, 40 *L.Q.R.* (1924), pp. 221 *sqq.*; support for buildings, *Dalton* v. *Angus* (1881), 6 App. Cas. 740.

[3] See Lenel, *Palingenesia*, 1. 159.

[4] In Buckland, *Equity in Roman Law*, pp. 11 *sqq.*, will be found instances of such unheralded decisions and there are many more.

[5] See Allen, *Law in the Making*, 5th ed. pp. 156, 157, on the evidence from Cicero and others. We have not much information on the matter from juristic sources.

'jurisprudence', i.e. the current of decisions of one or more tribunals on the point, is constantly cited in support of an argument.[1] It must not however be supposed that case law is inherent in the common law and inconceivable in other systems. If Roman law countries have not adopted the principle it is either because they lack our wealth of reported decisions or because they think it a bad one. We shall not here consider what it is which is binding in a case, interesting and unsettled as the question is,[2] but will merely observe that some of the dislike of the English doctrine expressed by foreign lawyers is probably due to some misconception of its nature.[3] On the other hand the common law has not always admitted it. The doctrine of precedent does not appear in the Year Books. Throughout the period covered by them the tendency to refer to previous decisions is growing, though usually with no precision of citation and often by memory, and the judge is apt to say something like: 'Never mind that! Go on with your argument.'[4] It seems indeed that it is only in what, in the history of the nation, is a recent time that the principle has prevailed with any strictness.[5] And even where the common law prevails, e.g. in the greater part of the United States of America, local conditions have led to a certain distrust of the notion of precedent, or at least to a certain freedom in handling it, greater than that admitted by

[1] See K. Lipstein, 'The Doctrine of Precedent in Continental Law', *Journal of Comparative Legislation*, 3rd ser., xxviii. pp. 34–43. It is becoming evident that the differences between the English and Continental practices have been greatly exaggerated. See, in particular, Gutteridge, *Comparative Law*, pp. 90–93.

[2] See Goodhart, *Essays in Jurisprudence and the Common Law*, pp. 1 *sqq*.

[3] For an excellent recent description of the English system by a French author, see R. David, *Introduction à l'Étude du Droit privé de l'Angleterre*, pp. 142–154; see also Goldschmidt, *English Law from the Foreign Standpoint*, pp. 34–47.

[4] Ellis Lewis, 46 *L.Q.R.* at p. 220; and generally *ibid.* pp. 207–224, 341–360; 47 *L.Q.R.* pp. 411–427; 48 *L.Q.R.* pp. 230–247; Goodhart, 50 *L.Q.R.* pp. 40–65, 196–200; Holdsworth, *ibid.* pp. 180–195.

[5] See Allen, *Law in the Making*, 2nd ed. pp. 150–153.

British Courts. Apart from the Courts of the State, there are the Federal Courts, and also the Courts of other States, the decisions of which though not binding are of 'persuasive authority'. This has led to the existence of a great unmanageable mass of case law, often conflicting, and American lawyers seem to be coming to think rather in terms of a course of decisions, a 'jurisprudence', like the French and German lawyers, though, in principle, in the United States as in England, a decision is binding in future cases.[1]

The fact that the Romans had no case law does not mean that their method was less casuistic than ours. If we may judge from what is preserved, it was unusual for a Roman lawyer, except in elementary books, to enter on abstract general statements of the law on a topic: he nearly always put the matter as a concrete case. The main difference is that with us the case is an actual one which has been decided in Court, with the Romans it is one which has been discussed in the lawyer's chambers and may be quite imaginary. In the great formative periods neither the Roman lawyers nor ours have been great theorists: they rarely get back to first principles. Both argue from cases more or less like the one under discussion and rules gradually emerge which sometimes find expression in a terse *regula*. But this *regula* is not a first principle: we are told that we must not take our law from a *regula*; it is only an attempt to state a rule deducible from the cases.[2] It is true that Justinian tells judges that they are to decide not by precedent but according to the *leges*,[3] but he has specially in mind imperial legislation: it is plain that the Roman common law was built up like ours by argument

---

[1] See Goodhart, *Essays in Jurisprudence and the Common Law*, pp. 50–74.

[2] D. 50. 17. 1. See Lord Esher M.R. in *Yarmouth* v. *France* (1887), 19 Q.B.D. at p. 653: 'I detest the attempt to fetter the law by maxims. They are almost invariably misleading: they are for the most part so large and general in their language that they always include something which really is not intended to be included in them.'   [3] C. 7. 45. 13.

from case upon case, with the difference that ours are decided cases and theirs are discussed cases, more open to dispute. The underlying principles are there and sometimes come to the surface, but it has been left to modern Romanists to work them out, and it is not surprising that in setting them forth for the purposes of the modern Roman law they have often arrived at principles which are not Roman law at all. Nothing could be more unlike the method of Papinian than that with which Windscheid started on his great work. The 'Willenstheorie' which pervades his *Allgemeiner Teil* (it is much less traceable in the detailed treatment of the law) is not Roman at all. It comes from Kant, who expressly warns his readers that he is not expounding any actual system of law.[1] Even the Byzantines, though they speak more readily of *voluntas* than the Roman jurists did, have nothing on which the 'Willenstheorie' can reasonably be based.[2]

3. JURISTIC WRITINGS

From the absence of authority attaching to cases it followed as a corollary that the opinions of learned lawyers enjoyed a much greater authority than with us. Our Courts do not indeed go so far as to refuse all help in a difficult case from the writings of one known to have, or to have had, profound knowledge of the matter in hand, but recourse is not often had to this kind of writing, and it is always done with a clear recognition of the fact that, however sound the propositions may be, they are 'not authority'.[3] It is

---

[1] *Philosophy of Law*, trans. Hastie, p. 44.

[2] But it is certainly present in the Prussian Code of 1794, whence it can be traced back, through the Natural Lawyers, to the maxims contained more especially in the final title (50. 17) of the Digest. This at least appears from a study of such a book as Zouche's *Elementa Jurisprudentiae, etc.*, 1629.

[3] Allen, *Law in the Making*, 5th ed. pp. 258–263, has pointed out that in two branches of our law, namely, real property and conflict of laws, our Courts have been readier to resort to the works of text-writers and to allow to them a considerable influence.

true that some ancient writers, e.g. Bracton and Littleton, are differently treated. But these books are used much as Gaius is used by students of the Roman law. What is found in their books is not authoritative because they said it, but because they recorded it: it is often the chief source of our knowledge of the early law. It is largely because the case is authoritative that the writer is not, and it does not seem wholly insignificant that in the United States, where the system of precedent shows some signs of breaking down, the authority of writings is much greater than it is with us. In American Courts writings of great lawyers and essays in legal periodicals are very frequently cited, not indeed as of binding authority, but as carrying great weight. In our Courts this is rarer, except where the Court has occasion to enquire into some other system of law.[1] Another factor has made for the greater recognition of legal literature in the United States. Modern representative assemblies seem inclined to regard legislation as their primary duty. There are many legislative bodies in the United States and it is computed that they have produced in the present century more statutes than have been enacted in all the legislatures of the known world in all previous history. It seems that in some States the Courts show a tendency to treat this mass of legislation with some freedom, though it is important to distinguish between matters entirely regulated by statute, such as Adoption, and those in which the legislatures have merely purported to amend the common law in detail, or to clarify it. But where both case law and statute law are handled loosely the writer on law is likely to have more influence.

[1] But the practice is undoubtedly changing rapidly: one might almost say that any author of ability who is prepared to go beyond the cases, whether he attempts to build up a body of doctrine or to answer undecided problems, is certain to be cited in Court nowadays. Such books as Pollock or Salmond on Torts have always been cited. Indeed it is astonishing how quickly a good text-book can become 'citable'. See Denning L.J.'s review of Winfield, *Textbook of the Law of Tort*, 3rd ed. at 63 *L.Q.R.* p. 536.

The Roman attitude was very different from ours. We need not consider the *interpretatio* of the early law. The Pontiffs, who, by ingenious distortions of the text, or what passed for the text, of ancient laws, introduced new rules and even new institutions into the law, were officials, and their action was in fact, though not in form, delegated legislation. It was in principle not unlike that of the Praetor, though on the one hand less comprehensive, and on the other affecting directly the civil law.[1] When, in mid-Republic, the task of interpreting law passed into the hands of lay lawyers, something of this power, though no formal authority, passed to them, but very soon the Edict was beginning to be the most convenient agency for law reform, and it was mainly by suggestions to the Praetor that the lawyers induced changes in the law. There are however cases of more direct influence. It was the example set by Antistius Labeo which definitely established the validity of codicils, i.e. in the Roman sense of the word, informal instruments by which the provisions of a will might be modified or, even without a will, the distribution of the property could be determined.[2]

It seems also that the purely consensual commercial contracts of Sale, Hire, etc., the early history of which is obscure, owed their recognition to the jurists of the later Republic. But in all this there was no suggestion of any formal authority. Augustus made a change by introducing the *ius respondendi*, by which some, probably only a few, privileged jurists could give sealed *responsa* under the authority of the Emperor, and Hadrian made these *responsa* binding if they were all agreed. We cannot go into the

---

[1] On the old *interpretatio*, Jolowicz, *cit.* pp. 85 *sqq.*; Schulz, *History of Roman Legal Science*, pp. 5–37.

[2] For their rules and history, Buckland, *Text-book*, p. 360. An interesting parallel is afforded by the story (see Hart in 40 *L.Q.R.* (1924) pp. 221–226) that Lord Thurlow invented the married woman's restraint on anticipation for the purpose of a marriage settlement of which he was to become a trustee.

story of these *responsa*: there is hardly a point in their history, the effect of the *ius respondendi*, etc., which is not hotly controverted.[1] No text of the classical age which survives independently of Justinian in anything like its original form ever speaks of a point as having been definitely settled by *responsum*, and it seems possible to overrate their importance as sources of law in their own age. Apart from that, it seems the better view that, notwithstanding some loose language in Gaius[2] which may be corrupt, writings of lawyers as such were not authoritative. No doubt they might be cited, but they would not, even if unanimous, bind the Court and they were the less important in that the jurists themselves were available to advise the *oratores* who addressed the Court.

If we pass to the time of Justinian we again find that juristic writings are not authoritative. It is true that the principal source of law in Justinian's time, the Digest, is made up of juristic writings and these writings are declared to be selected from the writings of jurists who had had some sort of authority. But the authority of the texts in the Digest is not due to their having been written by the jurist, but to their having been incorporated in the Digest and made law by enactment. Justinian is at great pains to tell us this several times and to warn people against attempting to use as authority writings not in his book or in a different form from that they have in it.[3] As to contemporary writers he goes further. He does not say that their writings are not to be authoritative, but that they are not to have any writings, for he forbids any commentaries on his legislation,[4] and it is difficult to imagine any practical juristic writing which would not be

---

[1] For various views, Girard, *Manuel*, 8th ed. p. 76; Buckland, *Textbook*, p. 22; Jolowicz, *cit*. p. 365.

[2] G. 1. 7.

[3] Const. '*Deo auctore*' [C. 1. 17. 1] 7; Const. '*Tanta*' [C. 1. 17. 2] 19.

[4] Const. '*Deo auctore*' 12; '*Tanta*' 21. These enactments are prefixed to the Digest.

such a commentary. Of course he did not succeed in preventing the writing of commentaries or the use of matter not in his canon, but these writings and citations had no authority.

The question for us, therefore, is the state of things in post-classical times, when there were no more *responsa*, and no more great jurists, and before Justinian's legislation. Here too there is a distinction to be drawn. After the Law of Citations of A.D. 426[1] it is quite clear what writings were authoritative and what was the extent of their authority. But, for the fourth century, things are really very dark. All that we know is that there was legislation under Constantine, one enactment declaring that certain notes of Paul and Ulpian on Papinian were to be abolished, which no doubt means that they could not be cited, and another declaring the works of Paul, including the *Sententiae*, to be confirmed in their *recepta auctoritas*,[2] and we are told by Justinian of an enactment excluding notes of Marcian on Papinian.[3] There may have been earlier legislation but the words *recepta auctoritas* rather suggest that the writings of the great jurists of the past had acquired a *de facto* authority in the Courts, though it is not possible to say how far this authority went. It can hardly be that any sentence of any book of one of these men bound the Court, and it may be that the rule enacted by Hadrian as to actual *responsa* was applied and that they bound the Court if uncontradicted by any other writing. In view of the innumerable conflicts of which we have so many traces this would mean little more than that they could be cited. Indeed, the authority seems to have been something like that which attached to writers on International Law till recent times. In the absence of any evidence of limiting legislation it is not unlikely that contemporary lawyers,

[1] C. Th. 1. 4. 3.
[2] C. Th. 1. 4. 1 [A.D. 321]; C. Th. 1. 4. 2 [A.D. 327].
[3] Const. '*Deo auctore*' 6.

the post-classical men generally, came to be cited, and that it was this mass of matter, which by the fifth century had become unmanageable, that was cut out by the Law of Citations which drove men back to the classical literature. For it is obvious on its terms that it did not cut out much classical literature of importance. All this, however, is little more than conjecture.

Before leaving the question of the contribution made by *responsa* to the development of Roman law, we should note the important part played by professional opinion in one branch of English law, namely the practice of conveyancers. Holdsworth[1] cites a number of judicial acknowledgements of this fact and states that in course of time 'the practice of these conveyancers, who settled the common forms which carried out in practice the principles of the law, tended to be treated by the courts as such cogent evidence of the law, that it can be regarded almost as a secondary source of law'.

4. CUSTOM

Law may be said to begin, everywhere, in custom, in the sense that when a central authority begins to intervene in the settlements of disputes, the rules which it applies are mainly those rules of conduct which have been habitually observed by members of the community in their dealings with one another. Our own common law is described by Blackstone as the general custom of the realm.[2] It is notoriously, as a matter of history, nothing of the kind. The common law was brought into existence by the King's Justices, all over the country, precisely because there was no general custom of the realm. The customs of different parts of the country, settled by different elements of our hybrid population, were very diverse, and manorial justice had brought it about that there was an almost

---

[1] vii. pp. 355, 384–387.
[2] *Commentaries*, Introd. Sect. iii.

infinite variety of customs prevailing in small areas. Indeed, anyone who has had occasion to study the law of copyholds (which to a large extent evaded the unifying process by which this common law was created) can form some idea of what the law of England would be like to-day but for the compulsion towards uniformity applied by the King's itinerant Justices. They gradually substituted for this mass of customs a law which doubtless has its roots in Germanic custom,[1] but a great part of which was apparently of their own creation.

The Roman common law, the *ius civile* of republican language, had perhaps a better claim to be called the general custom of the realm; for it is now generally agreed that the law of the XII Tables was based upon existing Latin custom, and we can see from what is left of the Tables that they assume an immense amount of custom which they do not state. It is however obvious that this too was greatly modified and augmented by the lawyers. Pomponius tells us indeed that the law had a customary basis: 'coepit populus Romanus incerto magis iure et consuetudine aliqua uti', is said of the state of things mended by the XII Tables,[2] but, speaking of it after that enactment, he says it is 'compositum a prudentibus'[3] and that it 'sine scripto in sola interpretatione prudentium consistit'.[4] Except in that sense, general custom, though it is occasionally mentioned, plays only a very small part in the developed Roman law. The only case in which it seems to raise a practical issue is the question whether a statute can be abolished by non-use. We are plainly told by Julian that it can, for the reason that it is immaterial whether the people expresses its will tacitly by conduct or by a formal statute.[5] In fact, there are several statutes

---

[1] Pollock, *Expansion of the Common Law*, pp. 11 *sqq.*
[2] D. 1. 2. 2. 3.   [3] D. 1. 2. 2. 3.   [4] D. 1. 2. 2. 12.
[5] D. 1. 3. 32. 1. Whether the reasoning is Julian's or Tribonian's we need not here consider.

declared to be obsolete by non-use. The reasoning would not apply to enactments by an autocratic Emperor, and the cases commonly cited of such statutes are all of popular enactments of the Republic.[1] Justinian preserves the text, but it is very unlikely that he contemplated this fate for his own laws, which were to be valid not only for his own time 'sed etiam omni aevo tam instanti quam posteriori'.[2] Modern systems of Roman law seem however in general to have treated desuetude as a mode of repeal, a rule definitely rejected by the common law.[3]

On local customs our information is not satisfactory. Many enactments of Diocletian show refusal to accept local customs as against the Roman law, but these are questions of foreign law: citizens in regions only recently made subject to the Roman law tried still to apply their own law. From Constantine onwards there are enactments accepting such things, but this is adoption into the law, not recognition of local validity as against the law. On the other hand it has been made clear that throughout this period the foreign and abrogated law was still freely applied in the remoter parts of the Empire, as against the imperial law.[4] As to local customs of the ordinary kind we have the rule that to be valid they must be reasonable and not contrary to statute.[5] And though there are other texts

[1] Illustrations, Jołowicz, *cit.* p. 360. As to the proper interpretation to be put on the facts, see Solazzi, *La desuetudine della legge.*

[2] Buckland, *Main Institutions of Roman Law,* p. 19; *Text-book,* p. 52.

[3] Craies, *Statute Law,* 3rd ed. p. 339, n. (b), cites the case of Mr Gladstone's appointment of two suffragan bishops under the statute 26 Hen. VIII, c. 14, although no suffragan bishop had been appointed under that statute since the reign of Queen Elizabeth. It must, however, have been difficult to give full effect to the English rule by the first half of the nineteenth century, before the Statute Law Revision Acts purged the Statute Book of the immense mass of obsolete statutes which had survived from different periods. It is interesting to note that pre-Union Scottish statutes are subject to the Continental, post-Union Statutes to the English rule.

[4] Mitteis, *Reichsrecht und Volksrecht, passim.*

[5] C. Just. 8. 52. 2.

which allow local custom in some concrete cases without
saying anything about statute, it seems that this was the
rule at least of later law.

5. GENERAL REFLEXIONS

Though to laymen and even to lawyers, in countries the
laws of which are codified, a statute seems the normal form
of law, it must be borne in mind that in the classical age of
Roman law, and throughout our own legal history, statute,
so far as private law is concerned, occupies only a very subordinate position.[1] Of the many hundreds of *leges* that are
on record, not more than about forty were of importance
in the private law, and though the Edict, regarded as
delegated legislation, and the *senatusconsulta* of the early
Empire constitute a considerable addition, it still remains
true that the main agency in legal progress was in Rome,
as with us, not the legislator, but the lawyer. As we have
seen the method was not the same as with us. With us it is
the judge who is directly effective. With the Romans it
was the lawyer, by his opinions communicated to magistrates, *iudices* or suitors who consulted him. But essentially
the agency is of the same kind, for the English Bench is
recruited from the Bar and preserves close contact with it.
Moreover, at Rome and in England the lawyers have
never liked legislation.[2] It is only when they have arrived
at an *impasse* from which legislation is the only escape—
more frequently with us than at Rome—that the lawyers
have been willing to advise the legislator to act.

The later Roman law and our own recent history seem
at first sight to indicate a change in both systems. The later
Emperors were immeasurably more active in legislation
than their predecessors or any earlier legislative agency.
Our statute books for the last hundred years have been
much bulkier than those of earlier centuries. But the re-

---

[1] Except in real property law.
[2] Schulz, *Principles of Roman Law*, pp. 6–18.

semblance here is largely superficial. Though our modern
legislature has intervened and codified some few parts of
our private law, the great mass of our modern legislation
is concerned with what may be called administration,
legislation rendered necessary by the complexity of our
modern life. And even those codifications of fragments of
the private law are in the main little more than orderly
statements of results already reached by the Courts and
are themselves being every day modified by the action of
those Courts. But in Rome the civilisation was in decay.
The successors of the great lawyers were of an inferior type
and the necessary reforms came from the Emperor and
his officials, partly because an absolute monarchy is intolerant of any authority other than its own, but partly
because there was no one else with the necessary knowledge and skill.[1]

In the preceding paragraphs the word 'source' has been
used to denote the agency by which a rule of law is created.
These agencies, however, do not work *in vacuo*: they apply
ideas derived from various sources. Thus it is widely held
that the *aequitas* which plays so great a part in Roman law is
essentially only a borrowing, through the rhetoricians, of
the ἐπιείκεια of the Greek philosophers. The movement
from form to intent, from *verba* to *voluntas*, from *strictum
ius* to *aequitas*, is said to have this origin. But though the
influence of Greek thought on the Roman lawyers cannot
be denied, and had much to do with this progress, this is
an over-statement of the matter: the Romans had not
waited for the Greeks to tell them that law was a social
science and the servant, though at times the reluctant
servant, of morality. Our own law has progressed independently in the same way, and it is not insignificant that
the reasonings and devices by which the Roman lawyers

---

[1] However, much of the contents of the Code is devoted to the organisa-
tion of society on an increasingly collectivist basis, and here the resemblance
to modern Britain is very marked.

made the law serve the needs of the time can be paralleled over and over from our law reports, without the smallest sign or probability of borrowing.[1]

Foreign law has of course affected both systems. In our law it can be traced from the courts of the medieval markets, attended by merchants of all countries, to the present day. In the Roman world, foreign law meant essentially Hellenistic law. In both systems it is naturally the commercial law which is most affected. In this connexion it is impossible not to think of the *ius gentium*, as practically applied. But there is nothing essentially foreign about *ius gentium*. It is that part of the Roman law which is extended to dealings in which peregrines are concerned, not because it is thought of as universal but because it is simple and intelligible to aliens. The 'philosophical' view of it as universal and therefore 'natural' is not that which is important and is at variance with the facts. Probably its most important institution is the consensual and executory contract of sale, but that is peculiarly Roman: Hellenistic systems knew nothing of it. With the spread of the Roman State, from the second Punic War onwards, the *ius gentium* must have gone far towards realising, for the then known world, the universal commercial law which the more enlightened lawyers of all modern countries are striving to attain.[2] In the later Empire the borrowing of Hellenistic and oriental ideas was much accentuated, but this was not the result of a striving to discover and adopt what was best in other systems, but of the fact that the centre of the Empire had shifted to the East. Unconscious and express adoption of oriental notions was inevitable when the surroundings were oriental and the men who made, and those who administered, the law were themselves orientals.

[1] Buckland, *Equity in Roman Law, passim.*
[2] See especially *L'Unification du Droit*, 1948, published in French and English by the Rome Institute for the Unification of Private Law.

EXCURSUS: ROMAN AND ENGLISH METHODS

It is right to emphasise the general resemblance in the methods followed by Roman and English law. Neither is in general a coherent intellectual system; both are rather ways of doing the legal business of society, observed and developed more or less instinctively by relatively small groups of men who have been trained by their predecessors in traditional procedures and habits of decision. No doubt the Roman law of the post-classical period, and English law from and after the career of Pollock, have tended to become more self-conscious and theoretical in character, but Roman law never reached a state at all comparable to that reached by the pandectists of the nineteenth century, nor has English law yet reached it, if it ever will.

Yet there is some danger of overdoing the likeness between Roman and English methods. In one department at least, that of real property, English law is much more systematic than Roman law ever was. One may even say that it is more systematic, more abstract and more intellectualised than any part of any foreign system derived from Roman law. This is the more surprising in that it has hardly been touched by civilian influences; though the old learning seems to have taken its final form at the hands of the Roman Catholic conveyancers, who doubtless imported into it some of the scholastic logic which was more characteristic of their thought than that of their Protestant contemporaries.[1] The tradition of accurate professional draftsmanship, which depends for its certainty very largely on the strict doctrine of precedent, long upheld by English Courts, is however found in many other branches of legal work, especially commercial law. It is one of the most marked characteristics of English law. It is perhaps even more strikingly developed in the United States.

[1] Cf. Plucknett, *Concise History of the Common Law*, 4th ed. p. 15.

Perhaps it is precisely because both Roman and English law are original creations and have for the most part grown up without much regard for system that each has produced an incomparable elementary treatise, namely Gaius' *Institutes* and Blackstone's *Commentaries*. Both books have had an extraordinary influence in determining the main lines of legal education and in ensuring the spread of Roman and English law to other lands.[1] Both, after a period of undue depreciation, have come into their own as works of exceptional but peculiar quality. They are, indeed, like all the best elementary books, works of inspired journalism, simple, clear, and persuasive, containing, but hardly disfigured by, a few unimportant mistakes. Other countries have produced literary works that are more thorough and more scientific, but hardly so influential.

[1] The missionary work of Gaius was of course mainly done through the Institutes of Justinian.

CHAPTER II. THE LAW OF PERSONS

1. TERRITORIAL AND PERSONAL LAW

Apart from Family Law, the rubric 'Persons' is of comparatively small importance in our law, since the law is territorial and every subject of the State is a citizen of it. If he is subject to disabilities, e.g. is a minor or a lunatic or a convict, this has nothing to do with his citizenship. And a domiciled alien is, so far as the private law is concerned, in much the same position as a citizen. Even a merely resident or visiting alien, with a foreign domicile, will rarely find, at least for acts *inter vivos*, that the law for him is very different from that under which his citizen neighbour lives. The Roman classical law presents at first sight a very different picture. The law was personal. There were of course many slaves, who were rightless and, so far as private law is concerned, dutiless. Moreover, not every free subject was a citizen. A man might be a member of a Latin colony or of a peregrine community: he might be a Junian Latin or a *dediticius*. It would be beyond the present purpose to go into these differences, but it may be pointed out that while in the family law and in the law of succession they are of very great importance, they amount in the rest of the private law to very little indeed. Indeed for members of Latin colonies and some other communities, who had the right of what was called *commercium*, there was practically no difference: all the ordinary law applied to them. But even for the others the practical disadvantage was not great. They could not have civil ownership (*dominium ex iure Quiritium*) or transfer or acquire by the civil law formal methods, but their inferior mode of ownership was efficiently protected by methods devised for the purpose.[1] They could not contract in the

---

[1] Girard, *Manuel*, 8th ed. pp. 125, 380.

highly technical form called *expensilatio*, the contract *literis*, but that mattered little, since it was obsolescent in the classical law, and every ordinary commercial contract was open to them. They could even take part in the ancient formal contract of *stipulatio*, made by question and answer, except indeed that they could not promise, or receive a promise, in the form 'Spondesne? Spondeo'. This excluded them indeed from certain forms of suretyship, and from certain forms of procedure in which this form was essential,[1] but was not otherwise of much importance. The law of delict (tort) was essentially statutory and statutes did not apply to peregrines unless expressly mentioned, but in fact it was made to apply to them by forms of action devised by the Praetor.[2] Under Justinian, apart from slaves, most of this complexity was gone. All subjects were, normally, citizens. But there were still *deportati*, citizens who had been deprived of their civil status by way of punishment. As they belonged to no other community no special system of law applied to them, but in fact they could deal and acquire by the informal ways which alone survived under Justinian. Nevertheless their disabilities in the law of succession were grave: they could not make or take under a will and no one could succeed to them.[3]

The question also arises: What law was applied to an alien resident in the Empire? We must not read into the system the modern precision as to the acquisition of citizenship, but from what the texts tell us it seems that an *incola*, a person not a member of the community but permanently settled there, had the same rights in commercial law as a member, but was governed in the matter of family law and succession by the law of his own community if he had one. The texts, however, deal mainly with liability to public

---

[1] G. 4. 91–95; 162 *sqq.* Perhaps some special provision was made for peregrines in interdicts.

[2] G. 4. 37.

[3] For references, Buckland, *Text-book*, p. 97.

burdens[1] and we really have little information. A foreigner not so settled had probably no trading rights except so far as they were conferred by treaty with his nation, though, presumably, he had the protection of the criminal law.[2]

It might have been expected that the strictly personal character of the Roman classical law, in contrast with the territorial character of English law, would, by reason of the many overseas interests of the Romans and of the influx of foreigners to the capital, have compelled the development of a system of Conflict of Laws.[3] In fact, however, any rules resembling rules of Conflict of Law were both rudimentary and fragmentary, and probably for two reasons: first, the continual process of enlarging the circle of Roman subjects, and secondly, the development of '*ius gentium*, in its practical sense, i.e. "that part of the law which we apply both to ourselves and to foreigners"'.[4] A system of Conflict of Laws recognises the existence of different legal systems and endeavours to avoid conflicts between them by laying down rules of priority in each case. The Roman solution of the problem started from the view that no foreigner was worthy of the *ius civile*, and went on to build up a body of law to regulate the relations between Romans and foreigners and between one foreigner and another.

2. SLAVERY

The slave is a figure so remote from our Western European civilisation and has been so long obsolete in the United States that he might seem hardly worth mention in a comparison of the Roman with the common law. But the word

---

[1] C. Just. 10. 40; D. 50. 1.
[2] This paragraph would apply equally to a provincial belonging to one community but living in another.
[3] Jolowicz, *Historical Introduction to Roman Law*, pp. 101, 102.
[4] Jolowicz, *cit.* p. 103.

'slave' has meant in practice very different things at different times, and the Roman slave was a very important factor in the law. When we moderns think of slaves, we think of them usually as African negroes employed in the tasks which a white man would not perform, hewers of wood and drawers of water in a climate where such tasks were irksome, plantation labourers and the like, having no importance in commerce except perhaps that the more intelligent might be employed as messengers, and that they themselves were vendible chattels. No doubt there were vast numbers of slaves in the Roman State who answered to the same description. But slaves of this kind are not those who play a part in the Roman law-books. The slave in Rome dates from the very earliest times, and in view of the autocratic power of the *paterfamilias* it is not easy to see much difference in primitive law between the positions of son and slave. They were alike in that whatever they received from any source belonged not to them but to the *paterfamilias*. This always remained the law for slaves, and even for sons it was relaxed only in the Empire and then only very partially. There was no necessary difference of race or colour in the slave. For long the chief source of supply of the slave market was capture in war, and for some centuries of the Republic the wars of the Romans were with neighbouring nations of the same stock as themselves. It is not therefore surprising that very early in Roman history, indeed as soon as commerce had assumed any importance, the rule that what slaves acquired vested in the master was applied not only to physical things but to rights acquired by negotiation. What was promised to them was promised to, and could be claimed by, him. This of itself was not enough, for though rights vested in the master liabilities did not, and, as most dealings are bilateral, third parties would not readily contract on this basis. The Praetor filled the gap by introducing actions by which the master was made liable (within limits which we shall consider later[1]) on contracts made by the slave, the object being not to improve the position of slaves, but to make them more effective instruments. The result was that the slave began to be freely employed in commerce, carrying on business in an almost independent way. The respectable Roman did not care about engaging in trade himself, but he let his slaves do the work and took the proceeds, the limits of his liability being such that he ran no very serious risk, so long as he did not give his express authority to the transactions of the slave. Thus the texts show constantly the intervention of the slave, though there is reason to think that in the bad times of the later Empire, when it was hard to make a living, freemen objected to the competition of slaves and the slave appears in commerce less and less.[2] It was not only in trade that slaves were active. They are prominent in literature, in education and in the public service.[3] But in all these respects things have changed, much to their damage, in the later Empire.[4]

The interest of this conception of slavery, for the purpose of comparison of the two systems, is in the fact that by this utilisation of the slave the Roman lawyers in various branches of the law reached goals which have been reached by the common law by a different road, reached them, that is, without possessing conceptions which are regarded as essential in the common law and even in the modern Roman law.

In the modern law of contract representation is fundamental: the modern commercial system and commercial law, both in common law countries and in those whose systems are based on Roman law, are saturated with the notion of representation. In Roman law contract was, as we shall see later, intensely personal: and to the end there

---

[1] Pp. 28–29, 219 *post.*

[2] See, e.g., Buckland, *Main Institutions of Roman Law*, p. 42.

[3] See, e.g., Aulus Gellius 2. 18 and the references in Girard, *Manuel*, 8th ed. pp. 107 *sqq.*; Buckland, *Roman Law of Slavery*, pp. 319 *sqq.*   [4] See, e.g., Buckland, *Slavery, loc. cit.*

were only unrelated elements out of which a system of
agency could be developed. There was in fact no need for
agency as we understand it: the slave filled the gap. The
slave himself could clearly be no more than a channel, for
he was incapable of rights and liabilities. All this involves
a conception of slavery very different from that to which
we are accustomed.

Another conception, fundamental in our law and such
that modern commerce is hardly conceivable without it, is
that of limited liability. But apart from slave law it was
entirely unknown in Rome, except as to some imperfectly
known *participes* in contracts with the State at the close of
the Republic for tax-farming, exploiting minerals and the
like.[1] The notion was no doubt less necessary in the less
complex commercial life of Rome, and, to the extent to
which it was necessary, slave law provided it. The Roman,
unwilling to trade himself, and equally unwilling to leave
his fortunes at the mercy of someone else and yet desirous
to invest his money, found a means by exploiting the slave.
It had been common from early times to entrust slaves
with a separate fund called *peculium*, at first small, but in
classical times often large, with which the slaves could deal
as if it were their own. With this money they could trade.
The master was liable on the slave's contracts to the *actio de
peculio*,[2] but apart from express authorisation only to the
extent of the *peculium* or of any profit which had been
transferred to him. Thus the risk was limited to the amount
of the *peculium*. Any profit belonged in law to the master,
and he could always recall the *peculium* at any moment,
subject to the rights of existing creditors, so that he could
always get back what was left of his money, an advantage
not always open to the shareholder or common stock-
holder. The importance of this institution is obvious from
its prominence in the texts and in particular from the

[1] See p. 303, *post.*
[2] Or, in certain cases, the *actio tributoria.*

careful way in which the liabilities under these actions are worked out in the relevant titles of the Digest.[1]

The slave is important also in the matter of succession. A man's appointment of his own slave as his *heres*, involving a gift of liberty to him, has little interest for us. But it was obviously very usual from the late Republic onwards to appoint another man's slave as *heres*, and the effect would be that the inheritance would go to his master. The original purpose of this odd-looking practice is not known, but it served a very practical end in classical law and later. The *heres*, except that he is usually the principal beneficiary, is very like an executor, and, like an executor, when once he has accepted the office he cannot get rid of it (*semel heres, semper heres*). But an executor who renounces probate does not necessarily lose benefits under the will, while a *heres* who refused was wholly excluded from the *hereditas*: if he wished the benefit without the duties he must assign his right of acceptance before he exercised it, before he became *heres*, contenting himself with the price received. It was in fact allowed to certain *heredes ab intestato* to do this by *cessio in iure*.[2] But a successor appointed by will had, for an unknown reason, no such right, and here came in one advantage of the appointment of your slave rather than yourself. A man did not become *heres* through his slave till the slave had accepted with due authorisation. But since it was the slave who was instituted *heres*, it was, for this purpose, indifferent who was his master, and the person who acquired was his master at the time of acceptance. If therefore the slave was assigned before acceptance he took the right of entry with him, so that in effect the inheritance could be assigned, its net value being no doubt reflected in the price received.

The slave serves another purpose in connexion with inheritance. Where the successor was not in the power of the testator at the time of his death, there would be an interval of time which might be considerable before the *heres* actually accepted. How were the affairs of the estate to be carried on in the interval? Slaves belonging to the *hereditas* were the only persons who could act and they filled the gap.[1]

The slave in England has a very different history.[2] It would not be profitable to examine it at length because most of the similarities between Roman and common law would be found to be mere borrowings. Anglo-Saxon law, like most other Germanic systems, recognised slavery. The Normans were not a squeamish race, and, though in the reign of William I (if not earlier) the voice of the Church was lifted to mitigate the lot of the slave, the Norman and Angevin lawyers had no difficulty in fitting into the manorial system as villeins both the pure serf and the class, only slightly above him, of 'those free yet dependent cultivators of the soil whose tenure was defined...to be unfree'.[3] Bracton, 'identifying the *servus* with the *villanus*', was disposed to import a considerable amount of the Roman law of slavery. But there seem to be two reasons why the history of slavery in the two systems has been so different; first, with us villeinage remained a predial, an agricultural condition, so that the opportunities of exploiting the status of villein for trading and other purposes as above described would not arise; and, secondly, the strong leaning in favour of liberty which has marked the common law from very early times, by encouraging presumptions of manumission and other pleas which would defeat villein status, ultimately succeeded in so completely undermining that status that, as Holdsworth says, 'the law of villein status was never repealed. It simply fell into disuse because the persons to whom it applied had ceased to exist.' When at a later stage the common law was faced

---

[1] See pp. 154–155, *post*.
[2] P. and M. i. pp. 395–415; Holdsworth, ii. pp. 40–42, 272; iii. pp. 491–510; vi. pp. 264, 265.   [3] Holdsworth, iii. p. 491.

with the problem of colonial slavery, this same bias, receiving fresh stimulus from the Revolution, eventually enabled Sir John Holt and Lord Mansfield to hold that the moment a negro slave stepped upon English ground he became free.

3. MARRIAGE

There has been, and still exists, much controversy as to what constitutes a 'marriage', as to the nature of the relation which our Courts will recognise as such a union,[1] and it is not very easy, on the other hand, to get a very clear idea of what was the exact meaning of the word *nuptiae* for the Romans. But in our Courts these difficulties have arisen mainly in cases where the parties have 'married' under other laws than our own: so far as the internal law is concerned, the matter seems fairly clear. The general notion of the relation in the two systems is much the same. In *Hyde* v. *Hyde*[2] it was defined as 'the voluntary union for life of one man and one woman, to the exclusion of all others', and Modestinus defines it[3] as 'coniunctio maris et feminae et consortium omnis vitae, divini et humani iuris communicatio'. These are much the same, and the accuracy of the definitions is not affected by the fact that these unions were not always in Rome, and are not always in modern England, actually lifelong. But marriage in the law of the Roman Empire had at first sight a look very different from that of modern English marriage. It was dissoluble not merely by consent but, at any moment, by either party, and it is to be noted that this conception of *liberum matrimonium* was so deeply rooted in the Roman mind that the Christian Church, though it made marriage a religious institution and surrounded it with ceremonial, and, in the later Empire, was a tremendous power in the

---

[1] See, e.g., Vesey-Fitzgerald, 47 *L.Q.R.* (1931) p. 253; Beckett, 48 *L.Q.R.* (1932) p. 341, and the cases there discussed. See also Cheshire, *Private International Law*, 3rd ed. pp. 395–417.

[2] (1866), L.R.P. and D. 130.   [3] D. 23. 2. 1.

State, never promoted, or at all events never induced, legislation to alter this. It discouraged causeless divorce and it secured legislation imposing serious, even disabling, penalties. In A.D. 542, i.e. by a Novel after the enactment of the *Corpus Juris*,[1] Justinian did in fact forbid divorce except for certain specific reasons, but this inroad on the old notions was repealed by his successor in A.D. 566.[2] This is all the more noticeable since in a recent case our High Court took the view that such a dissoluble union, even in a country (Soviet Russia) where this was the only form of marriage, could not be regarded as marriage at all. It is true that the Court of Appeal repudiated this doctrine and laid it down that such a union would be recognised by our Courts as a marriage, the point being that the conditions under which the union could be dissolved did not affect the nature of the union while it existed. That depended on the intent: the law required intent to create a permanent union and, if the other requirements of the law were satisfied, this was a marriage. The High Court, in refusing to admit that such a union came within the notion of Christian marriage, ignored the fact that for some centuries it was the only possible form of Christian marriage.[3]

There are, however, wide differences between the Roman conception of marriage and that of the modern common law, both as to form and as to effects. In Rome, apart from marriage with *manus*, of which there are few traces after the first century of the Empire, it was primarily a relation of fact to which if the parties had certain qualifications, age, *conubium* (capacity of civil marriage), and were not too closely related or otherwise barred by law from marrying each other, the law attached certain potential rights and duties.

What was that fact to which the law attached these potential rights and liabilities? The first answer is that a joint common life intended to be permanent must be set

---

[1] Novel 117. 10.   [2] Novel 140.
[3] *Nachimson* v. *Nachimson*, [1930] P. at p. 98; *ibid.* p. 217.

up. But that is not enough: it might be true of concubinage. The texts say that apart from the necessary qualifications, which were not quite the same for marriage and concubinage, there must, to make a marriage, be a further element, *animus* or *affectio maritalis*. It is widely held that this is a conception not known to the classical law. The reasoning is not convincing, but in any case the point is indifferent for us: the matter is clear in the *Corpus Juris*.[1] The idea is not easily analysed, but it seems to mean that, if the parties lived together meaning to be man and wife, they were man and wife. The question whether this intent, which distinguished marriage from concubinage, actually existed must be decided, like other questions of fact, on the evidence. There was a presumption in favour of marriage if the parties were of equal rank and in some other cases.

It is this *de facto* conception of marriage which enables the lawyers to speak of *nuptiae* where there could be no question of marriage for any legal purpose, e.g. where two Junian Latins (i.e. free persons who by reason of the circumstances of the manumission did not become citizens) were 'married'. They had not the capacity of Roman marriage, and they were not members of any other community under the laws of which they could marry. Some modern writers speak of this as *de facto* marriage, but, in fact, all marriage in Roman law was essentially *de facto*. There was indeed legislation recognising such unions of Junian Latins, if contracted with certain formalities, and making them, when there was a child a year old, avenues to citizenship.[2] But their union is called *matrimonium* whether it is in conformity with this legislation or not.[3] If two Latins lived together it was marriage if they so meant, not otherwise, as with *cives*. It is this *de facto* conception of marriage which makes it possible to use terms expressive of the marriage tie even in speaking of slaves, who are, properly

---

[1] D. 24. 1. 3. 1; 24. 1. 32. 13; 47. 2. 36. 1, etc. See also Vat. Fr. 253b.
[2] G. 1. 29 *sqq.* [3] G. 1. 80.

speaking, capable only of *contubernium*;[1] it is this conception which has led modern writers to coin the expression
matrimonium iuris gentium to describe unions which, while
contemplated as marriage, do not satisfy the civil requirements, e.g. where the parties have not *conubium*, capacity
of Roman marriage. It is a misleading expression, since it
suggests that such marriages are valid everywhere, while
in fact, as every community has its own rules of marriage,
they can hardly be said to be necessarily valid anywhere.
These relations are *nuptiae*, but *nuptiae non iustae*. All this
makes it difficult to define *affectio maritalis*. It can hardly
mean intent to be husband and wife, for two Latins who
did not have their marriage certified under the *l. Aelia
Sentia* knew perfectly well that they could not be husband
and wife for any purpose of the private law, though the
criminal law of adultery did apply to *nuptiae non iustae*.
But that applied also to *concubinatus*, where there was no
marriage and no *animus maritalis*.[2] Thus the expression
seems to mean intent to live together as husband and wife,
to treat each other as husband and wife, and presumably
mere separation ended such a marriage so as to prevent
liability for adultery in respect of later connexions, since
the laws of Augustus, imposing certain forms on divorce,
applied, as it seems, only to *iustae nuptiae*.

With us, at least in modern times, marriage is very
definitely a legal institution. It is hedged round by legal
formalities, execution of documents, etc.[3] To be recognised
as a marriage the transaction must be certified by the
State acting by an official, such as the Registrar or a clergyman of the Established Church, or by one authorised to
act as such in special cases, e.g. the captain of a British
ship. But as an essential of marriage this is comparatively

---

[1] See the numerous texts and inscriptions cited Marquardt, *Privatleben
der Römer*, 2nd ed. p. 176.

[2] D. 48. 5. 14. pr.–4; Mommsen, *Strafr.* p. 694.

[3] The statute law of marriage has now been consolidated in the
Marriage Act, 1949 (12 & 13 Geo. VI, c. 76).

modern. Our old marriage law was the canon law handled
by the ecclesiastical Courts. All that that law required
was a declaration of present intent to be man and wife,
verba de praesenti (which was almost certainly based on
Roman law, but ignored the Roman principle that there
must have been a beginning of joint life),[1] or sexual union
after a betrothal, *verba de futuro*. To this the lay Courts
added, for some purposes in connexion with the law of
real property, a ceremony *in facie ecclesiae*, as a means of
publicity, but this was not essential to the notion of
marriage itself, which could still be contracted by mere
words of consent, a method which has acquired the name
of 'common law marriage'. A marriage might always
have been contracted in this manner till Lord Hardwicke's
Act of 1753 (26 Geo. II, c. 33), since which date certifi-
cation by the Church or by the State has been essential to
the validity of a marriage in England or Wales. It may
therefore be said, in view of the history of the matter, that
these formal requirements are mere matter of necessary
evidence and have not affected the common law conception
of marriage. But the rules do in fact constitute almost
as complete a break-away from the original notions as
occurred in Rome when the old marriage with *manus* was
superseded by the marriage based on mere consent and
entry on joint life, which is that of classical and later law.[2]

---

[1] But Gratian's view to this effect was overruled with difficulty.
P. and M. ii. p. 369, n. 1.

[2] See, on the historical question, P. and M. ii. ch. 7. It is unnecessary
to discuss here the controversial question whether the presence of an
episcopally ordained clergyman was essential to the validity of a common
law marriage *per verba de praesenti*, and, if so, when that requirement
became attached to it. See *R. v. Millis* (1844), 10 Cl. and Fin. 534 (H.L.),
Beamish v. *Beamish* (1861), 9 H.L.C. 274, which pronounced in favour
of the affirmative view. They may well be right, for otherwise the Act of
1753 must, it seems, have imposed on Protestant dissenters a *new* requirement of a peculiarly odious character, from which they were relieved only
by an Act of 1836. Perhaps some nonconformist ecclesiastical historian
will clear up the problem.

Many of the settlements in North America out of which the United States have grown were in existence long before the Act of 1753 which abolished 'common law marriage', i.e. marriage by mere declaration *per verba de praesenti*, and they had taken the conception of common law marriage with them. They were not affected by the Act of 1753, and such marriages are still possible in some States. But the legislation of the States is extremely variable. Some Southern States have dealt with 'marriages' of slaves before they were emancipated, and Roman texts provide a parallel for this.[1] In Oregon, marriage was at one time presumed from one year's cohabitation, whether marriage was intended or not, which obviously recalls the old marriage by *manus* resulting from one year's cohabitation.[2] There is authority for saying that the common law marriage contracted *per verba de praesenti* before an episcopally ordained clergyman, valid before the Act of 1753, is still available for British subjects in places to which that Act (as partly re-enacted by the Marriage Act, 1823) does not extend, that is to say, in foreign countries and in British territory where the common law prevails and has not been altered by legislation.[3]

The effects of marriage are widely different in the two systems. At Rome if there were children there were important rights and duties relative to them. But apart from this the union in itself created hardly any immediate rights and duties. Adultery, though it was a crime, was not a civil wrong. Such duties as there were, so far as enforceable

---

[1] D. 23. 3. 39, 67.

[2] Vernier, *American Family Laws*, i. Sect. 26.

[3] See Hall, *Foreign Jurisdiction of the British Crown*, pp. 110–114, 194; Hailsham xvi. sect. 926. For survival of the common law marriage in American jurisdictions, see Vernier, *loc. cit.* Another American author, Keezer, *Marriage and Divorce*, 2nd ed. Sect. 81, suggests that in common law States, that is, States in which common law marriage is legal, marriages by telephone would be valid. There is clear authority for the validity of marriages by mail.

at law, were few and subsidiary. Indeed the texts repeatedly insist on the notion of *liberum matrimonium* and freedom from legal rule.[1] It has often been pointed out that marriage or no marriage was a question of fact in the same sense as the question, possession or not, was one, though, as was inevitable, both notions became somewhat sophisticated in the hands of the lawyers. The immediate effects were so slight that the question whether marriage was a contract or a conveyance is almost meaningless for Roman law. Marriage carried with it the possibility of a *dos*, a fund provided by or for the wife and vested in the husband during the marriage,[2] as a contribution to the joint expenses, the destiny of the fund when the marriage ended being regulated in classical and later law by highly technical rules varying with the circumstances. But *dos* was not necessary to marriage. Apart from *dos* and, in late law, *donatio ante nuptias*, a similar fund provided by the husband, the finances of the parties were quite distinct. The husband acquired nothing through the wife: what came to her was hers. He was in no way liable for her debts of any kind. She could not pledge his credit. Such a status as *feme coverte* is wholly alien to Roman notions.

The common law conception of marriage, which makes the parties one person for many purposes of property law, is in sharp contrast with the Roman view, under which, apart from *manus*, the marriage produces no effect whatever on property relations. Both systems agree in excluding proceedings for theft between the spouses, though by our modern legislation theft can occur when they are not living together or when the property is taken with a

---

[1] See, e.g., Buckland, *Text-book*, p. 106.

[2] It seems fairly clear that the classical jurists regarded the husband as *dominus*, but Justinian recognised something very like the English distinction between the legal estate and the equitable interest, the husband having the former and the wife the latter. See Pringsheim, 59 *L.Q.R.* p. 244; and p. 82, *post*.

view to their ceasing to live together.[1] The underlying reason in both systems is probably the unseemliness of such proceedings, but the difference in the effect of marriage on the property relations makes the rules work out differently. The common law doctrine was that no theft was conceivable between persons married to each other and thus even an accomplice of the dishonest spouse could not be liable, since there was no theft.[2] The Roman view was that there might well be a theft, as their properties were distinct, but no proceeding of an infaming character, such as the *actio furti*, could be allowed between them. The result was that if there had been an accomplice he was liable, though the spouse was not,[3] without reference to any question of adultery determining the wife's power of dealing with the property.[4]

4. THE FAMILY

The rubric of family law is prominent both in the modern Roman law and in our own law: in the Roman law of the Romans it can hardly be said to find a place. There is indeed what may be called a constitutional law of the family, that is to say, rules as to the constitution of the family and the ways in which it can be entered and left, but there is very little more. The reason for this is to be found in the *patria potestas*.[5]

The immense power of the *paterfamilias*, coupled with his right to determine the relation at any time, makes the Roman family a very different thing from ours. In our

---

[1] Married Women's Property Act, 1882, Sect. 12, and Larceny Act, 1916, Sect. 36, both amended by the Law Reform (Married Women and Tortfeasors) Act, 1935.

[2] *R.* v. *Avery* (1850), Bell. 150.

[3] D. 25. 2. 29; there was machinery for recovery of the property, D. 25. 2; C. 5. 21, *actio rerum amotarum*.

[4] Cf. *R.* v. *Mutters* (1865), Le. and Ca. 511.

[5] See Pound, *Spirit of the Common Law*, p. 27, for an interesting comparison of this with our feudal conception and its reciprocal duties.

law the father has control of the legitimate child, custody and so forth, with an obligation of maintenance, these rights, and, apparently, the obligations, determining at latest when the child is of full age and in some circumstances earlier; the mother's rights are similar when those of the father come to an end by death or otherwise, and since 1925 father and mother are in many respects upon an equality in regard to the guardianship of their legitimate infant children; of illegitimate children it is the mother who has the primary right of custody. And, while these parental rights can be forfeited by misconduct, it seems that the parents cannot rid themselves by their own volition of their obligations in respect of infant children. The child's property is his own: anything given to him by the parent or from outside vests in him, though his powers of administration are very limited in infancy. A parent is not liable upon any of those contracts which an infant may validly make for himself or in respect of any tort which he may commit; but, of course, the parent may have constituted the relationship of principal and agent, or of master and servant, with the child, and thus, since an infant can act as agent or servant, become liable by virtue of one of these relationships. Moreover, parents who give to their infant children, or allow them to use, dangerous toys, such as air-guns, with resulting damage, may find themselves held liable for their own negligence.

In general the consent of parents or guardians is required for the marriage of an infant,[1] but our law lacks the courage of its convictions, since an infant's marriage contracted without such consent may nevertheless be valid.[2]

---

[1] See Sect. 9 of the Guardianship of Infants Act, 1925, and the Schedule.

[2] This is the view of the canon law, even since the Council of Trent. The French monarchy refused to accept the Tridentine decree on this point and acted with peculiar savagery against anyone who married a girl without her parents' consent; and the Courts treated the marriage as tainted with violence and therefore void. See Colin et Capitant, *Cours élémentaire de Droit civil français*, i. No. 155. In England the requirement

The picture in Roman law is very different. Within the family the *paterfamilias* enjoyed a lifelong despotism, tempered till the Empire by an obligation, in serious cases, to consult a family council, whose advice he was in no way bound to follow, and later, more effectually, by the criminal law. The *paterfamilias* could control a son of any age. He could forbid his marriage at any age: in the earlier classical law, and possibly later, he could compel him to divorce. In the Republic, and perhaps later, he could force a marriage on him.[1] His children had no rights against him, and, though there was a shadowy *condominium*, in historical times they could own no property, whatever their age: everything was his. A son was, in this matter, like a slave: all that he acquired vested in the father, except in the Empire his earnings, etc., on military service and in the later Empire his earnings in some other public services. It was not till the fifth century that ordinary acquisitions from outside benefited him in any way in law, and even then the father enjoyed them for his life. The son, like a slave, might have a *peculium* and the father's liabilities on the son's contracts were the same as those on a slave's. For delicts (torts) committed by the son the father was liable in classical law, with the right, similar to that in the case of a slave, of surrendering the son, i.e. letting the injured person take him as a quasi-slave, instead of paying the damages (noxal surrender). The children of the son were in the *potestas* of the grandfather so long as he lived. Apart from noxal surrender and the position of her children, a daughter

---

of consent is very remotely sanctioned by the possibility that the spouses may forfeit property if the law is set in motion against them. But the publicity ensured by the system of banns (or, alternatively, notices) renders it unlikely that such a marriage could take place and, since clergymen and registrars are forbidden to celebrate marriages without the proper consents, the parties would have to make false declarations in order to marry.

[1] His power to compel him to divorce or to marry is denied by Volterra, *Revue Internationale des Droits de l'Antiquité*, i. p. 213.

was in much the same position, but her children were in the
family group of their father. Further, in both cases, the
father could at any moment end his rights and liabilities by
emancipating the child, though the Praetor remedied this
to some extent by giving the child so emancipated a certain
right of succession. All this seems rather intolerable, but
in practice it was not as harsh as it seems. To give the son
a *peculium* with power of administration was normal. The
son was capable of civil rights and liabilities and could
bring some actions, though the limits of this power were
narrow. Emancipation was usual, and was often accompanied by a gift of money. In fact, it seems that by
Justinian's time *filiifamilias* were or might be practically
independent as regards their finances, though this result
is not fully stated in the texts.

It will be seen from what has been said that the position
of the son in classical Roman law was, except that the relation was terminable at the discretion of the *paterfamilias*,
very much that of the wife in the unadulterated common
law; while, on the other hand, the wife, except in the
ancient marriage with *manus*, which put her in the position
of a daughter, but was rare even in early classical law and
totally obsolete in later law, was not for legal purposes a
member of the family at all. This difference in the way of
looking at the family relation is strongly brought out in the
law of succession. This will be discussed later.[1] It is
worth mentioning here that while our earlier law gave the
widow one-third of the personal property absolutely as
against children and a life interest in one-third of the real
property, the new statute gives her a life interest in one-
half of the whole property, real and personal. It may be
that here our law has learnt something from the Roman, for
this is exactly the change made by Justinian in another connexion. When a father emancipated a son, the law of the
late Empire before Justinian gave the father the right to

[1] Pp. 183–185, *post.*

retain absolutely one-third of those acquisitions from out-side (*bona adventitia*) in which he had a life interest, but Justinian altered this to a usufruct, i.e. a life interest, in one-half.[1]

5. ADOPTION AND LEGITIMATION

Adoption in Roman law was a very ancient institution, having its roots in ancestor worship. The maintenance of the family *sacra*, observances in honour of the ancestors of the family, was regarded as of the highest importance, and when a man was old and was likely to die without issue to carry on these observances, he was allowed to 'adrogate' some other independent citizen, a *paterfamilias*, and there-by make him a son. But as this necessarily ended the *familia* of the adopted *paterfamilias* it was allowed only under the supervision of the civil and religious authorities, the latter, the *pontifices*, satisfying themselves that the pro-vision was necessary, that it worked no injustice and that it left persons qualified to carry on the *sacra* of the family from which the adopted *paterfamilias* had sprung. This method of adoption continued in use throughout Roman history, and though the religious aspect of it had dis-appeared in later times, the control by the State was always preserved. But at some time early in the Republic another form of adoption was devised, by which *filiifamilias* in other families could be adopted. This had not necessarily any connexion with the *sacra* and was not supervised by the State, though there was a formal participation. Both brought the *adoptatus* into the family as a *filius* (or *filia*) *familias* exactly like any other child, except that, if the relation was terminated, as it might be, by emancipation, the Praetor did not interfere to give rights of succession as he did in the case of natural-born children so dealt with.

---

[1] The claims of spouses and children as against wills excluding them will be more conveniently dealt with under the law of succession, pp. 167, 183 *sqq., post.*

Later law severely cut down the rights of the *adrogator* in the property which had belonged to the *adrogatus*, and Justinian, in all cases of adoption of a *filiusfamilias* where there was no close tie independent of the adoption, limited the effects of the adoption. There was no change of family and the *adoptatus* acquired only a right of succession on intestacy, with no ground of complaint if he was passed over in the will.

With these institutions in existence there was no great need for any system of legitimation, since a man, at least if he had no other children, could always adrogate his own illegitimate child. When the Empire became Christian a system of legitimation *per subsequens matrimonium* was introduced, but only as regards children then born; it became ultimately a standing rule. The fifth and sixth centuries introduced other methods. They differed in their effects, into which it is impossible to go in detail,[1] but some points must be stated. Till Justinian it was not allowed if there were any legitimate children, and in one of the methods in his time it was not allowed even then. If it was by subsequent marriage, or under petition in the father's will where circumstances had made the marriage impossible, e.g. the woman had died, the child was legitimated for all purposes. But if it was by another authorised method, i.e. *per oblationem curiae*, it was complete so far as the family itself was concerned, but created no relationship or rights as between the child so legitimated and remoter relatives of the father. It was of narrow scope. It seems to have applied mainly, perhaps (notwithstanding loose language in some of the enactments) only, to children born of concubinage, which was a permanent connexion differing from marriage only in that there was no intent to be married. The woman must have been one whom the father could have married at the time of conception. Thus it did not apply to children born of incest or adultery, or to a

---

[1] See, e.g., Buckland, *Text-book*, p. 128.

child born of promiscuous intercourse, or, till very late, to a child by a slave woman, though some of these cases could be dealt with by adoption.[1]

The common law in its original home recognised, till recently, neither *adoptio* nor *legitimatio* as legal institutions. Both of them are however now admitted. A system of adoption was introduced by statute in 1926.[2] But the system so introduced differs fundamentally from that of the Roman law, at any stage. As in Roman law 'adoptio naturam imitatur', and, unless the parties are within the prohibited degrees of consanguinity, such a difference of age is necessary that the adopter might have been the natural parent. Each case is approved by the State, as in *adrogatio*: the Court with us, in Rome the supreme authority or a magistrate, has discretion to refuse to allow the adoption if in the circumstances it thinks it undesirable. The consent of persons interested is required in both systems. But here all resemblance ceased between the Roman institution and the English institution as originally established by the Act of 1926. There was, and is, no question in our law of *patria potestas*, and as the father has not the absolute ascendency of the *paterfamilias*, the consent of both parents is needed and also that of the adopter's spouse. Either parent can adopt and either spouse can adopt separately. No married person and no one over 21 can be adopted. It is essentially adoption of children. The adoption transfers the rights of the parents to the adopter but the rights transferred are merely those of custody and recovery, with the correlative duties of maintenance, education, and so forth. Until 1949, adoption affected no rights of property or succession: the adopted child gained no right of succession on intestacy in the new family, and

---

[1] It is impossible to state the effect of this complex and copious legislation both shortly and correctly. See, for the full story, P. Meyer, *Der römische Konkubinat*, pp. 125 *sqq.*

[2] Adoption of Children Act, 1926 (16 and 17 Geo. V, c. 29).

retained those he had in the old, i.e. the main characteristic and purpose of Roman adoption did not appear at all in the English system. Moreover, it does not appear that it set up any quasi-blood relationship, such as it did in Roman law, so as to constitute a bar to marriage.[1] However, the Adoption of Children Act, 1949, has brought the English institution more in line with the Roman. It has, for instance, enacted that adoption shall bring the adopter and the adopted child, for purposes of marriage, within the prohibited degrees of consanguinity, and that this effect shall survive any further adoption of the adopted child by another person. Moreover, the Act assimilated adopted children to actual children for the purpose of the devolution of disposal of real and personal property; thus they have rights of succession on intestacy, and ordinarily the term 'children' will be held to apply to them when used in any instrument *inter vivos* or a will. Thus it is no longer possible to say that in our law the relationship of adopter to adopted child is little more than a special form of guardianship, as it was described to be by the Committee on Child Adoption, which recommended it;[2] it is contemplated that the adopted child should be assimilated, for most purposes, to an actual child of the adopter.

Legitimation was introduced into our law by a Statute of the same year.[3] This is a good deal more like the Roman institution in its rules and its effects. Like the Roman it is not possible for children of an adulterous connexion, and, like the Roman in its latest state, it creates the same parental rights and duties as in the case of legitimate birth, though they are very different in the two cases. It gives the same rights of succession, both ways, as to all rights accruing after the date of legitimation,[4] as the Roman law

[1] Clarke Hall, *Law of Adoption*, p. 37.
[2] Clarke Hall, *cit.* p. 36.
[3] Legitimacy Act, 1926 (16 and 17 Geo. V, c. 60).
[4] Except a dignity or title of honour, or any property settled to go with it.

did, but, while in Rome this extended only to the immediate family, in the English system it is wider and applies to relations with remoter kin of the legitimating parent. Unlike the Roman, legitimation in England can be effected only by the marriage of the parents, and, again unlike the Roman, it is effected by the marriage *ipso facto*, so that there is no question of consent of the child or of others who may be interested, e.g., children of a former marriage.

Many other common law jurisdictions, in particular Australian and American, had accepted the principles of adoption and legitimation before it was accepted in England. As might be expected, the rules are far from uniform, as to the necessary conditions and as to the effects.[1]

6. MINORITY AND GUARDIANSHIP

In the Roman law and in the common law a very young child is not criminally responsible. As regards civil liability, the fact of minority itself is no defence in an action on tort, except where the action on tort is an indirect attempt to enforce a contract not binding on the minor.[2] But in Roman law, in which an action on delict is essentially an action for a penalty in respect of a wrong done,[3] it is clear that no such action will lie if the child is so young that it is impossible to attribute to him a culpable state of mind, and it is probable that the age, or degree of development, might vary with different wrongs.[4] In the common law authority is scanty: so far as general propositions go in the

---

[1] See, as to legitimation, Fitzpatrick in *Journal of Comparative Legislation*, N.S. vi (1905), pp. 22–45; as to adoption, Stanley Smith, *ibid*. 3rd ser. iii (1921), pp. 165–177, and as to adoption in American jurisdictions, *Notre Dame Lawyer*, January 1932, pp. 223–237.

[2] *Jennings* v. *Rundall* (1799), 8 T.R. 335; *Burnard* v. *Haggis* (1863), 14 C.B.N.S. 45.   [3] Pp. 344 *sqq., post*.

[4] D. 9. 2. 5. 2; 44. 4. 4. 26; 47. 2. 23, etc. For the texts and an account of the growth of the rule from a primitive view which ignored the element of guilt, Pernice, *Labeo*, i. pp. 226 *sqq*.

books, the age of the defendant is immaterial: 'the law knows of no distinction between infants of tender and of mature years'.[1] But what is negligent in an adult might not be in a child, so that damage done by him would not be tortious as it would in an adult;[2] and in view of the fact that when the matter arises the other way and the child is plaintiff, what would be contributory negligence in an adult is not necessarily such in a child,[3] it seems probable that the rule in our law is in practice the same as that in Rome, and that a child would not be held liable for a tort which involves as an essential ingredient a particular state of mind, if he was so young as to be, for that reason, incapable of possessing that state of mind.[4]

As to transactions by a minor the two systems are extremely different. In our law full age is fixed at twenty-one, except that marriage can be contracted at sixteen. In Roman law the important age, for at least classical and earlier law, was that of puberty, ultimately fixed at fourteen for males. It is plain that that age does not represent the acquisition of an adult judgement. Indeed, that is not the basis. Great restrictions were set on the child's power of binding himself or of alienating property up to that time, because till that age he could have no children and his *tutores* were normally the relatives, in whose interest the scheme was originally devised. They had till then a close interest in the property: they took it if the child died. This was not so outrageous as wardship in knight-service, which was treated as an opportunity to bleed the ward's

---

[1] Parke B. in *Morgan* v. *Thorne* (1841), 7 M. and W. pp. 400, 408, though he was not specifically referring to torts.

[2] Hailsham, xxiii. sect. 989.   [3] *Lynch* v. *Nurdin* (1841), 1 Q.B. 29.

[4] Modern civil law systems usually try to make some adult, e.g., a guardian, liable for negligently failing to control the child and, if that is impossible, award the victim out of the child's property such sum as seems fair and equitable in the circumstances. See B.G.B. §§ 828–829; Swiss Code of Obligations, § 54; Italian Civil Code, art. 2047. This treatment seems to have come, *via* natural law, from old Germanic ideas.

estate, but it differed widely from guardianship in socage. There the guardianship was in the next of kin who could not inherit. In Rome it was in those who inherited if the child died, which enabled Sir John Fortescue to score a point in his *De Laudibus Legum Angliae* by saying (ch. 44) that the Roman rule was 'quasi agnum committere lupo ad devorandum'. But by the time of classical law *tutela* had become guardianship in the modern sense with adequate remedies against the *tutor*, and there were other kinds of *tutor* appointed by the will of the *paterfamilias* or by the magistrates.

On the same principle, guardianship (*tutela*) ended at the same age as did the incapacitation. However, a boy of fourteen cannot look after his own affairs, and from early times there was protection (*cura*) for young persons up to the age of twenty-five. But there is much controversy about *cura*: comparison of the two systems is best provided by the *impubes*. Under the Roman law any transaction (contract or conveyance) made by the child without the *auctoritas* of his *tutor* did not bind him, but did bind the other party. If there was *auctoritas* the transaction was valid (though it seems that here too it could be set aside for cause shown) and the guardian (*tutor*) had wide powers of acting on behalf of the child into which it is not necessary to go. These were subsidiary: normally the child acted, with *auctoritas*. This works justly, for the child who has acted without *auctoritas* cannot enforce the contract unless he is prepared to do his part, nor recover what he has handed over without restoring what he has received. There is, however, the disadvantage to the other party that the child is responsible only to the extent to which he is still enriched at the time of the action, so that the risks are on the other party. Thus if a *pupillus* bought and paid for a horse, and received it, the horse was his and the money had not ceased to be his. But if he claimed it he must restore the horse, unless it had ceased to exist without fault.[1] Moreover, if he had already received performance without himself performing his part of the contract, the other party had no redress. In our law in its present state, some contracts of a minor are absolutely valid, e.g. for necessaries, if indeed this is contractual and not quasi-contractual as some hold;[2] others, of a continuing character, are binding unless repudiated within a reasonable time of attaining full age, while others, namely, those 'for the repayment of money lent or to be lent, or for goods supplied or to be supplied (other than contracts for necessaries), and all accounts stated with infants', are void.[3]

Our system is thus rather complex: the Roman was simple, as there were no exceptions to the rule. It would cause little inconvenience, since every child with property or expectation of it had a *tutor* as a matter of course, and his intervention would make the transaction valid. It is not quite accurate to say that the contract is voidable at the choice of the *pupillus*: it is void as against him. If he sells and delivers property and receives the price he acquires the money and still owns the thing. If he buys, he acquires on delivery, but the money he pays remains his.

No particular difficulty arises under either system so long as nothing has been done under the contract, but where there has been part performance the two systems do not give the same results. Where an infant buys goods, even though not necessaries, for cash, and takes delivery, it seems that in our law the transaction stands.[4] The acts of alienation are handled independently of the void agreement under which they were effected,[5] a rule convenient in itself,

---

[1] This seems to result from G. 2. 82; Inst. 2. 8. 2; D. 18. 5. 7. 1; 26. 8. 5. 1.

[2] See Fletcher Moulton L.J. in *Nash* v. *Inman*, [1908] 2 K.B. at p. 8, 'P.A.L.' in 50 *L.Q.R.* (1935) pp. 270 *sqq.* and Cheshire and Fifoot, *Law of Contract*, 2nd ed. pp. 294–295.

[3] Infants Relief Act, 1874, sect. 1.

[4] *Ex p. Taylor, in re Burrows* (1856), 8 De G., M., and G. 254.

[5] In the terminology of modern civilians, they are not causal, but abstract.

though unlike the Roman law. In *Stocks* v. *Wilson*[1] it was held that the property in unnecessary goods passed to an infant even in a case where the price had not been paid, and the equitable remedy of restitution is of doubtful scope. In Roman law the pupil could always recover his money on restoring the goods, and even without doing so, if they had ceased to exist without enriching him and not by his fault.[2] Otherwise the Praetor protected the acquirers. But there was no question of the infant's losing his right by reason of such a change in circumstances as made it impossible to restore things to their original state, or by the acquisition of rights by some third party.

In the large class of contracts of a minor which are voidable in our law, e.g. those involving continuing interests, leases, partnerships, etc., our law allows recovery (on due avoidance) of money paid only if he has not enjoyed any benefit under the contract, that is, if he has received no consideration under it. If he has and he withdraws, he forfeits what he has already paid.[3] The rule is well illustrated by *Everett* v. *Wilkins*.[4] Under an agreement for partnership the minor was to be boarded for pay. He was to pay, and did pay, a deposit, but he was to draw no profit from the concern till the whole purchase money was paid. The minor renounced the partnership. It was held that he could recover the deposit, as he had had as yet no enjoyment, less a payment for the board and lodging which was treated as a distinct and collateral contract. Roman law would apparently have given the same result; he had not alienated the money he had paid, so that he could recover it, but he would be met by an *exceptio doli* unless he allowed for the benefit he had received. But our law, involving forfeiture of what has been paid, if there

---

[1] [1913] 2 K.B. 235.

[2] D. 12. 6. 13. 1; h.t. 29; 18. 5. 7. 1, etc. The texts are not very explicit, but this seems to follow from the fact that his alienation is void.

[3] *Holmes* v. *Blogg* (1817), 8 Taunt. 508; *Corpe* v. *Overton* (1833), 10 Bing. 252.   [4] (1874), 29 L.T. (N.S.) 846.

has been any enjoyment, does only a rough justice in some cases. In *Valentini* v. *Canali*[1] a minor hired a house and agreed to buy the furniture in it for £102. He paid £68 on account of the price. After some months' occupation he renounced the lease. It was held that he could not recover the £68. In the view of the Court to allow recovery would be 'cruel injustice', 'contrary to natural justice'. Yet it is clear that what has been paid need bear no relation to what has been enjoyed: in this case more than two-thirds of the price was much more than a just equivalent for a few months' use of the furniture. It seems probable that the fact that the house also had been enjoyed for some months may have come into account, though this does not appear in the judgement. In Roman law the *pupillus* could have claimed a refund, but would have been met by an *exceptio doli* to enforce the reasonable set-off. The English law has recently been considered by the Court of Appeal in *Steinberg* v. *Scala (Leeds) Ltd.*,[2] from which it appears that the test is whether the minor has received some consideration as the result of the transaction: if so, he cannot recover what he has paid; if, on the other hand, there has been a total failure of consideration, he can. So, in that case, where the minor had subscribed for shares in a company and paid the money due on allotment and certain calls on the shares, while it was admitted that it was still open to her to repudiate the contract and have her name removed from the register, she was not allowed to recover from the company the money paid on the shares, the reason being that she had received under the contract some consideration, some money's worth; she could have sold the shares for cash, though she did not.[3] But in comparing the two systems it must be borne in mind that there is a wide difference between a young man or woman approaching full age and a child under fourteen.

[1] (1889), 24 Q.B.D. 166. [2] [1923] 2 Ch. 453.
[3] See also *Pearce* v. *Brain*, [1929] 2 K.B. 310.

In Roman law, as in ours, a father could appoint a guardian (*tutor*), but a mother had no such right as our modern statutes have conferred on her. Guardianship by the nearest male relatives as such was prominent in Roman law, but has no place in our modern law. As with our guardians, a *tutor* might if necessary be appointed by the Court, though there was no such institution as a ward of Court. The functions of a *tutor* were not quite those of a modern guardian. He was essentially the administrator of the property. He had not the custody of the child or any responsibility for his education, beyond the provision of funds from the estate. On the other hand he had large powers of alienation and acquisition on behalf of the ward, such alienations requiring, in some cases, leave of the Court. The fact that the ward himself, so soon as he was old enough to have what was called *intellectus*, could act, with the *auctoritas* of his *tutor*, lessened the need for this power of alienation, and it seems that an alienation which the *tutor* could not effect without leave of the Court he could not authorise without it. But though he could acquire and alienate, he could not contract, on behalf of the child.[1] The contracts of the *tutor* were his own: he alone was liable and entitled. But, apart from the fact that the child's power of acting with *auctoritas* lessened the need for independent contracts by the *tutor*, all these matters could be dealt with in the final adjustments of accounts; there was machinery by which at the close of the wardship outstanding rights and liabilities of the *tutor* in the ward's affairs were transferred to the ward, so that the *tutor* was no longer concerned with them. Herein our law is vitally different: no amount of approval by parents or guardians can enlarge a minor's contractual capacity, except that under the Infants' Settlements Act, 1855, a male minor of twenty years and a female of seventeen may

[1] On the personal nature of obligation in Roman law, see Buckland, *Text-book*, p. 407.

make a binding settlement upon marriage with the approval of the Court of Chancery (now the Chancery Division), which has immemorially exercised on behalf of the Crown, as being the guardian of all infants, a paternal jurisdiction. Where our law has considered it of vital importance that there should always be someone with power to alienate, as in the case of the legal estate in land, steps have been taken to ensure that the property shall not be vested in the infant,[1] but in someone of full age who holds it on trust for him.

The Roman law had however another type of minority: persons under twenty-five were not indeed under disabilities at law, but could get transactions set aside if the Court thought they had been led into them by youthful inexperience (*inconsulta facilitas*) though there was no fraud. *Curatores* could be appointed to them with their consent, who were a protection rather to third parties than to the minor. In later law the protection was gradually increased until a minor under a *curator* was in a position much like that of a ward under *tutela*, with differences of terminology. He is *curator*, not *tutor*, and gives *consensus*, not *auctoritas*. At least in later law, he administers the affairs of the minor. But the Emperor could give males of twenty and females of eighteen the rights of full age (*venia aetatis*),[2] a relief similar to, but obviously much wider than that given by Chancery under our law.

A remarkable institution of the earlier Roman law, merely formal even in classical law, and obsolete before Justinian, is the lifelong wardship of women. It is ascribed to *levitas animi*, but Gaius has the grace to admit that this explanation 'magis speciosa videtur quam vera'.[3] Its real explanation is in the original conception of *tutela* itself. This

[1] Law of Property Act, 1925, Sect. 1 (6).

[2] D. 4. 4. 3. pr.; C. 2. 44. 1. Grants are still made under Roman-Dutch law in Ceylon and the Orange Free State; see Lee, *Introduction to Roman-Dutch Law*, 4th ed. p. 45.

[3] G. 1. 144, 190.

was for the protection of the property in the interest of the relatives who would succeed if the person died without issue capable of succeeding (*sui heredes*). As a woman could have no *sui heredes*, for her children had no right of succession to her at civil law, the interest of the relatives was lifelong and so therefore was the *tutela*. With the change in the conception which began in mid-Republic the institution became an anachronism and it was gradually lessened of content till it disappeared. Our law has never had this institution, but reached male control of a woman's property by a different road, partly by the original law of the lord's right of marriage in knight-service, which seems to have applied at first only to female heirs, and partly by the control of her husband, who was for practical purposes owner of her freehold land during her marriage and absolute owner of her personalty.[1] This attitude is very different from that of the Roman law, under which her marriage made no difference at all to her property rights and her husband had, apart from the ancient *manus*, no interest at all in her property, nor had she in his. But for many centuries there were her *tutores* in the background whose authority was necessary for certain of her formal acts.[2]

7. JURISTIC PERSONALITY

As to corporate personality we ought not to expect to find much difference between Roman law and ours, since our theory of corporations seems to be mainly derived from medieval interpretations of the Roman law. The Romans had no such word as *personalitas* and they did not use the word *persona* in the technical sense of 'right- and duty-bearing unit'. It has indeed begun to creep in among the orientals of the late Empire,[3] but it does not appear in the *Corpus Juris*. A *persona* was simply a human being. A

---

[1] With certain exceptions which we need not discuss.
[2] On this subject see now P. W. Duff, *Personality in Roman Private Law*.
[3] See Buckland, *Text-book*, p. 173.

corporate body is never called a person though it has legal capacities. The nearest word to 'personality' is *caput*, but no text speaks of the *caput* of a corporation. The municipalities had certain powers, e.g. of acquiring property *inter vivos* and of contracting: they had had them when they were absorbed in the State and they retained them, but this rests on no legal theory: it is older than theorising about law. As new corporations were recognised similar powers were expressly conferred on them. The more uncommercial powers, e.g. of manumitting slaves, and of acquiring by will, were bestowed on them and other corporate bodies piecemeal by various acts of legislation at various dates, the history of which can be found in the manuals; but the Romans never seem to have reached the notion of rights and duties inherent in corporate character.

It is indeed a debated point among Romanists whether in the time of Ulpian they were thought of as anything more than groups of persons, on whom, as groups, certain rights had been conferred by legislation. The *populus Romanus* was itself, essentially, only a municipality and thus a corporate body in the sense in which any city was, but there seems no trace in historical times of an *institutio* of the Roman people as *heres* by anyone subject to the Roman State. The only cases of any historical value are of foreign States, the kings or queens of which left their State and property to the Roman people.[1] But the State as a corporation plays little part in the law because it settles the questions with which it is concerned by administrative methods, not appealing to its own Courts. And it disappears in the classical age. The sovereignty is no longer in the people: it is in Caesar. And Caesar is a man, possibly what we should call a corporation sole, the *fiscus* being merely a department of State.[2] It is true that the

---

[1] E.g. Cicero, *De l. agr.* 2. 16. 41.

[2] See however, for a very different view, Mitteis, *Röm. Privatrecht*, pp. 347 *sqq.*

devolution of the property was governed by special 'publicistic' rules. So is that of the Duchy of Cornwall, but the Prince of Wales is a private man. In fact the conception of the State in later Roman law was very like ours: it does not seem to distort the facts to say that technically the State as such is not incorporated, but the property which practically belongs to the community is thought of as vested in the Emperor, as it is in our King, or, as he is usually described for this purpose, 'the Crown'.

The question whether a corporate body was thought of as an ideal unit is not quite the same as the question whether it was a person in law. The former affirmation need mean no more than that it could have rights conferred on it: the latter would mean that it had of necessity a mass of potential rights and duties such as are associated with a person in law. The Romans seem to have taken the first view, as also does our law.[1] However that may be, leaving out of account corporate cities taken over ready made, the 'concession' theory was firmly established in Roman law. No body could have corporate powers unless they were conferred on it, and it had only such powers as were expressly conferred by its charter. Even the notion of an ideal unit is not always grasped. Throughout later Roman history and indeed throughout medieval times there is a constant tendency to fall back on the conception of a corporation as a mere group of people. In Digest 48. 18. 1. 7 Ulpian is clear that the slave of a corporation belongs to the corporation and is not *servus plurium*. Elsewhere he holds that a municipality cannot take a succession as 'universi consentire non possunt'.[2] A little later Marcian, while clear that *cives* individually own nothing in a slave of the city, calls him '*servus communis civitatis*'.[3] And when not

---

[1] The recent developments in the criminal liability of corporations seem to show that English law is assimilating juristic persons much more closely to national persons. See R. S. Welsh, 62 *L.Q.R.* pp. 345 *sqq.*
[2] D. 38. 3. 1. 1.　　　[3] D. 1. 8. 6. 1.

long after the publication of the Digest Stephanos set out to explain the text, he says that such a slave belongs to the *polis* κοινῶς ἀδιαιρέτως, language which at least tends to confuse the line between common and corporate owner-ship.[1] Both the ordinary gloss[2] and the canonists have the doctrine quite clearly. But Bracton and his master Azo were not very clear that the *res civitatis* were not the *res omnium civium*.[3] This was at the time when Innocent IV was grafting on the Roman concession theory the 'fiction' theory. Whether that theory be sound or not it implies a clear grasp of the distinction between the mere group and the ideal unit. But in fact in our law and on the continent it seems that the whole notion had to be thought out over again.[4]

The history of *collegia*, craft guilds, burial clubs, etc. is very obscure. But the course of events seems to have been much the same as with us. In the later law their existence as legal units is subjected to strict rules—the concession theory—but in early times they seem to have had an existence, and even property, with no strict analysis of their position. They were, for the purposes of private law, of very small importance: like the guilds spoken of in Pollock and Maitland, they spent most of their small funds in *potationes*.[5] In both systems it seems to have been not difficulties or problems of private law, thorny though these might be, which led to the establishment of State control, but fears for public order.

Except so far as some of these *collegia* had charitable aims, classical law had no corporate charities. There were clumsy devices for securing perpetuity to charitable en-dowments,[6] but charitable foundations as corporate bodies

---

[1] *Basilica*, 46. 3. 5, sch. τῆς ὁμάδος; Heimbach, 4. 560.
[2] *ad ll. citt.* [3] P. and M. i. p. 686.
[4] See the story told in P. and M. i. Bk. ii, ch. 2, sect. 12; *cit.* ch. 3, sect. 8.
[5] P. and M. i. p. 494. For the Roman *collegia*, Daremberg et Saglio, *Dict. des Antiq.* s.v. [6] Pernice, *Labeo*, iii. 1. p. 56.

belong to the Christian Empire. As with us, the starting point seems to have been gifts to churches, already recognised as corporate, for specified purposes. Most charities continued to have this character, but there appeared also charities for all manner of purposes with which the church had no concern, except, possibly, a general duty of supervision, and even this was sometimes expressly excluded. Their character was never clearly analysed, i.e. the question is never clearly answered: who were the legal owners of the property? Many views are held. Mitteis goes so far as to say that these foundations were independent 'Stiftungen' in the German sense, i.e. the property was vested in the fund itself, but it seems safe to say that any such notion would have been unintelligible to the Romans or the Byzantines. On the whole the better view seems to be that the owners were the administrators for the time being. They were thus much like the trustees of a modern unincorporated charity, but there is a fundamental difference. They are not the legal owners in the sense that any act of disposition is valid, subject to the intervention of the Court at the instigation of aggrieved persons: the acts of disposition which they can effect are closely defined and any alienation in excess of powers is simply void. And it seems from the verbose but obscure legislation of Justinian that the rules were enforced by administrative methods, usually by the Bishop, as if the Charity Commissioners put the matter right without any intervention of the Chancery.

It seems to represent fairly the position of the Bishop, as to property of the Church, and of the heads of charities, to say that they hold the property in right of the Church or House, and Justinian provided, for both Bishops and controllers, that they might not alienate from the Church or House anything which they had themselves acquired since acceptance of the office, except what came from near relatives.[1] The position of heads of monasteries is not

[1] C. 1. 3. 41. 5, 6, 11.

stated: presumably, as monks, they were incapable of acquiring anything. It is only because Bishops and *Oeconomi*
are secular that the question arises.[1]

The Roman inability or unwillingness to frame a theory
for a number of miscellaneous groups and group activities
finds a certain parallel in our own law. We recognise the
existence of many associations which are neither partnerships nor corporations, and when they give rise to trouble-
some questions, as they frequently do, we usually solve
them (or evade them) in some purely empirical way, either
judicially or by legislation. Thus, many clubs, many building societies, and many literary and scientific institutions
are unincorporated associations. Neither friendly societies
nor trade unions are corporations, though the latter have
been judicially referred to as 'quasi-corporations' and bear
certain resemblances to corporations, for instance in regard
to the liability of their funds for the tortious acts of their
agents[2] and in regard to the doctrine of *ultra vires*.[3]

[1] Professor de Zulueta, in a letter, says that there is a good deal of
evidence that in early times abbots held the abbey property and passed it
by will to their successors.

[2] Before the Trade Disputes Act, 1906.

[3] The Taff Vale decision, [1901] A.C. p. 426, has sometimes been
claimed as evidence in favour of the recognition of legal personality without
any concession by the State; but it must be noted that the Court was only
determining the effect of certain statutes. However, in Scotland a partnership was a person at common law even before the enactment of the
Partnership Act, 1890; it is hard to see any concession there. It would be
interesting to know whether the distinction between Scots and English
law on this point is more than accidental.

CHAPTER III. LAW OF PROPERTY

1. LAND AND MOVEABLES

The first point of interest to note is the comparative insignificance in Roman law of the distinction between land and other property. It is not wholly ignored. Land requires a longer period for acquisition by possession for a certain time. Land cannot be stolen. There are special restrictions on the power of alienation of land by those in a fiduciary position, such as tutors and curators. There were in classical law, diminished under Justinian, material differences in the possessory remedies affecting it. There were other differences but they do not altogether amount to very much. The distinction in our law between freehold and leasehold interests can hardly be said to exist in Roman law, for a term of years was not regarded as creating an interest in land at all: it was throughout the Roman law only a contractual right giving in general no remedies, proprietary or possessory, against third parties. It thus resembles our term of years in the early part of its career, when, according to Pollock and Maitland,[1] 'in an evil hour' it was affected by Roman law ideas and the termor was likened to the *conductor* who had not even possession of the land.[2]

Throughout the greater part of the history of Roman law the most prominent distinction was that between *res mancipi*, which were transferable at civil law only by a formal ritual act, and *res nec mancipi*, which were transferable by delivery. *Res mancipi* are, roughly, land, slaves

---

[1] ii. pp. 114, 115.

[2] English law did eventually get out of the difficulty. French law has never succeeded in getting leases clear of the law of obligations and attributing to them a 'real' character. Hence it is still impossible to hypothecate (mortgage) a lease, which is indeed treated as a moveable. See Amos and Walton, *Introduction to French Law*, p. 104, n. 5.

and cattle, but it must not be supposed that this means land with certain accessories. For it is obvious from the form of the conveyance by way of *mancipatio*[1] that it was originally designed for moveables. Indeed the form dates from a time when land was for the most part not the subject of private ownership, and what land could be owned, the *heredium*, was not transferable. *Res mancipi* were in fact slaves and cattle, the most valuable property to a primitive people and, very probably, at one time the only things to which the formal proprietary remedies were applicable. But even the difference between *res mancipi* and others is relatively unimportant. It affected the form of conveyance, and the rights of women under guardianship, so long as the *tutela* of women existed, to alienate. It involved no difference in the law of succession, no difference in the interests which could be created, and of course none of the differences, as to notice, etc., which exist under our law of trusts. It must also be noted that the distinction between *res mancipi* and others is gone in Justinian's law: *mancipatio*, in any real sense of the term, is extinct.

It is true that in the very nature of things, land raises questions which do not arise in relation to other property. Thus the law of easements and the like constitutes a chapter as important in the Roman law as in our own, which has indeed gone to the Roman law for many of its principles in this matter. And questions arise between adjoining owners of land which can hardly arise with moveables. Injuries and interferences with rights are far more likely between neighbouring landowners than in relation to moveables and there was in Roman law a very elaborate system of remedies[2] for such cases, remedies which are so fully treated as to show that they were of great practical importance. And there are not wanting

---

[1] G. 1. 119 *sqq.*

[2] *Damnum infectum*, interdict *quod vi aut clam, operis novi nuntiatio*, etc.

signs in the later law that land, which has come to be called *res immobilis*, as opposed to *res mobilis* or *se movens*, needed special treatment in many respects. Thus special publicity was required for the alienation of land.[1]

There was much regulation of mining rights, notably, in the later Empire the rule that lodes could be pursued under neighbouring property subject to royalties fixed by law.[2] There were legal restrictions on the enjoyment of land and houses, some of which will shortly be considered. But the distinction remained vastly less important than it has been in our law.

2. PROPERTY AND POSSESSION

A very striking characteristic of the Roman law is the clearness with which it brings out the notion of ownership and the difference between property and possession. Property or ownership is, roughly, title: possession is, roughly, actual enjoyment. Both of them become, as is inevitable in legal notions, a little sophisticated. Their absolute distinctness is brought out in the strong statement that 'nihil commune habet proprietas cum possessione'[3] and in the rule, which seems indeed to have existed in our earlier law[4] but was maintained to the last in Roman law, that where possession was the matter in issue, title was immaterial: the defendant could not set it up in defence. Ownership being thus clearly conceived, the Romans saw no difficulty in proof of it. Every person who claimed property as his must allege ownership and prove it. And though there may have been a time when such things as *compurgatio* existed we know nothing of them: from the earliest historical times proof had to be real. We may however suppose, since there were in classical law practically no rules of evidence, that evidence of reputation of ownership may often have been decisive. But there were none

---

[1] Vat. Fr. 35, 249; C. Th. 8. 12. 7.   [2] C. 11. 7. 3.
[3] D. 41. 2. 12. 1.   [4] P. and M. ii. p. 49.

of the artificial modes of proof known to our earlier law,[1] which compels us to speak, not of the burden of proof, but of the benefit of proof.

Thus in Roman law a holder had title or had not. If he had no title he might still be in a position to claim possessory remedies. If he had title either to ownership, or to a lesser interest, e.g. a usufruct, which was normally a life interest, he had proprietary remedies and he might also have possessory remedies. And the nature of his possessory remedies will be in no way affected by the question whether he has any sort of title: a man possesses or he does not, with some reservations which we need not discuss. But the Roman system has two anomalous figures. One who had taken possession in good faith and was in process of acquiring by long possession (*in via usucapiendi*) had not only the possessory remedies but one which must be classed as proprietary, the *actio Publiciana*. By this action (we need not consider its highly technical form) he could recover the property from anyone who held it except the real owner. Here then there seems to be a case in which ownership and possession are not kept distinct. His right to bring the proprietary action depends on his possession, or, rather, on the fact that he has had possession. The exception is really only apparent. He is more than a possessor. Not only must his possession have begun in good faith but he must have, if not a title, at least a *titulus*. He must be able to show *iusta causa*, i.e. that his taking was accompanied by some act or event, such as a conveyance, which is ordinarily a root of title.[2] His title is absolutely good against any but the true owner and

---

[1] P. and M. ii. p. 47; Holdsworth, ii. p. 107.

[2] Cf. P. and M., speaking of the assize of novel disseisin, in which they see the influence of Roman law acting either immediately, or through the medium of canon law, referring no doubt to the interdict *uti possidetis* (ii. p. 47). They write (ii. p. 50): 'This thought, that the disseisor gets his seisin by the acquiescence or negligence of the ousted possessor, becomes prominent in after times. Under its influence the justices begin to require

absolutely bad against him. Thus he is superficially like an equitable owner, but there is nothing in the nature of a trust. As his title is good against everybody but one, there is much controversy in modern times on the question whether he is properly to be regarded as owner, whether he has or has not a *ius in rem*. It does not appear that any text calls him owner, but that is not the kind of question with which the Roman lawyers were much concerned. The 'equitable' character of his right is also, it must be noted, merely temporary. In what, for us, seems a very short time it becomes full ownership by lapse of time. A variant of this figure is that of the bonitary owner. The typical bonitary owner is one who has received a *res mancipi* from the owner but without the formal conveyance required by civil law. There are many other ways in which one may be in this position, but they are all alike in the sense that the title is in practice perfectly good. As in the last case the ownership will become civil by lapse of time, but, in the meanwhile, as the holder is not *dominus* he will have to bring, like the *bona fide* possessor, the *actio Publiciana* but, unlike the *bona fide* possessor, he can bring it effectively against the *dominus*. The bonitary owner has disappeared from the law of Justinian.

The second anomalous figure is that of the person to whom public lands have been granted. Such grants were theoretically, and to some extent practically, subject to revocation, and the holders are called *possessores*. With these may be grouped the holder of provincial land, the *dominium* of which, at least in the Empire, is in the State.

that a plaintiff shall show something more than mere possession, that he shall show either that he came into the land by title, for example, by a feoffment, or else that he has been in possession for some little time.' By the time of Edward I they were even insisting on some title older than 1230, i.e., over fifty years before. See Plucknett, *Legislation of Edward I*, pp. 73–74. For his acceptance, against Maitland and Holdsworth, of Joüon des Longrais' views on seisin, see *ibid*. p. 53.

Both of these are practically owners: they have, in addition to the possessory remedies, proprietary remedies, though the forms of these are not perfectly known. The first class disappeared in the third century of the Empire when a statute definitely declared their rights to be ownership, and the second is gone under Justinian when the distinction between Italic and provincial land was abolished.[1] It will be noticed in connexion with these lands that they give us almost the only trace in Roman law of a notion approximating to that of tenure which has played so great a part in our law and still dominates its terminology. If, as is commonly held,[2] in an action to recover such property from a third party the right was expressed as 'habere frui possidere licere' or the like, the analogy with our traditional 'to have and to hold' is extremely close. But, substantially, the notion of tenure plays no part in the Roman law.

Dominium may be roughly translated as ownership. But if we conceive ownership as the *ius utendi, fruendi, abutendi*, it is obvious that it is only a very rough translation. For we have just seen cases in which the *dominus* has hardly any real interest in the property, e.g. where a *dominus* has transferred a *res mancipi* by *traditio*, creating a bonitary ownership. He does retain some rights in some forms of property but they are very little, and there may be in some circumstances a possibility of reverter. We can think of it as a 'dry legal estate'. But it is on the whole more akin to a feudal seignory. The bonitary owner in fact 'holds of' the *dominus*, and Italian Romanists habitually translate *dominium* by the word *signoria*. It is in fact the ultimate right to the thing or, as it has been more paradoxically expressed, it is minimal residual right, what is left

---

[1] Buckland, *Text-book*, pp. 189 *sq*. Perhaps a similar notion of tenure was the original reason for attributing *possessio* to the tenant at will (*precario*) and the tenant of *ager vectigalis*, the prototype of the *emphyteuta*. See p. 83 *post*.

[2] See, e.g., Girard, *Manuel*, 8th ed. p. 379.

when all other rights vested in various people are taken out.[1]

Thus the Roman law which sharply distinguishes ownership from possession and requires a plaintiff seeking to recover land to prove his title, and does not for practical purposes recognise degrees of ownership, presents a picture very different from that offered by our law at any stage in its development. No doubt there were in our early law real actions in the Roman sense, actions in which the plaintiff had to allege and prove ownership of some sort: the proceedings based on a writ of right.[2] But in general when our old lawyers speak of real actions they mean actions in which the plaintiff seeks to recover the thing itself, and not merely compensation for a breach of right, and such actions need not be real actions in the Roman sense at all.[3] And the writs of right were unpopular by reason of their technicality, their strange modes of proof, and their uncertainty. Other forms took their place, and what was left of them practically disappeared in the seventeenth century when the fictitious ejectment was invented and John Doe made his first appearance.[4] But, apart from this, and long before, a welter of remedies had been invented which provided us with a system utterly unlike the Roman. Apart from the complications introduced by the notion of tenure and its varieties, which we shall not consider, they are dominated by the important conception of seisin. It would be beyond the writers' competence to discuss this conception and its history.[5] We are told that 'Seisin is possession'.[6] And there are a mass of actions, novel

---

[1] See Buckland, *Elementary Principles of Roman Private Law*, p. 64; J. C. Naber, *Mnemosyne*, 1929, pp. 177 *sqq.*

[2] P. and M. ii. p. 62; Holdsworth, ii. p. 261; Jenks, *Short History of English Law*, ch. iv.   [3] P. and M. ii. pp. 570 *sqq.*

[4] Holdsworth, vii. pp. 9–19; Jenks, *cit.* 3rd ed. pp. 177 *sqq.*

[5] Maitland, 'The Mystery of Seisin', 'The Beatitude of Seisin' in *Collected Papers*, i. pp. 358 *sqq.*, 407 *sqq.*; P. and M. ii. pp. 29 *sqq.*

[6] P. and M. ii. p. 29.

disseisin, mort d'ancestor, writs of entry, in which the primary question is whether a party was or is seised or not. Possession is always involved, but the remedies and the rights vary according as there is or is not some kind of *titulus* behind it, and with the nature of that *titulus*.

This leads to the main contrast between the two systems in this matter. So far is the common law from the sharp distinction of the Roman law between ownership and possession that we learn that there is a hierarchy of actions, a sort of descending scale from the purely proprietary to the purely possessory. '"Possessoriness" has become a matter of degree',[1] all very different from the rule that possession has nothing in common with ownership. And this leads to another contrast equally significant. When, in our ancient courts, two persons were disputing about land, both might have some sort of seisin and the question was, which had the better seisin. The question was never simply which of these two is owner, but which has the better right of the two, which has *maius ius*. 'No one is ever called on to demonstrate an ownership good against all men; he does enough even in a proprietary action if he proves an older right than that of the person whom he attacks.'[2] It is a relative ownership: 'I own it more than you do.' This is very different from the Roman way of thinking. For the Roman lawyers ownership was absolute, subject to the very limited exception of the *bona fide* possessor with a *titulus*. Apart from this there was no question of an ownership good against one but not against another. It is worth observing that in this matter Roman law stood alone; in Greek systems of law the conception was relative, like our own,[3] and it may possibly have been so in the early procedure by *legis actio*.[4]

---

[1] P. and M. ii. p. 74.
[2] P. and M. ii. p. 77; Holdsworth, iii. p. 7.
[3] Mitteis, *Reichsrecht und Volksrecht*, p. 70.
[4] Betti, *Ist.* 2. 655.

There are no longer in our law any forms of action, but every action which is in practice an action for the recovery of personalty seems to be an action in tort or contract based on possession or the right to possess. The plaintiff need not assert ownership, though often no doubt he must prove facts which amount to proof of ownership, or at any rate to evidence of it, in order to justify his claim. But any possession is good against a trespasser and there are different degrees of right to possess, so that all the plaintiff has to prove is that he has a better right to possess than the defendant has; in fact the old principle of *maius ius* is still in full operation.[1] It is permissible to quote, in support of the proposition that in our law it is always a question of *maius ius*, two passages. Pollock and Wright[2] say: 'In the language of the modern authorities "possession is a good title", nothing less, "against all but the true owner".' And the late Professor Kenny, in his *Cases on the Law of Tort*, in a rubric to *Graham* v. *Peat*[3] sums up the law on the matter as being that 'Mere possession gives the possessor a right of action against all who disturb it without having some better right than his'.[4] A recent article by Professor Goodhart[5] shows how conflicting are the language of the books and the cases on questions of possession, but it is mainly on the question what is possession. It is broadly true to say that our Courts deal with rights to possess where the Roman Courts dealt with ownership. Our normal actions for the recovery of land or goods are based upon right of possession and not upon ownership, though it must not be overlooked that since 1883 the

[1] It does not seem necessary to consider the extent to which in such actions a defendant can set up *ius tertii* if indeed he can ever set it up.

[2] *Possession in the Common Law*, p. 96, citing *Asher* v. *Whitlock* (1865), L.R. 1 Q.B. 1, 6.

[3] (1801), 1 East 244.   [4] P. 389.

[5] 'Three Cases on Possession', *Cambridge Law Journal*, iii (1928), pp. 195 *sqq.* (reprinted in *Essays in Jurisprudence and the Common Law*, ch. iv).

Courts have the power to make a declaration of right or title, even when no question of the right to possession is raised and no substantive or ancillary relief is sought.[1]

If it be asked how it was that the Romans insisted on title, or in the one case of the *bona fide* possessor, *titulus*, i.e. *prima facie* title, and retained real actions to the end, the answer seems to be that it was infinitely easier for a Roman to prove a good title than it is with us. Indeed it is not easy to see how it could have been done at all in the great majority of cases till recent times. No length of title could prove that it was good to begin with. In the law as it was before the statute 32 Hen. VIII, c. 2, there was 'scarce any limitation at all',[2] and this statute and others which followed it set up long periods of time the expiry of which, without creating a title in the defendant, might bar the plaintiff and required him to prove not title but some kind of seisin within the prescribed period. This is far short of title, for there might have been other and adverse seisins within the prescribed period. All that he proved was that he had an older and therefore a better seisin than that of the defendant. He proved a relative title, or at best, a state of facts which made it unlikely that there was any better title. He could not prove more.[3] But in Rome *usucapio* was a positive root of title, with nothing relative about it: it gave absolute ownership. And the periods, one year for moveables and two for land, were extremely short. Anyone acquiring in any of the ordinary ways, if he was not owner at once, became owner in a very short time and could prove it very simply. When at an uncertain date it became possible to add his predecessor's time the matter was simpler still.[4] How it worked under the law of

---

[1] Odgers on the Common Law, 3rd ed. pp. 493–495 and 590, 591.

[2] Cruise, *Digest*, vol. iii, *tit.* XXXI. 4.

[3] As to the present law, *post*, pp. 79 *sqq.*

[4] How much difficulty was caused in practice by the requirement that the thing must not have been stolen it is not easy to say. In any case it did not apply to land. See further, pp. 76 *sq.*, 120–122, *post*.

Justinian when the two years had become ten or twenty according to circumstances it is difficult to say. Probably the system became rather unworkable, and it is not wholly insignificant that we are informed by a recent writer[1] that some modern systems based on the Roman law have found it necessary to abandon the 'absolute' notion of the Romans and regularly proceed on the lines of *maius ius*.

In both systems it is difficult to find a satisfactory theory of possession, especially with regard to moveables. Indeed possession illustrates well the casuistic, empirical method which is common to the Roman and the English lawyer. If a conception is workable, they do not much mind whether it is logical or not. Neither system ever worked out an adequate theory of possession, and, in the course of the development of each, views upon possession underwent considerable change. Both recognise a mental element (*animus*) and a physical element (*corpus*) and both shrink from defining these elements. In both, a man who takes wrongfully can have possession, with the striking difference that in Rome the claim of right could not be raised in the possessory proceedings and the person entitled was driven to an independent action, while, with us, except in the very earliest times 'the English law has always had the good sense to allow title to be set up in defence to a possessory action'.[2]

Perhaps the two systems differ most in the choice of persons to whom possession is attributed. They concur in allowing only what we call 'custody' (*possessio naturalis* in at least the later Roman law), and not possession, to the servant, though the English rule has not always been so[3]

---

[1] Cornil, *Bulletin de l'Académie Royale de Belgique*, 1931 (Lettres), pp. 178 *sqq.*

[2] Holmes, *The Common Law*, p. 210; cf. Maitland, *Collected Papers*, i. p. 426.

[3] Pollock and Wright, *Possession in the Common Law*, p. 9.

and moreover breaks down when it attributes to a servant possession of chattels and money entrusted to him for his master. But beyond that there is great divergence. The Romans were more reluctant than we are to attribute possession to anyone unless he was owner or in a fair way to become owner or one whose holding did not depend on concession from anyone else, one who held *pro suo*. Thus they denied possession to a borrower for use (commodatary), a depositee, or a tradesman working on a chattel, all of whom in modern English law have possession. The *sequester*, one with whom property in dispute is deposited, and the pledgee, were exceptions: the Roman law gave them *possessio* for obvious practical reasons. The *sequester* would, with us, have possession as an ordinary bailee, and, as to the pledgee, our text-books and reports speak of him, as indeed they do of other bailees, as having a 'special property' in the thing, the 'general property' remaining in the pledgor.[1] This, however, means no more than legal possession, though the pledgee has certain rights of detention and disposition not necessarily held by other bailees.

EXCURSUS: PROPERTY AND POSSESSION

It must be admitted that in both Roman and English law it is difficult to find a satisfactory theory of possession, especially with regard to moveables, and that both Roman and English lawyers have been quite satisfied with a conception of possession so long as it is workable.[2] Perhaps one might add that in both laws failure to think out the subject on logical lines has caused difficulty in exceptional cases. However, in both laws the lawyers have had some picture of possession at the back of their minds, even though the outlines have been rather hazy, and they have

---

[1] *Attenborough* v. *Solomon*, [1913] A.C. 76, 84.
[2] See p. 70, *ante*.

referred to this picture when they have had to deal with particular problems. Perhaps too the picture changed somewhat in the course of time.

However the two pictures are essentially different. A totally false impression will be gained if one starts from the assumption that both laws are trying to do the same thing with varying degrees of success. Although the two conceptions overlap to a very great extent, they have really very different functions.

The possession that starts with a unilateral taking, by thief, finder or squatter, is doubtless very much the same in both systems, and even where they diverge, they are giving more or less imperfect answers to the same question. However, their attitudes towards acquisition of possession by agreement between a transferor and a transferee are quite different, as will be seen at once from a consideration of bailment. In English law the bailee is always a possessor, though sometimes a bailor may possess as well.[1] A lessee, likewise, possesses, though for certain purposes the lessor also possesses. Thus the essential notion underlying the concept of possession is that of actual control, irrespective of title. So strong is this notion that even a servant, who in general only has custody for his master, the actual possessor, has possession attributed to him if goods are entrusted to him by a third party for transmission to his master; and there is always a strong tendency to attribute possession to him wherever it is markedly convenient for practical purposes. Why the servant is normally refused possession is an unsolved problem. He usually *had* possession down to the seventeenth century.[2] However, he is normally refused possession by those modern codes, such as the German,[3] which in principle give possession to all actual

---

[1] Thus a bailor at will can bring an action for trespass to goods.

[2] See Year Book 21 Hen. VII, Hil., fol. 14, pl. 21; Co. 3 Inst., 108; Hale, *Pleas of the Crown*, 56; Com. *Digest*, Justices, O. 6.

[3] B.G.B. §855.

holders; and the Italian Civil Code of 1942[1] refuses him the *réintégrande*, which is available to all other detentors. In fact it requires an effort for the English lawyer to realise that anybody who actually has a thing may not possess it.

In Roman law on the other hand, whatever may have been thought in the latter half of the nineteenth century, under the influence of Jhering, the bailee or lessee in principle does not possess. Moreover no one who has a thing in virtue of a contract recognising the ownership of another person can possess, and the same is true even of a person who has a real right of limited extent, such as usufruct, though such persons have quasi-possession, protected by a special interdict. There are, it is true, four types of persons who are regarded as possessors, even though they hold under a contract, namely the pledge creditor, the tenant for a perpetual or very long term of years, the tenant at will, and the stake-holder. But these cases can all be explained away on practical or historical grounds. In the classical or later laws they must be treated as exceptions. Conversely, the bailor or lessor usually retains possession of the thing he has bailed or let.

These characteristics make Roman possession very closely akin to seisin in English law, and although seisin has very marked possessory characteristics it has clearly been a different concept from possession at any time since 1500, or even earlier. Roman possession is indeed very closely akin to ownership, and is always thought of in close connexion with it. In principle, the only sort of person who can possess is one who can conceivably be an owner, hence neither a slave nor a *filiusfamilias*, except in relation to *peculium castrense*, etc., can possess on his own account. Similarly a thing which cannot be owned (i.e. *res extra commercium*) cannot be possessed. A possessor is always thought of as a possible defendant in a real action,

---

[1] Art. 1168.

and therefore as one who is, and will remain, owner, unless the plaintiff can oust him by proof of his title. All of this is quite alien to English law. English law does not think of the possessor as a defendant in a real action, but as a plaintiff in an action of trespass.

The difference can perhaps be even better expressed in another way. English law thinks of any person who can be observed as controlling a thing as a possessor, unless he falls within some very narrow class. Roman law does not think of possession in terms of the continuing relationship but concentrates its attention on the acquisition and loss of possession. It regards possession merely as something which has arisen from the taking of possession, and which has not been terminated through loss of that possession; and the taking of possession is essentially an appropriation of the thing. It is difficult to define so fundamental a notion as appropriation in terms of other less fundamental notions, but some suggestion of its meaning can be given if one says that a person appropriates who consciously assumes the practical and 'economic' advantages of ownership, irrespective of title. If he is a thief or squatter he has no belief in the existence of a title—which indeed probably does not exist at all—but even if he is acquiring from someone else, although property will not pass without title, the possession will pass irrespective of whether the transferor had title or not. After this explanation, it is probably safe to define Roman possession as being, in principle, the practical and economic aspect of ownership.

All this is, of course, very obvious if one is thinking of possession as something that will ripen into ownership by usucapion. For it is well known that it is essential to this kind of possession that it shall have started with a *iusta causa*, or *iustus titulus*. A person cannot begin to usucape unless he has done all that in him lies to become owner. This is not quite true of the possession which is protected by the interdicts, for even apart from the pledge creditor, etc., whose possession must, as has already been said, be considered exceptional, one must admit that the thief, finder, and squatter have no *iusta causa* or *iustus titulus*. The proper way to put it then is not that a possessor for the purpose of the interdicts must start with a *iusta causa* or *iustus titulus*, but that he must not start with the wrong kind of *causa*, for instance *commodatum* or *locatio conductio*. The jurists never use the term *causa* in relation to the acquisition of possession, but when they speak of *animus*, they do so in an objective sense; and objective *animus* is the same as *causa*. Thus whichever way one puts it, *causa* plays a very definite part in the concept of possession.

Thus, in attempting to grasp the Roman concept of possession, one should not start by asking whether the possessor has the actual control over a thing. But even in English law it is no longer possible to say that possession always depends on actual control. Whenever the law makes use for its own purposes of a simple state of fact, it tends eventually to look upon it in an artificial way. Thus English law, which thinks of larceny as primarily a crime against possession, sometimes attributes possession to persons who do not in the ordinary sense of the word possess; otherwise thieves would often escape punishment. If, as Holmes says,[1] the common law 'abhors the absence of . . . possessory rights as a kind of vacuum' we must not be surprised to find that possession at common law is sometimes very unlike what the ordinary man would call possession.[2]

It is a matter of principle in Roman law to differentiate ownership from possession. In fact we find statements to the effect that ownership has nothing in common with possession. Moreover the owner's and the possessor's remedies are sharply differentiated, and the jurists even

---

[1] *The Common Law*, p. 237.
[2] See, e.g., *Hibbert* v. *McKiernan*, [1948] 2 K.B. 142.

go so far as to say that success or failure in either is no bar to success or failure in the other. On the other hand in English law, at any rate in the law of moveables, there is hardly such a thing as ownership. All we have is successive possessions, accompanied by titles of varying efficacy. Thus we get the paradox that in English law, where possession has to a very great extent to do the work done by ownership in other systems, possession bears hardly any resemblance to ownership, whereas in Roman law, where ownership and possession are very closely akin, they are made to perform very different functions, and the jurists are at the utmost pains to differentiate them. Perhaps there is a suspicion that this differentiation was necessary in order to avoid a confusion which is hardly possible in English law.

Moreover when one reflects on the probable course of Roman litigation, one begins to wonder whether this dichotomy is not something mainly doctrinal, and insisted on without any real regard for the realities of practice.

How did a plaintiff in a *vindicatio* prove his case? It is hard to believe that he merely appealed to reputation of ownership. Wherever there was any real difficulty—and one may presume that it was only in such cases that the plaintiff would be put to his *vindicatio*—he would have to show that he had usucaped the property. So far as land is concerned, this would, in early classical times, cause little difficulty, for land could not be stolen, and there are many ways in which land could come into the possession of a non-owner without any violence on his part or on the part of any other person. But for moveables there would be very great difficulty. Indeed Gaius says[1] it is nearly impossible for a *bona fide* possessor—as opposed to a bonitary owner—to acquire moveables by usucapion. Thus one must face the fact that in any vindication of moveables a title set up might just as well be defeasible as indefeasible; and

[1] G. 2. 50.

that even where the thing claimed was land, the chances that the title would be defeasible were by no means negligible.

Thus the notion of absolute ownership must have been something of a fraud, only saved from public shame by the facts that a very large proportion of moveables which have any earmark are consumed by use, and that a large proportion of the residue are transformed by *specificatio*, or merged in something else by *accessio*. One is sometimes tempted to think that most Roman moveables that had preserved their existence and identity over a long period must at one time or another have been stolen, and much must have depended on the practical impossibility of proving theft in a large majority of cases; but this is not what one usually means when one uses the term 'absolute'. What seems to have happened is that the Romans started from a very simple and childish distinction between *meum* and *tuum*, and that in very early times they did really have a system of *usucapio* which conferred an absolute title in a very short time; but that having excluded *usucapio* of stolen goods for very obvious reasons, they did not face the fact that the absolute ownership in which they had been dealing had become fallacious. In other words they became the victims of their rather blunt intellectual methods. One must not attribute to Roman jurists of any age the sharp perception and ruthless logic of a nineteenth-century German metaphysician. For the Romans, if they had ever used the term in this connexion, 'absolute' must have meant 'absolute for most practical purposes'.

In one very important respect Roman and English law unite in differing from most modern civil law systems. Both adhere to the maxim 'nemo dat quod non habet'. In other words a non-owner cannot confer a title of ownership. English law has, it is true, made certain inroads on this principle by the Factors Acts, and by certain provisions of the Sale of Goods Act,[1] but on the whole it has been strict.

---

[1] Ss. 21–26.

Roman law admitted of no exceptions—the power of a pledgee to sell the thing pledged to him is no true exception, for he had the pledgor's authority, at any rate in earlier times—though in some cases the law of usucapion may have operated to cure defective titles in an exceptionally short time. However this is not the law in most continental countries of the present day. The prevailing principle is that a possessor can give a good title to a *bona fide* purchaser for value. Two exceptions are usually found, namely that a person who has lost goods, or had them stolen, may vindicate them in the short period of one year, though even within that year he may lose them irrevocably if they are sold by auction or in open market.[1] It seems very probable that these exceptions were, to some extent, derived from Roman law, for when the general doctrine was received into French law in the early part of the eighteenth century, an attempt was made by the civilians to reconcile it with Roman law by saying that what took place was an immediate usucapion without lapse of time; and usucapion was of course impossible where the goods had been stolen. In any case the great field of application of the rule is in connexion with bailments. The continental bailee can normally confer ownership on a *bona fide* purchaser for value of goods. This is not only very un-Roman, but it is also very un-English, for English law has clearly refused to make the most of the doctrine of estoppel.[2]

The nature of ownership in English law, if indeed the term be appropriate, cannot be understood without a discussion of the defence of *ius tertii*, for if a defendant cannot set up against a plaintiff who is claiming a thing from him by virtue of a prior possession, the better right of a third party, then clearly the plaintiff, can succeed upon the basis of his better right (*maius ius*). If, on the other hand, the defendant can set up against the plaintiff the title of a third person under which he himself does not claim, the

---

[1] French C.C., arts. 2279–2280.   [2] See 65 *L.Q.R.* pp. 354–355.

better right of the plaintiff is not decisive. Now there is no doubt that in the Middle Ages the *ius tertii* could not be set up in defence to an action for recovery of either land or moveables. The question was always one of better right. However, towards the end of the seventeenth century new ideas came into play,[1] and at the present day the defence of *ius tertii* can be set up at least in certain cases both where land and where moveables are concerned. There is great difficulty in ascertaining which those cases are, and this is not the place for a full discussion,[2] but it seems that the position is as follows: Wherever the defendant is in peaceable possession of the thing claimed, so that the plaintiff must succeed on the strength of his right to possess, it is open to the defendant to set up the better title of a third person, even though he does not claim under that title. If, on the other hand, the defendant is not in peaceable possession of the thing claimed, that is to say where he is in possession by virtue of a trespass which he has committed against the plaintiff, then the plaintiff claims not in virtue of his right to possess, but merely of the possession which he had at the time of the defendant's trespass. Thus a plea of *ius tertii* would be inadmissible, because it would be irrelevant. It is obviously no defence to the plaintiff's claim that he possesses or possessed the thing to say that he has, or had, no right to possess. It seems, however, that at least where land is concerned, a defendant trespasser may still set up the defence of *ius tertii*, if that *ius tertii* appears upon the title which the plaintiff himself sets up in his pleadings.[3]

The effect of this mass of decisions is to differentiate clearly between possession and a right to possess. Actual possession at the time of bringing the action, or at the time

---

[1] Holdsworth, vii. pp. 424–431.

[2] See Salmond, *Torts*, 10th ed. pp. 215–216, 303.

[3] Radcliffe and Miles, *Cases illustrating Principles of the Law of Torts*, p. 289.

when the defendant committed a trespass against the plaintiff, does itself imply a right to possess, and moreover any previous possession implies a right to possess. Further it is not necessary for the plaintiff himself to prove that his right to possess is absolute: it is enough for him to prove that his right to possess is better than the defendant's right. But since it is open to the defendant to prove that somebody else's right to possess is better than the plaintiff's, it is clear that what is in issue in an action based on title is the *best* right to possession, and if either the defendant or indeed the plaintiff himself in his pleadings shows that somebody else had a better title, then the plaintiff's title is clearly not the best in the world. For practical purposes it may therefore be said that English law recognises ownership, both of land and goods; and that the difference between Roman and English law is by no means so great as is stated in the text.

However there is still superficially a very considerable difference between the two systems, for the effect of *usucapio* is to confer a title on one who has possessed another's thing for the requisite period, whereas the effect of limitation in English law is only to cancel that other person's title. Hence the title of a disseisor or of a dispossessor in English law starts from the disseisin or dispossession, and its essential character does not change with the lapse of time. It is in every respect the same title as it was from the beginning. All that has happened is that a superior title has been destroyed. On the other hand in Roman law the title dates from the end of the period of usucapion. But the distinction is of importance mainly in connexion with covenants running with the land, and with the treatment of successive interests in land; and similar problems can hardly arise in Roman law. Where the same sort of question can be raised in both systems, it will be found that there is very little difference. Indeed, curiously enough the position of a Roman who was in process of acquiring by *usucapio*, even though his title to *dominium* was still in the future, was better than would be the position of his English counterpart at the present day, for the Roman could sue almost exactly as if he had already completed usucapion: at any rate the defendant could not raise a plea of *ius tertii*; whereas an English plaintiff who pleaded a possession that he had acquired from a non-owner at a time insufficiently remote to cancel the true owner's title would soon find the *ius tertii* set up against him. Moreover, as we have seen, although at first sight a Roman who was vindicating property would merely prove possession for the period required for usucapion, there was always a chance that the defendant might show that the thing had at some time or other been stolen; and it does not seem that the latter was under any obligation to show that it had been stolen from him or his predecessors in title. Thus even technically the plea of theft was not at all unlike the plea of *ius tertii*. In the end, therefore, it seems that there is not much to choose between the Roman and English conceptions of ownership, so far as the absolute nature of title is concerned, and indeed much of the technical detail is very similar. How far the changes in English law which appeared towards the end of the seventeenth century were due to Roman influences, it is very difficult to say.

The classical jurists had an extremely concentrated notion of ownership, that is to say, although they recognised that various people could own the same thing in common at the same time, they did not attempt any division of ownership as such. This excluded for instance anything in the nature of feudal tenure, under which the ownership of land could be split up between landlord and tenant: even in respect of leases, the landlord was full owner, and the tenant had only the benefit of an obligation. Similarly it excluded anything in the nature of a doctrine of estates, whereby the ownership of land could be divided in respect of time, the tenant for life being no more owner than the reversioner, nor the reversioner than the tenant for life: in Roman law, if the technique of usufruct was adopted, the reversioner was full owner subject to an incumbrance in the hands of the usufructuary, and even if the device of fideicommissary substitution was employed, each successive holder was regarded as full owner. In classical law quite probably each owner had the full powers of alienation which usually belonged to an owner, and was merely bound by an obligation not to exercise them, so that one had to apply the maxim 'quod fieri non debuit factum valet'. Finally there could be no distinction between the legal and equitable estate. In other words one could not dissociate the owner's powers of management from his rights of enjoyment, and vest the former in a trustee, and the latter in a beneficiary.

However, as Dr Pringsheim has shown,[1] this extreme concentration of ownership seems to be peculiar to the classical Roman law, and to modern systems derived from Roman law. It is not found in any independent systems, ancient or modern, and it is not found in early or late Roman law either. He himself calls attention to the existence of a problem which was solved in the time of Justinian by applying a technique essentially the same as the English distinction between the legal and the equitable estate. It had always been difficult to know how to explain the peculiar position of husband and wife in relation to *dos*. In one sense the husband owned it, but in another the wife. The classical lawyers seem to have been firmly convinced that they must place the undivided ownership— which was the only kind of ownership they knew—in the husband, though binding him by several obligations for the benefit of the wife. However in course of time the husband's powers over the *dos* became so limited that this solution became unreal, the more so when the wife was

----

[1] 59 *L.Q.R.* p. 244.

given for the recovery of her *dos* not merely a personal action, but what is called a *vindicatio utilis*; and in the end Justinian uses language which can be best translated as saying that whereas the husband has the legal estate in the *dos*, the wife has the equitable interest. Whatever we may think of the technical explanation of the situation, it is quite obvious that neither party has the full rights and powers of an owner, but the ownership is divided between them.

However, this is not the only trace of divided ownership in Roman law. Our next example must come from the residue of archaic ideas which can be detected in the mature law of possession. According to the prevailing view the typical Roman possessor in the classical period was one who held the thing in his own right and did not recognise in practice the claims of any other person. Thus, in principle, any person who held by virtue of an *ius in re aliena* or in virtue of a contract which did not divest the former holder of his full interest did not possess. How, then, are we to explain the cases of the tenant at will (*precario rogans*), and the tenant under a long or perpetual lease (*emphyteuta*), or of his earlier prototype, a tenant of municipal lands (*ager vectigalis*), or of the early possessor of public lands (*ager publicus*), all of whom were exceptionally admitted to possess? The suggestion has been made—and it seems to fit the facts better than any other—that these are all cases of tenure similar to feudal tenure, that in each case the possessor holds of the true owner, but that he holds what we should call the freehold, and is not a mere lessee. In other words, in early law the ownership was split up between the landlord and the tenant; only whereas the owner could recover his land by a real action, the tenant needed for his protection a special remedy, an interdict, devised by the Praetor. In later times it was easy to say that only the person who had the real action was owner, whereas the person who had only the interdict was a mere possessor, but it seems probable that he had the interdict and was possessor only because at an earlier time he had been a subordinate owner. Here again there is division of ownership.

Finally, as soon as it became the law that in a fidei-commissary substitution the prohibition against alienation that was imposed upon each successive holder operated *in rem*, and not merely *in personam*, so that each subsequent holder could undo any alienations made by his predecessors, then although each successive holder is called an owner, it is clear that the ownership was really divided between them in respect of time. In the classical law it looks as though the interests of the subsequent holders were, as we should say, merely equitable, for they could not have alienations set aside as against *bona fide* purchasers.

The tendency of the classical jurists to concentrate their attention on the distinction between ownership and possession led to curious results in connexion with *bona fide* possession. One might have expected them to make of it a third type of interest, and perhaps even to decide whether it should be considered as partaking more of the character of ownership or of possession. However, not only do they appear not to have concerned themselves with its proper position in the law, but they never thought of it in a coherent way. One can describe *bona fide* possession only as a state of fact to which different consequences were attached in different situations, as often as not with the addition of some other requirement.

Thus the *bona fide* possessor of a thing acquired the fruits of a thing by mere separation, but he had to be in good faith, not only at the time of the acquisition of possession, but also at the time when the fruits were separated. Strictly parallel to this case is that of the *bona fide* possessor's right to be recompensed for improvements made on land. However, in one particular case, namely the acquisition of things through a *bona fide serviens*, the *bona fide* possessor acquired only such things as the *bona fide serviens* had acquired by his own labour or in connexion with the property of the *bona fide* possessor. Perhaps acquisitions made under the former head could be said to be the fruits of the labour of the *bona fide serviens*, but hardly those under the latter head. On the other hand in all these cases the title, if any, by which he came into possession, was quite irrelevant. By the time of Justinian, it seems that he retained title only to such fruits as he had not consumed when he was evicted from the object. For another purpose, namely the acquisition of ownership by *usucapio*, and for the similar purpose of recovering an object by the *actio Publiciana*, good faith was required only at the beginning of the possession, but on the other hand the possession had to be in virtue of some *iustus titulus*.

It is clear that *bona fide* possession is not the same in these various cases, and it is impossible to form out of them a coherent concept. What seems to have happened is that the Roman jurists regarded the presence of good faith as entitling possessors to more favourable consideration than was implied in the mere power of retaining or recovering that possession, but that for each specific solution they set up different requirements.

It is not always easy to see the reasons for these various solutions, or whether they were arrived at on purely practical grounds. In particular it is very difficult to decide to what extent, if at all, the jurists thought of *bona fide* possession as partaking of the nature of ownership.

Clearly the *bona fide* possession which was protected by the *actio Publiciana* was a species of ownership, defeasible only by the true owner if acquired from a non-owner, but good even against the true owner if acquired from him by an informal mode. The latter form has always been recognised as ownership and has acquired in modern times the name of bonitary ownership; but the former type also, it must be admitted, is a form of ownership. However, as is said in the text, both forms are strictly temporary in character, and moreover the essential element seems to be not the *bona fide* possession, but the *iustus titulus* with which it started. In all the other cases it is the *bona fide* possession which counts, and in one of them at least it seems at first sight to be regarded as a form of ownership. The *bona fide* possessor acquires the fruits for the time being, and sues any other person who has harvested them, in the character of owner. Since he is in good faith he thinks he is an owner, and therefore if he has to bring an action he obviously brings a *vindicatio*. In the vast majority of cases it would not appear in the course of the proceedings that he was not the owner, and we may perhaps neglect as academic the case where he first hears of the defect in his title from the defendant who pleads it against him. It is probably because the evidence in existence at the time of action points to his being owner that he is distinguished from the usufructuary, who is not allowed to vindicate the fruits from a third party who has harvested them.[1] The usufructuary knows he is not the owner, and there is always the owner to bring the action in his own right: it is out of the question to assimilate the *bona fide* possessor at that moment to the usufructuary. However, the problem is as yet only half solved. It appears in a new form when the true owner evicts the *bona fide* possessor; for it no longer follows from the fact that the latter has successfully appropriated the fruits or recovered them from a third party, that he will be able to keep them as against the true owner. In English law the temporary title of the *bona fide* possessor, which does undoubtedly give him a form of ownership, though one defeasible by the true owner, does not prevent him from being liable to an action for mesne profits at the suit of the latter. In Roman law he is not, as we have seen, liable to account for these fruits, not at all it would seem in the classical period, and under Justinian at

---

[1] He can almost certainly bring the *actio furti*.

any rate not if he has consumed them. It would appear doubtful whether this freedom from liability to account can be derived from the defeasible ownership which he had formerly enjoyed.

Probably the *bona fide* possessor's claim to be compensated for improvements was thought of in very much the same way as his non-liability to account for fruits, and it is even more difficult to see how this claim could arise from a former ownership. It must have been thought of as a claim to be recompensed for expense which has led to the unjustified enrichment of the true owner.

It is just possible that the Romans may have approached both problems from the point of view not of the evicted *bona fide* possessor, but from that of the true owner who has evicted him. If Roman law thought of the latter as having been not merely out of possession, but out of his ownership during the period that the thing was held by the *bona fide* possessor, then it is easy to see that the true owner could not claim in his *vindicatio* any fruits which had been separated in the meantime—since he could only claim the thing itself as it was at the time when he lost it, and at the time when he recovered it—but also could not recover anything that had been added to it by way of improvements between those two dates. However, this solution gives rise to serious difficulties: it does not by itself explain the distinction made between the *bona fide* and the *mala fide* possessor, and it does not explain the various procedural complications—for the *bona fide* possessor could at civil law be evicted from the thing as it stood at the time of the vindication, improvements and all, and if he wished to be recompensed for the latter, he had to set up an *exceptio doli*. Moreover his right was a right of retention, and not a right of action.

The other case, that of acquisition through a *bona fide serviens*, is confessedly assimilated to acquisition through a slave in whom one has a usufruct. However this does not square with the distinction made between the *bona fide* possessor and the usufructuary in the acquisition of fruits. A restriction is placed on acquisition through the *bona fide serviens* which has no parallel where the fruits are those derived from a thing.

The proper conclusion therefore seems to be that each problem which arose in connexion with *bona fide* possession was dealt with on its own merits, and that there was no attempt to find a single analogy. It is quite obvious that there is nothing here comparable to the logical treatment which English law accords to persons holding under titles of varying degrees of validity; and, strange as it may seem, Roman law, which ordinarily places very great emphasis on ownership, is much more favourable to a person who is ultimately evicted than is English law, which recognises nothing better than the best right to possession.

The unsystematic, and indeed disorderly way in which Roman law dealt with problems of *bona fide* possession seems to show not only that the strict dichotomy between ownership and possession is rather unpractical, but also that there is no need for English lawyers to apologise, as the older analytical jurists were inclined to do, for the structure of their own law. Certainly the English treatment of real property is exceptionally logical and systematic, and although the law of personal property has not been thought out so consciously and carefully, it is probably as logical as it is practical in character. In any case the English law of real property shows a fertility in expedients, and affords to the conveyancer and to the man of property a wealth of constructions which are far beyond the scope of Roman law. Whether one should regard this as a matter for congratulation, or, on the contrary, one should prefer a law of property which limits its concepts to those which are absolutely indispensable, is really a question of policy on which the lawyer is not entitled to have the last word.

3. *IURA IN REM* AND *IN PERSONAM*

Closely allied with the distinctions which we have been considering is that between *iura in rem* and *iura in personam*, which was clearly expressed throughout the Roman system. The jurists did not indeed state it in these words: they spoke in terms of procedure, of actions *in rem, in personam*.[1] But their forms of action show that the distinction expressed in them is one of substantive law. The claim in a *legis actio, in rem*, was a claim not to a right available against a particular defendant, but to one available generally: 'I declare this thing to be mine.' In an *actio in personam* it was a declaration of some liability resting on the defendant: 'I declare that Negidius is lawfully bound to pay me 100 asses.' And in the later formulae the distinction is equally clear. The *iudex* in an *actio in rem* is directed to condemn the defendant if the *res* proves to be the plaintiff's. In an *actio in personam* the direction is to condemn if it appears that the defendant is lawfully bound to pay. It is true that some modern writers deny the validity of this distinction and maintain that a right *in rem* is only a mass of rights *in personam*, that it is 'in the air' till someone does something which gives a right of action, in fact that the only solid ground is a law court. On the same ground it is said that Austin's primary or sanctioned rights are not rights at all, but only possibilities of right, that under a contract we have no right to performance but only to damages in certain events. No doubt, also, with a tendency to treat all rights as claims it is difficult to cling to the notion of a *ius in rem* without arriving at claims *in rem*. Windscheid, who seems first to have made the conception 'Anspruch' fashionable, in fact arrives at what he calls a 'dinglicher Anspruch',[2]

---

[1] For the complicated relations of this distinction to the entirely different distinction between real and personal actions in English law, see especially Maitland, *The Forms of Action at Common Law*, pp. 73–78.

[2] Windscheid, *Lehrbuch*, 1. Sect. 43. *Anspruch*=claim; *dinglicher Anspruch*=claim *in rem*.

which, however, is, so long as no wrong has been committed, a claim to forbearances. But it does not seem that this 'dinglicher Anspruch' is widely accepted.

Whether this analysis is of real value, whether it really explains the proceedings of the Courts in such things as originating summonses[1] and whether the view that a man, who, like the majority of people, has at the moment no right of action against anyone, is without legal rights, satisfactorily explains his position, may be doubted. Law and litigation are not the same thing, however much they may seem so to one who spends his life in the study of cases and the practice of the Courts and is apt to regard the floor of the Court as the only solid ground. Law is a set of norms and notions, and one of these is, e.g., the right of property. Whatever the truth of all this may be, the fact remains that it is impossible to understand the Roman procedure or the Roman texts without treating the distinction between rights *in rem* and rights *in personam* as fundamental. It was the clear view the Romans had of this distinction that enabled them to maintain the distinction between *titulus* and *modus adquirendi*. Thus while with us the agreement to sell a specific piece of personal property in a deliverable state at once transfers the *ius in rem*, in Rome it never did: there had to be a distinct act of conveyance.[2] And the classical jurists, at any rate, could hardly have conceived of the hybrid right of the beneficiary under the trust.[3]

---

[1] E.g., in a case where executors are asking the Court for directions as to how to distribute legacies or, generally, to administer an estate.

[2] See p. 287, *post*, as to this and the modern Roman law on the matter.

[3] See pp. 176–179, *post*.

4. OWNERSHIP *IN FUTURO* AND TERMINABLE OWNERSHIP

There was nothing in Roman theory to prevent the creation of an ownership to begin in the future, provided the right form of conveyance was used. The formal civil methods, *mancipatio* and *in iure cessio*, would not serve because their operation could not be suspended, but *traditio* was not so limited and could be used for almost all purposes with the same practical effect. If Titius handed property to Maevius on the terms that it was to belong to him in ten days or when Sempronius died, or even when the grantor died, there was no change of ownership till the specified event occurred and when it did occur the property passed *ipso facto*. With *traditio* available the Romans were not faced with the difficulty, inherent in the doctrine of seisin, that every future estate must have a particular estate to support it, and that the seisin, i.e. for practical purposes the ownership, must pass from the transferor to someone, at the moment of the conveyance. Even the law of executory interests did formal obeisance to this principle, though in practice it evaded it. The sweeping changes of the present century have not abolished the principle. It is still not possible to create an estate in lands to begin *in futuro* without resorting to a trust, except that a lease may be created to begin at a future date not beyond twenty-one years. It is true that the difficulty does not arise in relation to moveables, which can be transferred by delivery. It is a common clause of hire-purchase agreements that, though the goods are delivered, the property shall not vest in the buyer till all the instalments are paid. But even here our law gives a result very different from that of the Roman law. In that law no act by the holder under the agreement could affect the title of the owner. If he alienated he could not give a good title to his buyer even though both parties were acting in good faith, though if they were, the receiver could acquire by *usucapio*; while in our law, by the operation of modern legislation, a *bona fide* purchaser from the holder on such facts will get an immediately good title.[1]

So too in a case of simple gift there seems to be a considerable difference. Under either system a man may hand over an article to another to be his if a certain event happens, e.g. 'It shall be yours if you pass your Bar examinations in due course.' Here, under Justinian, when once the thing has been so handed over it is a conditional transaction which waits for nothing but the fulfilment of the condition. Apart from some special cases which do not affect the principle[2] there was no possibility of revocation. But the case is not instructive, since under Justinian the mere informal promise to give would be binding even without any delivery. In classical law a promise to give would be valid only if it had been made by *stipulatio*. Moreover, if in earlier times the thing had been handed over with no formal promise, on a condition, it seems that under the system of possessory remedies the donor could within six months recover the possession even though the condition occurred.[3] But once the condition occurred, as there had been a valid *traditio donationis causa*, it seems that he would have had no defence against a *vindicatio*, a real action, by the donee. In our law, though authority on such things is very scanty, it seems probable that when a

---

[1] Factors Act, 1889, Sect. 9; Sale of Goods Act, 1893, Sect. 25 (2); *Marten* v. *Whale*, [1917] 2 K.B. 480; *Helby* v. *Matthews*, [1895] A.C. 471; but when, as is much more usual, the holder has not 'agreed to buy' but has merely an option either to return the goods hired by him or to become their owner by payment in full, the *bona fide* purchaser from him does not get a good title; it is necessary for this reason to distinguish between a mere option to buy which imposes no obligation and a conditional agreement to buy. See also pp. 291–292, *post*.

[2] Buckland, *Text-book*, pp. 253 *sq*.

[3] Since in the interdict *utrubi* that one of the parties prevailed who had had possession of the thing for the longer period during the past year. As soon as he had had the thing for six months the donee's position would be better than the donor's.

thing is so handed over to be a gift if a condition precedent is satisfied, the holder in the meantime is in the position of a bailee. The bailor can determine the bailment. If he does this before the condition is satisfied, it seems that the gift is imperfect and unenforceable.[1]

On the other hand classical Roman law did not recognise a terminable ownership and there was no such thing as a future estate dependent on the expiry of one created by the same transaction. Thus we are clearly told that if a *traditio* of property was made, to be operative only for a certain time or till a certain event, the conveyance was simply void.[2] What seems to be the same text recurs, however, in the Code of Justinian (C. 8. 54. 2), with its decision reversed. The property right reverts *ipso facto* by the occurrence of the event. The same thing is found in other branches of the law.[3] Many texts leave the old doctrine and it is not clear that Justinian laid down a comprehensive doctrine for all such cases. But, at most, it is never more than a question of reverter: there can be no question of a transaction by *A* creating an ownership in *B* to be followed by an ownership in *C*. Limited interests might indeed be created, for not more than a life (usufruct), but they were not thought of as ownership. They were *iura*, rights *sui generis*, which ultimately came to be thought of as servitudes, analogous to praedial servitudes which correspond to our easements and profits. They were *res incorporales*, while ownership is thought of as a *res corporalis*: the ownership and the thing are not distinguished in the texts. The ownership exists in someone else, hampered by the usufruct, but the ultimate right is the only ownership. It was not possible, as it is with us, to create *inter vivos*, by the

[1] See May, *Fraudulent and Voluntary Dispositions*, p. 362; Hailsham, xv. Sect. 1278.

[2] Vat. Fr. 283. This does not prevent transfer on the terms that at a certain time or on a certain event the property shall be reconveyed (D. 18. 2. 3, 5), but here there would be needed a reconveyance.

[3] See, e.g., Buckland, *Text-book*, pp. 189, 254, 497 *sq.*

same transaction, a further interest to begin at the expiry of the life interest. It could indeed be done by will, but the difference of conception leads to a noticeable difference in terminology. If a testator gives a life interest to *A* and the property, subject to this life interest, to *B*, then under our terminology, *A*, the life tenant, has the corporeal hereditament, and *B* has an incorporeal hereditament. But in Roman law the life tenant has only a *res incorporalis*: *B* has the *res corporalis*. It begins at once. *B* is regarded as being in possession, since *A*'s life interest, being incorporeal, is not susceptible of possession. The case has some similarity to that in which land is conveyed subject to a lease: the freehold passes at once. A usufruct could indeed be given for a term of years subject to survival, in which case it much resembles a lease for years determinable on life. However, our term of years has only gradually acquired the character of a *ius in rem*. Primarily it is a contract, as such a term always was in Roman law. Again, the termor 'holds of' the freeholder, but the usufructuary does not, any more than the life tenant in our law holds of the remainderman.

If a specific object was settled by way of fideicommissary substitution, each successive holder was regarded as full owner of it, though forbidden to alienate it and bound to leave it on his decease in accordance with the terms of the *fideicommissum*. Whatever was the position in the classical law, his ownership came in the end to be terminable; for no alienation by him could have effect for a longer period than his own life.

5. CONTENT OF OWNERSHIP

Ownership was no more unlimited than it is with us: the legislature could and did impose restrictions of various kinds. Apart from the general principle that a man's rights over his property are limited by the rights of others, there were a number of specific rules, often local, limiting the heights of buildings, and the use of certain sites for building. There was a rule forbidding the destruction of houses for speculative purposes, or, perhaps, for any purpose other than the improvement of the neighbourhood. There was much regulation of mining exploitations, some of which has already been mentioned.[1] But a more peculiar feature of the Roman law is the existence of a large number of special provisions regulating the relations between neighbours, a matter which, in our law, seems to be left to the ordinary law of trespass and nuisance, supplemented by the preventive machinery of injunctions.[2] As early as the XII Tables there were restrictive rules on the matter.[3] There was an ancient rule forbidding any kind of obstruction, in rural areas, upon the *fines*, i.e. within a few feet of the border of the property on either side, the open space, uncultivated, serving as a passage way.[4] An analogous rule required a space between buildings, but this disappeared early.[5] Other special machinery played a more important part in the law; but it is more properly discussed in connexion with nuisance.[6]

There has been much discussion in recent times of the question whether the Roman law allowed expropriation for public utilities. Here it is important to draw a distinction which has been somewhat disregarded. In historical times there was no restriction on the powers of the supreme legislature. It could expropriate for any purpose. But in fact, so far as utilities are concerned, there is little sign of any such thing in classical law. Indeed even such evidence as there is may be deceptive, for it seems that the cases

---

[1] P. 62, *ante*.

[2] *Attorney General* v. *Corporation of Manchester*, [1893] 2 Ch. 87; *Colls* v. *Home and Colonial Stores*, [1904] A.C. 179, though as early as Bracton there was an assize of nuisance.

[3] See Bruns, *Fontes Iuris Romani*, 7th ed. pp. 27, 28.

[4] Karlowa, *Röm. Rechtsg.* ii. p. 459.

[5] *Ibid.* p. 518.

[6] See pp. 392–395, *post*.

recorded are of lands which were technically the property of the State, though in the hands of *possessores* holding, in practice permanently, but technically at the will of the State. Augustus hesitated to expropriate for public utility at the height of his power.[1] What looks like a case, the Senatusconsult of 11 B.C. dealing with aqueducts,[2] is explained as creating certain general restrictions on ownership for the future, in the neighbourhood of aqueducts. Even the later Emperors expropriated sparingly.[3] Moreover, there is a difference between the supreme legislature and an executive department, and it does not appear that any magistrate or official had the compulsory powers which are vested in so many subordinate authorities in our law. On the other hand necessity and utility are different things, and there is no doubt that officials of various classes had large powers of destruction of property for religious, military or police purposes. The aediles destroyed to check a fire. The augurs ordered the destruction of houses which obstructed the auspices. But these and similar cases are all of overriding necessity.

A much discussed problem is that of abuse of right, opinion being divided on the question whether any rule on this matter existed in the Roman law. There are in fact two distinct questions. The first is whether there were in Roman law, in any relations, specific rules which can be construed as making abuse of right an actionable wrong, abuse of right meaning exercise of proprietary rights with intent or knowledge that the exercise will do harm to some other person or his property without any economic benefit to the doer. The answer is that there were such rules, i.e. rules which can be so understood. Thus in regard to an enactment of Antoninus Pius protecting slaves against cruel masters we are told, as a reason for the rule, that we

---

[1] Suetonius, *Augustus*, 56.　　　[2] Bruns, *cit*. p. 193.
[3] C. Th. 15. 1. 30 [C. 8. 11. 9], h.t. 50, 51 [C. 8. 11. 18], 53. See J. W. Jones, 'Expropriation in Roman Law', 45 *L.Q.R.* (1929) p. 512.

ought not *male uti* our right.[1] And elsewhere we are told that a *bona fide* possessor compelled to give up the property may take away (*ius tollendi*) what he has added, so far as the property is not damaged, but not merely to gratify spite and without benefit to himself.[2] In these cases there is no application of a general recognised rule. There are a few others of the same kind, but in all of them, as here, the moral reason is given as a justification of a specific rule, and not as a general principle of law. Out of them a general rule might have grown, but there is no evidence that it ever did. There is another group of texts dealing with rain-water, streams and percolating water, in which we are told that the landowner may act in such and such a way, but with the restriction that he must not do it merely to injure his neighbour, the restriction being often, but not always, the work of Justinian's compilers.[3] Of these the same may be said: the restriction expresses this moral principle, but no more, and in some of the cases it is clear that the rule was originally stated without this reason for it. But there is another fact which makes these texts unconvincing for the purpose of establishing such a rule. In all these cases it is not a question of a man's dealings with his land as such; it is of his dealings with flowing water on his land. Now in Roman law it is clear that flowing water, whatever its source, is not the subject of ownership: the landowner may use it for his own economic purposes but no more. If he does more he is not abusing his right but exceeding it, and he will be liable to an action if by so doing he prevents his neighbour from getting benefit out of it, or causes it to

---

[1] G. 1. 53; Inst. 1. 8. 2.

[2] D. 6. 1. 38. In fact this is not an illustration at all. The rule of civil law, based on the XII Tables (Bruns, *Fontes*, p. 26), was that nothing affixed to a building could be removed. The *ius tollendi* in the circumstances indicated in the texts is an equitable relaxation where the strict legal rule would do injustice or hardship, and is thus limited to what is necessary to prevent this hardship. It has nothing to do with 'abuse of right'.

[3] E.g. D. 39. 3. 1. 11; 2. 5; 2. 9.

damage his property. Thus the texts only illustrate well-known principles as to rights in running water.

What has been said appears to provide the answer to the second question: Was there a rule of Roman law that a man might not exercise his rights merely for the detriment of another, with no economic or betterment aim for himself? The correct answer seems to be that there was not. The rules for one or two cases expressing this notion are really evidence against, not for, the existence of a general rule. Had there been one the specific rules would not have been needed, and the notion is always stated as an ethical makeweight—a man ought not to do this sort of thing. Nowhere is it said that a principle of law forbids it. On the contrary, we get more than once the proposition that one who is exercising his right cannot be committing a wrong.[1]

The foregoing remarks are based on the full discussion by Bonfante.[2] It must be admitted that many writers have held the contrary view, but it does not appear that any evidence is adduced other than, firstly, the texts we have considered (the authority of which on the point we have rejected), secondly, general statements to be found here and there that a man ought to use his rights reasonably (which do not carry us very far), and, thirdly, the famous proposition of Celsus that 'ius est ars boni et aequi',[3] which does not mean that *ius* is always *bonum et aequum*, but that the art of the good jurist is to make it so as far as he can.

If there was such a general principle one might have expected to find it in connexion with the law of *iniuria*, outrage, which was so widely understood in the later classical law that any wanton interference with another man's right was an actionable *iniuria*. If this principle existed, it would seem to be arguable that such acts were

---

[1] E.g. D. 39. 2. 24. 12; 50. 17. 55, 151, 154. 1.
[2] *Corso*, ii. 1, pp. 290 *sqq.*   [3] D. 1. 1. 1. *pr.*

such interferences and, if intentional, would give rise to an *actio iniuriarum*. But the title on this delict[1] gives no hint of such a thing.[2] There is indeed one branch of the law, not concerned with property, in which there is such a rule —the law of actions. Abuse of process, the wilful bringing of an unfounded action, created a liability to the *actio calumniae* for a penalty.[3] But this liability seems to have rested on an express provision of the Edict and thus to be of itself evidence against any general principle.

Modern systems of Roman law[4] have dealt with the matter in different ways, but have in general accepted from the medieval lawyers the principle that abuse of right is an actionable wrong. Our English common law seems to take the same view as the Roman. There is no general principle of abuse of right, and in the sphere of the law of property some glaring instances can be found of the exercise of rights in order to injure a neighbour or to blackmail him into buying out the perpetrator.[5] But outside the law of property there are at least two kinds of abuse of legal rights which the common law will not tolerate. In the first place, abuse of process is with us both an actionable wrong and a crime, at least certain forms of it are.[6] But the lines are not those of the Roman law of *calumnia*. It does not seem that in our law the bringing wilfully of an unfounded civil suit is an actionable wrong, except in the case of malicious bankruptcy or liquidation proceedings, though a malicious criminal prosecution, at any rate of a

[1] D. 47. 10. The same reasoning applies to the *lex Aquilia*, D. 9. 2.

[2] As to another possibility, in relation to *dolus*, p. 389, *post*.

[3] Unless an oath had been tendered to and taken by the plaintiff, that he was acting in good faith. See G. 4. 174 *sqq.*; Inst. 4. 16. 1; Buckland, *Text-book*, p. 641.

[4] Gutteridge, 'Abuse of Rights', *Cambridge Law Journal*, v (1933), p. 22.

[5] *Mayor of Bradford* v. *Pickles*, [1895] A.C. 587, where Lord Halsbury L.C. said (p. 594): 'if it was a lawful act, however ill the motive might be, he had a right to do it.'

[6] See Winfield, *History of Conspiracy and Abuse of Legal Procedure* and *Present Law of Abuse of Legal Procedure*.

kind which involves scandal, and under certain conditions maliciously procuring a person's arrest, are actionable in our law.[1] On the other hand it does not seem that mere maintenance, i.e. without personal interest or personal tie, supporting the cost of a piece of litigation, or even champerty, was an actionable wrong in Roman law. For the Edict on *calumnia* which penalises the receiving of money as a consideration for stirring up trouble, or refraining from doing so, *calumniae causa*,[2] seems to be aimed at blackmail. In the second place, the existence of malice, which in this connexion means some dishonest or improper motive, may deprive a defendant to an action for defamation of the defence of qualified privilege or of fair comment, or may render actionable, as slander of title or slander of goods, an untrue and disparaging statement regarding the property of another. Moreover, it has recently been confirmed that conduct by a neighbour which is objectively reasonable may become subjectively unreasonable, and therefore a nuisance, if done maliciously, i.e., with a desire to injure.[3] Since the nuisance amounted to taking the law into one's own hands, the case is not easily reconcilable with *Pickles' Case* (see p. 99, *ante*). It may be only the first of a number of 'distinguishing' cases.

In the United States, where the social ends which law should seek to attain have perhaps received more attention from legal writers than they have in this country, and where much more weight is in fact attached to the writings of distinguished lawyers than our Courts allow to them, there seems to be a distinct tendency towards recognition of abuse of right as a tort. This tendency to diverge from the common law seems to manifest itself mainly within the sphere of property relations, but with great variety of judicial opinion. Thus Professor Ames tells us[4] that in

---

[1] Winfield, *Present Law, cit.* p. 202.   [2] D. 3. 6. 1. *pr.*

[3] *Hollywood Silver Fox Farm Ltd.* v. *Emmett*, [1936] All E.R., 825.

[4] Ames, *Lectures on Legal History*, republished 1913, pp. 403 *sqq.*

thirteen out of fifteen jurisdictions in which the question has arisen 'the malevolent draining of a neighbor's spring is a tort', but that in six out of ten jurisdictions actions 'brought for the malevolent erection of a spite fence' have failed. He adds that 'in at least six States statutes have been passed making the erection of spite fences a tort'. The enactment of such statutes with a limited aim seems to negative the notion of any common law of abuse of right for these jurisdictions. But it seems that at common law also the notion is constantly gaining strength.[1]

The maxim 'cuius est solum, eius est usque ad coelum' does not occur in the Roman texts though it is found in the gloss,[2] from which our law seems to have borrowed it. But the Roman law took the principle of the maxim in some respects more seriously than we do, though there is little mention of the higher reaches of the air, for the reason that, for the Romans, no question could arise as to these. The later addition 'et ad inferos' (it is perhaps suggested by the *casus* prefixed to the gloss on C. 3. 34. 8) certainly represents the Roman law; for, apart from the facts that most mining areas were the property of the State, and mining in Italy was restricted, possibly for political reasons,[3] it is clear that minerals were the property of the owner of the land, though, as we have seen, he could be compelled, subject to a right to royalties, to permit a lode to be followed under his land. But a very important difference between the Roman law and ours is that the Roman law totally excluded superimposed freeholds. They present no difficulty with us. The possibility is clearly laid down in Coke on Littleton[4] and the thing exists in various places, notably on the south side of New Square, Lincoln's Inn. The houses here consist of layers

[1] Prosser, *Handbook of the Law of Torts*, pp. 27–33.
[2] McNair, *Law of the Air*, ch. ii.
[3] Daremberg et Saglio, *Dict. des Antiq*. iii. 2, p. 1870.
[4] Sect. 48 b.

of freeholds, sold as such, by the Inn, many years ago.
There is of course a very complicated system of covenants
under which the owner of one layer is bound to support
the layers above. There is, perhaps, a hint of the same
thing in one Roman text,[1] but, if so, it is only to be rejected. It seems to have existed in some Eastern communities,[2] but in the Roman law itself, if the surface was
vested in one and the soil in another, the surface right was
merely a praetorian *ius*, the ownership being in the *dominus
soli*.

6. TRESPASS

It is further to be noted that trespass to lands was not an
actionable wrong in Roman law: the owner had a right to
exclude, and to remove, a trespasser, but no more. If, however, he had expressly forbidden entry or if it was an enclosure, such as a dwelling-house, into which everyone
knew that free entry would be forbidden, the entry would
in the law of the Empire be an actionable wrong. But it is
a wrong against personality, not against property. Under
the wide conception of insult, outrage, which had then
been reached, any wanton and wilful interference with
a man's rights was an actionable *iniuria*.[3] There was no
ownership in wild animals and thus, as there was no
law of trespass and no special game law, if a man entered
my land and trapped game there, I had no claim to it; and,
so far as the question of property was concerned, the result
was the same even though the land was an enclosed wood,
unless indeed it was an actual *vivarium*, in which case the
animals, while still in my control, were private property.[4]
There is thus no room for the complex doctrines which
have been developed in our law as to the property in wild

---

[1] D. 6. 1. 49.

[2] See *Syrisch-röm. Rechtsb.*, ed. Bruns und Sachau, par. 98 (M.S.
Lond.).   [3] P. 379, *post.*

[4] D. 41. 2. 3. 14; 41. 1. 55. The common law of Scotland follows the
Roman in this matter, Bell's *Law of Scotland*, sect. 1288. The law of
trespass is a very unimportant matter in Scotland; indeed it hardly exists.

animals killed on another's land.[1] But our law as to wild
animals is fundamentally the same as the Roman, and is
probably derived from it.

In like manner, though the wilful taking in bad faith of
a man's goods might be, and usually would be, actionable
civilly as a theft,[2] taking in good faith, however wrongfully, was not in the Roman law in itself an actionable
wrong; whereas in the common law a wrongful taking of
the goods of another, whether by mistake or, unless
necessity can be shown, even from a praiseworthy motive,
is an actionable trespass.[3] If, in the Roman law, the taker
thought, wrongly, that it was his own, or that he had some
right in it, e.g. a usufruct, so that he would be entitled to
possession or quasi-possession, the remedy against him
was a real action for the recovery of the thing or the usufruct. If the right which he supposed himself to have did
not involve possession, e.g. he thought the owner had lent
him the thing (for an ordinary bailee, other than a pledgee,
had no possession in Roman law), and he returned it on
demand, no action lay for the intervening enjoyment. If
he did not so return it, even though he might still be in
good faith, a real action lay for the thing.[4] If he claimed
that it had been lent him by a third person, or if indeed it
had been so lent, the result was the same, though, in the
last case, in classical law, the real action would be against
the lender.

7. COMMON OWNERSHIP[5]

The first point to note is that the Romans had really only
one kind of common ownership. It was immaterial whether
it arose by universal succession or in any other way. The
principal remedies were different, but the main principles

---

[1] *Blades* v. *Higgs* (1865), 11 H.L.C. 631.   [2] P. 352, *post.*

[3] *Kirk* v. *Gregory* (1876), 1 Ex. D. 55.

[4] *A fortiori* from D. 41. 2. 20, 47.

[5] See especially Riccobono, *Essays in Legal History*, ed. Vinogradoff,
Oxford, 1913, pp. 33 *sqq.*; Bonfante, *Corso*, ii. 2, ch. xx, with full discussion
of current theories as to the Roman conception of the institution.

were the same. Thus the complications introduced into our law by the conception of joint tenancy, tenancy in common, coparcenary and tenancy by entireties had for them no existence. While with us the joint tenant has an interest 'per my et per tout'[1] and a tenant in common owns only an undivided share and is not potential owner of the whole, the Roman common owner was thought of originally, and probably in classical law, as having a potential ownership of the whole.[2] It is however still matter of controversy whether this is properly contemplated as a number of distinct ownerships of the whole, cut down by the existence of the others, or as a number of partial ownerships, each extending over the whole, or as one ownership of the whole shared by all.[3] Of these views the first seems preferable, but it is clear that Justinian has altered some texts, by no means consistently, in such a way as to make the co-owner owner only of a part.

In our law the question of the correct analysis of any given case of common interest in property might be put in the form: If one of the parties wishes to transfer his interest to another of the parties, does he release his interest or does he convey it? A joint tenant releases, a tenant in common conveys. In Roman law a common owner desiring to transfer to another common owner did so by an ordinary conveyance, as to a third party.[4] If he desired simply to pass out of the community the machinery of the *actio communi dividundo* would be invoked. The *iudex* would 'adjudicate' the whole of the property to the other co-owners and award a money payment to the party ceasing to own.

---

[1] Which probably means in Coke's phrase (Co. Litt. 186a) 'totum tenet et nihil tenet', 'my' or 'mie' having nothing to do with moiety, but meaning 'not in the least' (*Daniel* v. *Camplin* (1845), 7 M. and G. 167, 172 n.; *Murray* v. *Hall* (1849), 7 C.B. 441, 455 n.).

[2] See, e.g., D. 32. 80.

[3] For these and other views, Bonfante, *loc. cit.*

[4] Arg. C. 4. 52. 3.

As in our joint tenancy, there was a right of accrual, but it was very different and less extensive. On the death of a common owner his inheritance represented him and took his interest: it was only where the right of a successor did not arise that there was accrual. This might occur, e.g., where one of two owners purported to manumit a slave: his right accrued to the other, though Justinian did away with this in a way which shows that he was more concerned with *favor libertatis* than with any theory about common ownership.[1] It might occur where one owner abandoned his share.[2] It arose where one legatee refused or was unable to take his share of a legacy left by direct gift (*per vindicationem*) to two or more,[3] probably also where one died without a successor, and indeed the rule is illustrated in many other ways.[4]

There were no necessary 'unities' in Roman law, though the unities of time, title, interest and possession existed in fact on the occurrence of joint succession. Any co-owner could alienate his share and be replaced in the community. The shares might be entirely unequal, and as there was no limited ownership the point of unity of interest could not arise.

The fragment of Gaius discovered in 1933[5] has shown us that in the primitive law of joint succession the theory that each owned the whole was carried so far that any one of the 'family heirs' could alienate an object in the succession. But in the law of historical times this has disappeared: as in our law, no common owner could effect an act of disposition affecting the whole, e.g. alienation or creation of a servitude, without the consent, indeed the

---

[1] Inst. 2. 7. 4.   [2] D. 41. 7. 3. *pr.*
[3] G. 2. 199; Ulp. Reg. 24. 12.
[4] The *ius accrescendi* between *coheredes* was not an accrual of property.
[5] For the editions and literature see De Zulueta, *Journal of Roman Studies*, 1934, pp. 168 *sqq.* and 1935, pp. 19 *sqq.* The fragment in question is now printed as sects. 154a and 154b of Book iii in De Zulueta's edition of the *Institutes* of Gaius.

concurrence, of all the owners, though, a
could dispose of his own share. And wh
right of enjoyment, subject to the concurr
others, he could do no act of administrati
others, e.g. build on the land, against the w
though it is still disputed whether in c
meant without the consent of the others
prohibition. This rule, which was some
Justinian's time, must have been very i
are told that it was so and that common
much dispute.[1] *Communio* is proverbially
The inconvenience of common ownership
a power of division was from early times
institution. So strongly was this felt that a r
to divide was not valid, except that unde
probably not in classical law, a temporary
enforced.[3] The contrary rule of our earlier
VIII,[4] under which no partition could
(except as between coparceners, who beca
by operation of law, so that the position wa
assumed), rests, no doubt, in reality more
of the chief lord in having the services un
this ground, but it is curious that the one c
early law allowed partition is precisely
primitive Roman law may have refused it

The rule that no administrative act coul
out, in some sense, the consent of all, is held
to be, in essence, the same as the system
in public law: every magistrate could act
currence of his colleagues, subject to their
his act, a *ius prohibendi*. It was some w
classical law in the matter of urgent rep

[1] D. 8. 2. 26; 31. 77. 20.
[2] It may not have existed in primitive succession ;
[3] D. 10. 3. 14. 2; C. 3. 37. 5.
[4] 31 Hen. VIII, c. 1; 32 Hen. VIII, c. 32.

As in our joint tenancy, there was a right of accrual, but it was very different and less extensive. On the death of a common owner his inheritance represented him and took his interest: it was only where the right of a successor did not arise that there was accrual. This might occur, e.g., where one of two owners purported to manumit a slave: his right accrued to the other, though Justinian did away with this in a way which shows that he was more concerned with *favor libertatis* than with any theory about common ownership.[1] It might occur where one owner abandoned his share.[2] It arose where one legatee refused or was unable to take his share of a legacy left by direct gift (*per vindicationem*) to two or more,[3] probably also where one died without a successor, and indeed the rule is illustrated in many other ways.[4]

There were no necessary 'unities' in Roman law, though the unities of time, title, interest and possession existed in fact on the occurrence of joint succession. Any co-owner could alienate his share and be replaced in the community. The shares might be entirely unequal, and as there was no limited ownership the point of unity of interest could not arise.

The fragment of Gaius discovered in 1933[5] has shown us that in the primitive law of joint succession the theory that each owned the whole was carried so far that any one of the 'family heirs' could alienate an object in the succession. But in the law of historical times this has disappeared: as in our law, no common owner could effect an act of disposition affecting the whole, e.g. alienation or creation of a servitude, without the consent, indeed the

---

[1] Inst. 2. 7. 4.   [2] D. 41. 7. 3. *pr.*
[3] G. 2. 199; Ulp. Reg. 24. 12.
[4] The *ius accrescendi* between *coheredes* was not an accrual of property.
[5] For the editions and literature see De Zulueta, *Journal of Roman Studies*, 1934, pp. 168 *sqq.* and 1935, pp. 19 *sqq.* The fragment in question is now printed as sects. 154a and 154b of Book iii in De Zulueta's edition of the *Institutes* of Gaius.

concurrence, of all the owners, though, as in our law, he could dispose of his own share. And while each had the right of enjoyment, subject to the concurrent rights of the others, he could do no act of administration affecting the others, e.g. build on the land, against the will of the others, though it is still disputed whether in classical law this meant without the consent of the others or against their prohibition. This rule, which was somewhat relaxed in Justinian's time, must have been very inconvenient; we are told that it was so and that common ownership led to much dispute.[1] *Communio* is proverbially *mater rixarum*. The inconvenience of common ownership was so great that a power of division was from early times inherent[2] in the institution. So strongly was this felt that an agreement not to divide was not valid, except that under Justinian, but probably not in classical law, a temporary limit might be enforced.[3] The contrary rule of our earlier law, till Henry VIII,[4] under which no partition could be compelled (except as between coparceners, who became joint owners by operation of law, so that the position was not voluntarily assumed), rests, no doubt, in reality more on the interest of the chief lord in having the services undivided than on this ground, but it is curious that the one case in which our early law allowed partition is precisely that in which primitive Roman law may have refused it.

The rule that no administrative act could be done without, in some sense, the consent of all, is held by some writers to be, in essence, the same as the system of 'collegiality' in public law: every magistrate could act without the concurrence of his colleagues, subject to their right of vetoing his act, a *ius prohibendi*. It was somewhat relaxed in classical law in the matter of urgent repairs, where the

[1] D. 8. 2. 26; 31. 77. 20.
[2] It may not have existed in primitive succession; Aul. Gell. 1. 9. 12.
[3] D. 10. 3. 14. 2; C. 3. 37. 5.
[4] 31 Hen. VIII, c. 1; 32 Hen. VIII, c. 32.

inconvenience had made itself greatly felt.[1] Justinian goes further by adding to some texts words allowing acts to be done by one if they are clearly to the benefit of the group as a whole.[2] And there are signs, which hardly amount to a general rule of law, that the decisions of the majority were to bind the rest,[3] a thing unknown to the classical law of the institution or indeed to public law except in relation to the tribunes.[4] The matter is complicated by the fact that common owners (*socii* in a wide sense) would also often be *socii* in the specific sense, partners, under the wide Roman notion of partnership.[5] And it is clear that, in the *actio pro socio*, *socii* could claim reimbursement of expenses incurred reasonably and in good faith in the maintenance of the common property.[6] But, quite apart from *societas stricto sensu*, it is clear that one co-owner could recover from the other expenses reasonably incurred in the management of the property, at least if it was by consent and probably if it was not against prohibition.[7]

When we turn to English law we find a somewhat primitive state of affairs prevailing in the relations between common owners. There was, by the strict rule of the common law, no reciprocal right of account, though the legislature and equity did something to remedy this defect. Both the common law and equity, instead of working out rules governing the position of acts of management and expense incurred by one common owner relating to the common property without the consent of the other, appear to have adopted the attitude: 'if you can't agree among yourselves, the sooner you partition the better.' Thus in

---

[1] P. Sent. 5. 10. 2; D. 39. 2. 32; D. 17. 2. 52. 10. The further drastic remedy mentioned in the text, provided by imperial enactment, expresses no general principle of law.

[2] D. 8. 2. 26; 10. 3. 6. 12; cf. D. 17. 2. 65. 5.

[3] D. 10. 2. 5; 10. 2. 44. 2; 16. 3. 14. *pr.*; Riccobono, *cit.* pp. 111 *sq.*

[4] G. 1. 185; Livy, 9. 46, etc.; Rein, *Philologus*, v. pp. 137 *sqq.*

[5] *Post*, p. 301. [6] D. 17. 2. 38. 1.

[7] D. 3. 5. 26; 10. 3. 29.

Leigh v. *Dickeson*[1] the Court of Appeal had to confess its inability to find any remedy whereby one tenant in common of a house could recover from the other a share of the cost of certain repairs effected by him, and told him that they would be taken into account in a partition suit if ever that should be instituted; this was a case of tenancy in common, but the principle has been accepted as applying to joint tenancy as well.[2]

It is plain that neither system has worked out a satisfactory solution of the question, and when it is remembered that the remedies in Roman law were *pro socio* and *communi dividundo* and that these normally ended the relation there does not appear to be much practical difference between the two systems. But it must be noted that in Justinian's law, though probably not in classical law, both these actions could be brought for a settlement of accounts without destroying the *societas* or the common ownership.

As there was in Roman law no limited ownership, these points have been considered only in relation to what compares with our fee simple or absolute ownership in moveables. But there were limited interests in Rome, i.e. usufructs, though they were not thought of as a form of ownership, but as interests *sui generis*. These too might be held jointly, and the rules of accrual in relation to them bring out clearly the fact that each usufructuary is thought of as potentially usufructuary of the whole. The general rules of such joint interests were, *mutatis mutandis*, the same as those in ownership. Thus if a slave were held in joint usufruct, not everything which he acquired went to the usufructuaries, but only what was acquired through his labour or in connexion with the property of the usufructuaries. Thus an inheritance left to him went not to

---

[1] (1883), 12 Q.B.D. 194; (1884), 15 Q.B.D. 60; see also *Kay* v. *Johnston* (1856), 21 Beav. 536; *Re Leslie, Leslie* v. *French* (1886), 23 Ch. D. 552.

[2] See Lindley, *Partnership*, 11th ed. pp. 30–39, for a discussion of co-ownership.

them but to the owner. But what they did acquire they shared exactly as common owners would. So too if, for any reason, one of the common owners could not acquire, the others benefited, and so, within the limited field, did other usufructuaries. In general, the rules of accrual were much the same as those between joint life tenants in our law—the survivor took all and the right of the *dominus* arose only when the whole of the usufructuary interests had expired, and the texts show a distinction similar to that between joint tenancy and tenancy in common. The right of accrual arose only where the joint usufruct arose by one joint gift, not where it was *separatim*.[1] There was indeed a peculiarity in the Roman law which is in no way represented in ours, owing to the fact that a life interest was so differently conceived. It was a *ius* attaching to an individual person and, in early classical law, it was regarded as having no existence for any purpose until it was capable of enjoyment. Moreover, though it normally was for life it might have a premature determination, e.g. it might be lost by non-enjoyment for a certain time. From the principles just stated the jurists drew the conclusion (expressed in the maxim that in usufruct accrual was *personae non portioni*)[2] that in a case of joint usufruct, if one usufructuary, B, had lost his share by non-use, but survived A, he could still claim accrual, but only as to what he had not lost. The result was that on the death of A, A's original share passed to B, but B's original share merged in the *dominium*. If there were three usufructuaries in equal shares and A lost his share by non-use, B and C would now hold one-half each, his original third and one-sixth derived from A. If now B died, C would take half B's original share together with the sixth derived from A which A could not claim, so that A would have one-sixth (i.e. the

---

[1] D. 7. 2. 1. *pr.*

[2] Cf. Blackstone, '*de persona in personam*' (ii. 184), but no contrast with '*portioni*' is intended.

half of *B*'s original share) and *C* the rest. If now *C* died, *A* would have all except the one-third which he had originally lost, and that would merge in the *dominium*.

8. MODES OF CONVEYANCE

The modes of conveyance were so different from ours that they are difficult to compare. The normal modes were *mancipatio* for *res mancipi*, land, slaves and cattle, and *traditio* for other things. In the time of Gaius *in iure cessio* could be used as an alternative to either, though it was peculiarly appropriate to the creation or conveyance of *res incorporales*. Of these modes, *traditio* finds a modern counterpart in the delivery of moveables, and there seems little doubt that our medieval requirement of a real delivery of land owes a good deal to its influence. Feoffment by livery of seisin, whether 'in law' or 'in deed', required for its complete operation an actual entry: it was in fact a delivery of possession. Similarly, *in iure cessio* can be compared to the common recovery by which entails were barred. Both were in form collusive actions, fully acknowledged as conveyances in the developed law; and in both the new title of the acquirer was recognised as compatible with the former existence of a title in the transferor. But *mancipatio* has no counterpart in English law.[1] *Mancipatio* is like feoffment a formal recognition of the transfer of property, the essence of which is its publicity, since it requires five witnesses. It includes a formal investiture of the receiver, since he lays his hand on the thing or, in case of land, probably a symbol of it; but there is also a formal handing over of the price, if it is a sale (though in historical times it is only a symbol of the price), and even if it is not a sale there is a pretence that it is a price. *Mancipatio* of land need not be on the spot and required no entry. There was no necessary transfer of possession either for land or moveables, and the ownership

[1] P. and M. ii. p. 89.

passed even though the transferor remained in possession.[1] In feoffment, on the other hand, it is the transferor who plays the active part. He says words to the effect that he 'gives and grants' to the other party, though no precise words are necessary. In *mancipatio* it is the acquirer who takes the leading part. He declares that the thing is his and that by the formality of copper and scales he is buying it, there being some difficulties about the logic of the form into which we need not go. Indeed, in all these modes of conveyance it is the acquirer, not the transferor, who acts; whereas with us it is the transferor.[2]

Two further points must be noted about *mancipatio*. In the fourth century when *mancipatio* still survives for certain purposes but has degenerated to a mere writing with witnesses, the method is reversed and it is the transferor who declares that he is conveying the property.[3] It should further be noted that *mancipatio* being a 'formal' act depends on nothing but the formality: at civil law the intent was not technically necessary. A *mancipatio* extorted by threats was formally valid and it was by praetorian methods that it could be practically set aside.

Traditio, which passed *dominium* in *res nec mancipi* and ownership *in bonis*[4] in *res mancipi*, is simply delivery. Hence we are told that it is causal. Ownership does not pass unless there is a *causa*, i.e. some fact showing the intent that there shall be a transfer of ownership. This will usually be some previous dealing or declaration, e.g. of intent to give. But, as the *causa* is mere evidence of the intent, a *causa* which was believed to exist though it actually did not was as good as a real *causa*: putative *causa* sufficed. If *A* paid *B* money in the belief that there was a debt which did not really exist, the conveyance was good,

---

[1] See, e.g., Vat. Fr. 266a, 310, where there has been no delivery. No doubt in very early times it was an actual delivery.

[2] See further p. 272, *post*.

[3] See Collinet, *Ét. juridiques*, i. p. 254, note 4.   [4] P. 64, *ante*.

though there was a means of recovery. To nullify the *traditio* the error must be one affecting the delivery itself. There is indeed much contradiction in the texts, and resulting controversy as to the kind of error which would vitiate a *traditio*, into which we cannot go.[1]

There is a curious difference in the evolution of conveyance in Roman law as compared with ours. Our law requires in principle either delivery or deed; Roman law requires delivery, or for some things only *mancipatio*. But in our law the actual transfer is not required on a sale of goods, and, apart from this, an incomplete transfer will be helped out in equity in favour of any one but a mere 'volunteer', a donee. In Roman law, on the other hand, sale always required a delivery to transfer the ownership and it was especially in favour of gifts that the rules were relaxed; whereas in our law it is precisely in the matter of gifts that we are strict and insist as a general rule upon delivery if there is no deed.[2]

There was a tendency, but, in general, till after the time of Justinian no more than a tendency, for delivery to become merely symbolical. But there were two respects in which the matter goes further. (i) It is clear on the texts that delivery of title deeds was treated in the later Empire as delivery of the thing,[3] but so far as the texts go, this applies only to *donatio*. The reason is not obvious, but it seems likely that it was in part at least due to the fact that the Church was very powerful and was a common recipient of gifts. The fact is so odd that the rule is sometimes treated as perfectly general, but it does not appear to be

---

[1] See, e.g., Buckland, *Text-book*, pp. 228 *sqq.*

[2] In England the delivery of the title deeds of land will not transfer the legal estate, though a valid equitable mortgage may still be created by a deposit of title deeds; as to personal property the handing over of a document of title to chattels may in certain cases be tantamount to delivery of the chattels themselves, for instance, the delivery of a bill of lading to the purchaser of goods under a c.i.f. contract.

[3] See Riccobono, *Zeit. d. Sav.-Stift.* xxxiv (1913), pp. 159 *sqq.*

anywhere evidenced except in relation to gifts, and its existence is sometimes denied altogether.[1] (ii) The other relaxation is that on the one hand if the thing is already in the intended owner's hands an actual delivery is dispensed with (*traditio brevi manu*), and that, on the other hand, if the transferor is intended to go on holding the thing as tenant or the like the handing forward and back is dispensed with and the legal possession passes with no physical transfer (*constitutum possessorium*). This also was utilised in relation to gifts. These (of land) required after A.D. 355 (C. Th. 8. 12. 7) *mancipatio* and *traditio*. The *mancipatio* was now a mere written document. In it was inserted a reservation of a usufruct for, say, three days, which would warrant the inference of a *constitutum possessorium* so that all requirements were satisfied. This too seems to have been applied at first only to gifts, but the enactment of 417 establishing it after a prohibition in 415 recurs in Justinian's Code (where it can have no relation to mancipation), with its provisions widened so as to cover sale.[2] The formal reservation of usufruct would soon disappear and delivery of title deeds be recognised as complete delivery of the property, though it cannot be said that this occurred in Justinian's time.[3] In the common law, too, where the intended donee is already in possession of the chattel, actual delivery is unnecessary. Our lease and release, whereby a tenant in fee simple could bargain and sell his estate to a purchaser for one year and the day after could release to him the reversion, thus transferring the fee simple to him without the need of livery of seisin, and, incidentally, without incurring even the notoriety of enrolment, is more like *traditio brevi manu* than *constitutum*

[1] Bonfante, *Corso*, ii. 2, pp. 170 *sqq.*

[2] C. Th. 8. 12. 9; C. 8. 53. 28.

[3] In French law it took until the Code Civil (1804) for this development to become complete. But the modern rule is much wider than the English: *any* valid unconditional agreement to transfer property automatically transfers it in principle without delivery (art. 1138).

possessorium.[1] In addition to this both systems recognise what has been misleadingly called symbolic delivery, e.g. the handing over of a key which gives access to the place where the goods are, with intent to give delivery of the goods. Here the key is not a symbol: it is a reality, namely the means of control.

The transfer of an undivided share can be effected in our law by deed, and in Roman law, for *res mancipi*, by *mancipatio* of the part. But this was not available for *res nec mancipi* and the Romans had no such thing as a deed. We are told that where a man had possession of a thing in which he owned an undivided share, delivery of the thing was a good delivery of the undivided share,[2] but we are not told how one is to transfer an undivided share where one owns the whole. In classical law it could be done by the highly formal process of *cessio in iure*, a sort of fictitious litigation bearing some resemblance to our common recovery. This, however, besides being inconvenient, as requiring attendance at a court of law, was obsolete under Justinian. The question arose in *Cochrane* v. *Moore*[3] whether delivery of an undivided share was impossible where this was not the whole interest of the transferor in possession, but was not expressly decided. It can be done by deed and, presumably, by transferring the possesssion to a bailee, who 'attorns' to the transferee as to that share. It is possible that some such device may have been used in Rome, though it could not be analysed in the same way, as a bailee (other than a pledgee) had in Rome no legal possession, but only detention or custody. It does not, however, seem impossible that *A* might deposit a thing with *B* and then or later present *C* to *B* and inform him that half the thing now belonged to *C*. His acknowledgement of this might be recognised as a sufficient transfer of that

---

[1] Digby, *History of the Law of Real Property*, 5th ed. pp. 366, 367; P. and M. ii. p. 89, n. 2.

[2] D. 21. 2. 64. 4.   [3] (1890), 25 Q.B. 57.

moiety to the possession and ownership of *C*. But we are not informed.

The covenants which play so large a part in our conveyances of land have little or no parallel in Roman law. Though the contrary is sometimes said, on the strength of the expression *lex mancipii* and similar forms,[1] it seems the better view that there could be no subsidiary clauses in a *mancipatio* or a *traditio*, other than those defining what was transferred, e.g. *deductio ususfructus*, grant of reservation of a servitude, a statement of area, exclusion of tombs contained in the land transferred, etc.[2] It is difficult to see by what action any obligations stated in this way could be enforced, and indeed the only obligation which we know was enforceable by action, namely that arising out of *fiducia*, was, though mentioned in the *mancipatio*, embodied in a separate pact, giving rise to the *actio fiduciae*. Many other such things are recorded, but they seem all to form part not of the *mancipatio* but of the transaction which led up to the *mancipatio*, and, if directly enforceable at all, are so by reason of this transaction. They were never more than contracts and thus, apart from express assignment or novation, could apply only between the original parties to the contract. There was no such thing as a covenant running with the lease (there was no reversion) and still less any such principle as that of *Tulk* v. *Moxhay*.[3] There is indeed one text in which a negative covenant in a contract of sale of land is held to be binding on grounds of good faith on 'personae possidentium aut in ius eorum succedentium'.[4] Its *prima facie* meaning seems to be that such a covenant runs with the land, if there is notice, in other

---

[1] E.g. G. 1. 140; 1. 172; D. 8. 4. 6. *pr.*, etc.

[2] See, for full discussion and references to relevant texts, with a somewhat different view, Georgescu, *Leges privatae*, esp. pp. 45 *sqq.*

[3] (1848), 2 Ph. 774. See however p. 140, *post*.

[4] D. 8. 4. 13. *pr.* See Buckland, *Equity in Roman Law*, p. 94, where, however, the explanation there rejected now seems to the authors preferable to that accepted.

words, the rule in *Tulk* v. *Moxhay*. Its isolated character
has led to the view, generally held, that it means no more
than that the agreement is binding on the transferee and
his *heredes* and the like, and it has been made clear that
the jurists never use the word successor to mean anyone
but a 'universal successor'. But the swelling phrase looks
more like Tribonian than Ulpian and it does not seem
impossible that it is one of those sporadic slapdash pieces
of 'equity' of which the compilers give many instances.
Possibly all that Ulpian said was that there could be no
servitude. In any case it is isolated, and we can say that
except in the case of slaves[1] the Romans never attained to
the conception of restrictive covenants running with property sold and binding subsequent purchasers. But our
restrictive covenants running with land are now really
servitudes, and Roman law would have recognised them
as such.[2]

    This attitude of the Roman law was an almost inevitable
outcome of its fundamental notions. The distinction between what we call *iura in rem* and *iura in personam*, or, to
speak in Roman terms, between actions *in rem* and actions
in personam, was much more clearly felt than it has been
with us. A conveyance was one thing: a contract was
another. The typical conveyance was *mancipatio*, a formal
act, admitting of no express conditions, and transferring
property but doing nothing more. Thus the form could
not contain covenants: this would have been to the Romans
a confusion of ideas. The operative covenant would be in
an independent document, though it might, as in *fiducia*,
be mentioned in the act of transfer. The covenant would
contain obligations and no more, and obligation was intensely personal: it was inconceivable that it should 'run
with the land'. Even if a record of conveyance and a
covenant did occur in the same document, each retained

---

[1] Buckland, *Slavery*, p. 68.
[2] See pp. 139–140, *post*.

its own character unaffected by the proximity of the other. With us the lease, originally pure obligation, first required a 'real' character and then communicated some of it to the covenants attached to it.

9. ACQUISITION BY LONG POSSESSION

The rules as to acquisition of property through long possession were in Roman law based on principles quite different from ours. With us there is, apart from easements and profits, no such thing as acquisitive prescription. The most that can happen is that a title, hitherto defeasible, may become indefeasible by lapse of time, owing to the extinction of some other title; and although one often speaks loosely of the acquisition of a possessory title by lapse of time, the title, and indeed the estate,[1] are the same after the lapse of time as they were before, and really date from the original taking. Judicial language can be found in which the statutes have been described as 'transferring' the estate of the former owner or as making a 'parliamentary conveyance' of the land to the 'person in possession', but it is now clear that these expressions are incorrect and that 'the statute does not convey but destroys the right'.[2] It is in fact negative, not positive.[3]

In Rome, on the other hand, lapse of time might lead by a process of *usucapio* to the acquisition of a new title, though there were other requirements of great importance.

Behind these two divergent solutions lies some history, for which the English evidence is much easier to follow

---

[1] This is devisable; *Asher* v. *Whitlock* (1865), L.R. 1 Q.B. 1.

[2] Hayes, *Introduction to Conveyancing*, i. (6th ed.) p. 269, cited with approval by the C.A. in *Tichborne* v. *Weir* (1892), 67 L.T. 735. And see Cheshire, *Modern Law of Real Property*, 3rd ed. pp. 204–206, 798–800, and Holdsworth, iii. p. 94.

[3] The practical effect of the distinction is not very important. It has been held in *Tichborne* v. *Weir* (*supra*), to prevent covenants from being enforced against one who had ousted a lessee and had not attorned

than the Roman. As to land, attention was directed, not to title, but to the remedies open to the disseisee, which were two: a right of entry, and a right of action. The former was peculiarly fragile, being destroyed by the death of the disseisor, or a conveyance by him to a third party. The latter was barred, not by a fixed period of limitation, but by some historical event, which was altered from time to time; a man's action was to be barred if he had not had seisin since, e.g., the time of Henry I or Henry II, so that between the legislative changes the time of limitation was always lengthening. Under Henry VIII the system was altered and definite periods were fixed, varying according to the kind of action; and the right of entry also was barred by lapse of time. All of this was superseded by the Statute of Limitations of 1623, which remained in force until 1833.[1] There was even less temptation to advert to the title to moveables, for although originally the actions of debt and detinue were conceived of as recuperatory, by the end of the sixteenth century they had lost this character, and for a long time past the actions for the recovery of chattels and money had been regarded as being actions either in contract or in tort; and thus the same régime was applied to chattels as to land. Section 3 of the Statute of Limitations, 1623, fixes a term of six years for (inter alia) trespass, trover, detinue and replevin. It has no special concern with property, deals with personal actions in general, and is a pure statute of limitation. It tells us that the actions mentioned above and others 'shall be commenced and sued... within six years next after the cause of such actions or suit, and not after... ' and leaves the Courts to draw their own conclusion about title, if that

tenant to the lessor; he did not hold the same estate in the land as his predecessor. But this does not apply to restrictive covenants running with the land in equity, the only person not affected by the covenant being a *bona fide* purchaser of the land without notice of the covenant, *In re Nisbet and Potts' Contract*, [1895] 1 Ch. 391; [1906] 1 Ch. 386.

[1] For land. It remained in force for moveables until 1939.

is in question. However, as the action of ejectment, which put in issue the right of entry, superseded the real actions for the recovery of land, and as the Courts came to hold that, to be successful, the plaintiff must have, not only a better title to the land than the defendant, but the best title, attention became focussed not on the act of disseisin but on the title of the disseisee; and so when a difficulty in applying the Act of 1623 to rights of entry made legislation inevitable, it was natural that Parliament should have taken the opportunity in 1833 of making the lapse of time extinguish not merely the plaintiff's right of action but also his title. This change has been perpetuated by the Limitation Act, 1939. The period is twelve years.

It was not until the passing of that Act that any attempt was made to extend this solution to moveables. It was accepted as law that the Statute of Limitations, 1623, as applied to personal chattels, did not destroy title.[1] In *Miller* v. *Dell*[2] it was held that an action of detinue would not be barred unless the defendant could show that the particular cause of action on which he was being sued in respect of a wrongful act by him had not arisen within six years before the issue of the writ, so that he could not avail himself of an adverse possession previous to his own. Thus if the person dispossessed could contrive, after the period of limitation was complete, to repossess himself of the object in a peaceable way, he could not be disturbed. In fact there was even greater need to extinguish the title to goods, since otherwise a buyer from a person against whom an action was barred by lapse of time could be sued for converting the original owner's goods.[3] Hence section 3

---

[1] Perhaps this was because it was difficult in 1623 to regard detinue as truly recuperatory: until 1833 most defendants could wage their law and until 1854 every defendant had the option of paying the value instead of returning the chattel.

[2] [1891] 1 Q.B. 463.

[3] Though this was not free from doubt. See Salmond, *Torts* (8th ed. 1935), p. 358.

of the Limitation Act, 1939, not only makes lapse of time bar the dispossessed owner's title, but also makes the time run from the original conversion or detention of the goods. The period is six years.

In Roman law all this is reversed. In principle there is no limitation of actions for the recovery of property: they are *actiones perpetuae* in classical law, though the principle of limitation creeps in in the later law when all actions, with a few exceptions, are barred by the lapse of thirty years. However, though a man's title could not be barred by mere lapse of time it might be barred by the fact that, in the meantime, someone had acquired ownership by long possession. The times for this established in the XII Tables look astonishingly short, two years for land, one year for moveables, but in the time of Justinian they had been lengthened to ten or twenty years for land, according to circumstances, and three years for moveables. As we have already noted, this *usucapio* is a definite acquisition of ownership, not a mere bar.[1]

The extreme brevity of the original periods is presumably to be explained by the fact that when they were established the whole State was a very small area, but they were obviously unsatisfactory when the community came to have an area comparable to that of a modern State. The XII Tables had already enacted that stolen things could not be usucaped. This rule may have originally operated only against the thief himself, and may have had the same purpose as our equitable doctrine of concealed fraud, i.e., to avoid penalising an owner who had had no chance of finding the right party to sue. But, at

---

[1] This system applied only to what was capable of civil ownership and to persons with full civil right. For provincial land and some other cases periods were fixed in the Empire much longer, the same as that ultimately generalised by Justinian, and this prescription was at first merely a bar, extinguishing the previous title, though it ultimately became acquisitive. This we shall not discuss. The kind of prescription that merely bars the remedy is discussed at pp. 413–419, *post*.

any rate in classical times and later, it seems that no one, however innocent, could usucape stolen property until it had actually or constructively returned to the possession of the person from whom it had been stolen. There is nothing in English law like this provision, which, as Gaius points out,[1] made it almost impossible for a *bona fide* possessor, as opposed to a bonitary owner, to usucape moveables. Further, though the times were not changed a corrective was introduced at some time in the Republic, involving a principle of which our common law[2] system knows nothing. Long possession did not constitute a basis for title unless it had begun with what in the language of the jurists of the Empire is called *bona fides* and *iusta causa*. *Bona fides* appears to be best described as a belief that in the circumstances the taking was not an infringement of anyone's rights. *Iusta causa* means that the taking was based on some fact on which ordinarily acquisition of property is based, such as sale or legacy or abandonment, which normally would be abandonment by a non-owner; otherwise ownership would have arisen at once. Without going into details it may be noted that the sharp definition of the two notions is the work of the jurists, the two ideas probably having hardly been separated to begin with, and that as time went on *bona fides* became the predominant element and there was a tendency to allow belief that a *causa* existed to suffice—to treat 'putative *causa*' as enough, as in *traditio*.

It will be seen that these principles differ fundamentally from those of concealed fraud as developed in Equity or the slightly different doctrine established by the Real

[1] G. 2. 50.

[2] The notion of concealed fraud as barring the operation of Statutes of Limitation is of equitable origin, and attempts made since the Judicature Act, 1873, to introduce it into the common law have not met with uniform success: see *Legh* v. *Legh* (1930), 143 L.T. 151 and cases cited therein, and Wade, 'Misrepresentation in Equity', in *Cambridge Legal Essays* (Heffer and Sons, Cambridge, 1926).

Property Limitation Act, 1833.[1] Here the rule is that time does not begin to run against the plaintiff until the fraud on which the opponent's enjoyment is based has been or should have been discovered. But in Roman law, if the holding had not begun in good faith, the defect could never be cured: no title could ever be acquired by *usucapio*, though, in the later law, when a real limitation of actions was introduced, the plaintiff might be barred by the lapse of thirty years.[2]

In Roman law the possession required to bar the old title and create a new one, both for land and for moveables, must be continuous and uninterrupted, and must have existed in the same person or someone under whom he claims. If I am *in via usucapiendi* and lose possession—not merely transfer it voluntarily to another—I must begin all over again, and, what is more, begin with *bona fides*. Moreover, at first the possession had to be in the same person all the time, and it was only by degrees that a person was allowed to add to his own possession that of a predecessor in title, first that of one to whom he had succeeded *mortis causa*, and then that of a vendor. As to land, in our law, the question whether the possession in order to extinguish the old title must be continuous in one person and others claiming through him, or may be in a series of successive but independent trespassers, is controversial. As to moveables, we look at the mattter differently. The question is not one of possession but of actionability. Did the cause of action on which the defendant is being sued arise more than six years before the issue of the writ? Thus if I wait more than six years after a conversion or detention, then unless I have resumed possession in the meantime, I shall lose my title, even though the present possessor has no

---

[1] As to this difference, see Ashburner, *Principles of Equity*, 2nd ed. pp. 506–508.

[2] C. 7. 39. 3. Further details as to the later law, Buckland, *Text-book*, p. 251.

connexion with the original wrongdoer, and however
great an interval may have occurred between the various
possessions.

Although the principles on which Roman and English
law proceed are so different, there is some danger of over-
estimating the difference in operation. We may say that
the Roman acquirer usucapes on his own merits, whereas
the English loser loses on his own demerits. But it does not
always work out quite in that way; for, as will be more
fully explained later,[1] no mere failure to possess, for however long a time, will bar an English tenant of land of his
remedy, or of his title, unless one or more persons have
been in continuous possession throughout the limitation
period. In the normal case it will be the same person, or
someone deriving title from him, who will be in possession
for the whole time, and accordingly for most practical
purposes we could say that he has acquired a title by long
possession.

10. PARTITION

We have seen that any common owner at Roman law
could compel partition and that in our law it was necessary
(except for coparceners, who could already compel partition) to create this power by statute. Roman law had a
special mode of conveyance by judicial award called *adiu-
dicatio*, which somewhat resembled in its method the procedure under the old writ of partition, now superseded in
our law. As under our older system, the judge had not the
power to order sale which he has under the modern legislation. But while under our system the actual partition
was carried out by the sheriff under decree of the Court,
and the judicial confirmation of his return constituted the
basis of title,[2] the *iudex* himself made or superintended the
partition, no doubt with the assistance of *agrimensores*, and

---

[1] P. 415, *post*.
[2] See Cruise, *Digest*, vol. ii. *tit.* XVIII, 34.

his order was the basis of title. On the other hand the *iudex* had a much freer hand than the judge under the old writ of partition. He could give or destroy no rights in others than the actual parties, but subject to this he had large powers. Where fair division was impossible he could make unequal division and order equalising payments, and other payments in respect of expenses incurred or damage done by any party, and he could create such subsidiary rights as were needed, e.g. rights of way. He could even allot the actual property to one alone of the parties.[1] Thus there was no need for such grotesque results as occurred in *Turner* v. *Morgan*,[2] where the Court awarded to one of the claimants all the chimneys, all the fire-places and the only staircase. The power of ordering sale, under more recent legislation, put an end to this difficulty, and under the legislation of 1925 there is always a trust for sale, so that the partition action is gone. If the sale is to be avoided the parties must agree upon a division.

11. ACQUISITION OF FRUITS BY A NON-OWNER

The only other case of acquisition which needs mention here is the acquisition of fruits by a non-owner. So far as the life tenant (who was not an owner in Roman law) is concerned, there is no great difference to state. In both systems the fruits are his, with the technical difference that as the Roman life tenant has not legal 'possession' of the land, the fruits are not his till he has taken them. As to the leaseholder the only point to note for Roman law is the logical but inconvenient rule that as he did not 'possess' he did not acquire until he took, and as his right was purely contractual[3] his right to the fruits depended on the consent of the lessor. If that consent was revoked he no longer

---

[1] D. 10. 2. 55.
[2] (1803), 8 Vesey 143.
[3] As to the effect on his tenancy of sale by the lessor, p. 295, *post*.

acquired. He would indeed have an answer to the owner who claimed them, arising out of the latter's breach of contract, but as to third persons he would have no right at all;[1] though, again under his contract, he could require the owner to proceed against the third person, or to assign his right of action.[2] When we turn to the English termor or lessee, we find that, though he started life on a contractual basis like the *conductor*, he eventually acquired possession. In these circumstances it is not surprising that the termor's right to fruits is stronger than that of the *conductor*, and that we are told that a lessor 'cannot of right meddle with the demesne nor the fruits thereof'.[3]

Another case presented by the Roman law is remarkable. A *bona fide* possessor without right acquired the normal products so far as they had been separated while he was still in good faith, with, in later law, a duty to account for such as still existed when his right was disputed.[4] It is not easy to see why he had more right in the fruits than in the thing itself, and the odd rule is explained in many ways, e.g. that it would be unfair to charge him as he has been living as if the thing was his and therefore the fruits also,[5] which is not very satisfactory, and, again, that it is because they are the fruits of his labour,[6] as they commonly would be, with the corollary that at one time it did not extend beyond such fruits.[7]

Our law seems to have nothing of the kind. It is especially in connexion with actions for the recovery of land that the point arises, and here it is clear that the plaintiff can recover mesne profits from the time of the

---

[1] D. 39. 5. 6.

[2] D. 19. 2. 60. 5; cf. D. 19. 2. 25. 8.

[3] Pollock and Wright, *Possession*, pp. 47–53; P. and M. ii. pp. 106–117.

[4] See, e.g., Girard, *Manuel*, 8th ed. p. 345.

[5] Girard, *loc. cit.*

[6] Inst. 2. 1. 35.

[7] Suggested by D. 22. 1. 45. Other explanations, Buckland, *Text-book*, p. 224. See also pp. 86–87, *ante*.

defendant's entry up to the time of recovery of possession, irrespective of the defendant's good or bad faith.[1]   And as to moveables, both in detinue[2] and in trover[3] damages for detention may be claimed, but, as they are meant to compensate the plaintiff for the use he has not been able to make rather than to force the defendant to disgorge the profits he has made, there is no question of an account.

[1] *Southport Tramways* v. *Gandy*, [1897] 2 Q.B. 66.
[2] *Crossfield* v. *Such* (1852), 8 Ex. 159.
[3] *Bodley* v. *Reynolds* (1846), 8 Q.B. 779.

CHAPTER IV. LIMITED INTERESTS AND SERVITUDES

The heading of this chapter must look somewhat surprising to a common lawyer, who is not likely to see much affinity between a life estate and a right of way. But, for the Romans to whom the notion of a limited ownership was a contradiction in terms, the affinity is clear enough. Both these classes of rights, usufruct and its offshoots and what we call easements and profits, were rights *in rem* in the property vested in someone other than the owner. Both of them were *iura*, incorporeal rights. They were created in just the same ways. They were claimed and enforced by similar remedies. It is not therefore surprising that in the later Roman law they were classed together as servitudes, life interests (usufruct and the like) being personal servitudes, as attached to a particular person and dying with him, and our easements and profits being praedial servitudes, attached to the tenements they affected and of perpetual duration. But this is very different from the earlier conception.

Usufruct is not primitive. It dates only from late in the Republic and its primary purpose was essentially alimentary, e.g. provision for a widow. It is not till the Empire that it becomes a general legal institution, divorced from this alimentary purpose, and it is clear that the lawyers of the first century did not find it easy to analyse it and fit it into the scheme of legal things. What seems to have impressed them first was its entirely incorporeal nature. It was a legal entity *sui generis*, not to be thought of in physical terms—a *ius*, and as such a *res*, capable of being claimed as such, but not capable of being possessed, as it was not physical; and though for certain purposes a part of the mass of rights called *dominium*, it was not at first thought of as a *ius* in the physical thing, a *ius in re*, but simply as a *ius*. It would be beyond the purpose of these pages to go into the odd results which sprang from this conception, discussed in the Vatican Fragments.[1] But early in the second century it came to be thought of as a *ius in re*, like a servitude, and at some later date, probably early in the third century, though the dominant opinion is that it was not till the Byzantine age,[2] the assimilation with servitudes was complete and usufruct was a personal servitude as opposed to rights of way, light, etc., which were praedial servitudes.

As usufruct is not a form of ownership, it could not be created by the modes usual for the conveyance of property, not by *traditio*, for, not being physical, it could not be delivered, nor by *mancipatio*, not being a *res mancipi*. The only way of creating it *inter vivos* at civil law was by *cessio in iure*, rather like a common recovery, though here as elsewhere the Praetor gave protection where it had been set up informally, in ways which we need not discuss. Unlike a life estate it was inalienable—it attached to the person of the donee and could not be detached from him. There was nothing indeed to prevent him from allowing someone else to enjoy it, or even from selling the right of enjoyment, but such a transaction did not affect his position as usufructuary. So too there could be no usufruct *pur autre vie*, though the working of the law of legacy might give something like it. Thus, in classical law if a usufruct was left to a slave by direct legacy, it vested of course in his master, and could not survive the master. But it could not survive the slave either, so that it was in effect for the shorter of the two lives. This is gone under Justinian, but he provides that where one is acquired through a son it survives to the son if he outlives the father.[3]

[1] Sects. 41–93; see Buckland, 43 *L.Q.R.* (1927), pp. 326 *sqq.*
[2] See Buckland, 'Marcian', *Studi Riccobono*, i. pp. 274 *sqq.*
[3] Buckland, *Text-book*, pp. 272 *sq.*

There is no evidence as to the civil law liability of the usufructuary in the matter of waste, but it is clear that under praetorian law he was liable for waste, even permissive.[1] As the texts express it, he must conduct himself as a *bonus paterfamilias*, and for this he had to give security,[2] the security covering maintenance, good cultivation and return at expiration of the right. And it seems that in classical law he might enjoy only as his donor had been in the habit of enjoying. Thus he might sell produce only if the donor had been in the habit of doing this,[3] though this severe rule is gone under Justinian. As to voluntary and ameliorating waste the rule was much more drastic than with us; amelioration was not allowed—the usufructuary might not even plaster a rough wall.[4] And any fundamental alteration of the property was not merely a wrong: it ended the usufruct, which was in the thing as it was, and this whether the change was by him or someone else.[5]

There was no right of entry for emblements if the right expired while crops were growing. The growing crops belonged to the person entitled in default of the usufructuary, but if they were actually cut, though not yet garnered, they went to the usufructuary's estate.[6] This may be compared with the rule that if the usufructuary had let the land and died between rent days, the question whether his *heres* or the owner of the land was entitled to the next rent depended on whether the tenant had gathered the crops or not.[7] Naturally as he could not alienate his own right he could not alienate that of the owner. There was nothing in the smallest degree corresponding to the powers of sale of a tenant for life under modern statutes.

---

[1] D. 7. 1. 7. 2, etc.   [2] D. 7. 9. 1.

[3] Riccobono, *Studi Brugi*, pp. 173 *sqq.*

[4] D. 7. 1. 44. But see h.t. 13. 5 where his act could not burden the reversioner.

[5] P. Sent. 3. 6. 28; D. 7. 4. 5. 2, 31.

[6] D. 7. 4. 13.

[7] Buckland, *Text-book*, p. 222.

There was not of course the same need for such powers, since in general the land could not be 'tied up' for more than the life of the usufructuary—there were no estates tail.[1] But the real difficulty is that a usufructuary had not ownership at all. The thing subject to the usufruct was a *res aliena*. And only within very narrow limits did the Romans ever allow anyone who was not owner to make a title in property without the owner's authority. The pledgee[2] and certain kinds of guardians are the only cases: there was nothing like our powers operating in equity or under the Statute of Uses. Still less was it possible for a mere bailee, as generally in French law, and under narrow conditions as in English law,[3] to transfer ownership to a *bona fide* purchaser.

As to mines, the general rule of our law that a tenant for life may work existing mines, but may not in general open new ones,[4] would serve for a description of the right of the usufructuary, but the principle is not quite the same. The usufructuary may not open new mines because to do so is to alter the character of the property, not merely because such a thing is more than is involved in the enjoyment of the thing as it is. On the other hand, where he is entitled to work a mine and therefore to let it there is no question of setting aside any part of the proceeds as capital money, as under our Settled Land Acts. It is absolutely his, as it is a tenant-for-life's if he works the mine himself under his common law powers. In fact minerals in such a case were on just the same level as fruits, the organic produce of the property, and were apparently regarded by the Romans as equally capable of renewing themselves.

---

[1] As to the possibility of settlements at certain periods, Buckland, *Equity in Roman Law*, pp. 83 *sqq.*; also pp. 173–175, *post*.

[2] And he was, originally at least, given authority at the time of the pledge.

[3] Cf. Sale of Goods Act, Sect. 25; Factors Acts, *passim*; see also pp. 77–78, *ante*.

[4] *Elias* v. *Snowdon* (1879), 4 App. Cas. 454.

Notwithstanding the assimilation to servitudes, usufruct retains two characteristics in which it resembles a
limited estate. It gives indefinite rights of enjoyment, almost the same as those of an owner, and is attached to the
personality of the holder so that on the cesser of that personality it ceases to exist. And, because of its character, it
is thought of for many purposes as a part of ownership, so
that if a man who has sold a piece of land can convey it only
subject to outstanding usufruct he is liable to his buyer for
'eviction' in exactly the same way as if a specific part, or
an undivided share in the land, was effectively claimed by
a third party. A praedial servitude on the other hand is
attached to the *praedium* concerned and can last as long as
the *praedium* does, i.e., normally it is perpetual. And if a
buyer found after the sale that the land was burdened with
a servitude of which nothing had been said, he had no
remedy unless there was an express guarantee that there
were no servitudes,[1] though knowingly to conceal such a
servitude was a fraud for which the vendor would be liable;
whereas in English law the rule is that, in the absence of
express mention, a buyer may decline to perform a contract for the sale of land if he discovers before completion
that the land is subject to an easement which is not patent
or discoverable by inspection.[2] In fact praedial servitudes
seem to have been regarded rather as accidental characteristics or qualities of the land, like relative fertility. A
buyer is not entitled to a remedy if the land proves less
fertile than he expected.

The Roman law of praedial servitudes has many resemblances to our law of easement sand profits. This is no
doubt in part due to the fact that our authorities have very
frequently appealed to the Roman law. Bracton appeals to
the Roman law and our modern cases and text-books are

[1] D. 18. 1. 59; 50. 16. 90.
[2] Williams, *Vendor and Purchaser,* 4th ed. p. 638; *Yandle* v. *Sutton,*
[1922] 2 Ch. 199.

full of references to it on this matter. But there are many similarities of which borrowing cannot be the explanation. Thus in both systems these rights can be acquired by long enjoyment, lapse of time without interruption of the enjoyment. If this system had been simply borrowed it would have been borrowed as it was in the time of Justinian or later, but in fact it appears, with us, to have gone through an evolution very like that it underwent in Roman law. In that law it does not appear till the second century and apparently then applied only to the primitive rights of way and water, and took the form of a presumption of lawful creation drawn from a long enjoyment,[1] without any definite limit. Only in late law are there fixed limits of time and only then is it clear that it applied to all praedial servitudes and is free from the conception of a lost grant.[2] So in our law the system seems to have passed from one in which enjoyment must have been from before the time of memory to one in which a certain length of enjoyment was taken as evidence of a lost grant and finally to the rules in the Prescription Act, 1832,[3] under which different times are established for different types of right and different efficacies for different lapses of time, with no reference to lost grant.[4]

Under Section 4 of the Prescription Act the period prescribed for the enjoyment of an easement or profit must be 'the period next before some suit or action wherein the

---

[1] D. 43. 20. 3. 4, etc.

[2] Buckland, *Main Institutions of Roman Law*, p. 158.

[3] 2 and 3 Wm. IV, c. 71. The periods are sixty and thirty years in the case of profits, twenty years in the case of light, or twenty and forty years in the case of easements. After twenty (or thirty) years the claim to the easement (or profit) cannot be defeated by proof that it could not have existed at some date later than 1189; after forty (or sixty) years the right is absolute and indefeasible unless it appears that the enjoyment depends on some consent given by deed or writing. See Holdsworth, vii. pp. 351, 352, as to the mental confusion surrounding the drafting of this Act.

[4] *Tapling* v. *Jones* (1865), 11 H.L.C. 290. See, on the history of the matter, Gale on *Easements*, Part II, ch. iii.

claim or matter . . . shall have been or shall be brought into question', and a right thus acquired may be set up when challenged in a subsequent action;[1] it results from this section that no right is acquired under the Act until it has been 'brought into question' in an action and established, though it may still be acquired under the common law, which has not been superseded by the statute. There is no such rule in Roman law, but apparently a cesser of enjoyment for such time as would bar a duly acquired right would prevent an acquisition (i.e., would render necessary a new beginning of enjoyment), namely, before Justinian two years non-user for rights of way and the like and two years *usucapio libertatis* for rights to light, etc.

The rule of the statute that the right must have been enjoyed otherwise than by consent in writing, and, except in case of light, by one 'claiming right thereto', or, as it is ordinarily put, 'as of right', is paralleled in the Roman law by the rule that it must not have been enjoyed *vi clam aut precario*.[2]

But there are many differences in the two systems. With us the right to support is a natural right only so far as the land is in its natural condition. If a heavier burden is imposed, by such things as buildings, there is no right to support of this except as an easement to be acquired in one or other of the ways in which easements can be acquired, e.g. by lapse of time.[3] But in Roman law no such distinction seems to have been drawn. The right to lateral support nowhere appears in the law of servitudes, for the *ius oneris*

---

[1] *Cooper* v. *Hubbuck* (1862), 12 C.B.N.S. 456.

[2] D. 8. 5. 10. *pr.*, and see Thesiger L.J. in *Sturges* v. *Bridgman* (1879), 11 Ch. D. 852, at p. 863: 'Consent or acquiescence of the owner of the servient tenement lies at the root of prescription, and of the fiction of a lost grant, and hence the acts or [? of] user, which go to the proof of either one or the other, must be, in the language of the civil law, "nec vi nec clam nec precario".'

[3] *Wyatt* v. *Harrison* (1832), 3 B. and Ad. 871; *Dalton* v. *Angus* (1881), L.R. 6 App. Cas. 740, 792.

ferendi is the right to the maintenance of a supporting structure. There is indeed very little in the Roman books about a right to lateral support. In D. 10. 1. 13 Gaius cites, as being accepted as part of the Roman law, an extract from a law attributed to Solon, providing that if one digs a ditch or the like on one's land there must be left an interval equal to its depth: this does not sound very practical, and it is very doubtful if it is really Roman law of any epoch. In any case it cannot mean that this was the only restriction in this matter. The Roman attitude seems rather to have been that an owner is entitled to make any use of his land which he likes provided he does not infringe some right of his neighbour, and if his neighbour does something which prevents this enjoyment this is an actionable wrong, so far as it does damage. Thus we are told that if you begin to dig a well in such a way that my wall cannot stand I have a remedy, without, as it seems, any reference to the length of time my wall has stood,[1] at least if I have given you notice before the work was done and also, pre- sumably, if it was done secretly.

The distinction between easements and profits *à prendre* has no place in the Roman law. The distinction drawn is between rustic and urban servitudes, of which the former are the older, and are those essentially associated with the enjoyment of unbuilt land, such as rights of way and water, the latter being those connected with buildings, such as rights to light. But it is to be noted that while all the urban servitudes and the rights of way and water are easements in our sense, nearly all the other rustic servi- tudes, such as rights of pasture, of lime-burning, etc., are what we should call profits. They are of more recent origin than rights of way and water and there is reason to think that in classical law they were more urban than rustic in their legal characteristics, i.e., they were not, like the rights of way and water, capable of creation by *mancipatio*

[1] D. 39. 2. 24. 12.

or of being mortgaged. That is the whole difference, and it does not separate them from easements but rather associates them with urban servitudes, which are all easements. Thus the rules as to their creation and acquisition by lapse of time were the same.

This last point, however, is affected by another consideration. All the rustic servitudes seem to be positive, i.e., the enjoyment of them involves some form of entry on the servient land—they are *iura faciendi*. The urban are usually negative—rights to prevent the owner of the servient land from doing something—*iura prohibendi*. This distinction has legal effects. When we think of acquisition by prescription, ancient lights is the first case which comes to our mind, but there is reason to think that till very late in the Roman law the rules of acquisition by long enjoyment applied only to rustic, or positive, servitudes. There seems to be only one text which applies it in a wider field[1] and the reference to it there is not above suspicion of interpolation. There is a corresponding difference in relation to loss by non-enjoyment. Rustic servitudes, being positive, were lost by failure to enjoy for the statutory time and this was all that was necessary. But as negative servitudes do not involve doing anything, they were not lost by mere non-user: you do not lose a right to light by not looking out of the window or even by not having any window, but only by submitting for the necessary time to something inconsistent with the servitude. In our law there is no statutory rule as to loss by non-user. The question always turns upon a presumed intention to abandon the right and a period of twenty years is commonly mentioned in the cases, based upon the analogy of the presumption of acquisition which arises from twenty years unexplained enjoyment. But twenty years is not always necessary or enough. It depends on the circumstances in which, e.g., the window was destroyed. Length of time is only a factor in the solution of

[1] C. 3. 34. 1.

the question whether the owner of the dominant tenement meant to abandon the right,[1] in the case of both continuous and discontinuous easements.[2]

It must be noted that, in the case of negative easements, the right was lost only by acquiescence, for the necessary time, in something inconsistent with the servitude;[3] and this was not said to be loss by non-user, but loss by *usucapio libertatis*,[4] though the rules of *iusta causa* and *bona fides* did not apply. This contemplated not loss of the right by the dominant owner, but release of the servient owner from a burden. And this had an important legal result. For since it was *usucapio*, it rested on adverse enjoyment of the liberty, not on mere cesser of enjoyment of the servitude nor even on adversely created inability to enjoy. Thus if the servient owner blocked the right and then lost possession of the land, time ceased to run in his favour, and if he regained possession the time had to begin again.[5] Time would begin to run in favour of an intruder when he took possession, and if the right was destroyed as against him it was destroyed altogether. There is apparently nothing of this sort in our law on the matter, and we address ourselves to the question whether the dominant owner of the right has lost it by non-user and not to the question whether the servient owner has acquired an immunity from it. The law as to commons and other profits on this matter provides little authority on the present point. It seems that the extinguishment of a right of common, once established, cannot be presumed from mere non-exercise; it is evidence but not conclusive evidence of abandonment. Adverse unjustified enclosure seems to be a case for the Real Property Limitation Acts.

---

[1] *Moore* v. *Rawson* (1824), 3 B. and C. 332.
[2] *Crossley* v. *Lightowler* (1867), L.R. 2 Ch. App. 478; *James* v. *Stevenson*, [1893] A.C. 162.
[3] D. 8. 2. 6. 32. [4] D. 8. 2. 6; 8. 6. 18. 2.
[5] D. 8. 2. 32. 1.

Praedial servitudes, whether amounting to profits or not, being essentially appanages to land, could not exist in gross.[1] Such a thing agreed for between the owner of the land on which it was to be exercised and a man in his personal capacity could be no more than a contractual right. In classical law a usufruct of an old pasture which had always been grazed might not differ substantially in content from a *ius pecoris pascendi*, which was a praedial servitude, and if created in favour of a man under a will it might, if he owned neighbouring land, sometimes be doubtful which it was meant to be. Construed as a usufruct it would give a *ius in rem*, but would be only for life: as a praedial servitude it would be a perpetual *ius in rem*, but it might indeed be construed as giving only a *ius in personam*.[2]

Easements of necessity existed as with us,[3] the language of the texts rather implying that they lasted only so long as the need lasted, but throwing no light on the question whether the right extended only so far as it was necessary to the enjoyment of the property in its present condition. On the former point our law does not seem quite clear.[4] On the second point it seems now to be settled[5] that it extends only to the user being made of the property at the time when the easement of necessity arose. It seems probable, though not certain, that with us an easement of necessity does not survive the necessity.[6] The Roman law and ours agree apparently in the rule that when the way has once been chosen or assigned, it cannot be altered by either party.[7]

---

[1] As to English law, see Gale on Easements, 12th ed. pp. 12–15.
[2] Buckland, *Text-book*, pp. 273 *sq*.
[3] D. 7. 6. 1 *sqq*.; 8. 3. 3. 3; 30. 81. 3.
[4] See Gale, *cit*. p. 165.
[5] *London (Corporation of)* v. *Riggs* (1880), 13 Ch. D. 798.
[6] Hailsham, xi. p. 273.
[7] *Pearson* v. *Spencer* (1863), 1 B. and S. 571; 3 B. and S. 761; D. 8. 1. 9, arg.

The Roman easement of necessity rests on the principle that a right is not properly created if this is so done that it cannot be utilised, not on any rule that a man cannot derogate from his own grant. There was in fact no such principle. Our rule to that effect, for which *Wheeldon* v. *Burrows*[1] affords authority, had no application. There are a number of texts dealing with an owner of two tenements who sells one or both, and in all of them it is clear that there is no servitude by implication and that if it is desired to create a servitude either way this must be done expressly.[2] In one of these[3] the two *praedia* are sold *simul* but the question is raised whether it is possible to create a servitude at all in such circumstances. In another text[4] it is clearly laid down that one who alienates property adjoining other property of his may lawfully block lights of the property sold. All this turns on the principle that a man cannot have a servitude over his own land, and that, if one is to be created on severance, it must be a new servitude and therefore must be created in one of the ways in which servitudes are established. For the same reason if one whose property has been or is subject to a servitude acquires the other property, the servitude is at once extinct and does not revive on resale,[5] while with us it revives on resale.[6] Though there are in Roman law some exceptional circumstances, such as *restitutio in integrum*,[7] in which there is a claim to have the servitude created again, these do not affect the principle: indeed they confirm it, since in all the cases the servitude must be re-established, and they are all cases in which the transfer which destroyed the servitude was practically abortive.

---

[1] (1879), L.R. 12 Ch. D. 31.
[2] See, e.g., D. 8. 1. 19; 8. 3. 34, 35, 36; 8. 4. 3, 6. *pr.*, 8.
[3] D. 8. 4. 8.
[4] D. 8. 2. 10.
[5] D. 8. 2. 30. *pr.*; 8. 3. 27; 8. 6. 1.
[6] *Charlesworth* v. *Gartshed* (1863), 3 New Rep. 54.
[7] See Elvers, *Servitutenlehre*, pp. 125 *sqq.*

The two systems agree in confining the servitude to purposes for the benefit of the enjoyment of the dominant
land.[1] In both systems there is no limit to the number of
servitudes and the number is obviously added to from
time to time; they agree also in holding that there may be
a servitude to do what would otherwise be a private
nuisance.[2] English law makes another distinction which
apparently does not occur in the law of ancient Rome,
though it can be detected in a slightly different form in
modern systems, such as the Roman-Dutch law of South
Africa. It distinguishes between easements, which are
legal interests, and restrictive covenants, which run with
the land only in equity. The latter, which started as mere
contractual burdens on land, have now been subjected to
the limitations, such as the need for a dominant and a
servient tenement, which are appropriate to easements.
Moreover, since 1925, they rarely run, except where
contained in a lease, unless they are registered. Since
they have now approached so closely to easements the
question arises why they cannot be created as easements;
and the answer seems to be that, apart from the easements
of light and of support for a building—which are only
doubtfully exceptions—no easement can be negative in
character. Thus the distinction between easements and
restrictive covenants corresponds to that between positive
and negative servitudes; and the Roman-Dutch law of
South Africa shows that that distinction is relevant for
purposes of acquisition. All servitudes can be acquired by
express grant or reservation, but only positive servitudes
can be prescribed for; for by Roman-Dutch law as well as
by Roman law, prescription requires that the benefit shall
have been enjoyed *nec vi nec clam nec precario*. To be
nec precario the enjoyment must have been adverse to

---

[1] D. 8. 1. 8; 8. 3. 5. 1, 24; *Bailey* v. *Stephens* (1862), 12
C.B.N.S. 91.

[2] D. 8. 5. 8. 5–7; *Bliss* v. *Hall* (1838), 4 Bing. N.C. 183.

the owner of the servient tenement. As Professor Wille says:[1]

in the case of a positive or affirmative servitude the act of user must necessarily be adverse to the servient owner. In the case of a negative servitude, on the other hand, the mere fact that a landowner has abstained for thirty years from using his land in a particular manner does not constitute an act adverse to himself, for he is not obliged to exercise his rights, and consequently no servitude against his land is created.

The arguments are obviously applicable to English law also, and the only reason why the resemblance between the Roman and English law on this topic has not been observed is that in English law restrictive covenants are contractual in origin. It is not very easy to know why we should not have allowed restrictive covenants to operate as easements at common law, subject to the limitation that they must have been created by act of parties—they would have been perfectly good servitudes in Roman law—but perhaps the answer is that with us prescription came before any clear notion of servitude, whereas in Rome, as has already been said, prescription came late. When it was desired to enforce restrictive covenants—the desire did not make itself felt until *Tulk* v. *Moxhay*[2]—the natural course to pursue was to apply to the Chancellor for an injunction and the Chancellor naturally and properly treated the covenant as creating an equitable interest, not binding on a *bona fide* purchaser for value without notice of the covenant.

Easements, etc., are rights *in rem*, but, as has already been noted, all forms of real action have long since disappeared from our common law. Consequently the remedy for interference with such a right is a personal one, either an action based on nuisance, claiming damages or an injunction, or, in appropriate cases, actual abatement.[3] Roman law had also various personal remedies. Damage

---

[1] *Principles of South African Law*, 2nd ed. p. 207.
[2] (1858), 11 Beav. 571.
[3] As to these remedies, see Gale on Easements, part vi.

to a structure of any kind erected under a servitude would give the Aquilian action.[1] Wilful, wanton interference with the enjoyment of a servitude would base an action for *iniuria*.[2] But the texts give far more prominence to the real remedies. If there was interference with enjoyment of any of these *iura* there was a real action to enforce it, a *vindicatio ususfructus, servitutis*, called, in later law, an *actio confessoria*. There was also an *actio negatoria* denying a servitude,[3] essentially a vindication of freedom, a claim that the ownership was free of the servitude, and an *actio prohibitoria*, the purpose of which is still obscure.[4] Recent writers have raised doubts whether in classical law these actions were available against third persons disturbing the enjoyment or only against the servient (or supposed servient) owner, but these doubts seem unfounded: in any case the rule is clear under Justinian.[5] In these actions the question of right was in issue, but there was also a system, though less complete, of 'possessory' remedies. For physical interference with any such *ius* in actual enjoyment there was the interdict *quod vi aut clam*.[6] There was a modified form of *uti possidetis* for the protection of usufruct[7] and there were special interdicts for the enjoyment of the older rustic servitudes of way and water,[8] but it is by no means clear that they applied to the servitudes of later formation. Such an evolution would have been natural, but another recorded extension is more questionable. If a usufruct included a right of way, and there was interference with this, a *vindicatio ususfructus* lay for the interference with the usufruct.[9] But later law seems to have allowed the usufructuary to vindicate the servitude against the

---

[1] *Actio utilis*, D. 9. 2. 27. 32.
[2] Arg. D. 47. 10. 13. 7, pp. 379 *sqq., post.*
[3] For its application to nuisances, see p. 393, *post.*
[4] Details, Buckland, *Text-book*, pp. 675 *sqq.*
[5] Discussion and references, Buckland, 46 *L.Q.R.* (1930), pp. 447 *sqq*
[6] D. 43. 24. 15. 8.   [7] Vat. Fr. 90, 91.
[8] D. 43. 18 *sqq.*   [9] D. 7. 6. 1. *pr.*

interrupter, though it certainly did not belong to the usufructuary.[1]

It should be repeated here that where the matter in hand is a comparison of the ways of thinking about legal notions of the common and the Roman lawyer, respectively, the subject of servitudes is one of the least instructive. Probably in no other subject, except perhaps that of the interpretation of wills, has there been so much borrowing from the Romans.

[1] D. 43. 25. 1. 4, commonly held interpolated, but possibly a special opinion of Julian.

CHAPTER V. UNIVERSAL SUCCESSION

1. INTRODUCTORY

The word 'succession', at least in the sense in which it was used by the Romans, is not traditional in our private law. Bracton, under Roman influence, employs *successio* and *succedere* in describing the transfer of an estate in lands by inheritance,[1] but later it becomes usual to speak of descent in real property and of administration, distribution and title by will in personal property. Littleton uses the word 'successors' in relation to what we should now call corporations sole, that is, in relation to succession *virtute officii*.[2] The *Termes de la Ley* and Cowell's *Interpreter* know nothing of it. Blackstone speaks of succession *ab intestato* and applies it to both real and personal property,[3] but with the protest that the expression is in strict propriety applicable only to the continuous succession of members of corporate bodies which never die. Nowadays it is usual and may be said to be technical, especially in connexion with the duties payable on devolution of property at death, e.g. the recently abolished 'succession duty'. In Rome, while it was also used for succession to office and the like, it was the term commonly used from the latter days of the Republic onwards to express the devolution of property on death and in certain analogous cases. The later Roman law gives us a distinction between singular and universal succession, the former referring to acquisition of individual things by, e.g., gift, purchase or legacy, the latter referring to cases in which the rights and duties of a

---

[1] E.g. Bracton (Twiss), i. pp. 531, 541; iii. p. 415, and even of transfer by substitution, i. p. 547.

[2] Co. Litt. 190a, 250a.

[3] ii. 430, 516.

person pass, if not wholly, at least contemplated as a unit, from one person to another. Succession on death is the typical case. With us it is practically the only case, for bankruptcy, though it can be thought of as universal succession, and is in fact so described in some works on jurisprudence,[1] is not commonly so thought of in practice.

In Rome there were many cases other than death, though most of them have disappeared in the law of Justinian. Under the ancient form of marriage with *manus*, where the woman had been independent (*sui iuris*) her rights of property had vested in the husband, apart from such as were destroyed by the transaction. Her liabilities were destroyed at civil law, but the Praetor made the husband responsible to the extent of the property the wife had brought with her.[2] Gaius treats this as a mode of succession[3] as he does the Roman equivalent of bankruptcy, *bonorum emptio*, also obsolete in later law.[4] Where a freeman *sui iuris* gave himself in adoption (*adrogatio*) the result was much as in the last case, and this is still treated as succession by Justinian, though its effects had been much cut down.[5] Under the *Sc. Claudianum*, where a freewoman cohabited with a slave against his master's orders, she was enslaved to his master, who took her property, the so-called *successio miserabilis*, abolished by Justinian.[6] Where there had been a death the property might pass not by the ordinary law of succession but in another way; for instance where, in classical law (the institution was obsolete in later law), an agnate entitled on intestacy, but not having yet accepted the succession, made a formal surrender (*cessio in*

---

[1] E.g. Holland, *Jurisprudence*, 13th ed. p. 162.

[2] Which calls to mind certain provisions of our Married Women's Property Acts.

[3] G. 3. 82–84.

[4] G. 3. 77 *sqq.* But see Buckland, *Text-book*, p. 402.

[5] G. 3. 82–84; Inst. 3. 10.

[6] G. 1. 91, 160; Inst. 3. 12.

iure) of his right to another person who thereupon took his place as *heres*;[1] or where, a testator having provided for the manumission of slaves, the will, and with it these provisions, were in danger of failure because he was insolvent and the appointed *heres* would not accept, and the estate might be assigned to one who gave security for the debts, so that the manumissions might take effect.[2] *Adsignatio liberti* gives another type of case. By the XII Tables a patron succeeded to his childless freedman; if he predeceased the freedman the *liberi patroni* succeeded, not by inheritance from their father, but under an express provision of the XII Tables, so that their right was independent of his. But a senatusconsult allowed him, not indeed to deprive his children of the succession in favour of someone else, but to assign this potential succession (to the still living freedman) to any one or more of the children, to the exclusion of the others.[3]

Of all these institutions the only one which has any parallel in our law is that of the wife passing into the *manus* of her husband. Here is indeed no talk of succession, but, otherwise, the language of our older books is very like the Roman. The Abridgements and Digests speak of 'Baron et Feme'. The old language survives in such books as Bacon's *Abridgement*,[4] where we read that 'the law looks upon the husband and wife but as one person, and therefore allows of but one will between them, which is placed in the husband', or in the pithy propositions in Comyns' *Digest*[5] to the effect that there can be no contract or conveyance between them, that the marriage puts an end to a contract previously made, that her chattels real and personal vest in him, though not, to the same extent, her

---

[1] G. 2. 34–37; 3. 85–87; Buckland, *Text-book*, p. 400.
[2] Inst. 3. 11.
[3] *Adsignatio liberti*, Inst. 3. 8.
[4] (1832) 1. 694.
[5] (1822) 2. 220.

real property. Superficially this looks like *manus* but only superficially because her position at common law was not that of a child; moreover, the case never seems to have been thought of as succession. But all this is long since obsolete and the only succession we need consider is succession on death.

The Roman law did not distinguish between real and personal property for the purpose of succession. In our law the same is true nowadays, but till very recently the distinction was fundamental. The heir succeeded to the real property, while personal property was distributed by the executor or administrator. Till relatively modern times the common law had nothing to do with the fate of personal property on death.[1] In modern practice, however, we speak of succession in connexion with both real property and personal property, though the expression is very modern and can hardly be said to be a term of art.[2] This succession indeed is not 'universal succession' in Justinian's sense. Owing to the fact that debts had been primarily payable out of personal property, the personal representative of the deceased, to whom creditors looked for payment and to whom debts had to be paid, was the executor or administrator, who did not, as such, take any beneficial interest. Recent legislation has accentuated this difference between the Roman and English notions of succession, for all the property now vests in the executor or administrator, and the actual beneficiaries, as such, in no way represent the deceased. Under the Succession Duty Act, though the duty applied mainly to realty and chattels real, it applied whether the acquisition was on intestacy or by disposition, and had no relation to any question of universal succession in the Roman sense.

[1] It was of course the business of the ecclesiastical Courts.
[2] See, e.g., Williams, *Real Property*, 24th ed. p. 250.

2. *HERES*, HEIR, EXECUTOR AND ADMINISTRATOR

The 'heir' of our law, now almost a figure of the past so far as property is concerned, no doubt derives his name from the Roman *heres*, but the two words have very different meanings. The *heres* was for Justinian the representative of the deceased, to whom passed all the liabilities which survived the death and all the rights which, surviving the death, were not transferred by direct legacy to other persons. And it was indifferent whether he derived his title from the rules of succession on intestacy or from a will. Our 'heir' throughout the greater part of our legal history has been simply the person who succeeded to the descendible real property of the deceased under the rules of succession on intestacy.[1] So, too, a will is not the same thing in the two systems. With us a will is essentially an instrument, to be operative only on the death of the maker and revocable till then, regulating the devolution of property. It usually nominates a personal representative, an executor, but it need not do so: the provisions of the will can be carried out by an administrator appointed for the purpose by the court. But the Roman will, while it might and usually did contain gifts of property and other analogous provisions, need not contain them: its primary purpose, perhaps at one time its only purpose, was the appointment of the 'universal successor', the personal representative, the *heres*, and a will which did not do this in clear terms was a nullity. And if the persons nominated as *heredes* refused to accept the nomination or died without accepting it, the will was, in general, void: there was no question of appointing someone else to take their place.[2]

---

[1] See, however, as to the position of the *heres* as personal representative in our early law, Holdsworth, ii. pp. 96, 97; iii. pp. 572 *sqq.*

[2] For exceptions, not affecting the principle, see Buckland, *Text-book*, pp. 321, 326.

It may be added that while, under Justinian, a will was revocable in much the same way as in our law, this was not so originally; when made before the Public Assembly, it was probably irrevocable, and even the classical mancipatory will could be revoked at civil law only by making another will, though here the Praetor intervened and gave effect to ordinary methods of revocation.[1]

Our executor and administrator resemble the Roman *heres* much more than does our heir,[2] a resemblance once closer than it is now.[3] Till 1857 the church Courts controlled the grant of probate of wills of personal property, though long before that date the Court of Chancery had acquired jurisdiction to administer the provisions of wills. The Church applied the principles of canon law, which in turn was based essentially on the civil law. It is therefore not surprising that many civil law principles appeared in the law, or that some of these survived the secularisation of the judicial control of wills. Owing to the absence of adequate records of the doings of the ecclesiastical courts it is often difficult, if not impossible, to say whether, when our rule and the Roman agree, we have borrowed the principle or developed it independently. In some cases the descent from Roman law notions seems fairly clear. Swinburne,[4] writing late in the sixteenth century, lays down propo-

---

[1] It is interesting to note that we find under imperial influence cases of dependent relative revocation very like that in *Giles* v. *Warren* (1872), 2 P. and D. 401. See D. 28. 5. 93; C. 3. 28. 3; cp. D. 32. 18.

[2] As to the origin of the executor, which was not Roman, see Holdsworth, iii. pp. 563, 564. The administrator was appointed by the ordinary: see *ibid.* p. 568: 'though the ordinary took the goods, he was in no sense a true representative. He was not liable to be sued [until 1285] nor was he able to sue.' To-day the real and personal estate of an intestate vests, until administration is granted, in the President of the Probate, Divorce and Admiralty Division 'in the same manner and to the same extent as formerly in the case of personal estate it vested in the ordinary': Administration of Estates Act, 1925, Sect. 9.

[3] See Littleton, s. 337: 'for that the executors represent the person of their testator', and Holmes, *The Common Law*, pp. 345, 346.

[4] *Testaments and Last Wills.*

sitions (no longer true) which express what are clearly Roman notions of the will. He says[1] that the naming of an executor is essential, 'without which a will is no proper testament, and by the which only the will is made a testament', and again[2] he tells us that if an executor is appointed there is a good will even though it contains no dispositions of property. This is the Roman notion of a will and the executor is the *heres*.[3] All this is gone, but, as we shall see later, some similar things seem still to remain.

The power to refuse the nomination as *heres* was important, since, up to the time of Justinian, the *heres* who had once accepted was liable for the debts not merely so far as assets would go, but absolutely. The *heres* had not always this right. If he was a member of the *familia*, and in immediate succession, a *suus heres*, there was no question of acceptance: he was *heres* whether he liked it or not and whether by will or on intestacy—*heres suus et necessarius*; though the Praetor, in view of the hardship resulting where the estate was insolvent, while he could not directly relieve him—since he could not make or unmake a *heres*—would allow him to abstain, and if he did so, would protect him against actions.[4] He was not thereby barred from his civil law right of suing debtors, but to do so would be ill-advised, for if he in any way intermeddled with the estate he lost his right to abstain. Abstention left the estate insolvent, to be sold by the creditors with resulting *infamia* to the memory of the deceased. All this might be avoided by the insolvent if he appointed one of his slaves as *heres*, with a gift of liberty. He also would be *necessarius*, and as the appointment was made in order that the *infamia* should rest on him rather than on the memory of the deceased, he had no right of abstention, this being the price of his liberty. The Praetor, however, protected him in another

---

[1] P. 7 and notes (6th ed.).   [2] P. 239.
[3] See also Brooke's *Abridgement*: Testaments, par. 20.
[4] *Beneficium abstinendi*, Buckland, *Text-book*, p. 305.

way by providing that any property he might himself later acquire was not liable to the late master's creditors, so that effectively he was not liable beyond the assets, except that, if these were insufficient, he was *infamis*. The Roman notion probably underlies our old rule that 'immediately on the death of the ancestor...the law casts the estate upon the heir',[1] and also the rule of our early law that he was liable for debts even beyond the assets.[2]

The rule of absolute liability lasted till the time of Justinian. It was indeed possible for the creditors to agree to take less by way of an inducement to the *institutus* to enter, and, according to the Digest, such an agreement made by a majority of the creditors bound the rest.[3] It is likely that this last provision is an interpolation. It is indeed remarkable in two respects. It anticipates modern creditors' compositions and is the nearest approach to our modern 'white-washing' that Roman law knew, for the ordinary bankruptcy left the balance still due.[4] It is further remarkable as being one of the very few cases in which the Roman law admitted to private law the majority principle which was freely admitted in some parts of public law. But by an enactment of A.D. 531 Justinian revolutionised the whole system. He provided that if the *heres* made a proper schedule of the assets, within a certain time, he should not be liable to creditors beyond the amount of the estate.[5] This places him much in the position of the modern executor,[6] with the difference, however, that he is normally also the principal beneficiary; and though this is often the case with the executor, often, probably more often, it is

---

[1] Watkins on Descents, 3rd ed. pp. 38, 272. As to reasons, see Powell on Devises, 3rd ed. i. p. 421; cf. G. 2. 55, 154.

[2] Holdsworth, iii. p. 573, citing Glanvill, vii. 5 and 8.

[3] D. 2. 14. 7. 19; h.t. 10. *pr.*

[4] *Bonorum venditio, B. distractio*, Buckland, *Text-book*, pp. 643 *sqq.*

[5] The so-called *Beneficium inventarii*; C. 6. 30. 22.

[6] Though it seems clear that this officer does not descend from the Roman *heres*, Holdsworth, iii. pp. 563, 564.

not. There is a further difference. If an executor refuses
to act, it is a simple matter to appoint an administrator in
his place. But if the Roman *heres,* i.e. all the *heredes,* refused to enter, the whole will was thereby destroyed, so
that legacies and similar gifts would fail. This was early
remedied where there was a trust bequest of the inheritance
or of an aliquot part of it; the *heres* could be compelled to
enter and transfer,[1] and in case of manumissions relief was
granted on a variety of grounds, *favore libertatis.*[2] Apart
from these cases and that in which the *heres* refused because he was also *heres* on intestacy, in which case he was
compelled to carry out the provisions of the will,[3] it seems
that a sole *heres* who, for spite, refused to accept the *hereditas* under the will, could destroy all legacies and all trust
bequests (*fideicommissa*) of specific things; unless indeed
the testator had taken the precaution of saying that all
these charges were also to be binding on the *heres ab intestato* and that the will was to be interpreted as a 'codicil' if
it failed as a will.[4] For a codicil was not necessarily an
appendage to a will: it might make trusts binding on the
heres ab intestato where there was no will.

Our will being merely a disposition of certain property,
it does not necessarily cover the whole estate of the testator
and there is nothing unusual in a partial intestacy. Such a
thing could not occur in the Roman system. The function
of the will was not primarily the disposition of property,
but the appointment of a successor, a *heres;* and, however
the will was expressed, even though in terms the *heres* or
heredes were appointed *heredes* only to a half, their appointment would be construed as covering the whole estate,
apart from specific gifts by legacy and the like in the will
or by codicil.[5] There is clearly nothing inevitable about this
rule. Where a will merely appointed a *heres* to a half the

---

[1] G. 2. 254 *sqq.*
[2] See Buckland, *Roman Law of Slavery,* pp. 609 *sqq.,* 620.
[3] D. 29. 4.   [4] Buckland, *Text-book,* p. 360.   [5] Inst. 2. 14. 5.

rule might well have been that he and the *heres ab intestato* were joint and equal heirs, and there is much dispute as to the origin of the principle, a dispute with which we need not deal.[1]

When we set out to compare the Roman and the English conceptions of *hereditas* we are faced with the difficulty that our law has, in fact, no such conception as *hereditas*. There are rules, formerly very different for real property and for personal property, but now unified, regulating the devolution of property at death, by will or otherwise; we shall, however, look in vain in our modern authorities for any such conception as that of the *hereditas* as a 'universal succession', an entity created by the death of the *de cuius* and ultimately merging in the personality of the *heres*, the actual successor. What traces we do find of this notion in our old authorities are no more than *disiecta membra* of the Roman law, never more than half assimilated and now quite forgotten. In the new system, under which all the rights and liabilities vest in the executor or administrator, at least in the sense that no title is complete without his intervention, it is possible that some 'concept' may appear of the inheritance as a whole, though our habit of doing without general concepts makes this unlikely. Under Justinian the attitude of the Roman law was very different. The *hereditas* created by the death of Titius was thought of as an ideal unit, distinct from the elements of which it was composed. It was 'successio in universum ius quod defunctus habuit'.[2] It was a *nomen iuris*.[3] It 'sustinet personam defuncti',[4] 'personae defuncti vice fungitur'.[5] It thus connects up the deceased to the *heres* in whom it ultimately merges and the knot is tied by a remarkable proposition in a *novella constitutio* of Justinian,[6] which says

---

[1] See, for brief discussion and literature, Buckland, *Text-book*, pp. 282 *sq.* In any case the principle did not apply to the wills of soldiers made on active service.   [2] D. 50. 16. 24.   [3] D. 50. 16. 119.
[4] Inst. 2. 14. 2; D. 41. 1. 34.   [5] D. 30. 116. 3.   [6] Nov. 48. *pr.*

that by intendment of law the ancestor and the *heres* have one *persona*. This last proposition, amplified by the gloss and to be found in treatises on Scots law,[1] is certainly not classical: how far the rest is, is much disputed. It is rejected by many on the ground that the jurists, for all their philosophy, never dealt in abstract notions and saw in a *hereditas* nothing but its elements, though Seneca[2] chides the lawyers for supposing that a *hereditas* is anything more than its content. Others strike out the word *universum* in Justinian's texts, taking the view that the classics held the *hereditas* to be the *ius* of the deceased—his legal position. It seems more likely that the lawyers, passing from the conception of the *hereditas* as a mere aggregate, which is probably all that Gaius meant by *per universitatem*[3] (his theoretical views being derived from an earlier writer), would have reached the notion of an ideal unit comprising these rights than that they would have passed without it to the highly abstract notion of a man's legal position as a juristic unit. In any case it is odd to find this sweeping proposition in the Novel when Justinian had recently, by limiting the liability of the *heres*, deprived the proposition about unity of *persona* of any plausibility it might have had in earlier law.

In fact, all the property did not necessarily vest in the *heres* except on intestacy. In classical law legacies given in a certain form (*per vindicationem*) vested directly in the legatees,[4] and under Justinian all legacies of property or *iura in rem* did so; whereas in our law the beneficiary's title in chattels real and personal[5] and now in real property[6] is not complete till the executor, in whom the property has vested, has assented to the bequest. The Roman rule looks

---

[1] Bell's *Principles of the Law of Scotland*, sect. 1638.
[2] *De beneficiis*, 6. 5.   [3] G. 2. 97.
[4] *Exceptis excipiendis*, G. 2. 200.   [5] Co. Litt. 111 a.
[6] Land Transfer Act, 1897. Before that Act devises took effect immediately on the death of the testator; but before 1540 they were not direct gifts like the legacy *per vindicationem*, but channelled through a feoffee to uses.

as if it might cause inconvenience where the estate was insolvent, but legacies failed in that case and the *heres*, if in
possession, as he would normally be, need not hand them
over without security for refund in certain cases of which
this was one. Excessive legacies were another such case.
In early law there was no restriction and as Gaius says the
testator might leave everything in legacies, leaving the
heres only *inane nomen*.[1] In the Empire, however, they
might not exceed three-quarters (with complications we
need not consider). Here too they failed *pro rata*, and the
heres could require security for refund if they proved to
exceed the lawful proportion.[2] Justinian, however, allowed
the testator to exclude these restrictions,[3] so that in his
time again the *heres* might conceivably get nothing, being
purely an executor.

The unlimited liability of the *heres*, coupled with
another point, led to the appearance of an institution in
Roman law to which our law hardly affords a parallel.
Before accepting, a *heres* might need time to consider
whether he could safely do so. And a *heres* might be appointed conditionally. In such circumstances, if he was
sole *heres*, there would be a time, possibly long, in which
there was for the moment no successor, but only a *hereditas
iacens*. There were rules limiting the time allowed for
deliberation, but no one could tell how long it might be
before a condition was satisfied. With us, an executor or
administrator, as he runs no risk, can, and usually does,
enter on his office at once, and even if, from any cause,
there is delay in the grant of probate, ordinary acts of administration can be carried out before probate. If a sole
executor were appointed under a condition not yet satisfied,
it seems probable that the Court would have power to
grant temporary administration, *cum testamento annexo*, to
another person, but this does not seem to occur in practice.
In Roman law nothing of the sort was possible and thus, in

[1] G. 2. 224.   [2] G. 2. 224 *sqq.*   [3] Nov. 1.

any case where there was no *necessarius heres*, there would
be a time, more or less long, during which the *hereditas* had
no legal owner. Some protection was given by criminal
remedies where property was made away with, and by
giving the *heres*, if he ultimately did accept, the ordinary
actions for various forms of wrong, retrospectively. For
the actual administration a way was found by treating the
hereditas as if it owned itself, so that slaves belonging to it
could act as for a living master; except that nothing
requiring express authorisation could be done, though
general authorisations by the deceased master were regarded as continuing. But since such slaves had only
derivative capacity, everything they did was null and void
if no one accepted the succession. On the question whether
this is to be regarded as a personification of the *hereditas*,
it is possible to hold two opinions, though we may be
fairly confident that the classical lawyers did not really
regard it in that way, while Justinian's men very probably
did. Some of the rules imply that the *hereditas* had rights,
but others show that these rights were far less than those
of a living man. Thus the *hereditas*, through its slaves,
could, for the purpose of acquisition by long possession,
continue a possession begun in the lifetime of the deceased,
but it could not through them acquire a new possession
for that purpose.[1] In fact its capacities were the irreducible
minimum for commercial convenience, in view of the fact
that no outsider could act for it. As a matter of historical
fact it seems fairly clear that the classical lawyers did not
think of the *hereditas iacens* as a person, even a *persona ficta*,
and that texts in the Digest which express this notion have
been materially altered.[2] But, upon the conceptions of
Justinian's age, it must be taken as a sort of interim
universal succession.

[1] On the position of *hereditas iacens*, see Buckland, *Text-book*, pp. 306 *sqq*.
[2] E.g. D. 28. 5. 31. 1; 43. 24. 13. 5. See, generally, Duff, *Personality
in Roman Private Law*.

3. TESTAMENTARY FORM AND CAPACITY

The normal form of will in the time of Justinian is pre-scribed by an enactment of A.D. 439.[1] The rules, which are given in some detail in the appropriate titles of the Digest and Code,[2] are on the whole very modern-looking. They need not be set out here, but one or two of them are worth mention. The will must be made, i.e. executed and attested, *uno contextu*, and, as under the Wills Act, 1837, Sect. 9, the witnesses must all attest in the presence of the testator[3] and, in Roman law, apparently in the presence of each other,[4] which, though usual, is not necessary under our law. A will which had been made away with was still valid if execution and content could be in some way proved.[5]

The fact that the Roman community, especially in classical times, included distinct classes with very different civil rights, e.g. *cives*, latins, *peregrini*, *dediticii*, slaves, led to many complications in the law of capacity to make a will or to take under a will or to witness one. These have no equivalent in our law and have been sufficiently dealt with in an earlier chapter. But the position of the witnesses was different from that in our law and the differences are of some interest. The large number of witnesses, seven for the normal will of Justinian's time, is due to historical causes and need not be discussed.[6] The witnesses must be specially summoned for the purpose and one who merely happened to be there and attested was not a valid witness.[7]

---

[1] C. 6. 23. 21 = Nov. Theod. 16. 1.

[2] C. 6. 23; D. 28. 1.   [3] C. 6. 23. 9.

[4] C. 6. 23. 21. *pr.* 'uno eodemque die ac tempore subscribentibus et consignantibus'.

[5] C. 6. 23. 2; h.t. 11. The latter text seems to imply that for this rule to apply the *subtractio* of the will must have occurred after the testator's death, but probably does not mean this.

[6] Buckland, *Text-book*, pp. 285 *sq.*

[7] D. 28. 1. 21. 2. So apparently in our early law, Bracton (Twiss), i. p. 487. Swinburne, late in the sixteenth century, knows nothing of this.

Further, they attest not merely, as with us, the execution of the document, the nature of which may be unknown to them,[1] but the whole transaction. Consequently they must know that it is a will, though they need not know the content.[2] Horace observes that one ought not to show too much curiosity about the content, though there is no harm in getting a look to see whether you are sole *heres* or only take a share;[3] and from an enactment under Theodosius[4] it is clear that a practice had grown up, which he declares not to be the law, of requiring witnesses to know the provisions of the will. Witnesses attested by sealing (*signatio*) and *subscriptio*, i.e. an acknowledgement of the seal and the document, usually with a signature. The rules as to capacity of witnesses, so far as they are absolute, depend on the personal law and need not be discussed, but the 'relative' exclusions, dependent on the relation between the witness and the parties to a particular will, are so different from ours as to need mention. Our law is based on distrust of the evidence of interested parties.[5] The Statute of Frauds said that the witnesses must be 'credible'; and if a witness was a legatee or the spouse of a legatee, the Courts did not regard him as 'credible', and so the whole will might fail for lack of the right number of witnesses. The modern rule is[6] that, where there is a gift to a witness or the spouse of a witness, the attestation is good, no doubt 'ut res magis valeat quam pereat' (*favor testamenti*), but the gift is void. In the Roman classical law the attestation of anyone in the same family group as the testator or the *familiae emptor*, i.e. the person to whom the estate is nominally assigned for the purpose of carrying into effect the provisions of the will, is void. But this does not turn on personal interest, for at that time the *familiae*

---

[1] *Daintree* v. *Fasculo* (1888), 13 P.D. 67.
[2] P. Sent. 3. 4a. 13; D. 28. 1. 20. 8–10.
[3] *Sat.* 2. 5. 50.   [4] Nov. Theod. 16. 1.
[5] Swinburne, *cit*. p. 347.   [6] Wills Act, 1837, sect. 15.

emptor was a mere form, having no actual function or interest (and it is far from clear that he ever had any interest), but on the fact that the proceeding was by mancipation and the witnesses to a *mancipatio*, who were intended to secure publicity, must not be of the family of either party. Interest had nothing to do with the matter and the *heres* was a perfectly good witness, though Gaius goes so far as to say that it is not desirable to have the *heres* or a member of his family.[1] Justinian indeed, acting apparently on the hint in Gaius, makes the *heres* and those in his family incompetent, but he goes no further and any other beneficiaries are perfectly good witnesses.[2] The attestation of the *heres* or other incompetent person does not of course *per se* vitiate the transaction: they simply do not count in the necessary number of witnesses, so that the deficiency thus resulting may vitiate the transaction.

The process of 'opening the will' corresponded closely to our 'probate' and seems to have served the same fiscal purpose. It was a formal process before the magistrate at which the available witnesses were required to appear and acknowledge their seals and the fact that they took part in the making of the will.[3]

4. SOLDIERS' WILLS

This is a topic in which Roman law long exercised a decisive influence on English law, an influence which has recently been held to have been unfortunate. Roman law allowed a soldier to make a valid will without any formality if he was *in expeditione*, though the will so made remained valid only for a year after discharge.

Before 1677 English law insisted on no formalities in the making of a will, and when the Statute of Frauds

---

[1] G. 2. 105–108.

[2] Inst. 2. 10. 10, 11; D. 28. 1. 20, interpolated.

[3] C. 6. 32 *passim*. For a *procès verbal* of such a transaction, see Bruns, *Fontes Iuris*, 7th ed. pp. 317 *sqq.*

imposed formalities, Sir Leoline Jenkins succeeded in obtaining a privilege in favour of soldiers and sailors, who were exempted from all formalities. Since he was an eminent civilian, he seems to have taken the idea from Roman law. The present law is contained in sect. 11 of the Wills Act, 1837, which confers the privilege on 'any soldier being in actual military service'. Unfortunately for a long time the Courts interpreted these words with reference to Roman law, and regarded them as equivalent to the words *in expeditione*. Accordingly fine distinctions were drawn which refused, for instance, the privilege to a person who, though engaged in military administration during war, was actually living at home, even though his death was caused by a bombing attack upon his home.[1] It has now been held that the words 'in actual military service' must be interpreted without any reference whatever to Roman law, and if statements in a recent decision[2] are correct, the privilege extends to all persons 'actually serving with the armed forces in connexion with military operations which are or have been taking place, or are believed to be imminent'. Thus in the case in question, an airman was held entitled to make a will informally when training as a pilot, in 1943, at a training school in Saskatchewan, Canada. It has also been held that a soldier's will, validly though informally made, remains in force until revoked. It is not automatically revoked on the lapse of one year after discharge.[3]

5. INTERPRETATION

In Rome, as with us, the law of wills and succession in general is very bulky, much of the discussion being on questions of interpretation and construction of inept words used by the testator. It is a remarkable fact that while the

[1] *In the Estate of Gibson*, [1941] P. 118.
[2] *In re Wingham*, [1949] P. 187.
[3] *In re Booth*, [1926] P. 118.

Digest covers the whole of private law and a good deal
of public law, considerably more than a quarter of it is
occupied by succession and the various provisions of wills.[1]
This is all the more remarkable as the Roman law was without the complications and difficulties of interpretation due
to our highly sophisticated real property law.[2] It is impossible to go, for the purpose of comparison, through the
whole mass of rules of interpretation and construction, but
space must be found for some of the more important,
bearing in mind that the rules as we have them are in the
main the rules of Justinian's law and that the rules of
classical law were certainly to some extent, and may have
been to a very great extent, different.

Some of the Roman rules are due to the fact that the
Romans disliked intestacy. This *favor testamenti* led to the
adoption of rules, not necessarily rational, which would
maintain the validity of the *institutio heredis*, on which
depended the validity of the will, where another interpretation would have been more reasonable in itself, or
more in accord with existing legal principles. Thus, while
an impossible, illegal or immoral condition avoided a contract,[3] in an *institutio* it was simply struck out, to avoid an
intestacy,[4] and this was extended to all provisions of a will
without the same necessity. As our law of wills of personal
property was developed by the church Courts (and there
were, at first, no wills of real property) it is not surprising
that it borrowed something from this source.

'Semel heres, semper heres', and thus if a *heres* was appointed only for a time, the limitation was struck out.[5] In

---

[1] But one has only to observe the bulk of such a book as Jarman on
Wills to realise that Roman law shares this peculiarity to some extent with
English law.

[2] Moreover, an executor is personally liable if he distributes the estate
on a wrong basis; and so, in doubtful cases, he always seeks the opinion of
the Court. There was no such incentive to litigation at Rome.

[3] Inst. 3. 19. 11; D. 45. 1. 61.

[4] Inst. 2. 14. 10; D. 28. 7. 14.   [5] Inst. 2. 14. 9.

our law there is also a leaning against intestacy in all cases where the construction of a will is doubtful,[1] but as appears from the language of Romer L.J. in *Re Edwards, Jones* v. *Jones*[2] a 'testator may well intend to die intestate', and if his intention is clear it must receive effect; the principle does not dominate the rules as it does in Roman law. It is to be noted that the *favor testamenti* of classical law becomes in later law *favor testantis,* and Justinian's texts contain many decisions in which effect is given to what is conceived to have been the wish of the testator, though this construction is not the true effect of what he has said, or necessary to avoid intestacy.[3]

In Roman law, as in ours, wills are construed according to the intent of the testator, but there are differences between the two systems as to the evidence receivable by the Court in proof of the intent. The governing principle of our law in the matter is that the intent is to be gathered from the will itself, the whole will, not the individual proposition[4] and, in particular, that where the will is clear no extraneous evidence is admissible to vary it,[5] to show for instance that where one property or person is clearly indicated another is actually meant.[6] It is true that there are limitations to this. Evidence is admitted against the will where it is shown, e.g., that clauses have been improperly introduced into it against the intent of the testator: they must be struck out of the probate, even if they affect the sense of the remaining words, but the right words cannot be substituted for them.[7]

At first sight the Roman principles seem much the same. There are many texts which lay down the rule, or imply it,

---

[1] *In re Harrison, Turner* v. *Hellard,* 30 Ch.D. at p. 393; Hailsham, xxxiv, *Wills,* p. 204. [2] [1906] 1 Ch. at p. 574.

[3] Suman, *Favor Testamenti, passim.*

[4] *Perrin* v. *Morgan,* [1943] A.C. 399; *Re Hipwell* (1945), 173 L.T. 192.

[5] *Higgins* v. *Dawson,* [1902] A.C. 1.

[6] *Re Overhill's Trusts* (1853), 1 Sm. and Gif. 362, 366.

[7] See the cases collected in Jarman on Wills, 7th ed. ch. xv.

that the will is to be interpreted by the will, the whole will and nothing but the will.[1] There are also many texts which lay it down that to determine in which of admissible senses a word is used, we may look at the circumstances, the testator's habits and knowledge.[2] On the other hand there are many texts which give power to cite extraneous evidence in a wider field and in nearly every case this doctrine seems to have been introduced by interpolation.[3] However, in some cases there is no sign of interpolation. In one case a testator instituted *A* meaning to institute *B*. It was held that neither was *heres*, *A* because he was not meant, *B* because he was not named. Here it is clear that extraneous evidence is admitted.[4] So too we are told that the insertion or omission of a condition where this was intended can be made good.[5] It is true that in D. 2. 8. 5. 9. 5 the words occur: 'nec nuncupatum videri quod contra voluntatem scriptum est', which would bring it into line with some of the cases referred to by Jarman,[6] but it does not seem that there actually was any difference in the *nuncupatio*. It is clear that where such a difference had occurred the matter could be set right by external evidence[7] and also that errors leaving the sense clear were immaterial.[8] It should be

---

[1] E.g. C. 6. 28. 1; C. 6. 37. 23. 1c; D. 28. 5. 19; C. 6. 37. 1; D. 30. 17. *pr.*, 33, 74, 81. 3; D. 31. 33. 1; D. 32. 25 (where all is clear there is no question of *voluntas*); D. 32. 35. 3, 41. 3; D. 33. 7. 12. 45, 18. 11; D. 35. 1. 16 (very specific), 82, 102.

[2] E.g. C. 6. 38. 2; C. 6. 24. 14; D. 28. 5. 35. 3; D. 30. 50. 3; D. 31. 10, 30, 34. 3; D. 32. 50. 1; D. 33. 7. 12. 14; D. 33. 10. 7. 2; D. 34. 1. 16. 1, 22. *pr.*; D. 34. 2. 33; D. 34. 5. 25; D. 35. 1. 11. *pr.*, 27, 39. 1.

[3] D. 28. 5. 2; D. 28. 5. 63. 1; D. 28. 7. 2. *pr.*; D. 30. 17. 1, 88; D. 32. 73. 4; D. 33. 6. 13; D. 33. 7. 27. 3; D. 34. 1. 20. 2; C. 6. 44. 1.

[4] D. 28. 5. 9. *pr.* The same thing is said more generally in D. 34. 5. 3. In D. 30. 4, where a man left a farm using the name of another, the devisee was allowed to prove and claim that which was really meant. But here there was no *error in corpore*, merely a misnomer.

[5] D. 28. 5. 9. 5.   [6] P. 161 n. 7, *ante*.

[7] D. 28. 5. 9. 6, 7; D. 30. 4; C. 6. 23. 7.

[8] C. 6. 23. 4, 17; 6. 37. 7. 1. As in our law, *Denn d. Wilkins* v. *Kemeys* (1808), 9 East, 366.

added that in Justinian's law *fideicommissa* were equiparated with legacies, so that each form should have the advantages of the others (a rule which must have been very difficult to apply); and since *fideicommissa* could be made orally, and could always be proved by extraneous evidence,[1] not much could really be left, so far as specific gifts were concerned, of the stricter principle. As in classical law there were only sketchy rules of evidence it is improbable that any rule of interpretation was ever very strictly observed.

As with us, where there was clear equivocation, e.g. a testator had two farms of the same name and made a legacy of one, it was allowed to prove by external evidence which he meant.[2] Where there was a definite error *in corpore*, e.g., 'dum vult lancem relinquere vestem leget',[3] the Roman law allowed this to be proved, but only to the effect of destroying the gift, not of substituting what was really meant: the one gift fails as not being intended, the other as not having been made.[4] In our law the rule seems to be that if the thing given is unambiguously described extraneous evidence cannot be produced to show that this was not the thing meant by the testator.[5] But the rule above given for the Roman law, though clearly stated in the texts, is a rule of strict classical law and it may be doubted how far it really represents Justinian's law. There are several texts in which fundamental error is given more positive effect and, though they seem to be due to the intervention of the Emperor, they appear in the *Corpus Juris* and must therefore be taken as representing the law for Justinian's time. The best known is in the Institutes.[6] *A* institutes as

---

[1] Buckland, *Text-book*, p. 354.
[2] D. 30. 39. 6; cp. D. 28. 5. 63. 1, where a man having several friends of the same name institutes one. Here the form of the text strongly suggests that the power to clear up the point by extraneous evidence is due to Justinian. See *Reynolds* v. *Whelan* (1847), 16 L.J. Ch. 434.
[3] D. 28. 5. 9. 1.   [4] D. 30. 4. *pr.*; 34. 5. 3.
[5] Hailsham, xxxiv, *Wills*, p. 171.
[6] Inst. 2. 15. 4.

heres a man whom he believes to be free but who is in fact a slave and he substitutes *X* to the *institutus* 'si heres non erit'. The slave accepts at his master's orders. Tiberius decides that on such facts the words 'si heres non erit' mean 'if he does not himself become *heres*'. As he cannot, there is an *institutio* of the substitute so that they share. A woman supposing her son to be dead instituted someone else. Hadrian gave the son the *hereditas*, preserving the legacies, i.e. reading into the will the *institutio* the mother would have made had she known the facts.[1] Severus and Caracalla dealt in the same way with a similar case, but here the will showed on its face that the actual *institutio* was due to the belief that the desired *heres* was dead.[2] And where a mother with children died in childbirth the same Emperors read the will as if the last child had been named *per coniecturam maternae pietatis*.[3] These texts have been the subject of a very careful study,[4] but it is doubtful whether for the Romans themselves they express any principle more precise than a general desire to give effect to a testator's wishes.

Both systems of law provide, indeed the rule is probably Roman in origin, that of two repugnant provisions the second prevails.[5] But for this there must be a real repugnancy; thus if in a will there is a gift to *A* and later on a gift of the same thing to *B*, there is no repugnancy, for the thing may perfectly well be given to *A* and *B*. Accordingly they share.[6] That the rule, now apparently quite general, is derived from the Roman law appears from the fact that Swinburne[7] thought that the common law courts would say that the second devise would destroy the earlier one, but that in the case of personalty the ecclesiastical courts

---

[1] D. 5. 2. 28.   [2] D. 28. 5. 93.   [3] C. 3. 28. 3.
[4] Schulz, *Gedaechtnisschrift für Seckel*, pp. 70 *sqq.*
[5] D. 30. 12. 3; C. 6. 42. 19; *Ulrich* v. *Litchfield* (1742), 2 Atk. 372.
[6] C. 6. 37. 23. 3; *Sherratt* v. *Bentley* (1834), 2 My. and K. at p. 165; *Re Alexander* (1948), 64 T.L.R. 308.   [7] *Op. cit.* pp. 552 *sq.*

would hold that the legatees took jointly. It should be added that the rule is not universal in Roman law; it applies only to legacies and the like. Thus it seems that, if it is a manumission, that gift is preferred which is more favourable to liberty.[1] So in the *institutio* of a *heres* that gift is preferred which is more favourable to the *heres*. *Favor libertatis* accounts sufficiently for the first case. The other case is applied to *institutio* of the same person twice, once simply and again under a condition, or under different conditions. Here it is no doubt *favor testamenti*, the desire to secure that the will shall be valid, As neither of these considerations could operate in English law no such distinction is drawn.

In our modern law a will, as to the property disposed of by it, 'speaks from death' in the sense that a gift of 'all my property' or 'all my lands in Newton' will cover all the property, or all the property answering the description, which the testator had at the time of his death, without reference to the time of testation, unless the contrary appears by the will. This is provided by the Wills Act.[2] The Roman law was different. By the form of direct gift (*per vindicationem*) nothing could be left but what was the property of the testator at the time of testation, apart from *res fungibiles*.[3] There was no such restriction in legacy *per damnationem*, an instruction to the *heres* to hand over a thing, or in *fideicommissum*. These distinctions are gone in Justinian's law, but it is clear that under him as well as in classical law a legacy of 'my slaves' or 'my wardrobe' or 'my silver' covered only what belonged to the testator at the time of testation unless the contrary appeared.[4] This seems to turn on the use of the word *meum*: 'hac demonstratione praesens, non futurum tempus ostendit'.[5] But this reasoning assumes the principle. The Gloss gives an

[1] D. 31. 14; 35. 1. 87, 88: see however h.t. 90.
[2] 1837, sect. 24.   [3] G. 2. 196.
[4] D. 34. 2. 7; cp. D. 32. 68. 2.   [5] D. 33. 7. 28; 31. 10.

array of opposing texts but few are in point and the
glossators and the commentators had no difficulty in explaining these away. It is clear that testators or their
lawyers were alive to the point and habitually used such
expressions as 'qui meus erit' to show that the gift was to
cover future acquisitions.[1] Our modern rule was not
quite new in the Wills Act. Swinburne[2] indeed lays down
the opposite, the Roman rule, but with many exceptions,
and it is clear that long before the Wills Act the modern
rule was applied to general gifts of personalty or of classes
of things, though not to general gifts of real property.[3] It
is curious that the non-Roman rule should have been first
applied to the kind of gift which had been administered by
the ecclesiastical courts.

The Roman law as to lapses in joint legacies was extremely complex for reasons into which we need not go.[4]
But it may be noted that where there was a gift to a class
there could be no lapse into the residue, i.e. to the *heres*.
For no gift vested till the testator's death or later, and in
principle all gifts failed if the beneficiary died before the
testator, the result being that those who survived him
constituted the class. This reaches by a different road the
result attained by our law, in 'joint' gifts, by the rule of
survivorship and in the case of gifts 'in common' by
adopting a construction of such words as 'the children of
X', based apparently on the principle that a will speaks
from death for this purpose also.[5]

---

[1] E.g. D. 10.   [2] *Op. cit.* p. 512.

[3] Jarman, *Wills*, 6th ed. pp. 404–406 and 946. The reason for the rule
governing general gifts of realty was that before 1540 there could, in general,
be no wills of realty without a previous feoffment to uses; and a person
could enfeoff another of only such realty as he had at the time of feoffment.

[4] Buckland, *Text-book*, pp. 337 *sqq.*

[5] Jarman, *Wills*, 7th ed. ch. xliv.

6. FREEDOM OF TESTATION

The absolute freedom of testation which was until recently permitted by our law,[1] but has been qualified in many common law jurisdictions and now by us,[2] is not found in the classical Roman law. It is possible that in very early times there was no power of appointing a *heres* by will if there existed direct successors (*sui heredes*); but, however this may be, and though Gaius describes these *heredes* as *domestici heredes* with a sort of shadowy *condominium*, so that they are in a sense *heredes* to themselves,[3] it was always possible for the testator to exclude them by his will, by using prescribed forms of *exheredatio*, and to appoint other persons as *heredes*. If he failed to insert the form, and simply omitted the descendant, the will might be in some cases set aside, in others modified. Further, though at civil law this applied only to descendants actually within the family group, the Praetor extended similar rights with some modifications to issue who had passed out of the family by emancipation. It will be seen that this restriction could always be met by using the proper forms. The testator's freedom went further; for whether he appointed *sui heredes* or *extranei* as *heredes* it was possible for him to give the whole estate to other persons by way of legacy, leaving to the *heres* only the *inane nomen*. This freedom was not effectually checked till just at the end of the Republic, when a *lex Falcidia* limited legacies to three quarters of the estate, or, since particular legacies could be charged on individual *heredes*, three-quarters of the share taken by that *heres*.[4] But in the Empire there was a change. Under the system of the *querela inofficiosi testamenti*, the origin of which is obscure, a will could be set

---

[1] The ancient local customs to the contrary mentioned by Blackstone (2. 518) being now extinct.

[2] Inheritance (Family Provision) Act, 1938.

[3] G. 2. 157.   [4] G. 2. 244 *sqq.*

aside if it did not make a certain minimum provision for those who would have been entitled on intestacy, unless good ground could be shown for the omission. This was at first confined to *sui heredes* and *emancipati*, etc., grouped with them by the Praetor, but the classes who could claim were gradually extended to include ascendants and brothers and sisters, where they would have been entitled on intestacy.[1] But there was another historical factor. Trust bequests, *fideicommissa*, were free from a number of restrictions which affected legacies, and the *lex Falcidia* did not apply to them. Thus when they were introduced at the beginning of the Empire, a testator could again give away all the property by *fideicommissum*, leaving to the *heres* only the *inane nomen*. But by *senatusconsulta* of the second century, especially the *Sc. Pegasianum*, this too was checked, and such gifts were limited to three-quarters, like legacies. So, with only slight modifications, the system remains in the law of the *Corpus Juris*. But very soon after the publication of the Digest[2] Justinian made an alteration which must, it seems, have practically destroyed it. He allowed the testator to insert a clause excluding the operation of the Falcidian and the Pegasian.

7. REVOCATION

By our modern law a will is *ipso facto* revoked by the marriage of the testator[3] unless it is 'expressed to be made in contemplation of a marriage'.[4] But it was an obvious result of the conception of marriage in the Roman Empire,

---

[1] Buckland, *Text-book*, pp. 327 *sqq.* Our law has taken the opposite course, for such restrictions as formerly existed in favour of widow and children have long since disappeared, and even the Inheritance (Family Provision) Act, 1938, gives the dependants a right, not to a fixed share, but only to such provision as the Court, in its discretion, may allot.

[2] Nov. 1 A.D. 535.

[3] With an exception unimportant for our purpose, Wills Act, 1837, sect. 18.

[4] Law of Property Act, 1925, sect. 177.

as not affecting the financial relations or the status of the parties, that a marriage of the testator had no effect whatever on his or her will—in law they still continued for most purposes to be strangers. The birth of children, however, which has no effect on a will under our law, while it did not of itself revoke a previously made will, would under the rules of *exheredatio* just mentioned be extremely likely to cause it to be set aside; though this could in fact be prevented by previous precautions, by instituting or disinheriting children yet unborn, *postumi*.[1] The formal will of classical law, owing to its basis as a *mancipatio familiae*, itself an irrevocable act, was revocable expressly only by making another will. But the Praetor intervened in this field, in a way totally unknown to our English equity. He gave validity for the purposes of his praetorian remedies (*bonorum possessio*) to a will executed with the substantial safeguards of the mancipatory will but not complying with the idle formality of *mancipatio familiae*, and the praetorian will was revocable. How far his protection of the praetorian will and his rules as to revocation, which applied also to the mancipatory will, were less effective than the civil law rules we need not here consider; for the praetorian rules both of testation and of revocation were, with a good deal of statutory modification, the basis of the rules of Justinian's law.

In that law as in ours a will may be revoked by making a later one. But there is a considerable difference. A Roman will was essentially the appointment of a *heres* and it must be made *uno contextu*. It follows that any later will containing an appointment of a *heres*, which could conceivably take effect, revoked any earlier will whether the later will actually operated or not.[2] In our law a later will revokes the earlier only if it does so in express words or it is in the opinion of the Court so inconsistent with the other

[1] Details, Buckland, *Text-book*, pp. 323 *sqq.*
[2] D. 28. 2. 9. See Buckland, *Text-book*, p. 332.

that it is intended to revoke it.[1] Our law admits of partial revocation, with the result that a number of instruments of the same or different dates may together constitute the testator's 'last will'.[2] This is impossible in Roman law, but here the difference is not so great as might appear. It was practically true only so far as the *institutio heredis* was concerned. The whole *hereditas* must be conferred by the one instrument. But it was possible to make *codicilli* which did not need to be executed with the forms of a will, and, by these, trust bequests (*fideicommissa*) could be added, removed or varied. And if the will contained any provision confirming *codicilli*, not only *fideicommissa*, but any provision not amounting to a direct gift of the *hereditas*, could in the same way be added, removed or varied.

The Wills Act also provides that a will may be revoked by 'some writing declaring an intention to revoke the same', which however must be executed with the forms of a will, though it will not of itself operate as a will unless it in some way purports to be a will.[3] Justinian provided that, after ten years, a will could be revoked by declaration in Court or before three witnesses. The ten-year limit is what he leaves of an extraordinary enactment of the fifth century by which all wills were *ipso facto* revoked by the lapse of ten years. He also preserves a rule of the fifth century that if a document purports to be a will, but the formalities are not complied with, it will still suffice to revoke an earlier will if five witnesses are prepared to swear to its genuineness, provided that the *heredes* under the second will are entitled on intestacy and those under the first will are not.[4]

---

[1] *Dempsey* v. *Lawson* (1877), 2 P.D. 98; *Re Hawksley's Settlement*, [1934] Ch. 384.

[2] *Townsend* v. *Moore*, [1905] P. 66 (C.A.); *Re Howard*, [1944] p. 39.

[3] Wills Act, 1837, sect. 20; *In the goods of Fraser* (1869), L.R. 2 P. and D. 40; *In the goods of Hubbard* (1865), L.R. 1 P. and D. 53.

[4] C. 6. 23. 21. 5; h.t. 27. 2.

The Wills Act also provides that a will is revoked by burning, tearing or otherwise destroying with intention to revoke.[1] As we have seen this would not have affected a mancipatory will at civil law, but the Praetor took a different line, and Justinian, in his fusion of praetorian *bonorum possessio* and civil *hereditas*, adopted the praetorian rules. If the testator had intentionally torn up or burnt or cancelled the material parts of the will, the Praetor would refuse claims under it and would give his remedies, *bonorum possessio*, to those otherwise entitled.[2] In one important respect, however, the rules were different from ours. The Wills Act provides that a will once revoked cannot be revived otherwise than by re-execution or by some document executed like a will and showing intention to revive the will,[3] so that the effect of a mere revocation is necessarily to introduce intestacy. The Roman rule was not so rigid. If the revocation was shown to be with intent to revive the earlier will, this was revived. The rule was much the same in our law before the Wills Act.[4]

There is a further difference. Our law requires a real act of destruction. There must be an actual destruction of what it is intended to revoke, so that mere cancellation of a provision, however important, is not revocation, even partial. But in Roman law cancellation of the name of the *heres* is given as an illustration of effective revocation, but only praetorian at first.[5] Rescripts of the second century treat it not exactly as a revocation, but as a forfeiture, though it is not always clear whether it goes to the *Fiscus*, as forfeited for *indignitas*, or as a *caducum* under the *leges caducariae*.[6] If it was the only *heres* the will would be destroyed, subject to sporadic imperial reliefs into which

[1] Wills Act, 1837, sect. 20.
[2] G. 2. 151, 151a; D. 38. 6. 1. 8; 28. 1. 22. 3; 37. 11. 1. 10; C. 6. 23. 30.
[3] Wills Act, 1837, sect. 22.
[4] Jarman, *Wills*, 7th ed. p. 178.
[5] G. 2. 151; D. 38. 6. 1. 8.
[6] D. 34. 9. 12; 34. 9. 16. 2; cf. C. 6. 24. 4; 6. 35. 4.

we need not go. If there were other *heredes*, subject to
what has been said, the intentionally deleted part would
be taken, in later law, as unwritten, and the share would
accrue to the others. On the same principle, any other
provision intentionally deleted by the testator, or at his
orders, was ignored. An unintentional deletion was itself
ignored and the provision remained valid if it could be
proved, as to which it seems that any evidence could be
brought. Here too, except on the question of evidence,
our older law may have been the same.[1] But section 21 of
the Wills Act, 1837, provides that, except so far as the
words or effect of the will before the obliteration shall not
be apparent, no obliteration after the will was executed
shall have any effect, unless itself executed like a will, so
that if the words of the will can still be read the provision
is valid, whatever the intention of the testator.

One cause of failure of a Roman will is without parallel
in our system. As we have seen, a testator was bound
either to institute or to disinherit all his children.[2] Thus
children born after the will was made (*postumi*) would
necessarily upset it in early law. This was gradually remedied, partly by *leges*, partly by the Praetor, partly by
juristic interpretation, the general upshot being that the
failure could be avoided by anticipatory institution or dis-
herison;[3] the only thing we need note is that in these rules
there is a difference between the treatment of males and of
females. But these changes did not affect the case of
persons brought artificially into the family, by *adoptio*,
anniculi probatio or the like, and these necessarily destroyed
the will, till, late in the classical law, the rule appeared
that anticipatory *institutio* of such persons would save
the will. Anticipatory *exheredatio* would not: for such
persons it was meaningless.

[1] Jarman, *Wills*, 7th ed. pp. 143 *sqq.*   [2] P. 167, *ante.*
[3] Details, Buckland, *Text-book*, pp. 323 *sqq.*

8. RESTRICTIONS AS TO REMOTENESS, UNBORN BENEFICIARIES, ETC.

The restriction on testation which we have already mentioned, together with the fact that, throughout most of
the history, it was impossible to make a gift by will to anyone who was not at least *in utero* at the time when the will
operated, left the Roman testator little power of 'tying up'
his property. But the desire to exercise power after his
death was as strong with him as it is with us, and what he
could do, he did. There was indeed no rule against perpetuities, no express rule against remoteness, though we
shall see something like it. The testator could appoint as
heredes, or give legacies to, unborn issue of his own and,
by praetorian and later law, unborn issue of other people
(*postumi extranei*), in as remote a generation as he liked, but
the gift would fail if the beneficiary was not conceived
when the will operated. But when, under Augustus, trust
bequests (*fideicommissa*) were introduced, these were subject to none of the restrictions about *incertae personae* and
postumi, and it at once became possible to give successive
fideicommissa in such a way as to constitute a perpetuity.
We have indeed a will of A.D. 108 which creates such a
perpetuity.[1] Not long after this, however, Hadrian for-
bade *fideicommissa* in favour of *incertae personae*.[2] Another
device of testators was to forbid the *heredes* to alienate, but
Severus and Caracalla declared such a prohibition to be
void, as a *nudum preceptum*, unless it was coupled with a
fideicommissum of the property in favour of some person.[3]
A usual form of such *fideicommissa* seems to have been:
'ne fundum alienaret et ut in familia relinqueret'.[4] Such
a direction was understood in the later classical law to
extend to those alive at the death of the testator and their

---

[1] *Testamentum Dasumii*, Bruns, *Fontes Iuris*, 7th ed. i. p. 307.
[2] G. 2. 287.   [3] D. 30. 114. 14.
[4] D. 30. 114. 15.

immediate issue, but no further.[1] The rule, thus modified, while it ignored to this extent the old principle which required that beneficiaries should be born or *in utero* at the time when the will operated, rendered it impossible to make a gift to issue of an unborn beneficiary, a rule somewhat like that in *Whitby* v. *Mitchell*.[2] It is true that some texts say that there could be a *fideicommissum* on the *heres heredis*,[3] but there is nothing in the illustrations given to suggest that this could be in favour of remoter generations.

Under Justinian there were great changes. The text which establishes the limits of the *familia*[4] says that the testator can extend this, but it is plain that these words are an addition by the compilers. They seem to give effect to an enactment by Justinian which allows gifts to *incertae personae*,[5] the primary purpose of the enactment having probably been to facilitate gifts to charities, the more far-reaching effects not having been contemplated. Perpetuities at once became possible and were created. A case is recorded in a Novel of Justinian[6] which drew his attention to the undesirability of such things, for, besides deciding the actual case, he provides that such things are to be good in future for only four generations, a sufficiently long term. This became the rule in the fideicommissary substitutions of medieval law, and it was operative over a great part of Europe till modern times.[7] It may indeed have had repercussions in our own law. For, in view of the fact that judges were commonly clerics and therefore canonists and civilians in some degree, it is at least a

---

[1] D. 31. 32. 6.   [2] (1890), 44 Ch.D. 85.
[3] D. 32. 5. 1 and 6. *pr.*   [4] Cf. note 1, *supra.*
[5] C. 6. 48. 1.   [6] Nov. 159.

[7] It is still the law in South Africa, though there an absolute perpetuity can be created if the testator expressly overrides the rule. See Lee, *Introduction to Roman-Dutch Law*, 4th ed. pp. 386–387. For the French position, see Amos and Walton, *Introduction to French Law*, pp. 126–133; for the German, see Schuster, *Principles of German Civil Law*, pp. 607–608.

possible source of the rule in frankmarriage that the land
is free of services for four generations, and, through this,
of the original plan of the statute *De Donis* which, according
to Bereford C.J., as recorded in *Belyng's Case*, seems to have
been to allow the tying up of property for four generations.[1]

The question, how far the succession could be secured
for later generations, is distinct from that of how far such
dispositions made the property inalienable. Our own law
has dealt with the matter in a series of statutes, dealing
with settled property in such a way that there is almost
always a power of alienation of the actual property, the
proceeds of any sale being preserved to the intended beneficiary. The classical Roman law on this matter is not well
known, but the rule seems to have been the very modern-
looking one that the alienation was *prima facie* valid, but
the beneficiary under the trust could get it set aside by
missio in possessionem, as against a buyer with notice.[2] And
if there was also an express prohibition of alienation, the
sale was absolutely void unless it was for payment of the
testator's debts.[3] Justinian abolished the old rules: under
him it is clear that property subject to legacy or *fideicommissum* could not be alienated as against the beneficiary.
Any such alienation was void, whether the intended
assignee had notice or not, if the legacy or *fideicommissum*
was unconditional, and was subject to a resolutive condition if the gift was conditional.[4] Thus the law as Justinian left it was without any of the reliefs which our law
has found it necessary to introduce.

[1] Year Book, 5 Ed. II, Easter Term, Selden Society, *Year Books Series*,
xi. pp. xxv, 176. But as to other possible sources, which need not however
be independent, see *ibid*. p. xxviii. See also Plucknett, *Legislation of
Edward I*, pp. 125–135. For a somewhat fuller account of the Roman
story, see Buckland, *Equity in Roman Law*, pp. 83 *sqq*., from which much
of the foregoing is taken.

[2] P. Sent. 4. 1. 15; cf. D. 43. 4. 3. *pr*. For a general discussion of this
technique, see p. 84, *ante*.

[3] C. 4. 51. 7; 7. 26. 2; D. 32. 38. *pr*., etc.

[4] C. 6. 43. 3. 2a and 3. Further details, Buckland, *Equity, cit*.

9. TRUSTS

The trust, which has been described as the most original creation of English law, is an institution by which something is entrusted to one person, the trustee, for the benefit of another, the *cestui que trust* or beneficiary. Thereupon the legal ownership vests in the trustee, who is however bound by an obligation to use the thing for the benefit of the beneficiary, who has in it an equitable interest, of which he cannot be divested unless the legal ownership comes to vest in a purchaser for value without notice, actual or constructive, of the trust. Any person who acquires the legal ownership in circumstances other than these, becomes a constructive trustee. In the trust for sale, any person who acquires the legal ownership from the trustee in accordance with the terms of the trust acquires it free from the equitable interest, which is transferred to the proceeds of the sale. Most trusts of land are now in effect trusts for sale.

It is evident that what appears to the English lawyer the simple act of constituting a trust at one and the same time vests the legal ownership of a thing or of a fund in the trustee, imposes on him an obligation, not towards the settlor, but to the beneficiary, who is a third party to the agreement and may not yet be in existence, and confers on the last-named person a right to follow the trust property into the hands of anyone other than a *bona fide* purchaser for value without notice. It also constitutes the trust fund a separate entity, which the law keeps separate in a remarkable degree from the residue of the trustee's property. Where the trust is a trust for sale, it is only against the assets of this fund, whatever form they happen to assume for the time being, that the beneficiary has rights, and not against the specific objects which it contained at the time the trust was created.

From a third point of view, the constitution of a trust

effects a division of ownership in the thing or fund, between the powers of management, including in certain cases alienation, vested in the trustee, and the rights of enjoyment vested in the beneficiary.

It has long been recognised that the trust is not derived from Roman law, nor has Roman law influenced its development to any extent. Nor does it now look to us at all like a Roman institution. However, the older writers, who took its Roman origin very much for granted, were not perhaps quite so absurd as they have recently appeared to be.

Certainly the notion of making someone the owner of a thing, and binding him by an obligation to use it in a certain way, is not un-Roman. The *fideicommissum* was obviously such an institution, though normally the heir did not hold the inheritance or specific thing subject to a *fideicommissum* for any length of time as a mere trustee, being bound in one typical case to hand it over as soon as possible, and in the other, the *fideicommissary* substitution, enjoying the beneficial interest until he passed on the inheritance to a successor.

It is however a clear though little known fact that an heir might have had a *fiducia* imposed on him to preserve an inheritance intact and accumulate the income for the benefit of someone who should later take the beneficial interest.[1] This is not quite our trust, for although the heir is a mere manager, his powers of management precede the ultimate vesting of the beneficial interest, and do not co-exist with the rights of enjoyment contained in the latter; but it is not very far removed.

Nor is it very hard to find in Roman law something akin to the beneficiary's power of following trust funds. The beneficiary is a creditor of the trustee, and if the latter alienated in fraud of him, the beneficiary could bring the

[1] Lepaulle, *Bulletin de la Société de Législation Comparée*, 1929, p. 14; D. 22. 1. 3. 3; 36. 1. 78. 12.

actio Pauliana against either him or anyone into whose hands the property had come, unless he was a *bona fide* purchaser.

The notion of a separate fund, kept apart from the trustee's personal assets, is very far from being un-Roman, for Roman law invented one of the classical examples of the separate fund, the *peculium* entrusted to the *filius* or slave. Moreover, the Praetor, in the actions devised by him to protect creditors of the *peculium*, applied a complicated system of accounting between the *peculium* and the other *peculia* or personal estate belonging to the *paterfamilias*. Doubtless it was on the analogy of the *peculium* that he allowed *separatio bonorum* to the *heres necessarius*, and to the creditors of a solvent inheritance which had devolved on an insolvent heir.

The distinction between the legal and the equitable estate must be regarded as inconceivable in classical law, though, as has been said elsewhere,[1] something very like it developed in later law. But too much can be made of the need for this distinction as an element in the law of trusts. It is not found in the law of Scotland, Quebec or Ceylon, all of which know the trust; and it could easily be dispensed with in English law, were it not for the doctrine of estates, which is not essentially connected with the trust.

Is it possible to point to the combination of conveyance and contract in a single instrument as un-Roman? We should not insist too strongly, even for classical law, on the use of a single institution to produce a single result; for many rights and duties were implied in the consensual contracts which had not been thought of by the parties. It does, however, seem clear that the classical jurists disliked the incorporation of a conveyance in an instrument which was primarily intended to create obligations, though they had to accept the composite nature of the will.

[1] P. 82.

But the older lawyers, who had elaborated the will and determined its essential character, seem to have had no such repugnance, for they made liability to the *actio auctoritatis*, a matter of pure obligation, arise out of the mere fact of mancipating a thing.

One is almost forced to the conclusion that the main difficulty in the way of a Roman acceptance of the trust would have been that it may vest rights in a third person not a party to an agreement. But even this argument is not free from objection. It applies with full force only to the law of obligations; for the *fideicommissum* is an obvious exception, and it too was preceded by the civil law institution of the legacy *per damnationem*. In ancient Rome both were confined to the law of succession, though in Byzantine law, if not earlier, the *fideicommissum* had an analogue *inter vivos* in the *donatio sub modo*. Here again there is a certain resemblance to English law, for in so far as we assign topics to different branches of law we tend to think of trusts as belonging to the law of property and succession rather than to the law of contract.

In sum, it seems that there was nothing in the essential nature of Roman law to prevent it from admitting the trust had there been any practical need for the institution: though it must be conceded that it would have squared ill with the pedantry of the classical jurists.

10. SUCCESSION ON INTESTACY

In succession upon intestacy, the Roman law had not that distinction between real and personal property which, till the Administration of Estates Act, 1925, came into force, was so important in our law. Thus there was in the law of Rome nothing of the extraordinary complication which characterised our law of inheritance, nothing about seisin, nothing about descent traced from the purchaser, *possessio fratris*, and so forth, which made Mr Challis say, at the end of his chapter on 'Descent of a fee simple', that the labour of constructing it was the most arduous part of the work. There was no trace, at least in historical times, whatever may have been the case at the beginning, of any primogeniture. On the other hand the rules of canon law as to the distribution of personal property were a modified version of the rules of succession as Justinian left them, and they were themselves adopted, in a further modified form, by the Statute of Distributions. They have now been supplemented by the very different provisions of the Administration of Estates Act, 1925, which governs the devolution on intestacy of all property, real and personal. It seems therefore that there cannot be much material for comparison or contrast. But, in fact, Justinian's final rules have nothing Roman about them: they show a complete breakaway from Roman notions. It is not necessary to set out the earlier rules, which have a long history of perpetual change, but some remarks may be made on the more striking contrasts, which are mainly due to the fact that the Roman conception of the family is very different from ours.

Our present law and the older law of personal property have no preference for males, but the law of inheritance of land had, partly for feudal reasons,[1] a marked preference for males. The Roman law had such a preference, though not expressed in the same way, and inspired by a different reason. Under the rules attributed to the XII Tables relationship was reckoned entirely through males, and in fact through males who, when the claimant was conceived, had not passed out of the family circle by emancipation or the like. But, with this limitation, where claimants were of the same degree, the male had no preference over the female. Thus a man's son and daughter, or his brother and sister, were equally entitled. A half-brother by the same father had the same claim as if he were a full brother, but one by the same mother had no claim at all. A mother had

[1] P. and M. ii. pp. 258 *sqq.*

no claim in a child's estate, nor had her children any claim in her estate. The Praetor in his more or less rationalising changes broke down the rule requiring that claimants should still be within the family group, at least so far as issue were concerned, imposing certain necessary safeguards, but he did very little toward breaking down the rule that claimants must be related to the deceased through males. He did indeed create a class of claimants called *cognati* which included relatives through males and females, with an arbitrary limit of remoteness, more liberal however than that under the Administration of Estates Act, 1925. In this way mothers could succeed to their children and *vice versa*, but only in the complete absence of persons entitled under the civil law. In the course of the Empire, this was remedied. Children were given the first right of succession to their mothers, and mothers were given a much improved right, under complex rules which we need not discuss. Later still, similar but not quite identical rights were given to grandchildren of, or through, a woman. Not long before Justinian the notion of agnation, the civil relationship, was relaxed and the breach of it partially ignored. The *Corpus Juris* carried this piecemeal rationalising legislation still further and paved the way for the completely remodelled and modern-looking system which appears in the Novels.[1]

The contrast between the position of women, in the law of succession, under our law and under the Roman law, before Justinian's revolutionary changes, may perhaps be summed up as follows. Our law, as to real property but only as to real property, differentiated against women, a rule which took its rise before our law was feudalised but whose continuance was encouraged by it.[2] The Roman law of succession did not distinguish land from other property, and, so far as issue were concerned, there was no direct

[1] Details, Buckland, *Text-book*, pp. 365 *sqq.*
[2] P. and M. ii. pp. 258 *sqq.*

preference for males; both sexes, within the family, took
equally. If they passed out of the family by emancipation
they had no rights at civil law, but the Praetor gave them
equal rights. If they passed into another family by adoption
or, in the case of women, by marriage with *manus*, already
rare in early classical law, again the praetorian rights of
men and women were the same: they were *cognati* with
only a remote claim. But civil relationship was agnatic, i.e.
traced exclusively through males, so that remoter issue,
male or female, through daughters or granddaughters
were not in the family, but only *cognati*. Agnates were
those connected by legitimate descent through males, or,
to put the matter in another form, those who would be in
the same *patria potestas* if the common ancestor were alive.
They were preferred, however remote, to other collaterals.
Thus while women could succeed as agnates, they could
not be the channels of agnatic succession. A brother or
sister of the whole blood, or by the same father, had equal
rights as agnates: uterine brothers and sisters were equally
excluded. Early in the classical law, however, there appeared, apparently as a result of juristic *interpretatio*, one
very important differentiation against women. No woman
more remotely related than a sister could succeed as an
agnate, and this exclusion continued till Justinian.

The system finally established by Justinian[1] was based
on nearness of kinship, and, like our present system, had
no preference for males. But there are substantial differences, and the provisions of the Novels are in some
respects obscure and have been understood in different
ways by the later legislatures and legal systems building
upon them. As with us, issue had the first claim (the position of the surviving spouse will be considered later), the
nearer excluding the more remote, and remoter issue
claiming *per stirpem*, but, in Roman law, without any provision making the absolute right of issue dependent on

[1] Novv. 118, 127.

marriage or majority. With us, parents are preferred to brothers and sisters: after brothers and sisters (subject to representation by their issue, shortly to be stated) come grandparents and, after them, uncles and aunts. Under the system of the Novels all ascendants formed one class, sharing with brothers and sisters of the whole blood, apparently, though this is not absolutely clear, each of the groups taking half. Among ascendants, the nearer excluded the more remote in the same or a different line. And where there were several in different lines of the same degree of remoteness, each line took half irrespective of number, while with us they take equally. As with us, brothers and sisters of the whole blood were preferred to those of the half-blood, and, as with us, issue of deceased brothers or sisters of either group represented them taking *per stirpes*, but, again, in Roman law, without any question of marriage or majority, and with the curious limitation that this representation did not occur unless there survived the intestate some other brother or sister to keep the class alive. Failing any claim under these heads the property went to the nearest relatives, *per capita* and with no representation, so that there was not, as in our law, any representation of uncles by their issue. In this class the Novel said nothing of any limit of remoteness, but it is probable, though disputed, that the old limit of cognation to the sixth, or in one case, the seventh, degree still held.

11. THE SURVIVING SPOUSE

The most remarkable difference between the two systems is as to the position of the surviving spouse. In England, as Blackstone said (*Commentaries*, Book i. ch. 15), 'the husband and wife are one person in law: that is, the very being or legal existence of the woman is suspended during the marriage, or at least is incorporated and consolidated into that of the husband: under whose wing, protection and *cover* she performs every thing'. It is not surprising to find, amongst other results of this doctrine, that her personal property in possession vested normally in him (there was no such rule the other way), and it is only gradually that our law has reached the present position in which the woman's property is separate and independent. It was thus necessary that the surviving widow should be provided for, and our earlier law, dealing indeed with personal property, gave her very considerable claims both in priority to, and in competition with, her children, and in relation to land gave her a similar right by the law of dower, which, however, could be defeated by conveyancing devices. Into these it is not necessary to go. The recent legislation does not distinguish in the matter between real and personal property, or between husband and wife, but gives the surviving spouse (i) all 'personal chattels', (ii) the sum of £1000, and (iii) a life interest in the whole residuary estate, real and personal, or in one-half if the intestate leaves issue; and if there is no other claim at all, the whole estate.

Where a Roman wife became *in manu* to her husband the situation was not greatly different from that at common law. The wife was in the *familia* and succeeded as a daughter, and she could have, as a *filiafamilias*, no property to leave. But in classical law this is practically obsolete and is utterly gone centuries before Justinian. In the civil law, as they are not related and their properties are entirely independent, neither husband nor wife has any claim on intestacy, or to a provision in the will of the other spouse. Though the Praetor modified this, it was only to a very small extent: he gave them a right of succession only if there were no relatives entitled to claim, i.e. only where the goods would otherwise be *bona vacantia* and would go to the public treasury. In the Novels nothing is said of the wife or husband, but it is clear from other evidence[1] that the old rule continued and they took the property in

---

[1] *Basilica*, 45. 5, Heimbach, 4. 543.

absence of any relatives who could claim. There is indeed
one amelioration. By two Novels Justinian provided[1] that,
where there was no *dos*, the widow, and where there was
no *donatio propter nuptias*, the widower, should have in any
case a quarter of the estate, or, if there were more than
three children, a *pars virilis*, but, as it seems, only for life
and only up to a maximum of 100 *aurei*, so that the provision is not very important. All this reflects the fundamental difference in the relation of the wife to the husband's
family which we have already noted.[2] She is not essentially
a member of the family and must look to her own family
for provision. The contrast is striking between the rules
described above and our old law of dower, of the widow's
half or third of the personal property (as the case might be)
and of the widower's tenancy by the curtesy and his retention of practically all his wife's personal property. The *dos*
was no corrective for the state of things in classical and
later law; for though it commonly, but not always, went to
the wife on her husband's death, it was not, like our dower,
a provision from the husband's property. It came normally
from the wife's family and was handed over to the husband.
At first there was no right in the widow, but when this
appeared it was still no provision by the husband, but
from outside, a fact which is brought out by the rule that
where a woman claimed in succession to her father she had
to bring into hotchpot what she had received by way of
dos from him. Similarly the husband had only the remote
claim we have mentioned, and the *donatio ante*, or *propter*,
nuptias of later law, which normally went to him at the
death of the wife, had been provided by him or on his
behalf in the beginning. On the other hand, the *donatio*
was a provision for the wife in case she survived her
husband.

---

[1] Novv. 53. 6; 117. 5.   [2] P. 41, *ante*.

12. SUCCESSION TO FREEDMEN

It should be noted that Roman law presents one case of
succession on intestacy which has no connexion with relationship or marriage. It is the succession to freedmen.
We need not state the rules, which were varied greatly
from time to time by the Praetor and by legislation. It will
suffice to say that broadly speaking the patron, and his
children if he was dead, were entitled to the property of
the freedman in default of issue to him: he could have no
relatives but issue, since *cognatio servilis* was not recognised.
The matter is complicated by the fact that these rules
applied only to freedmen who were *cives*. The goods of
freedmen who were Latins reverted to the patron or his
children in any case, but it was a reversion of what was
regarded as a mere *peculium*, and not a succession, so that,
e.g., it did not carry with it liability for debts beyond the
available fund. The fullness with which this matter is
treated in so small and elementary a book as the *Institutes*
of Gaius is an indication of its importance: it is well known
that in the early Empire freedmen often attained to high
position and great wealth: they were probably the most
intelligent class of the community. It is a far cry from the
Roman freedman to the English bastard, but they possess
one curious feature in common, namely, that in the eye of
the law they have no ancestors or collaterals and their only
relatives must be posterity.[1] The Legitimacy Act, 1926,
in addition to introducing legitimation by subsequent
marriage, as described above,[2] has given a bastard and his
mother certain reciprocal, though not identical, rights
of succession on intestacy. It may be noted that the
Roman law had always recognised the cognatic claim
between an illegitimate child and its mother and her
cognates, and that, under Justinian, where children

---

[1] Perhaps the *emancipatus* is even nearer to the English bastard.
[2] P. 45, *ante*.

were born in slavery, reciprocal rights of succession were allowed between parent and issue, though no remoter kinship was recognised.

13. *BONORUM POSSESSIO*

The most remarkable characteristic of the Roman law of succession, by will or on intestacy, as compared with ours, is the existence, side by side, from the later Republic to the time of Justinian, of two systems of succession, the civil, which alone is concerned with the *hereditas* strictly so called, and the praetorian, under which the claimant gets, not *hereditas* ('praetor heredem facere non potest'), but *bonorum possessio*, with a scheme of remedies quite distinct from those of civil law. Each has a definite order of claims, the praetorian to some extent coinciding with, to some extent differing from, that of the civil law. The praetorian scheme is more rational: it may be, and commonly is, thought of as 'equity' intervening in a region which the Chancellor has not entered. The Praetor's original purpose does not indeed seem to have been reform but, here as in other branches of the law, to provide a summary means of obtaining actual possession for those who appeared, *prima facie*, to be entitled. The first step in reform was to give *bonorum possessio* to relatives who had no civil law claim where no one was civilly entitled, so that there was no one to attack the possession given by the Praetor. The next step was to allow persons not entitled at civil law to claim with those so entitled, e.g. emancipated children with *sui heredes*, and here the *bonorum possessio* seems to have been effective (*cum re*). The final stage is to allow persons with no civil title to claim to the exclusion of civil *heredes*, e.g. those claiming under a purely praetorian will. But, in such cases, the *bonorum possessio* was, at first, purely provisional, capable of being upset by the civil claimant, if there was one (*bonorum possessio sine re*), and it was made effective (*cum re*) not usually by the authority of the Praetor himself, so far as the texts show, but by enactments of the Emperor or the Senate.[1] In Justinian's time the two systems are more or less fused—it is usually merely a matter of choice of remedies, though, as with our so-called fusion of law and equity, there were still cases in which the distinction was material. Into this it is not necessary to go. The feature of *bonorum possessio* which interests the English lawyer is that, while it occurred in a sphere in which the Court of Chancery did not intervene, it presents, in its system of praetorian remedies parallel to the civil law remedies, and in its effect as an agent for the reform of the civil law of succession, certain striking resemblances to the activity and influence of the Chancellor.

14. *CURA PRODIGI*

A Roman institution which is entirely unknown to the common law and indeed to the law of England generally, and which may be conveniently considered here by reason of its effect on the power of testation, is the *cura prodigi*. In Rome, as early as the XII Tables, a man who wasted hereditary property received on an intestacy could by certain machinery be interdicted from dealing with his property, this being placed in the hands of an administrator with very large powers, *curator prodigi*. This was extended, still in early law, to *prodigi* wasting what they had received by will, and, ultimately, as it seems, to any case of prodigality. Apparently the *prodigus* could apply at any time to have the interdiction removed, but, so long as it lasted, he could make no alienation whatever of his capital. We are not well informed, but it is clear that he could not make a will.[2] The father could not set up such a *curatio* by his will, but, if he purported to do so, there was a question whether the magistrate was bound to confirm it, settled in the affirmative under Justinian.[3] Thus it seems that the institu-

---

[1] See, e.g., G. 2. 119 *sqq.*; 2. 143; 2. 151a.
[2] *Liber sing. regularum*, attributed to Ulp. 20. 13; P. Sent. 3. 4a. 12.
[3] D. 27. 10. 16. 1.

tion was found useful, for it was continuously strengthened and widened. We are told in Paul's *Sententiae*, and the passage is preserved in the Digest,[1] that it applied also to women; this cannot be primitive, at earliest it dates from the time when there were *tutores* with only formal authority,[2] for till then women were under a lifelong real *tutela*.

With us, on the other hand, if a person once gets into control of his property, there is no machinery by which he can be prevented from wasting it and ruining those who are dependent on him, unless it is possible to persuade the Court that he is, through mental infirmity arising from disease or age, incapable of managing his affairs, thus bringing him within the scope of the lunacy laws; but, as has been pointed out,[3] there is 'the fundamental distinction that the status created by' the Lunacy Acts and Mental Deficiency Acts 'rests on unsoundness of mind, not on extravagance, and accordingly has no penal character'. It is possible that the indifference of English law towards habits of prodigality is to be found in the same conceptions of liberty which until recently enabled a man to disinherit his family completely and still refuse to admit any 'bairns' part' or widow's *legitim*. So repellent to the English law is the institution of *prodigi interdictio* as found in modern systems which have followed Roman law, such as that of France, that our Courts decline to give effect to the decree of a French Court pronouncing a person to be *prodigue* and appointing a *conseil judiciaire* to control his property, and will pay out a fund in Court to the *prodigue* himself.[4] There is no doubt that our system of settlements, creating limited interests, so that the capital cannot be touched, and the not uncommon habit of postponing unlimited control till the age of twenty-five or thirty, frequently averts or postpones the full consequences

---

[1] P. Sent. 3. 4a .6; D. 27. 10. 15.   [2] G. 1. 190 *sqq.*; p. 53, *ante*.
[3] Dicey, *Conflict of Laws*, 5th ed. p. 535, n. (x).
[4] *In re Selot's Trust*, [1902] 1 Ch. 488.

of extravagance, and the married woman's restraint on anticipation may often have had the same effect.[1] But the principle remains that when once a settlor or testator has conferred an absolute interest on a person *sui iuris* nothing can be done to protect that person against himself. It may be better so in the interests of the community at large; it may be well that nothing should prevent a man from falling to his proper level, but a wife or a widow and children will not quite accept this view. The ingenuity of conveyancers has, however, devised two methods to which resort may be had when the possibility of the development of prodigal habits is foreseen. The first is the 'spendthrift trust',[2] whereby a fund is given to trustees with an absolute discretion as to paying any part of the capital or income to the beneficiary or not; the second is by way of 'protective trusts', under which the beneficiary takes a life interest determinable upon alienation, bankruptcy or execution,[3] whereupon the life interest is administered by the trustees for the beneficiary and his or her spouse and children; and there are combinations of both these methods.

In the United States parallels to both the Roman and the English law can be found. The spendthrift trust is known in almost all the States, and the law is much more favourable to the beneficiary than in England. Thus, whether by statute or otherwise, the creator of a trust can almost always effectively provide that although the beneficiary is entitled to require the trustee to pay the income to him, he cannot assign his interest under the trust, and his creditors cannot reach it. There is no need to give any discretionary power to the trustee, but occasionally, as in New York, the restraint is effective only as to so much of the income as is necessary for the education and support

---

[1] They are now entirely abolished by the Married Women (Restraint upon Anticipation) Act, 1949.

[2] Key and Elphinstone, *Precedents in Conveyancing*, 14th ed. ii. p. 907.

[3] *Ibid.* p. 512; Trustee Act, 1925, sect. 33.

of the beneficiary. In all these cases it is immaterial whether the beneficiary is, or is not, wasteful in his habits.

On the other hand, some States, including the important States of Massachusetts and New York, have made specific legislative provisions for the appointment of guardians for spendthrifts, and a large majority of the States have provided for guardians or conservators of persons who, for one reason or another, such as intemperance or old age or infirmity, are, though not actually insane, incapable of looking after their property.[1]

15. DISLIKE OF INTESTACY

As we have said, in Rome intestacy seems to have been so far as possible avoided, not only by the habits of man, but also by legal rule. Wills are far more prominent. No doubt the desire to exercise power after death is always present, especially where, as until recently with us, there is a free power of testation. In Rome this did not exist in the Empire, but the feeling was very strong. Maine speaks of this as a 'horror of intestacy'. But it has been pointed out that there is no justification for this suggestion,[2] which rests mainly on the common form of curse: *intestabilis esto*;[3] but to be *intestabilis* meant a great deal more than to have no will. It meant exclusion from acting as a witness, and, as some said, from having a witness, which would amount to something like outlawry. The reason for the dislike of intestacy is probably the fact that the civil law of succession was intensely artificial, not corresponding in the least to the impulses of natural affection, so that everything reasonably possible to avoid the operation of that law ought to be done. For instance, it insisted on agnation. That a son who has been emancipated

---

[1] We are indebted for this information to Professor A. W. Scott of Harvard University.

[2] Maine, *Ancient Law*, p. 218; Radin, *Roman Law*, pp. 414, 456.

[3] See Lewis and Short, *Latin Dictionary*, s.v. *intestabilis*.

should have no claim does not perhaps much matter. If the emancipation was meant as a punishment, the result was reasonable. If it was a reward, provision for him would be made at the time. However, the slow and reluctant way in which steps were taken to remove the hardships affecting mothers and their children, widows, and relatives whose agnatic tie had been broken,[1] accounts sufficiently for the fact that throughout the history there was a very strong sentiment in favour of testation.

In England, on the other hand, it appears[2] that both before the Norman Conquest and for some time after it, there was a genuine horror of intestacy, or, to be more accurate, of deliberate, wilful, intestacy, for the intestate who died suddenly was the object of sympathy rather than reprobation. Intestacy was frequently penalised by confiscation of the deceased's goods. Whether or not the early horror of intestacy has left any trace upon our rules for the construction of wills it would be difficult to say;[3] there is a leaning, if not a presumption, against intestacy, which may, however, merely be due to the influence of the *ut magis valeat quam pereat* rule.

As we have seen, the feudal system of tenure had crushed out the will of real property, but it is worthy of note that, when once the system of uses had been recognised by the Court of Chancery, it was seized upon as a means of re-establishing the power of devising lands by will. Indeed, long after any superstitious or religious dislike of intestacy had disappeared, the awkward and piecemeal character of our law of intestate succession made it the practice of most persons possessing an appreciable amount of property to make a will. It is perhaps too early to ascertain whether the more rational rules introduced by the Administration of Estates Act, 1925, have modified the practice.

[1] Pp. 181 *sqq., ante.*
[2] P. and M. ii. pp. 356–363; Holdsworth, iii. pp. 535, 536.
[3] See Jarman, *Wills,* 7th ed. p. 2146.

CHAPTER VI. OBLIGATIONS: GENERAL

1. INTRODUCTORY

The elementary text-book of Gaius, followed by Justinian, after dealing with property and succession, enters upon a subject called *Obligationes*. Gaius describes this as consisting of contract and delict, to which Justinian adds quasi-contract and quasi-delict. Even so expanded the Roman *obligationes* are far from covering the whole field of what in modern theory are called *iura in personam*. It was not in accordance with the casuistic methods of the Roman lawyers, any more than it would be with us (we can hardly be said to have adopted the word), to seek for an exact definition of the abstract notion of *obligatio*. The word itself does not seem to be used as a legal term till the Empire. *Obligationes* are a group, within the field of what modern jurisprudence calls *iura in personam*, but no more covering the field of *iura in personam* than our treatises on contract, quasi-contract and tort cover that field.[1]

For Gaius, *obligatio* is a notion which belongs entirely to the *ius civile*. No praetorian right or duty can be an *obligatio*, although jurists writing well after the Edict had been stabilised by Julian sometimes speak of *obligatio* in relation to praetorian rules. Justinian includes among obligations a few praetorian liabilities, under the rubric of quasi-delict, but in the main he follows the lines of Gaius: no agreement which gave rise to a merely praetorian right of action came for him, any more than for Gaius, under the head of contract. The width of our modern conception of contract prevents the existence in our law to-day of any class of purely equitable agreements corresponding to praetorian

[1] In Italy the terms *obbligo* and *obbligazione* are used to cover the wider and the narrower field respectively.

pacts which are not contracts. But, at an early stage, this notion appeared in our system. In the first place, the ecclesiastical courts imposed spiritual penalties in some cases of breach of agreement where the common law gave no remedy; but this was checked very early by writs of prohibition and does not seem to have had any influence on the later law.[1] Secondly, we find that in the fifteenth and early sixteenth centuries, before the common law courts had evolved a workable theory of contracts, the Court of Chancery constantly enforced agreements of several different kinds without ever clearly deciding the principle on which it was acting: it sufficed that the agreement was one which in all the circumstances it was reasonable to enforce, because it would be unconscientious if the defendant failed to do what he had promised to do.[2] This is not unlike the praetorian enforcement of certain pacts, except that, for Roman law, there was no distinction of Courts.

Apart from the fact that the name 'contract' had an artificial limitation in the Roman law, and excluded as a matter of terminology not only agreements made actionable by the Praetor but also those made actionable in post-classical times by the Emperor, there is a very fundamental distinction between the Roman and the modern English view of contract. Our law requires for a valid contract either the form of a seal or the presence of 'consideration'. These requirements being satisfied, any agreement, for any legitimate purpose, within the compass of legal and not merely social relations, is valid, so that we may say that the general attitude of our law is that any specialty or bargain is a valid contract unless there is some positive reason why it should not be. At first sight the Roman system seems to be similar: any agreement for a lawful purpose, cast in the form of *stipulatio*—in principle, question and answer—was enforceable. This contract, however,

---

[1] Holdsworth, ii. p. 305; iii. pp. 415, 424.
[2] Holdsworth, v. pp. 294–298.

is entirely unilateral: it creates duties on one side and rights on the other, and although there is evidence to show that bilateral contracts were concluded by means of reciprocal *stipulationes*, the *stipulatio*, standing alone, would have been very inadequate for the purposes of commerce. Apart from *stipulatio*, all the contracts recognised by law are contracts for some one specific purpose, loan, pledge, sale, hire, and so forth. Hence we get, not a theory of contract, but a theory of contracts, a number of contracts, each with its own theory.[1] Thus the attitude of the Roman law can be fairly stated by the proposition that an agreement is not a contract unless the law, for some reason, erects it into one.

The contrast is not unlike that between the two conflicting views held by English lawyers[2] upon the theory of the law of torts or tort: the first that all damage is actionable in the absence of some cause, justification or excuse, recognised by law, and the second that no action will lie in respect of an act or omission unless the circumstances bring it under the rubric of some specific tort recognised by law.

The terminology of the two laws is curiously parallel on two points. A contract is, as ordinarily understood, any enforceable agreement of parties, but in both systems the name is applied where the so-called contract, though in form an agreement, is actually imposed on the party by the force of public authority. As with us 'recognizances', in form agreements, can be required by the Court with detention as an alternative, and are called 'contracts of record', so in Roman law promises could be required by the Court, *stipulationes praetoriae*, with *missio in possessionem*,

---

[1] But these contracts have so wide a range that they cover almost all the normal business transactions of the Roman world. Moreover, the law became sufficiently generalised to produce, apart from some peculiarities in the law of sale, only two theories of contract, one for contracts enforced in a *strictum iudicium* and the other for those with a *bonae fidei iudicium* (see p. 238, *post*).   [2] Pp. 338 *sqq.*, *post*.

i.e. seizure of all property, as an alternative. And in both cases the terms of the agreement are settled by the Court. Similarly there is a tendency in both systems to give the name 'contract' to states of fact which have nothing to do with agreement. Thus Gaius classes under contract the obligation to refund money paid by mistake, and, in our law, the same liability is described as a contract implied in law. It may be that, at least for Roman law, this survives from an earlier state of things in which *contractus* has nothing to do, strictly, with consent, and is hardly more than another name for *obligatio*. The verb 'to contract', *contrahere*, is used in this wider sense in both systems. There are other ways of 'contracting an obligation' than by contract. In any case the distinction is made clear in later law, and such things are called 'quasi-contract'; and the same usage is gradually creeping into our law.[1] The first branch of obligation for us to consider is contract in the ordinary sense.

2. REALITY OF CONSENT IN CONTRACT

This was dealt with in practice much as it is with us. Duress and fraud did not of themselves make the contract void, but they entitled the aggrieved party to have it set aside. But where mere mistake affected a contract it avoided it on the ground that there was no real consent. And the detailed working out of the rules was similar, though not quite identical. Thus, under our system, where a contract has been procured by fraud not inducing a mistake fundamental enough to preclude the formation of any contract at all[2] and is thus valid till set aside, it is sometimes possible for the fraudulent party to confer rights on third parties while the contract is still standing, and these rights cannot be set aside. A contract for the sale of specific goods

---

[1] We need not pay much attention to Coke's 'in any contract there must be quid pro quo, for contractus est quasi actus contra actum', Co. Litt. 47 b.

[2] *Cundy* v. *Lindsay* (1878), 3 App. Cas. 459.

in a deliverable state transfers the ownership, and if the buyer has transferred the ownership to a third party before steps are taken, the third party's title is good; though if the price has not been paid to him, the original seller may exercise his right of lien even against the third party. In Roman law the situation was rather different: a contract of sale did not transfer ownership, of itself, and there was thus no question of acquisition of title by a third party. But if the contract had been followed by an actual conveyance, the result was as with us. The aggrieved person had his remedy against the fraudulent party, but he could not disturb the title of the innocent third party. On the other hand, where the fraud had induced such a mistake as would have avoided the agreement even had there been no fraud, the position was different. Thus where the buyer had by trickery led the vendor to take him for some other person, and it was to this other person that the intent to transfer was directed, here the ownership did not pass and the third person could acquire no right.[1] The question in Roman law cases was not whether the agreement was void for mistake but whether the conveyance under it was.

While in our law fraud and mistake are very modern rubrics, at least on the common law side, and mistake was also rather late in Roman law, fraud came into account in that system at an earlier stage, at a time when the notion that contract rests on consent had not yet become clear, a time when, if a man had gone through certain forms, or had said certain words, he was bound. The rule allowing a contract to be set aside if it was affected by *dolus* or *metus* was designed merely to prevent a wrongdoer taking advantage of his own wrong: it was not the expression of any theory concerning reality of assent. It is true that later on a jurist dealing with *metus* can say that it does not make the agreement absolutely void, as there was, after all, an assent:

[1] D. 47. 2. 43. *pr.*; h.t. 44. *pr.*, etc.

'quamvis si liberum esset noluissem, tamen coactus volui'.[1]
But this is only explaining an ancient rule in the light of
a much more recent theory.

The Roman conception of fraud in contract was in some
ways more severe than ours. With us it must be shown
that the fraud induced the contract: in Rome it sufficed
that there was serious fraud, which had misled. This difference is perhaps little more than verbal, since *res ipsa
loquitur*, and inducement will readily be inferred if the
fraud was serious, and hardly if it was not. Another difference is more important. On the texts non-disclosure of
known material defects, e.g. in a thing sold, was *dolus*, and
enabled the other party to defend action on the contract
or recover damages, under the *ex fide bona* clause in the
action. The rule was retained in the modern Pandekten-
recht, and is embodied in the German Bürgerliches Gesetzbuch, and in the French Code Civil. Indeed continental
critics have made it a reproach to our law of sale of goods,
as expressing a low commercial morality, that it does not
contain this rule.[2]

Innocent misrepresentation is not a ground of avoidance
in Roman law or in the modern systems derived from it. If
it is wilful it is fraud. If though not wilful it amounts to an
undertaking, then it is a term in the contract and its falsity
is a breach of contract, giving a right of action: it has
nothing to do with reality of assent.[3] The same result is
reached in Roman law in cases like *Bannerman* v. *White*[4]
as in ours. But if it is neither wilful nor a term in the contract, then it is in itself, for Roman law, indifferent—it

---

[1] D. 4. 2. 21. 5.

[2] But in part the conditions and warranties implied by the Sale of Goods
Act go far, as interpreted, to reduce the maxim *caveat emptor* to a nullity,
especially where unascertained goods are concerned. See also pp. 285–286.

[3] D. 18. 1. 45. But since innocent misrepresentation always induces
error, and the bounds of relevant *error* are wider in civil law systems than
in English law, the same result can often be attained.

[4] (1861), 10 C.B.N.S. 84.

gives no right to rescission of the contract as it now does with us.[1] But if it has led to a mistake, and it is only in such an event that the question is likely to arise, the question whether the contract will be avoided or not depends on the rules of mistake, not innocent misrepresentation. Whether in our law a contract so affected by innocent misrepresentation is voidable, like one affected by fraud of certain kinds, or void, but so that the maker of the representation is estopped from setting up this fact, is not altogether clear on the cases.

The rubric of mistake as an element in the law of formation of contract came into Roman law only rather late, together with a clear recognition of the essential dependence of contract on consent. In our law it seems a very late comer indeed, at least on the common law side. It seems to result from an adoption, a little before the time of the Judicature Acts, as a test of validity at common law, of a principle which had long been applied in equity as a test for the applicability of equitable remedies. The essence of mistake, that is to say fundamental, material, mistake, the kind which precludes the formation of a contract, is that the error must be such as to negative consent. As our Courts have said, it must be such that the minds of the parties are not *ad idem*, though how much they must be *ad idem* our law has never defined with precision: it has preferred to deal with each case as it has arisen.[2] There can hardly be a contract in which both parties are fully and correctly informed on all the facts which might influence the mind in determining whether to make the contract or not. If the existence of any false impression were to vitiate the contract, there could hardly be any law of contract. Some test is therefore wanted to determine what error is sufficient. Obviously, importance is a main factor, but that is too vague to serve. The question whether the

[1] *Redgrave* v. *Hurd* (1881), 20 Ch.D. 1.
[2] See Cockburn, C.J. in *Smith* v. *Hughes* (1871), L.R. 6 Q.B. at p. 606.

contract would have been made if the fact had been known
has been suggested, but, apart from difficulty of application, it would not really serve. A man who bought a
house in the belief that there was a convenient service of
trains to London from a nearby station cannot be allowed
to cry off the bargain merely because this proves not to be
so, even though the vendor was under the same impression,
so that the mistake was mutual.

Modern writers both on the Roman and on the English
law are endeavouring to arrive at a solution. There is a
tendency to regard the problem as improperly formulated,
and to substitute for the question whether there was mistake and, if so, what kind of mistake, the question whether
there was *dissensus* or *consensus*. To discuss this would be
beyond our scope, for it seems fairly clear that neither
system has ever really solved the problem. The Roman law
was, and the English law has been, content to deal rather
empirically with the cases as they arose. Thus though it
may be possible to enumerate the cases in the two systems
in which error has been held to vitiate the contract, these
should not be regarded as fixed categories in either system.
To a great extent they follow the same lines. Error as to
the nature of the transaction appears in both.[1] So also does
error as to the identity of the subject matter.[2] The same is
true of identity of the other party, where this is material,[3]
and, apparently, of error as to quantity or price, where it is
to the prejudice of the party under the error, though the
English authorities are not very clear.[4]

There is also what is called *error in substantia*, which
is confined in Roman law to *bonae fidei* transactions[5] and
which high authorities hold to be a creation of the post-
classical law. Many attempts have been made to give some

---

[1] D. 12. 1. 18. 1; *Foster* v. *Mackinnon* (1869), L.R. 4 C.P., 704.
[2] D. 18. 1. 9. *pr.*; *Raffles* v. *Wichelhaus* (1864), 2 H. and C. 906.
[3] D. 47. 2. 43. *pr.*; *Cundy* v. *Lindsay, supra.*   [4] D. 19. 2. 52.
[5] In fact all the texts refer to sale.

precision to this conception, by deduction from the instances in the texts, but none of them is really satisfactory.[1] It seems to come to little more than that there must be a very important error as to the nature of the thing sold. We have the same rather ill-defined case in our own law,[2] and without attempting to define it we can say that the cases falling within it are those in which the mistake is not as to the identity or existence of the subject matter, but as to some quality or attribute of it, the absence or presence of which produces a 'difference in substance in the nature of the thing', or, as it was recently put in the House of Lords,[3] 'as to the existence of some quality which makes the thing without the quality essentially different from the thing as it was believed to be'.[4]

In both systems we hear of mutuality of mistake, but that does not mean quite the same in the two systems, and in ours it does not seem to be essential except in the last case. References to common or mutual mistake will be found in other classes of case, but it must not be assumed that the existence of this is always an essential feature in them.[5] In Roman law, if one party knows of the other's mistake and does not inform him, this is *dolus* and other rules come into play.[6] In our law the position seems rather to be that the one party's expectation ought not to be defeated owing to a misconception of the other party of which the former did not know. But in such case there is mistake on both sides, for each is mistaken as to the intention or belief of the other.

The present state of the English law is not easily made out. The common law has taken the course of adopting as a ground for declaring a contract void facts which would

---

[1] See Buckland, *Text-book*, pp. 418 *sq.*; Lawson in 52 *L.Q.R.* (1936) pp. 79 *sqq.*   [2] See Pollock on Contract, 13th ed. p. 396.

[3] By Lord Atkin in *Bell* v. *Lever*, [1932] A.C. 161, 218.

[4] See also *Kennedy* v. *Panama etc. Mail Co.* (1867), L.R. 2 Q.B. 580, 588.

[5] *Scott* v. *Coulson*, [1903] 2 Ch. 249; *Galloway* v. *Galloway* (1914), 30 T.L.R. 531.   [6] D. 44. 4. 4. 3; 44. 4. 7. *pr.*

have led the Court of Chancery to refuse its special remedies, such as specific performance. This is a result of the Judicature Acts, but it is not a logical result. For the Acts merely direct the Common Law Divisions to grant the same relief as ought to have been given by the Court of Chancery before the passing of the Acts, and provide that in the event of conflict or variance between the rules of equity and common law the former shall prevail. Thus common law Courts can give specific performance, and the Acts appear to mean that they can give and refuse these remedies where the Court of Chancery would have done so. The further step, of declaring void contracts for which that Court would have refused its special remedies, is one which they have taken on their own initiative. They have not made, as it seems, a general principle of this: it is especially in the field of 'reality of assent' that they have so acted.[1]

Moreover both Courts and text-books have a habit of citing, as authorities on the law of mistake, cases (often cases in equity) in which not a word was said about mistake and which depend on quite different principles. Thus *Raffles* v. *Wichelhaus* appears very commonly.[2] Here there was an agreement to buy goods 'ex Peerless from Bombay'. There were two ships answering that description and each party had a different one in mind. The agreement was held void, but this was a case of incurable ambiguity. If indeed one of the ships had been called 'Peeress', the

---

[1] See *Redgrave* v. *Hurd* (1881), 20 Ch.D. 1 from which it appears that Jessel M.R., basing himself upon the Judicature Act, 1873, sect. 25 (11), was mainly responsible for the new movement; *Newbigging* v. *Adam* (1886), 34 Ch.D. 582; (1888), 13 App. Ca. 308; and *Derry* v. *Peek* (1889), 14 App. Ca. 337, where Lord Bramwell at p. 347 (cited in Anson, *Law of Contract*, 19th ed. p. 175), after stating that fraud which induces a contract gives a cause of action, said: 'To this may now be added the equitable rule (which is not in question here), that a material misrepresentation, though not fraudulent, may give a right to avoid or rescind a contract where capable of such a rescission.'

[2] (1864), 2 H. and C. 906. It is badly reported.

question of mistake might at least have been raised. In
Smith v. *Hughes*,[1] where a new trial was ordered, the purchaser agreed to buy oats believing that the oats offered
were old oats, whereas the oats which the vendor intended
to sell and which were delivered to the plaintiff were new
oats: it appears from the judgements that a finding by the
jury to the effect that the vendor knew of the purchaser's
self-deception, and took no steps to remove it, would not
vitiate the contract. A Roman Court would no doubt have
held the same so far as error is concerned, if only because
the error could not be said to be fundamental enough to be
error in substantia. But it would probably have regarded
the case as one of fraud and rescinded the contract on that
account.[2] The Court went on to say that it would have
been different if the buyer had thought he was being
actually promised old oats and the vendor knew this. The
Roman law would have said the same, but would have put
it on the ground of fraud, and the language of Hannen J.
in which this last proposition is stated seems to treat it
rather as fraud than as mistake.

Cases of impossibility also sometimes appear under the
rubric of mistake. Where the contract is plainly, on the
face of it, for an impossibility 'in the nature of things', it is
void in both systems, apparently on the ground that it
cannot have been seriously meant.[3] Where the impossibility is not obvious but is due to the fact that the subject-
matter of the contract has ceased to exist, the contract is
void in Roman law if both parties were in ignorance.[4]
But, we are told, if the vendor alone knew, there is no sale,
and if the buyer alone knew, the sale is good and he must
pay the price, though he does not get the thing.[5] It is

---

[1] (1871), L.R. 6 Q.B. 597.
[2] See the very similar case in D. 19. 1. 11. 5.
[3] G. 3. 97; D. 45. 1. 35; D. 44. 7. 31. See Anson, *Law of Contract*,
19th ed. p. 93.
[4] D. 18. 1. 57. *pr*.; 44. 7. 1. 9.   [5] D. 18. 1. 57. 1, 2.

probable that these later decisions are due to Justinian. The last rests on *dolus*. But it is difficult to say that the earlier ones rest on mistake: the Roman view seems rather to be that the agreement is void for lack of subject-matter. Another text lays down the rule of voidness and says nothing about state of knowledge,[1] and we are told also that there is no sale unless there is a thing to be sold.[2] Where the impossibility is not patent, our system seems to give a similar result in practice, though the principle is not easily made out. It is clear that impossibility, however absolute, is not necessarily a defence: a man may be understood to have warranted possibility.[3] But where a subject-matter, essential to the bargain, has ceased to exist at the time of the contract, or, in fact, never did exist, the Courts have repeatedly held the agreement inoperative. In *Couturier* v. *Hastie*[4] the Court said that the contract 'imports that there was something which was to be sold at the time of the contract' and that 'what the parties contemplated . . . was that there was an existing something to be sold and bought', an attitude very like that of the Roman law. In *Clifford* v. *Watts*[5] the view taken was that there was an implied term that the subject-matter should exist, which is much the same, and in *Scott* v. *Coulson*[6] a similar decision was put on the ground of mistake. But again, as in Roman law, a promisor who, knowing that the circumstances are such as to make performance by him extremely difficult or even impossible, nevertheless makes an unqualified promise to do something, is bound by it.[7]

---

[1] D. 18. 1. 15. *pr.*
[2] D. 18. 1. 8. *pr.* Savigny, for these reasons, holds that the decision has nothing to do with mistake. *System*, iii. p. 303.
[3] *Hills* v. *Sughrue* (1846), 15 M. and W. 253.
[4] (1856), 5 H.L. 673, 681.
[5] (1870), L.R. 5 C.P. 577.
[6] [1903] 2 Ch. 249.
[7] *Jervis* v. *Tomkinson* (1806), 1 H. and N. 195.

EXCURSUS: MISTAKE

The account given in the text needs supplementing for two reasons: first, the outlines of the English law of mistake seem now tolerably clear, whatever may be thought of their justice or of the way they work in practice; secondly, it seems possible to make more pointed and detailed the comparison between the Roman doctrine of *error in substantia* and the English doctrine, so far as one can be said to exist.

The text very properly gives prominence[1] to the notion that the error must in both Roman and English law be a very important one, and indeed in both systems it is the exception rather than the rule for a person to be able to escape from contractual obligation on the ground that he has made a mistake. The view may be hazarded that so long as this point is kept in mind—and all the recent theorists of mistake so far have kept it in mind—the differences between the various theories are unlikely to be of great practical importance. Cases that are worth fighting on the ground of mistake are extraordinarily rare.

I believe that the account given of mistake in the second edition of Cheshire and Fifoot's *Law of Contract* is correct, but perhaps it may be useful to restate it in simpler, though not perhaps so accurate terms.

English law has accepted Savigny's distinction between the kind of mistake that induces a party to consent and the kind of mistake that excludes consent. To take the most obvious example: in the one case I say I would not have accepted your offer unless I had been acting under the influence of a mistake. In the other case I say the result of my making this particular mistake is that I did not accept your offer at all; either I accepted somebody else's offer or the offer that I accepted was different in terms from the one you actually made.

[1] P. 201.

English law treats mistake of the former kind as going to motive, and therefore as irrelevant for purposes of mistake, unless the mistake amounts to thinking that the subject-matter of the contract existed whereas in fact it did not. Perhaps a mistake common to both parties as to the identity of the subject-matter has the same effect. Of course mistake inducing consent may be very relevant if induced by the other party, whether fraudulently or innocently, but in either case the contract will become voidable, not void, and innocent third parties who have acquired goods by reason of the contract will be protected.

It still seems correct[1] to say that a mistake of the second kind (i.e. one which excludes consent) is relevant only if the other party knew of the mistake, or perhaps if he ought to have known of it. If he did not know of the mistake then the parties are genuinely at cross purposes, and the view that the law takes of the resulting situation is that the Court must try to ascertain the sense of the contract, and for that purpose will ask what meaning would be given to it by a reasonable man. This may end in imposing upon the two parties a contract which is different from what either of them meant, but the method will usually work and will at any rate preserve almost all contracts from failing. However, in a few very exceptional cases the Court will find itself unable to give a clear and definite meaning to the contract because there is some latent ambiguity which cannot be resolved, even by the admission of oral evidence. But if a definite meaning can be given to the contract, then neither party will be allowed to slide away from it on the ground of mistake, unless his mistake was known to the other party.

There still remains the question what kind of mistake excluding consent will be treated as relevant, even when known to the other party. This question[2] has never been

---

[1] In spite of Mr T. H. Tylor's article in 11 *Mod. L.R.* pp. 257–268.
[2] As is said on p. 199.

properly worked out. Perhaps the majority of cases can be left to take care of themselves on the ground that they are comparatively unimportant or that mistakes as to some minor point in the contract would be very unlikely to be known to the other party. All one can say, for the moment, is that mistakes as to the identity of the other party or of the object of the contract, or as to the existence or non-existence of some express term, have been declared to be relevant, and that probably a mistake known to the other party as to the price would also be considered relevant; but it seems unlikely that the Courts would go much further.

The *non est factum* cases undoubtedly cause difficulties in formulating a law of mistake in contract; for in none of them was the party seeking to hold the mistaken party to the contract aware of his mistake, and yet in several of them he failed. I think that quite a fair defence can be made for some of these decisions and even for the decision in *Carlisle and Cumberland Banking Co. v. Bragg.*[1] In all the cases in which effect has been given to the doctrine a fraudulent person has been careful not to bring the parties to the contract face to face, but to constitute himself a messenger of a document which he has induced the one party mistakenly to execute in favour of the other party. It may be thought that the law would have been better had the Court in *Bragg's Case* held that Bragg must pay for his carelessness in executing the guarantee, but there may also be some doubt whether it was altogether businesslike of the bank to act upon the supposed guarantee without communicating with Bragg. It is perhaps not unreasonable to say that a party who acts upon a document purporting to be signed by somebody not in his presence should take the risk of its turning out to be something other than it purports to be, and it is not unreasonable that some distinction should be made between negotiable instruments

[1] [1911] 1 K.B. 489.

and other documents.[1] However, there seems to be no good reason for extending the doctrine of *non est factum* so as to cover the whole law of mistake—which is what would happen if the one party's knowledge or ignorance of the other party's mistake were considered irrelevant.

It is when one comes to the application of these rules that one finds difficulties; in particular it is not always easy to know whether a party has mistaken the identity or only the attributes of the other party. The difficulty is all the more disturbing because the person really affected by the distinction is not usually the party mistaken, still less the other party to the contract, who has almost invariably been fraudulent, but a third party who has acquired goods innocently from a fraudulent buyer; and he is the person least likely to know anything about the distinction. In the circumstances it is not altogether surprising to find that the decision in *Cundy* v. *Lindsay*,[2] which protected the mistaken party against the innocent third party, does not seem ever to have been followed, at any rate in England, in a case where a third party was affected. Am I wrong in detecting both in the *King's Norton Metal Co.* v. *Edridge*,[3] and in *Phillips* v. *Brooks*,[4] an obvious desire on the part of the judges to escape from the hideous logic of *Cundy* v. *Lindsay*?

This distinction between identity and attributes forms a natural bridge between English law and the Roman doctrine of *error in substantia*.

There seems to be no doubt that the English law of mistake makes no distinction between one attribute of a thing and another, and therefore it is of no use to single out one particular attribute as appertaining to the substance of the thing. On the other hand, as Professor

---

[1] To decide otherwise would perhaps imply the acceptance of all documents as bearer documents.

[2] (1878), 3 App. Cas. 459. [3] (1897), 14 T.L.R. 98.

[4] [1919] 2 K.B. 243.

Glanville Williams has shown,[1] identity is only determined by a combination of attributes; thus English law is in fact bound to take notice of attributes if they are so important as to determine identity. However, there is no doubt whatever that the English law of mistake always looks beyond the attributes to the resulting identity; but it would be quite possible for a law, while regarding a mistake as to identity as the only relevant mistake, to concentrate on the mistaken attributes which led to the mistake of identity, and if it did so, there might well be a tendency to say that any attributes which determined the substance of the thing were relevant even though they did not actually determine its identity. It is quite possible that this is the way the Roman jurists approached the problem of *error in substantia*.

Nevertheless the doctrine seems to us dangerous, and it is no great consolation to be told that in any case the Roman law of contract placed much greater emphasis than English law on actual consensus and left very little room for the notion of reliance on the other party's words and acts. In practice the two laws were probably not so far apart. Let us take for instance a case like *Smith* v. *Hughes*.[2] English law lays emphasis upon two separate points: it says that in any case the contract would not be void against Smith if he did not know of the mistake, and secondly that even if he did know of the mistake, the mistake would be irrelevant unless it was as to a term of the contract, and not merely as to an attribute of the thing sold. As to the first point, the only definite rule we find in Roman law is that the mistake will not be relevant if it is clearly due to the mistaken party's own fault. That would cut out most of the cases; but further, the party alleging mistake would surely have had to prove his mistake. How could he do it to the satisfaction of the judge? In most cases he would have to show that the price he had agreed to pay was intelligible

[1] 23 *Can.B.R.* p. 273.   [2] (1871), L.R. 6 Q.B. 597.

upon the basis of the mistaken attribute, but not otherwise. But if he could prove so much, the inference would be almost inevitable in many cases that the other party knew or ought to have known of the mistake. There would still however remain some cases where one party could convince the judge that he had been mistaken, but not that the other party had known of his mistake; and in these cases Roman law would treat the contract as void, whilst English law would treat it as valid.

On the second point there is an undoubted difficulty: Roman law does not make any clear distinction between a mistake as to an attribute and a mistake as to a term, or, to put the distinction as it arose in *Smith* v. *Hughes*,[1] between a quality and a promised quality. As to this, two particular points may be made: the first is that the English distinction must be very difficult to draw in practice, and a judge or jury faced with evidence which seemed to point to a mere mistake as to an important attribute would be inclined to scent fraud if the other party had been aware of it, and would very probably take the short additional step of finding that the mistake went beyond the mere attribute and extended to an actual term of the contract—in other words, that the mistaken party thought, not merely that the thing he would get had a particular attribute, but that the other party was promising that attribute. The second point is that the Roman solution is very much in line with the Roman treatment of liability for secret defects of quality. If the rule is, as in English law, *caveat emptor*, then the corollary is that, leaving on one side the implied conditions in the Sale of Goods Act, I must bargain specially for every quality that I want the subject-matter of the contract to possess, and inevitably the only sort of mistake that will be relevant will be one that relates to whether I have successfully bargained for the quality or not. But in Roman law the position was quite different.

[1] (1871), L.R. 6 Q.B. 597.

Whatever may have been the limits of the implied warranties of quality in classical law, the whole atmosphere of the contract of sale (which is alone in question in these cases) is one of good faith. A buyer is entitled to assume that a seller will deliver goods of proper quality, and of the kind which he is likely to want. No doubt the parties are entitled to overreach each other as regards price, but the whole atmosphere of the contract is against such overreaching in respect of the nature or quality of the goods. In these circumstances it would be unreasonable to place the requirements of mistake as high as in English law. One cannot go so far as to say that a buyer is always entitled to expect that the goods shall be of precisely the kind that he wants, but it will not be unreasonable to say that he can treat the sale as void if he was mistaken as to some very important quality.

For we must always remember that it is not every attribute that goes to the substance of a thing. Whatever the correct meaning to be given to the word 'substance'—and it is admitted on all hands that there is great obscurity here—it is quite clear that it must be something very important.

This juxtaposition of *error in substantia* and the liability for secret defects of quality is not fanciful. In modern French law they are regularly confused, and in many cases where a buyer is unable, e.g. owing to lapse of time, to use his remedy for secret defects, and the defect proves to be serious enough to be considered one of substance, an attempt is made to treat the sale as voidable for *error in substantia*.[1]

At first sight another difference seems to exist between Roman and English law, for although no criterion of *substantia* has been found to satisfy all critics, it seems at any rate to have had some connexion with the nature of the thing itself, which is the subject-matter of the contract. On the other hand there seems to be no reason why a contract should not be treated as void in English law,

[1] 52 *L.Q.R.* 99.

owing to a mistake of one party known to the other, even though the mistake does not relate to the actual thing, but to some term in the contract not connected with the thing itself. It would seem then that the contract in *Smith* v. *Hughes*[1] could, in Roman law, have been treated as void only if the judge was prepared to say that the goods had a substance different from that which they were supposed to have by the other party, whereas in English law the actual substance or quality of the goods seems irrelevant, and the only relevant consideration can be the existence or non-existence of a term in the contract. However, the difference is probably illusory, for Roman law treated mere passive acquiescence in the self-deception of the other party as *dolus*, and therefore a party could not have held the other party to a contract when he knew that that other party was mistaken as to the existence or non-existence of a term. Undoubtedly the presence of *dolus* would have made the contract not void, but voidable, but the Roman texts afford us no example of a case comparable to *Cundy* v. *Lindsay*[2] in which the rights of an innocent third party are at stake.

It seems that the text is correct[3] when it says that before the Judicature Acts a Court of Equity would have rescinded a contract on grounds of mistake in circumstances in which a common law Court would not have treated the mistake as making a contract void; and further that the common law Courts had taken over a good deal of the jurisdiction before those acts came into force. It has recently been suggested in the very remarkable case of *Solle* v. *Butcher*[4] that this development, which involved declaring contracts void *ab initio* which would have better been rescinded, was unfortunate, and that now that all judges of the High Court have power to award both common law and equitable remedies, this particular de-

---

[1] (1871), L.R. 6 Q.B. 597.   [2] (1878), 3 App. Cas. 459.
[3] See pp. 201–202, *ante*.   [4] [1950] 1 K.B. 671.

velopment should be forgotten, and we should return to the practice of awarding only equitable remedies in cases which would have been dealt with in equity before the middle of the nineteenth century. This would have the further advantage of allowing the Court in a very large number of cases to grant rescission to the plaintiff only on terms.[1]

There is much to be said for the view that all cases of mistake should be subjected to the discretionary action of the judge, at any rate all the cases in which the two parties to the action are innocent. In the nature of things mistakes of this kind are very hard to guard against, and parties do not draft their agreements on the faith of a settled law of mistake, which would be disturbed by discretionary action. Moreover, in almost every case where both parties are innocent it is at present largely a matter of chance which of them succeeds; and success does not always come to the more innocent or more careful party. Whether the suggested procedure can be made to apply to all cases of mistake where both parties are innocent, may be a matter of some doubt. There will probably always be a hard residue of cases which will have to be decided at common law, and will receive the rough justice which is all that common law can give.

So far there are very few instances from which one could conjecture the terms that a Court of Equity would impose as a condition of rescission; relief seems to be modelled very closely on that granted for innocent misrepresentation, from which no doubt mistake is not easily distinguishable in respect of the treatment it receives from equity. It would be very interesting to see whether cases arising out of mistakes as to the identity or attributes of the parties could be thrown into equity, and if so whether, in a proper case, a Court would feel itself at liberty to apportion the damage caused by a guilty third person between the two parties to the suit.

[1] The terms offered to the plaintiff in that case were of a very complicated nature.

3. POSITION OF THIRD PARTIES

Both the Roman and the English law have the principle
that a third party cannot be liable or entitled under a contract, and the Roman law had not the conception of
agency, which lessens the field of application of the rule
in our law. But both systems have found the rule inconvenient, at least as to the acquisition of rights by third
parties, and have circumvented it in different ways. In
Roman law the method is not systematic: an equitable
action (*actio utilis*) was given to the third party in a number
of cases in which justice or convenience seemed to require
it. We do not know how the action was formulated—in
many cases it is later than the abolition of the formulary
system—but the fact that it is an equitable action and not
a direct action on the contract shows that it is in no way
meant to break with the principle that third parties cannot
acquire rights under contracts. In our system the trust
principle is invoked with very similar results. Where the
Court thinks that justice requires that third parties should
have a remedy it constructs a trust in their favour, even
though the parties to the contract have not used the language usually associated with trusts; but it must be admitted that the occasions on which the Courts have been
willing to do this have been very rare. In the United
States a different road has been followed. Disapproval has
been expressed with our way of dealing with the matter:
the trust, it is said, is a figment, and we are in fact giving
rights to third parties under the contract, but in an un-
necessarily clumsy way.[1] American Courts prefer not to
use this device (though at least one jurisdiction resorts to
'equity procedure' for the purpose), but to say that there
are cases in which a third party can acquire rights under
the contract. It is however clear that the rule cannot be
that in every case in which a third party is an intended

---

[1] See, e.g., Corbin, 46 *L.Q.R.* (1930) pp. 12 *sqq.*

beneficiary he will have an action. That would do great injustice, e.g., where nothing has been actually done or
communicated to the third party and the contracting
parties wish to vary or revoke their agreement. Indeed, as
Professor Corbin says:[1] 'it cannot be said that the exact
limits within which the rule is to be applied have been
clearly established; these limits are in process of establishment as new cases arise.' That is perhaps to understate the
matter: it is difficult to find a principle in the American
cases, so far as they have gone. The American method
seems on the whole less logical, for our view recognises
the fact that the relation is unilateral: the third party is in
no sense a party to the contract. He is not in any way
bound by it, though it may well be that some act of his is
a condition on his obtaining the rights. The doctrine which
constructs a trust in proper cases seems more *elegans* in the
Roman sense. It is also more elastic: it gives the judge a very
free hand. It is for him to decide whether he thinks on the
facts of the case, which are infinitely variable, that a trust
should be constructed.[2] A rule dealing with the matter as
one of pure contract, as is proposed in the 'Restatement' of
the American Law Institute, may not be so easily manipu-
lated. This may be an advantage; at any rate it is a difference.

The Roman law seems to have started on lines somewhat similar to our own. Breach of faith in deposit was an
actionable wrong long before the conception of deposit as
a contract had been reached;[3] and it is noticeable that the

---

[1] At p. 13.

[2] Unfortunately one cannot now take so optimistic a view as that expressed above. The Courts seem strangely loath to imply a trust except
where there is a very definite custom in favour of using documents purporting to create third-party rights. On the other hand, it may reasonably
be said that, owing to the existence of the trust, and of other institutions
unknown to Continental law, the field within which third-party rights
have a chance of performing a useful function is much narrower here.

[3] Coll. 10. 7. 11, from P. Sent., *'lege duodecim tabularum'*. It is perhaps
worth while to note the helpful part played by Deceit in the efforts of the
common law to develop *assumpsit*. For *dolus* generally, see pp. 383 *sqq., post.*

earliest text on our subject, i.e. independent of Justinian, deals with deposit. It says that if *A* deposits with *B* and *B* redeposits with *C*, which may often be a proper thing to do, *A* has an *actio* against *C*.[1] This can hardly be contemplated as giving a right under the contract between *B* and *C*, for so far as appears *A* was not mentioned in it. Still less can we think of an obligation on *C* under the contract between *A* and *B*: here *C* was in no way contemplated. But in fact, though the action is *actio depositi utilis*, it is not really thought of in terms of contract. Nor, in fact, can we think of the matter in terms of trust, for *C* can hardly be under a trust in favour of *A*, of whom or of any interest of whom he has no knowledge whatever. It is, however, a rule somewhat late to develop, for in earlier law it does not seem that *A* would have had any action against *C*, though he could claim a transfer of the action of *B* against *C*.[2] Again Diocletian provided that if *A* deposited property with *B* or lent it to him on the terms that he was to redeliver it to *C*, *C* had an *actio utilis* against *B*.[3] This looks more like contract or trust, for *C* is expressly contemplated in the original contract. But in fact no attempt is made to rest it on any principle of law: the reason given in the text is *propter aequitatis rationem*. So too where *A* made a *donatio* to *B* on the terms that he was at a later date to hand the thing on to *C*, Diocletian says that earlier Emperors had enacted that *C* should have an *actio utilis* 'juxta donatoris voluntatem';[4] and it has been shown that this had nothing to do with contract,[5] but was a *condictio* for the recovery of property unjustly detained. It looks more like trust than contract, but it is in fact no more than a sporadic decision on general grounds of equity. There

---

[1] Coll. 10. 7. 8, from P. Sent.
[2] D. 16. 3. 16, which, as often, retains the older rule.
[3] C. Just. 3. 42. 8. 1.
[4] Vat. Fr. 286; C. Just. 8. 54. 3.
[5] Eisele, *Beiträge*, p. 83.

are a few other cases in the texts. An *actio utilis* was given where it had been agreed that at the end of the marriage the *dos* was to be handed over to a third party,[1] and where a pledgee had sold the pledge on the terms that the debtor was to have the right to rebuy it for the amount of the debt.[2] Where a debtor to a ward had made a promise (*constitutum*) to the *tutor* that he would pay the debt on a certain day, the ward had an action *utilitatis gratia*.[3] Where a principal had made an agreement not to be sued, his surety could use it, as otherwise the agreement would be illusory.[4] The cases are few and some of them are due to Justinian, but it still remained true that on principle a third party could not acquire rights under a contract.

4. AGENCY

It was observed above that Roman law had not the relief afforded by the conception of agency: something should here be said of the sense in which and the extent to which this is true.

For the purpose of this discussion 'agency' means the system under which *B*, authorised by *A*, may go through a transaction on behalf of *A*, with *C*, with the result that all the effects of the transaction, all the rights and liabilities created by it, will take effect between *A* and *C*, *B* having no concern whatever with them and acting merely as a conduit pipe. There are of course limits. In our law *A* cannot authorise *B* to marry a lady on behalf of *A*, or to make a will for *A*, though *A* can authorise *B* to sign his (*A*'s) will in his presence.[5] But our law gives a very wide effect to the principle of agency. It is not necessary for *C* to be informed of the identity of *A*, and even though the fact that *B* is acting for a principal is not disclosed, some

---

[1] C. 5. 14. 7.
[2] D. 13. 7. 13. pr.   [3] D. 13. 5. 5. 9.
[4] D. 2. 14. 21. 5. For other cases see Buckland, *Text-book*, p. 427.
[5] Wills Act, 1837, sect. 9.

of the effects of agency are produced. *A* is liable and entitled, but so is *B*. Though French and German law have accepted, inevitably, the principle of agency, they do not accept this last development. Karlowa goes so far as to say that an undisclosed principal 'würde juristisch gar keine Bedeutung haben'.[1]

Modern life could hardly be carried on without agency. In view of the importance of commerce in the Roman Empire and of the distance between commercial centres and slow means of communication, it would seem that the same must have been true for Rome, and yet agency, as we understand the notion, was in fact unknown to the Romans in the law of contract. Such approximations as they made to it were really by a quite different road. The Roman governing principle is expressed in the rule that a man cannot bind, or acquire for, a third party. The structure of the Roman family, however, lessened the inconvenience. Every 'real' right and every right of action acquired by a subordinate member of the family, son or slave, vested in the *paterfamilias*, and a man of affairs would commonly have, as Cicero had, slaves in other places than that in which he lived. But this rests on the unity of the family. Modern writers speak of it as 'representation' or *Stellvertretung*, but this is not the notion. The rule operates though the transaction was unauthorised or was even forbidden. And at civil law the liabilities do not affect the *pater*: moreover, although the slave cannot be civilly liable, the son is, though he has no property.[2] It is true that the *paterfamilias* could not enforce the contract without doing his part, but it could not be enforced against him. It is true also that the Praetor remedied the unfairness by giving actions against the *paterfamilias*, but these

---

[1] *Röm. Rechtsg.* ii. p. 1129, 'would have absolutely no juristic significance'. But this view is not invariably taken; cf. Goldschmidt, *English Law from the Foreign Standpoint*, p. 202.

[2] G. 3. 104.

do not depend on representation. The son or slave cannot have been a very useful instrument in commerce so long as the civil law stood by itself, and the Praetor's rule makes him much more useful. So far as a juristic basis must be sought it may be found in the principle of taking risks: one who sets up a man with the means of trading with third persons (*peculium*), and so induces them to deal with him, ought within limits to take the resulting risks. There was a further extension. If *A* set up an outsider to manage a business (*institor*) he was liable, again within certain limits, on all contracts in connexion with the business. But here too it is a question of taking risks, not of representation.[1] There is no notion of 'extension of the personality' or the like, as is shown by the fact that in general the appointor does not acquire rights under the contracts made by the outsider and by the further fact that the actual contracting party (or his master, if he is a *servus alienus*) is both liable and entitled.[2] The same result is ultimately reached where, apart from permanent appointment, *A* authorises *B* to make a contract on his behalf: i.e. *A*, the appointor, becomes liable under the contract so made but, apart from some rather doubtful cases, seems to depend for his rights against the third party on the not very satisfactory expedient of assignment.[3]

Outside the field of contract there was a little closer approximation to agency. There was indeed an overriding rule that, apart from certain exceptions within the family, no *iuris civilis* 'act in the law' could be done by a representative. The *heres* himself must make the act of entry on the *hereditas*. The parties themselves must make a *mancipatio* or a *cessio in iure*. But a power of alienation and acquisition through persons not members of the family, by

---

[1] *Actio institoria*, D. 14. 3. See also the analogous *actio exercitoria* for shipmasters, D. 14. 1.

[2] Details, Buckland, *Text-book*, p. 535.

[3] Buckland, *Text-book*, p. 519. See pp. 309–310, *post*.

the informal method of delivery, *traditio*, was reached by a devious route which had nothing to do with the conception of agency. It had always been possible to use an intermediary for the purely ministerial act of delivery or receipt, a *nuntius*, and it did not matter who he was. But, for the actual negotiation, the actual intent to transfer or to receive ownership (we need not here consider whether this is the exact way in which to describe the necessary intent), it was long inconceivable for this to be in some person other than the real transferor or transferee. Possession or non-possession was thought of as matter of fact. If my employee held a thing of mine, he had not possession of it but only, as we should say, custody; he *detinet* the thing. But if he gives the thing away and so loses control, then, whatever happens to the ownership, at any rate I lose possession. The same would be true if I told him to hand over the thing to someone else, e.g. a buyer. Thus if the owner had the necessary intent the ownership would pass with the possession. In the first century jurists began to ask whether, if the owner had manifested his willingness that ownership should pass at the discretion of the representative, it should not be possible for him to negotiate transfers and deal with the thing as if he were owner; and by the second century we get the clear rule that a procurator or general business manager, having a general authority to alienate, could validly transfer ownership. It was not quite so simple in acquisition, for possession by the procurator was not necessarily possession by the principal. But this step also was taken, and where a duly authorised procurator took possession, e.g. of a thing he had bought for his principal, both the ownership and the possession were regarded as vesting in the employer. At some later time the obvious corollary was drawn that the same principle would apply to other than general procurators and the rule appeared that an alienation or acquisition could be effected for me by anyone whom I authorised to act even for one transaction only. If

I instructed *B* to sell or buy a horse for me, he could carry out the negotiations and the receipt or delivery of the horse by him would complete the transaction and create or determine my ownership. This is no doubt agency, but does not express any principle of agency. There was no such principle; the rule was brought about without any theorising, even subconscious, about representation. This is shown by the very limited effect of the rule. It dealt only with the passing of property and possession: the rights and liabilities under the contract remained with the intermediary and would need to be expressly transferred. Except to the extent that we have seen, there was no agency in the law of contract.

We also find something like representation in connexion with procedure, but that will be more conveniently dealt with later.

5. CONSIDERATION

It is commonly said, and in a certain sense the statement is correct, that Roman law had no doctrine of consideration: there was in fact no rule that every promise must have, as a condition of its validity, consideration in the sense of a *quid pro quo*. If, by *stipulatio*, *A* promised *B* 100 *aurei*, it would be no reply to *B*'s action that there was no consideration, that *A* had no benefit, or that *B* incurred no detriment. Something which looks much the same may be said of our law: if a man makes a promise in a certain form, i.e. under seal, the fact that there was no *quid pro quo* is no answer to an action. But in fact the situation is very different. Roman law had no general theory of contract, but a definite list of contracts, each with its own special rules; just as, according to one opinion, we have no general theory of tort but only a list of torts, each with its own special rules. The only contract which was flexible and capable of application to any purpose was *stipulatio*, and it did not require a *quid pro quo*: it was strictly unilateral. But consideration in its simple sense of *quid pro quo* plays a considerable part in various contracts, and indeed in all countries by far the greater number of contracts made from day to day are supported by consideration. In sale and hire a money price is an essential. In *societas* there must be a contribution from each side. In the innominate contracts there must be undertaking of service both ways. In loan of money or other fungibles (*mutuum*) it is obvious that consideration has been given by the lender, who alone can sue on what is essentially a unilateral contract. So too, although for the Romans *commodatum* and *depositum* were essentially gratuitous, and although we are now returning to the older common law habit of treating them generally as bailments, something which would satisfy our modern sophisticated notion of consideration may be found in them by men of good will: it is indeed obvious that the *commodator* and the depositee furnish consideration, but the depositor also parts with the physical possession of his goods, and even the *commodatarius* may be said to subject himself to a certain risk of damage in handling something, possibly dangerous, which he has borrowed. And something of the sort can be found in pledge, and in *constitutum*, a formless promise to pay an existing debt, your own or another's. In the various cases in which consideration is required its character is obvious and does not in fact give rise to the questions which have arisen in our law on the matter. It might be possible to show from the texts that, where consideration is necessary, it must not be a past consideration, that it must move from the promisee and that it need not move to the promisor, but to do this is to falsify the institutions: the Romans did not think in terms of consideration. But it may be worth while to note that precisely because consideration was not a factor which had always to be found at all cost, the Romans could dispense with those subterfuges which disfigure our law. Since a debt could be released for nothing there was no need or temptation to hold that a canary was a good consideration for a release of a debt of £500. On the other hand where consideration was required, it had to be a real consideration, not necessarily adequate but at any rate real. Each partner must make a substantial contribution. If the price or hire fixed under an alleged sale or hire was obviously derisory, or it was known that it was not meant to be paid, the transaction was not a sale or hire: it was a mere *donatio* and was governed by the very different rules of that institution.[1]

None of the modern systems based on Roman law has any theory of consideration and the German Bürgerliches Gesetzbuch, a highly eclectic system in which Roman and Germanic law are blended, has nothing of the kind. But some other systems have a principle which somewhat resembles consideration, and is called 'cause', which is supposed to originate in Roman law. The evidence for the conception of *causa* as a requisite in Roman law is twofold. There is a text, which may not be classical but is certainly in the *Corpus Juris*, which says that 'cum nulla subest causa praeter conventionem' it is a *nudum pactum*, i.e. unenforceable.[2] This text at least suggests that contract needed *causa* as well as consent. Further, there are texts which say that an agreement is void or voidable if it rests on an illicit or non-existent *causa*. The texts of the first group have been those mainly used to demonstrate the need of *causa*, but, explicit as they look, they are worthless for the purpose. The main difficulty to be faced in using these texts to support the dogma of *causa* is that there are four contracts in Roman law which are binding by mere consent, so that it is impossible to find a *causa praeter conventionem*. Various attempts have been made to surmount the difficulty, but the fact is that these contracts will not fit the notion. What the language of the text cited means is that an agreement is not a contract unless the law has made it

[1] D. 18. 1. 36; 19. 2. 20. 1; C. 4. 38. 3.
[2] D. 2. 14. 7. 4; see also D. 15. 1. 49. 2.

such; it is an expression of the distinction already mentioned between the Roman conception of contract and ours. As Bonfante has put it,[1] the *causa* of the contract is the *voluntas legis* in antithesis to the *voluntas* of the parties. Merely to say that you owe money does not make you owe it.[2]

But there is another group of texts to be considered. We are told that an undertaking for no *causa* or a false *causa* is void and there is a *condictio sine causa* for recovering what is paid without *causa*, and an *exceptio* to resist payment where what was paid can be recovered. In all this the word *causa* is prominent.[3] There is also *condictio ex turpi causa* for recovery of what is paid for illicit purposes where the payer was innocent. *Causa* is, however, a vague word and it does not seem to be used in either of these cases in the same sense as it is in the text with which we began.[4] In that text, if we make it mean more than the fact that the law has attached obligation to the undertaking, it must mean any circumstance of any kind which has led the law to attach obligation. But in *condictio sine causa* and similar cases it means some economic advantage (not necessarily to the promisee) or detriment undertaken, in fact something at first sight very like our doctrine of consideration in contract. This is entirely different and again it does not justify the view that *causa* was essential to contract. If I pay you money thinking I owe it when I do not, I can recover what I have paid (*condictio indebiti*). If I pay you money to constitute a wife's *dos* in a forthcoming marriage, and the marriage does not take place, I can recover the money (*condictio sine causa*).[5] If I give you money on the understanding that you will do something, and you fail to do it, I can recover the money (*condictio ob rem dati, causa data causa non secuta*).[6] In our language this is failure of

---

[1] *Scritti giuridici*, iii. p. 134.   [2] D. 15. 1. 49. 2.
[3] D. 12. 4–7, *passim*.   [4] D. 2. 14. 7. 4.
[5] D. 12. 7. 5.   [6] D. 12. 4.

consideration. Notwithstanding the name *condictio sine causa* and the language of D. 12. 7. 1. 2, these are all cases where the money can be recovered, not because there was no *causa*, but because a *causa* was assumed as the basis of the contract and this *causa* did not in fact exist. In another case, *condictio ob turpem causam*,[1] it means something different again. It is some ulterior motive or purpose. It has nothing to do with *causa* as a binding element. If I let to *B* a house with the intent that he shall use it as a brothel, this is void in all systems of law. Here the contract is formally correct: the *causa* which makes a contract good can have nothing to do with the *causa* which makes it bad. If I was innocent, no party to the ulterior purpose, I can rescind the contract because this remoter *causa* exists. Obviously we are here talking of something entirely different: it is not the consideration for, or the content of, either promise. It is the vitiating ulterior purpose.

The medieval lawyers made the principle of *causa* the basis of their system of contract, and from them the principle has passed into modern continental law, not in Germany, but in France and Italy and elsewhere. But the conception is unmanageable and it was long ago observed by Bonfante that it is the most discussed and most 'indecipherable' problem of modern legal doctrine, the battle ground for metaphysical elucubrations and juridical psychology.[2] If this is so for Italy it is certainly not less so for France. *Cause* is not *quid pro quo*, for intent to donate is a *cause*. It is not motive, for motive, in general, is indifferent. It is sometimes defined as the immediate aim, as opposed to ulterior motives, sometimes as the 'objective' motive. Yet the French Code Civil deals with '*cause illicite*', which is much the same as the Roman *turpis causa*, 'ulterior motive', but groups it with '*sans cause*' (*sine causa*) and '*fausse cause*' (*falsa causa*) as if *cause* were

[1] D. 12. 5.   [2] *Scr. Giur.* iii. p. 125.

used in the same sense in all three cases.[1] In fact so wide is
the conception of *cause* if it is to be found wherever there
is a binding contract, that it becomes meaningless: as has
been said, no one but a lunatic could possibly set out to
contract an obligation without a cause in this sense. It is,
however, firmly embodied in the Code Civil, art. 1131,
which rejects an obligation *sans cause*. The question of the
value of the conception has been much discussed both in
France and in Italy, but need not be here considered.[2] Our
only concern with the matter is to suggest that it is not really
to be based on the Roman law, as expressed in the texts.

Our law escaped the confusion surrounding the notion
of *causa*, but it might have been otherwise. In the twelfth
century the ecclesiastical Courts were enforcing certain
agreements on the basis of breach of faith, but were
warned off the ground by the Constitutions of Clarendon,[3]
and ultimately acquiesced in this prohibition, though from
time to time and 'as late as 1460'[4] the common law judges
found it necessary to crush their attempts to acquire a
general jurisdiction over contracts by means of suits *pro
laesione fidei*. In the sixteenth century when the common
law courts had evolved a general remedy for the non-
performance of promises, and appear to have been casting
about to find some limiting test of their actionability, the
danger of *causa* might have arisen again, because the
medieval chancellors had been busy working out 'a theory
of contract based on the canonist idea of *causa*';[5] but by
this time the battle was over, and while the 'Doctor' of
Divinity might refer to 'cause' the 'Student' in the Laws
of England would have none of it.[6]

---

[1] C.C. art. 1131.

[2] For the views of some critics, see Walton, 41 *L.Q.R.* (1925) pp. 306
sqq.; Amos and Walton, *Introduction to French Law*, pp. 162 *sqq.*

[3] Glanvill, x. 12, who uses the word '*causa*' in x. 2 and elsewhere,
though perhaps without much knowledge of its meaning.

[4] Holdsworth, ii. p. 305.   [5] Holdsworth, iii. p. 413.

[6] *Doctor and Student*, Second Dialogue, c. xxiv.

Whether the common law did well to adopt consideration as the basis of the simple contract, and whence that doctrine was evolved, are questions which do not concern us here. The Roman law of contract required neither a doctrine of *causa* nor a doctrine of consideration, for the same reason that enabled our law of covenants, or contracts under seal, to dispense with any doctrine of consideration. Various types of agreement were successively made binding for reasons which appeared sufficient in each case, just as sealed documents were made binding in our law. The common law, however, finding the sealed covenant inadequate to meet the needs of the community, developed Assumpsit as a general remedy for unsealed promises, and then required the presence of certain facts or circumstances as a condition of the enforceability of promises by that action; and most people, when making a promise designed to have legal effects, expect to get something for it, which is the predominant though not the exclusive element in consideration.[1]

Causa as a legal concept thus appears to be a sophisticated medieval attempt to generalise the various reasons which led the Roman law to recognise as binding various types of agreement. Consideration, as originally developed, was a piece of practical machinery for deciding whether or not a promise ought to be enforced by one of the personal actions and particularly by *assumpsit*; it was in fact just because we had evolved, not a general theory of contract, but a general remedy for its enforcement, that

---

[1] Is it not possible that we might have escaped the doctrine of consideration entirely if the judges of the sixteenth and seventeenth centuries had preferred to adopt as a test of enforceability the difference between a promise intended to affect the promisor in his legal relations and one intended to affect only his social relations or his duties as a man of honour? See, for instance, *Weeks* v. *Tybald* (1604), Noy 11 ('general words spoken to excite suitors'); *Balfour* v. *Balfour*, [1919] 2 K.B. 571; *Rose and Frank Co.* v. *Crompton*, [1923] 2 K.B. 261; [1925] A.C. 445. The consideration test may have appeared simpler, but it has led to much artificiality.

we felt the need of some such test. It was precisely
because the Roman law had no such general theory, but
only a specified list of enforceable agreements, that it had
no need of any such test.

Our doctrine of consideration has become so artificial
in modern times that it is not now possible to speak of it
as *quid pro quo*. It has thus been said that it is essentially
a 'form'[1] in the sense that it is an element additional to
consent, necessary to make the agreement binding. It
should, however, be borne in mind that there is another
and more fundamental meaning of 'form'. In the earlier
Roman law, and to some extent in our own law, 'form'
was not an element added to consent: it was an element
which made the transaction binding whether there was
consent or not. Indeed it is not easy to see much difference
between 'form' in Mr Justice Holmes' sense and the
notion of *causa*.

EXCURSUS: CAUSE AND CONSIDERATION

The problem of *cause* has much exercised the minds of
French jurists in recent years. Its presence is expressly
required in the Code Civil,[2] and the need for it was more
or less accepted as a matter of course throughout the nineteenth century. However, after one or two unimportant
and ineffectual attacks it was subjected about 1900 to the
more dangerous onslaught of Marcel Planiol,[3] who expressed in no uncertain terms the view that it was a quite
unnecessary concept and that the law would in practice be
exactly the same if it were entirely abolished. Although
Planiol's view has not on the whole been accepted,
he forced all serious jurists to reconsider their position,
and in spite of a valiant effort by Henri Capitant[4] to

---

[1] See, e.g., Holmes, *The Common Law*, p. 273.
[2] Arts. 1108, 1131.
[3] See *Traité élémentaire de Droit civil* (ed. 1949), ii. no. 291.
[4] See *De la Cause des Obligations* (3rd ed. 1928).

reconstitute a single coherent theory of *cause*, I think it must now be accepted that *cause* has not one single meaning, but at least three. None of the three concepts which are known by this name can be dispensed with, and all of them can be traced back to the Roman texts.

For the sake of clarity, one must distinguish from them not only the *iusta causa* which plays such an important part in the law of property, but also *causa* in connexion with the general law of obligations. This latter is the *causa* mentioned in the text on p. 223. For an obligation to be valid it must be supported by some cause, but it is clear that in a contractual obligation the cause is the contract itself just as in other circumstances it might be quasi-contract, delict, or quasi-delict. We are obviously not speaking there of the cause of a contract.

(1) The famous passage[1] on which the whole theory of *cause* was based, and which was taken to mean that every contract must have a *cause*, in reality says nothing of the kind. It distinguishes between agreements which have been recognised as nominate contracts, such as sale and hire, and agreements for which no special régime has been laid down. Then it goes on to say that in all these latter cases there will still be an action provided that there is also *cause*. The text, which may well be due to the compilers, clearly deals with what later came to be known as the innominate contracts, and *causa* here means what English lawyers call executed consideration. The contracts are of the type *do ut des*, *do ut facias*, *facio ut des*, or *facio ut facias*. Then the passage goes on to say that if there is no *causa*, it is a case of *nudum pactum*, which will give rise to an exception but not to an action.

Causa is here evidently made to play a part only in the theory of the innominate contracts. It has nothing to do with the consensual contracts, which have always been recognised to present a serious difficulty, but it has also,

[1] D. 2. 14. 7. *pr.*–4.

for the purposes of this passage, nothing whatever to do with the real or verbal contracts either. In other words, all it says is that executed consideration is required where no régimes have been set up for particular contracts.

(2) The word *causa* is also used in connexion with the *condictio ob turpem causam*.[1] If a person has paid money to another person, or has done any performance for his benefit, under circumstances which, though not illegal or immoral as regards the performer, are illegal or immoral as regards the recipient, then the performer can recover his money or the value of his services. Here in strictness it is the cause of the obligation, not the cause of the contract, which is illegal or immoral, but it is very easy to apply the doctrine to the contract itself, so as to say that an illegal or immoral contract will be void because its cause is illegal or immoral. This reasoning can of course be made to apply to all kinds of contract, whether gratuitous or for an executed or for an executory consideration.

(3) The third Roman origin of the doctrine of *cause* is not associated with the word *causa*. It is best known by the term 'interdependence of promises'. In truth the Romans never developed it fully. Originally the obligations of the buyer and the seller were mutually independent, so that it was not open to either to refuse to perform his part on the ground that the other had already defaulted, or was not ready or willing to perform. He must still do his own part and then, if he wished, have recourse to an action for damages. By the classical period the rule had been mitigated at any rate to the extent of allowing either party to refuse to perform unless the other party was for his part ready and willing to perform.[2] This is known by the illogical name *exceptio non adimpleti contractus*. It was not pleaded as an *exceptio*, and the plaintiff would have to prove that he was ready and willing to perform. But the non-performance by one party neither

---

[1] See D. 12. 5.   [2] See G. 4. 120a; D. 19. 1. 25.

discharged the contract, nor provided the other party with a ground for rescission. No doubt in many cases a party could safely treat the contract as at an end, and in particular the buyer need not be troubled by the continued existence of the contract if the seller refused to deliver; for money has no earmark, and so long as the buyer kept enough money to pay the price, he was in no difficulty. But the position of the seller was a good deal more awkward, especially if he had sold a unique object, such as a piece of land, for, apart from express agreement, he would have to retain the land or other object in case the buyer later came along with the price and demanded delivery. The difficulty could be avoided by the insertion of a term known as *lex commissoria*,[1] which gave the seller an option of declaring the contract at an end if the buyer did not pay within the agreed time. This term probably became common form in Roman law, but was never implied. It always had to be expressly inserted in the contract. Where, of course, it was inserted the two promises became virtually interdependent. Not until the time of Lord Mansfield was a similar development complete in English law,[2] though in the end we carried it much further than the Romans. Even to this day the position of a disappointed party to a French contract is not quite so good as in England, for he has to sue for rescission, and the Court exercises a certain control.[3]

(4) Another source of the doctrine of *cause* has yet to be mentioned. It is well known that from early in the third century A.D. a written acknowledgement of debt could be met by the plea that the money had never been advanced (*exceptio non numeratae pecuniae*), though this was only available within a fairly short period of limitation. On the other hand it seems that by the time of Justinian[4] at any rate the acknowledgement could not be contested if it

---

[1] See D. 18. 3.   [2] See Holdsworth, viii. pp. 71–75.
[3] See Amos and Walton, *Introduction to French Law*, pp. 181–183.
[4] C. 4. 30. 13.

contained a declaration of the *causa* of the debt and unless, no doubt, the maker of the document could prove it was untrue. Thus one gets a distinction between what are called *cautio discreta* and *cautio indiscreta*, the former containing an indication of the cause of the debt, and the other containing no such indication. The canonists took up this notion seriously, for they feared that abstract promises, that is to say promises not disclosing the cause for which they were made, might conceal something that would not bear the light of day; therefore they insisted that whereas a promise might be perfectly valid, although it was not in any prescribed form (*nudum a solemnitate*), it must not be *nudum a causa*. In other words, no abstract promise would be enforced. This type of *causa* has no connexion whatever with consideration. No objection can be made to a promise of donation so long as it is quite clear that the promise is intended to be one of pure liberality.

Now out of these elements, a theory of *cause* came to be formed. It is first given clear expression by Domat,[1] who says:

4. *Four sorts of agreements, by four combinations of the exploitation of persons and things.*—Intercourse and commerce for the purpose of exploiting persons and things are of four sorts, which make four kinds of agreements. For those who treat together either give to one another reciprocally one thing for another, as in a sale and in an exchange; or they do something the one for the other, as if they undertake the management of each other's concerns; or otherwise one of the parties does something and the other gives something, as when a labourer gives his labour for a certain hire; or, lastly, one of them either does or gives something, the other neither doing nor giving anything, as when a person undertakes to manage the affairs of another gratuitously; or when one makes a gift out of pure liberality.

---

[1] 1625–95. An Auvergnat and a friend of Pascal, he wrote a large treatise entitled *Des Loix civiles dans leur ordre naturel*, in which he attempted to give a rational account of the Roman law as it was applied in France. The compilers of the Code Civil used it to a considerable extent. It was translated into English in 1722 by Strahan, who added comparative notes on English law. See Holdsworth, xii. pp. 427–428. The

5. *No agreement binds without a cause.*—In the first three sorts of agreements the transaction between the parties is not gratuitous, the engagement of one of the parties being the foundation of that of the other. And even in the agreements where only one of the parties seems to be obliged, as in the loan of money, the obligation of the borrower is always preceded on the lender's part by the delivery he had to make in order to bring the agreement into existence. Thus the obligation which is formed in these kinds of agreements for the benefit of one of the contracting parties has always its cause on the other's part: and the obligation would be null, if it were really without a cause.

6. *Donations have their cause.*—In donations, and in the other contracts where one party alone does or gives something, and where the other neither does nor gives anything, it is the acceptance that forms the agreement. And the engagement of the donor has its foundation in some reasonable and just motive, such as a service rendered, or some other merit in the donee, or the mere pleasure of doing good. And this motive takes the place of a cause on the part of the person who receives without giving any thing.

Here *cause* has really three different meanings. Where the contract is, in the Roman sense, real or innominate, the *cause* is the same as executed consideration. Where it is consensual, the *cause* of each promise is the other party's engagement to perform; in other words, we may say that here the *cause* is executory consideration, but we shall probably be nearer to Domat's thought if we say that he is insisting upon the interdependence of promises. But where the promise is gratuitous—and this is really very remarkable and has not been fully understood by later writers—Domat does not say that there is a *cause*, but that a just and reasonable motive which is the foundation of the promise 'takes the place of a *cause*'. He even suggests that *cause* ought 'to move from the promisee'. We shall not go far wrong if we say that for Domat a contract in principle requires consideration in the English sense of the term, but that since he was committed by Roman and French legal developments to accepting the possibility of a gratuitous promise, he had to admit that in these

translation was reissued by Cushing at Boston in 1850. Through these two editions Domat may have exercised some influence on English and American law.

particular contracts some substitute for a *cause* had to be found; he found this in a just and reasonable motive on the part of the promisor. Domat's doctrine was to some extent deformed by Pothier,[1] who substituted for motive a liberal intent; and he seems to have thought, as Domat probably did not, that this liberal intent was a *cause*, and moreover that a uniform notion of *cause* was fundamental to all contracts.

French law has of course accepted fully the notion that an illegal or immoral *cause* is fatal to the validity of a contract, but the notion that *cause* was uniform throughout the law of contract caused them many difficulties. For gratuitous contracts they soon found a way out, for it was accepted at a relatively early period after the enactment of the Code Civil that an immoral promise of a gift was void: in these contracts at any rate the distinction between *cause* and motive, which had been set up as essential to sound doctrine, soon broke down. We have seen that it never existed for Domat. On the other hand, there was for long a serious difficulty as regards contracts for a consideration, and more especially consensual contracts, where the consideration was executory. For, as is said very reasonably in the text,[2] *cause* is here used in two different senses, first as expressing the notion of executory consideration, which is uniform for all contracts of a particular type (the consideration for purchase always being merely sale, and *vice versa*), and secondly as expressing the motive or object of the contract, which varies for each individual transaction. It is not unreasonable to say with the text that 'the *cause* which makes a contract good, can have nothing to do with the *cause* which makes it bad'. However, the French Courts had to extend the notion of illegal or immoral *cause* to contracts for a consideration.

Thus in modern French law one could well say that *cause* expresses three different notions: (1) something

---

[1] *Obligations*, Ss. 42–43.   [2] P. 225, *ante*.

almost identical with the English consideration, such consideration not being a legal requirement in all contracts, but being merely the result of analysing the vast majority of contracts, which in practice have a consideration; (2) the notion of the interdependence of promises, which is very closely related to the notion of consideration; and (3) the motive, or rather perhaps we should say the object, of the parties in entering into the contract. French legal opinion seems more and more disposed to recognise the difficulty of using one word to express these different notions. Thus the draft proposed by the Commission de Réforme du Code Civil distinguishes between *objet*, *cause* and *motif*. *Objet* is what is promised, the content of the promise. *Cause* is, in onerous contracts, the consideration for the promise, in gratuitous promises, the liberal intent; and it is uniform for all contracts of a type. *Motif* is the concrete individual motive which has induced a party to make a promise or enter into a contract; its effects are of course restricted by considerations of fairness to persons other than the person whose consent it determined.[1]

The result of all this seems to be that although the French often use *cause* in the sense of consideration, and although they recognise perfectly well for many purposes the distinction between a contract supported by consideration and a gratuitous contract, yet they have nothing in the nature of a doctrine of consideration since lack of consideration is never fatal to the validity of a contract. On the other hand, failure of consideration is a very serious matter, because if a contract is intended to be for a consideration, and no consideration in fact materialises, then the contract may be treated as void.

Students of Roman-Dutch law will recognise in Domat's doctrine something not very far removed from that set

---

[1] See *Travaux de la Commission de Réforme du Code Civil* (Année 1947–1948), pp. 46 s, 48 s, 51 s, 62 s, 65 s, 266 s, 277–278; and 28 *Canadian Bar Review*, pp. 256–260.

up by Lord de Villiers, though his doctrine was much more rigorous in that it admitted only donations in the strict sense of the term as exceptions to the doctrine of consideration.[1]

The protection against the consequences of ill-advised declarations of intention, which serves as a modern justification for the doctrine of consideration, is largely effected in other systems by the requirement of writing, whether formal or informal. Thus in both French and German law a formal writing is required for promises of gifts, in the former a notarial document,[2] in the latter either a notarial document or a document attested in open court.[3] Moreover, German civil law insists on writing for abstract acknowledgements of debt, i.e., where no cause is disclosed.[4] In French civil law all contracts for more than 5000 francs must be in writing;[5] and indeed French lawyers admit quite freely that they view all oral evidence with the utmost suspicion. In most countries commercial contracts are almost entirely free from the requirement of writing.[6] In Scots law writing and consideration are alternatives, though some contracts must be in writing even if there is consideration.

[1] See *Mtembu* v. *Webster* (1904), 21 S.C. 323.
[2] C.C. art. 931.   [3] B.G.B. §518.
[4] B.G.B. §781.   [5] C.C. art. 1341.
[6] E.g. C.Com. art. 109.

CHAPTER VII. OBLIGATIONS: GENERAL (*cont.*)

1. IMPOSSIBILITY

In Roman law, as in ours, agreements for plain impossibilities, or on conditions involving plain impossibilities, are void, though, naturally, many things quite possible to us were thought of as impossible in Rome. There are some points of terminology which should be mentioned. Augustan and earlier Latin had no such word as *impossibilis*. Labeo has to express the idea in Greek,[1] and Julian does the same,[2] though by his time the word *impossibilis* had acquired citizenship. It never seems to have been very common. The more usual expression is 'in rerum natura non esse' or the like, in which the influence of Greek philosophy is evident.[3] Though texts not infrequently use the word *impossibilis* without limitation to any particular type of what we should call impossibility, it does not seem ever to be specifically applied except to something to be done or given. To touch the sky with one's finger is impossible: that a son should be older than his father is still *contra rerum naturam*.

The rule laid down in the most general terms, 'impossibilium nulla obligatio est',[4] and covering legal impossibility as well as physical, seems to apply in practice in our own law, though on the last application there is little authority.[5] With us the line taken seems rather to be that the parties must have assumed possibility as the basis of the contract, so that it is theoretically, and perhaps practically, possible for a man to contract validly to perform an absolute impossibility. In Roman law the rule is stated

---

[1] D. 28. 7. 20. *pr.*
[2] D. 30. 104. 1.
[3] Rabel, *Mél. Gérardin*, pp. 494 *sqq.*
[4] D. 50. 17. 185.
[5] *Harvy* v. *Gibbons* (1675), 2 Lev. 161.

absolutely: there is no contract for an impossibility. In regard to legal impossibility, however, e.g., agreement to sell the Campus Martius, or a freeman, there was some relaxation in the *bonae fidei* contract of sale: a buyer, ignorant of the character of the thing, had his *actio ex empto*, notwithstanding the impossibility. This is clear for Justinian,[1] though it is doubtful how far it was true for classical law. Further, it is by no means certain that the general rule was as absolute in the classical law as it was under Justinian.

Similarly the word 'impossibility' is late in appearance in our rubrics, and the first edition (1867) of one of our leading text-books on contract (Leake on Contract[2]), while stating the rule to be that 'where an absolute impossibility of performance exists at the time of making the agreement the general rule seems to be that there is no contract', explains that a thing is absolutely impossible 'quod natura fieri non concedit', an explanation which would have satisfied a Roman lawyer.

When the impossibility is known to the parties at the time of agreement, it is clear that the essentials of a contract are lacking; when they were not aware of the impossibility, it is usual in our law to base the nullity of the contract on mistake.[3]

When we turn to supervening impossibility, or *casus* as the Romans called it, we find a strongly contrasted method of treatment in the two systems. We deal first with the Roman *casus*, the effect of which differed in different cases. The Roman law of the Romans, unlike our law and unlike the modern Roman law in both its French and its German forms, had two distinct forms of what may be loosely called contractual obligation. The first and most ancient kind was that in which the remedies were *stricti iuris*, a

---

[1] D. 18. 1. 4–6, 34. 3, 62. 1. It was on the last of these texts that Jhering based his celebrated doctrine of *culpa in contrahendo*.

[2] P. 358.   [3] But see p. 204, *ante*.

name given to them, however, only in post-classical times. The other consisted of transactions which gave *bonae fidei iudicia*. All the obligations in the first class were unilateral. The typical case is *stipulatio*, a formal promise in which an obligation is imposed only on one party, the promisor. It is clear on the texts that in *stipulatio* if performance became impossible after the contract was made, without fault on the part of the promisor, he was released from his liability.[1] But most business relations are bilateral: a *stipulatio* would not usually stand alone; there would commonly be an undertaking, e.g. a *stipulatio*, on the other side, or some service on the other side would have already been rendered. In such a case the question arises: What is to happen if one party to a pair of stipulations has been released by *casus* before anything has been done? Must the other still perform? The question is nowhere directly answered, either way. Modern Roman law has no difficulty in releasing him, because the notion of *stricti iuris* obligation is no part of its scheme. It is true that we are told:[2] 'sive ab initio sine causa promissum est, sive fuit causa promittendi quae finita est vel secuta non est, dicendum est condictioni locum esse'. This in its terms deals with the right to recover what has been rendered and would *a fortiori* justify refusal to perform. But this deals only with simple failure to perform and must not be pressed as dealing with the effect of release by *casus*. The *casus* involves release of the party and no more, and it seems that the other party would still be bound: nothing in the evidence entitles us to say that there would be an *exceptio doli*. If, as is sometimes held, sale is a simplification of two counter-stipulations this state of things might account for the rule that the risk passed to the buyer though there had been no transfer of ownership, since the liability under one stipulation would not, at civil law, be affected by the fate of the other.[3]

[1] D. 45. 1. 23, 33, 37, etc.   [2] D. 12. 7. 1. 2.
[3] But see, for another view, p. 294, *post*.

The point could not arise in the other *stricti iuris* contracts, *mutuum* (loan for consumption) and *expensilatio* (a fictitious entry of money lent), for they deal only with 'fungible things' and 'genera non pereunt'. But it has great importance in the field of the *condictiones*. The *condictio* was a remedy for unjustified enrichment. Its primary application is to money paid by mistake; the *condictio indebiti* lies for recovery of money paid in the erroneous belief that it was due. But in the present connexion another application is of greater interest, that of the *condictio ob rem dati*, called by Justinian '*condictio causa data causa non secuta*'. We have seen that not every bargain was an enforceable contract. There were many dealings not covered by the scheme of contracts and therefore not legally enforceable. Such were agreements for mutual services, including exchange (for sale required a money price); and for such things there was in earlier law no mode of enforcement. So long as nothing had been done under the agreement this was perhaps endurable, but when one party had handed over his contribution the fact that he could not compel the counter-performance constituted a grave injustice. Accordingly the civil law provided a *condictio ob rem dati*, by which even if the person who had done his part could not enforce the counter-performance, he could at least recover what he had paid. This created a civil obligation, which was entirely unilateral, for the first performance was not made under any obligation at all. It was thus closely analogous to *stipulatio*. We should thus expect that here as there, however harsh it may seem, *casus* rendering the counter-performance impossible would release the promisor from his obligation. And, as it was release of the person liable and no more, the person who had originally performed would not have the *condictio ob rem dati*, as he would where there was simply failure to perform. So the law is laid down in a number of texts, some of them giving an obviously unjust result. There are, however, some texts which lay down the more equitable doctrine that, on such facts, what had been handed over could be recovered by the *condictio*. These are mostly in non-commercial cases and have all the air of equitable relaxation of a harsh civil rule, and some of them at least are probably post-classical.[1] The conflict has been noted by many modern writers and disposed of in various ways. Girard[2] considers the right of retention to be a late development, but as a strict rule of civil law the retention is intelligible, while it is wholly unlike the general attitude of later law.[3] However, its origin is unimportant for us: in the *Corpus Juris* the weight of evidence is strongly in favour of retention, at any rate where the case has a commercial aspect. In the modern Roman law it has disappeared. There is only one system of contract and any agreement normally makes a contract. Thus the real field of *condictio ob rem dati* no longer exists and *bonae fidei* notions have practically ousted those of *strictum ius*. Thus, e.g., Dernburg[4] ignores the retention texts altogether.

The important point to notice is that the special field in which these results occur is that of partly performed agreements which could not legally be enforced. If the transaction comes within the field of one of the recognised *bonae fidei* contracts wholly different considerations apply, and there is no reason to appeal to the principles of the *condictio*. This point is sometimes ignored. Thus in the *Cantiere San Rocco Case*[5] an agreement to supply a set of marine engines was made between a Scottish and an Austrian company. The outbreak of war made the performance of the contract impossible and the Court held that a deposit paid must be refunded. The decision, which was

---

[1] For texts and fuller discussion see a note signed 'W. P.' in 2 *Cambridge Law Journal*, p. 215, and Buckland, 46 *Harvard Law Review*, 1933, pp. 1281 *sqq.*

[2] *Manuel*, 8th ed. p. 631.

[3] See the article by Buckland cited in note on p. 181.

[4] *Pandekten*, ii. Sect. 142. [5] [1924] A.C. 226.

manifestly just, was under Scots law and does not itself
concern us. Both the Court of Session and the House of
Lords made excursions into Roman law, as the basis of
Scots law. They held that the deposit paid was recoverable
under the principles of the *condictio*. But for these principles they went not to the texts but to the authoritative text-
books of Scots law, in most of which, much influenced by
the *modernus usus*, the rule that *casus* is an absolute release
of the party bound, and no more, has disappeared.[1] In fact
the *condictio* had no bearing on the case. It was one of
emptio venditio and was governed by the rules of that contract, if treated as a question of Roman law. Treating the
case as sale, the decision was perfectly sound: in Roman sale
the risks are on the vendor till the goods are in a deliverable state and till then he is entitled to no part of the price.
If, therefore, the goods never reach a deliverable state but
the contract is destroyed, he must refund anything he has
received, on the principles of *bonae fidei iudicia*.[2]

On the other hand, whereas the general rule of Roman
law was, as we have seen, that a party whose performance
became impossible without fault or fraud, was released,
for 'lex non cogit ad impossibilia', the rule of the common
law was almost the exact opposite. We say 'was', because
it has in recent years executed almost a complete *volte-face*.
The attitude of the common law towards the party thus
prevented formerly was: 'you should not have been so
foolish as to make an absolute promise and you must pay
for your folly'. 'When the party by his own conduct
creates a duty or charge upon himself, he is bound to
make it good, if he may, notwithstanding any accident by

---

[1] I.e., the modern developments of Roman law. Both Courts were
very much disturbed by the fact that Erskine, the older writer on whom
most reliance is usually placed, enunciated the law of *casus* in its pure
Roman form, as described above.

[2] For fuller discussion of this case and the principles of Roman law involved, see the article above cited, 46 *Harvard Law Review*, 1933, pp. 1281
sqq., '*Casus* and Frustration in Roman and Common Law'.

inevitable necessity, because he might have provided against it by his contract.'[1] It was inevitable that sooner or later a rule of this kind would come into conflict with considerations of justice, and very slowly the judges have modified it by the doctrine of an implied condition.[2] The classic statement of the rule is that of Blackburn J. in the well-known Surrey Music Hall case in 1863:[3] 'where, from the nature of the contract, it appears that the parties must from the beginning have known that it could not be fulfilled unless when the time for the fulfilment of the contract arrived some particular specified thing continued to exist, so that, when entering into the contract, they must have contemplated such continuing existence as the foundation of what was to be done; there, in the absence of any express or implied warranty that the thing shall exist, the contract is not to be construed as a positive contract, but as subject to an implied condition that the parties shall be excused in case, before breach, performance becomes impossible from the perishing of the thing without default of the contractor.'[4] Here too the principles of the two systems are not quite the same. For the Romans such an obligation is a mere nullity: for us it is one which the parties must be contemplated as not having intended.[5]

However, judges and text-book writers seem to be approaching more and more to a recognition of the fact that no intention can be imputed to the parties, that if the parties had really contemplated the possibility of the supervening event, they would in most cases almost certainly

[1] *Paradine* v. *Jane* (1647), Aleyn 27.

[2] Some account of the process of breaking down the old common law will be found in McNair, 'War-time Impossibility of Performance of Contract', 35 *L.Q.R.* p. 84, and *Legal Effects of War* (3rd ed. 1948), ch. vi: 'Frustration'.

[3] *Taylor* v. *Caldwell*, 3 B. and S. 826, at p. 833.

[4] This principle, as we shall see later in dealing with frustration, has been carried a good deal further.

[5] Yet Blackburn J. cited Roman law in support of his decision, without any sense of this difference.

have intended opposite consequences, the one that the contract should come to an end, the other that the contract should stand, with the result that failure to perform should be regarded as a breach of contract. According to this view the Court can not escape responsibility for imposing upon both parties the solution that justice demands.[1]

2. *CASUS* AND FRUSTRATION

With supervening impossibility, *casus*, modern law has had occasion to grasp another phenomenon, which has acquired the name of frustration. It may be that while it is physically quite possible to carry out the contract, on both sides, there has been such a change of circumstances that effect cannot be given to the real purpose of the parties; or, more generally, some state of facts, or some event, which was assumed as the basis of the whole transaction, has ceased to exist, or has not happened. In a number of cases our law has treated this as equivalent to supervening impossibility. What limits are to be assigned to this doctrine it is impossible to say. It is obvious that there must be limits: if I hire a field to play a cricket match I shall not be able to refuse to pay the hire because owing to a railway accident the visiting team telegraph that they are unable to come. It has, however, been applied in this country where seats were taken to view the Coronation procession of King Edward VII, and this did not take place, and in America to contracts for advertising space in a programme of yacht-races which were cancelled owing to the outbreak of war. Having adopted, as we have seen, the doctrine of an implied condition as a means of giving effect to supervening impossibility which was actual, physical, it was an

---

[1] See Lord Wright in *Denny, Mott and Dickson, Ltd.* v. *J. B. Fraser and Co. Ltd.*, [1944] A.C. 265, at p. 275—his remarks are probably *obiter dicta*—and Cheshire and Fifoot, *Law of Contract*, 2nd ed. pp. 415–417. The House of Lords has reiterated the old doctrine in *British Movietonews Ltd.* v. *London & District Cinemas Ltd.*, [1951] 2 All E.R. 617.

easy step for the common law to apply the same doctrine to impossibility which was constructive; much easier than it would have been to extend *casus* for this purpose.

There is here no direct point of comparison with Roman law, because frustration not amounting to actual impossibility is little represented in the texts; but, assuming that the Romans would have treated this as *casus*, it is possible to make an interesting comparison of the ways in which the two systems deal with the effect of *casus* and frustration upon the rights and liabilities under the contract. Such cases are usually either sale or hire. Confining ourselves to cases in which no part of the service has been rendered on one side, but the other has paid or promised to pay, we get—or rather we used to get—a remarkable difference in the two systems. In the Coronation cases[1] the Court reached the conclusions that the loss must lie where it fell, that a deposit paid in respect of the seats hired could not be recovered, and further that instalments not yet paid but already due when circumstances put an end to the contract could be recovered by the party who had contracted to provide the accommodation, while liability for payments to accrue due at a later date was annulled. The Court took the view that the contract could not be rescinded *ab initio*, that therefore instalments paid could not be recovered, and that one from whom there was due a payment which had not been made ought not to be better off than if he had actually paid.[2] The effect of these decisions was to apply the rules of the *condictio* to a case which would have been in Roman law one of hire, a *bonae fidei negotium* to which the doctrine of the *condictio* had no application. It is clear that Roman law would have reached

---

[1] See especially *Krell* v. *Henry*, [1903] 2 K.B. 740, and *Chandler* v. *Webster*, [1904] 1 K.B. 493, and criticism in *Maritime National Fish, Limited* v. *Ocean Trawlers, Limited*, [1935] A.C. 524.

[2] For a discussion of the reasoning of the Court and the interpretation put upon earlier cases on the authority of which the Court purported to act see the article already cited from 46 *Harvard Law Review*, pp. 1281 *sqq.*

a conclusion very different from those of our Courts in *Krell* v. *Henry* and *Chandler* v. *Webster*, on the assumption that frustration was equivalent to *casus*. The contract was hire, and in Roman law, if the service hired was not rendered, and this was not due to the fault of the hirer, he was under no liability to pay for service he had not had and could recover anything he had paid in advance.[1] The decisions in the English Courts seem to have been based on the view that the other rule would be unjust. Lord Alverstone indeed gave this reason in *Blakeley* v. *Muller*.[2] The reclaim of money would be, he said, unjust, in view of the fact that the other party might have expended money in preparation. It is, however, not ideal justice, for the intended letter of the accommodation may receive all the hire without rendering any of the service and may have incurred no expense at all; in any case the expense incurred will bear no relation to the price paid or promised for the seats. The Roman law at first sight seems to err in the opposite way: to have to refund all money received irrespective of what expenses have been incurred looks unfair. But it must be noted that though the contract is in effect set aside, the action brought will be *actio ex conducto*, a *bonae fidei iudicium* in which under the words *ex fide bona* the *iudex* has power to condemn for what in all the circumstances is fair; the formula was gone in the time of the *Corpus Juris*, but the principle remained. This may be contrasted with the language of Darling J. in *Lumsden* v. *Barton*,[3] for whom it was all or nothing: he 'could not find any rule of law by which she could recover half'.[4]

However, in 1942 the House of Lords reversed *Chandler* v. *Webster*, holding that a party could recover an advance payment made in respect of a contract which had been

---

[1] D. 19. 2. 15. 2, 15. 3, 19. 6, 30. 1, and see Buckland, *Text-book*, pp. 505 *sq*.

[2] [1903] 2 K.B. at p. 761 n.   [3] (1902), 19 T.L.R. 53.

[4] See an interesting discussion of these cases by Gutteridge in 50 *L.Q.R.* pp. 108–112 following McElroy.

subsequently frustrated, if there had been a total failure of consideration;[1] and in the next year Parliament extended the rule to cases when the consideration has failed only in part, directing that the payee's expenses be set off against the payer's claim.[2]

3. CONDITIONS

Conditional promises are of course prominent in the law. But the Roman way of looking at conditions was not quite the same as ours. Leaving fees conditional at the common law and the like out of account, our law appears to recognise two types of condition, conditions precedent or suspensive and conditions subsequent; but the whole treatment of conditions in different branches of English law, conveyances, bonds, contracts and wills (including even differences between gifts of real and personal property), presents a very confused story from which it is difficult to extract any solid principle. The distinction between conditions which are mere conditions and those which are also promises existed in Rome as with us, but not with the same significance.[3]

Another difference is of more importance, at least in legal theory. To the Romans a condition subsequent was almost a contradiction in terms. There was only one kind of condition, some future uncertain event on which the effect of a transaction was to depend. This excludes on the one hand mere suspension: a contract dependent only on the arrival of some time which must come is not conditional: this is *dies* and has very different effects. On the other hand it excludes provisions with no futurity in them. A promise 'If St Paul's is more than 400 feet high' is not

[1] *Fibrosa Spolka Akcyjna* v. *Fairbairn Lawson Combe Barbour Ltd.*, [1943] A.C. 32.

[2] Law Reform (Frustrated Contracts) Act, 1943 (6 and 7 Geo. VI, c. 40). See 60 *L.Q.R.* pp. 160–174. For the treatment of 'Frustration of Contract' in various foreign legal systems, see *Journal of Comparative Legislation*, 3rd ser., xxviii. pp. 1–25; xxix. pp. 1–19; xxx. pp. 55–67; and McNair, *Legal Effects of War* (3rd ed. 1943), ch. vi: 'Frustration'.

[3] See p. 254, *post.*

for the Romans conditional, though it is with us. The agreement is either void or valid, and though it may be some time before the facts are known, the contract has its full effect, if at all, from the moment when it was made. And what we call a condition subsequent on the contract, the Romans called a condition on the annulment of the contract. Where a sale was to be set aside on a particular event, it was not a conditional sale, but 'pura emptio quae sub condicione resolvitur'.[1] In such a case the contract produced its full effect at once, as to risks and the like. The Romans distinguished in language more clearly than our books do between those 'conditions subsequent' which merely put an end to the relation thenceforward and those which annul it *ab initio*, the matter being in fact more important in gifts than in contract.

A contract may be made (i) if an event happens, or (ii) till it happens, or (iii) unless it happens. The first type is in both systems said to be under a condition precedent or suspensive: the contract is not enforceable unless the event happens.

The second type would presumably in our law be said to be under a condition subsequent, but the effect in both systems is the same: the contract is determined for the future when the event happens. Roman law had indeed a complication which we are fortunately without: the contract of *stipulatio*, formal promise, was regarded as essentially perpetual, and effect could be given to such terminating provisions only by praetorian assistance.[2] But the ordinary commercial contracts were under no such restriction. They could be made to determine on a future event as well as on a future day. The case seems to present no difficulty in Roman law; it is hardly necessary to appeal to the notion of condition at all. In our law indeed a lease for years must have a certain period beyond which it cannot last; but this only makes it necessary, if it is desired to

---

[1] D. 18. 2. 2. *pr.*; 41. 4. 2. 5.   [2] D. 45. 1. 56. 4, etc.

make the lease end on an uncertain event, to make the
lease for a term longer than the latest time at which the
event can happen, determinable earlier by the event. There
does not seem to be any difficulty in a contract for the hire
of goods or services till an event happens.

The most interesting type is the third. Here, leaving
out of account the case of *stipulatio*, the Roman law is clear.
A sale or hire 'unless such and such an event happens'
was an unconditional contract, producing all the normal
effects of such a contract precisely as if no such clause had
been inserted. The condition was one not on the contract
but on its nullification. If the event happened the parties
were entitled, subject to questions of *culpa* and the like,
to be restored to their original positions.[1]

The main difference seems to be that the Romans had
thought out the consequences of such a resolutive condition, and confined the notion of resolutive condition to
cases in which nullification *ab initio* was to be the result. In
our terminology the distinction is not so clearly drawn
between those conditions which, if satisfied, destroy the
right or obligation *ab initio* and those conditions the satisfaction of which simply determines it. Thus the satisfaction
of the condition on a bond destroys the obligation *ab initio*
and it is commonly called a condition subsequent:[2] the
Romans would have called it resolutory. But elsewhere a
condition subsequent is defined and illustrated as one
which merely determines the right for the future.[3] Our
courts seem usually to have treated such conditions, in
wills, as defeasances, merely determining the right, even
though the testator has expressly said that the gift is to be
void if the event happens; where this is impossible, they
have usually made it a simple suspensory condition, with

[1] Illustrations, Buckland, *Text-book*, pp. 494 *sqq.*
[2] Anson, *Law of Contract*, 17th ed. p. 63.
[3] E.g. Jarman on Wills, 7th ed. pp. 1444 *sqq.*; Comyns' *Digest*, s.v.
Condition (C). See also the frustration cases discussed, pp. 244 *sqq., ante.*

inconvenient results to the beneficiary.[1] Roman law could reach the desired result in other ways, e.g. *inter vivos*, by giving a usufruct, which was not thought of as ownership, till the event happened, but this had the disadvantage that it ended necessarily on the death of the beneficiary. Under wills it could be done, more or less, by *fideicommissa*,[2] by which the person to whom property was left could be put under an obligation to transfer when the event happened.[3] There is not the same difficulty in Roman law under contract, as the contract of sale never of itself transferred ownership. But if under a contract with a resolutive condition there had been an actual conveyance this was not annulled: the remedy was an action *in personam*. Hence there was a tendency in classical law to treat such things as suspensive wherever this was possible, but in later law they are often treated as resolutive. But there are many signs of a weakening of the notion of the perpetuity of ownership and Justinian, in some cases, seems to allow of a reversion of ownership.[4]

Where a transaction was made subject to a condition on the face of it impossible in fact or law, the Roman law, in acts *inter vivos*, in general avoided the transaction, i.e. the condition took effect at once: it could not be performed and the transaction failed. Our own law seems to be the same, but there is little evidence,[5] the reason being that unilateral contracts are much less prominent than in Roman law, so that what there appears as a condition is often consideration with us. But in wills of personalty,

---

[1] Ownership being essentially perpetual a gift of property did not in Roman law admit of such conditions, a rule relaxed under Justinian (*ante*, p. 93). As to the way in which such difficulties were more or less surmounted in gifts by will (negative conditions), Buckland, *Text-book*, pp. 298, 340. [2] P. 173, *ante*.

[3] On the extent to which this operated *in rem*, Buckland, *Equity in Roman Law*, pp. 83 *sqq*.

[4] Wieacker, *Lex Commissoria*; Sieg, *Bessergebotsklausel*; Levy, *Symbolae Friburgenses für O. Lenel*, pp. 127 *sqq*.   [5] See p. 238, *ante*.

perhaps owing to their earlier association with ecclesiastical
Courts, it is not surprising that civil law rules have been
partially adopted (i.e. the offending condition is struck
out[1]). We need not consider the difficult cases of what may
be called conditional conditions, i.e where the condition
assumes a state of fact which does not exist, and the court
has to determine whether the testator intended the condition to apply in any event or only if the fact were so. It
is a question of intent, and it is difficult to get much principle out of the solutions in either system. Leaving these
and conditions subsequent out of account, we get a story
not quite reconcilable in all details. Swinburne,[2] whose
language has been followed by later writers, tells us that
the appointment of an executor on an 'impossible or un-
honest' condition is 'in effect pure and simple'—the civil
law rule; indeed only civil law authorities are cited. Yet in
legacy, where a condition was legally impossible, the condition operated and the gift failed.[3] But in *Brown* v. *Peck*[4]
an illegal condition was struck out and the gift was pure
and simple. The head-note to *Gath* v. *Burton*[5] makes the
case decide that if the impossibility is obvious, the gift is
pure and simple. But in fact the case decides a different
point. A legacy was subject to the condition that the
legatee paid a certain debt to the testator. The testator
afterwards released the debt. It was held, on the facts, that
he meant to waive the condition. Halsbury observes[6] that
'if a condition, intended to be operative in any event, is
precedent, and is originally impossible...' the performance is not excused and the gift fails (which is contrary
to the Roman rule), and[7] 'in general, if a condition is void
as contrary to public policy...(or) illegal..., the effect

---

[1] See p. 160, *ante*.
[2] *Testaments and Last Wills*, 6th ed. p. 249.
[3] *Robinson* v. *Wheelwright* (1856), 6 De G., M., and G. 535.
[4] (1758), 1 Eden 140.   [5] (1839), 1 Beav. 478.
[6] Hailsham, xxxiv. p. 112.   [7] P. 104.

on the gift is that if the condition is precedent the gift
fails'—again not the Roman doctrine.[1]

In Roman law prevention of the performance of a
condition by one interested in non-performance was equivalent to performance,[2] and if the condition was one which
involved co-operation with a third party, the third party's
failure to co-operate had the same effect. This was true at
least if the case was under a will, and the testator could not
have contemplated refusal, e.g. on a condition of payment
to X, tender to X was as good as payment.[3] This is perhaps
as far as the classical law went, except in manumissions,
but there are texts (which may, however, be interpolated)
which indicate, at least in connexion with wills, that in

---

[1] There is in this last passage a peculiarity of language which is found in
many other places. To say that a condition is void is to say that it is ineffectual, but this passage says that though the condition is void it vitiates the
gift: in other words it is not void. It is a valid and effective condition, though
if it had been a promise it would not be enforced. Jarman, *Wills* (7th ed.
p. 1443), observes on the difference between land and personalty and says,
in regard to the latter, that equity has adopted the Roman rule, that where
a suspensive condition is impossible or illegal as *malum prohibitum*, the gift is
absolute. But 'where the performance of the condition is the sole motive of
the bequest, or its impossibility was unknown to the testator...or where it
is illegal as involving *malum in se*, in these cases the civil agrees with the common law in holding both gift and condition void'. This is no doubt correct
in effect, the civil law being the modern civil law. But it is clear that in these
cases the condition is not void but operative. So, on p. 1439: 'A condition
which is impossible *ab initio* is void, such as a condition that a man shall go
to Rome in an impossibly short space of time.' As the writer cites Sheppard's *Touchstone* (p. 132) in support, he presumably agrees with Sheppard
who says: 'if the condition be subsequent to the estate the condition only is
void and the estate good and absolute', by which he means the original
estate, not the one which is to arise if the condition is satisfied, 'and if the
condition be precedent the condition and the estate are both void': that is,
the condition is not void, but operative. So in Coke on Littleton (206b)
this is expressed in words which speak of the impossible condition as void,
when the context shows that the condition is valid and prevents the estate
from arising. It cannot be said that the writers treat the condition and the
estate as one conception, for they distinguish them. They cannot mean that
it is void in the sense that satisfying it will bring the gift into effect, for they
are dealing largely with impossible conditions.

[2] D. 50. 17. 161.   [3] D. 28. 7. 3.

such a case the condition was regarded as fulfilled if the failure to fulfil it was not imputable to the beneficiary himself.[1] There is some evidence for the application of similar principles *inter vivos*, e.g. where *A* sold *B* a library provided the local authority sold *B* a site on which to store it. They were willing to do so, but *B* did not buy it. It was held that the sale was good, fulfilment having been prevented by *B*.[2] The case is inadequately stated: it would seem that there must have been more precision in the condition than appears in the actual wording. With us too, prevention of performance of a condition, arising from an act for which the obligee is responsible, has the effect of releasing the obligor; such an act is 'equal to performance';[3] in wills the question of prevention of performance by one interested in non-performance does not seem to have arisen, but it would probably be equivalent to performance.

There are a few texts in relation to *stipulatio* for a penalty if a certain thing is not done, which treat the penalty as not due where *casus fortuitus* had prevented the performance,[4] but on a general view of the texts the better opinion seems to be that even under Justinian there was no general principle that *casus* or act of God preventing performance of the condition was treated as equivalent to performance. It must be noted that this applies only to pure conditions. If, e.g., I informally promise you money if you render me a certain service and you undertake to do it but *casus* prevents this, there is a contract of hire of service under which you have no claim unless you have rendered the service.[5] It is practically only in *stipulatio* that the point could arise.

[1] D. 28. 7. 11; 35. 1. 14; see Grosso, *Contributo allo studio dell' adempimento: La finzione di adempimento nella condizione.*

[2] D. 18. 1. 50; see also D. 50. 17. 161.

[3] Ashurst J. in *Hotham* v. *East India Co.* (1787), 1 T.R. 638, 645; Comyn's *Digest*, Condition L6; Hailsham, vii. sect. 298.

[4] D. 45. 1. 69.   [5] D. 19. 2. 15. 6.

In considering our law of contract we must leave out of account two things which are called conditions in our books:

(i) conditions which are also promises to do something, vital to the contract, failure to do which is a breach of contract, entitling the other party to treat the contract as discharged; they are in actual life the most important 'conditions', but they are really terms in the contract and bring in considerations wholly alien to the present topic; they were not conditions in Roman law, which had no general doctrine of discharge by breach;[1]

(ii) representations of existing fact sometimes called conditions, e.g. in *Bannerman* v. *White*,[2] which are not really conditions at all in the Roman sense, since there is no uncertainty or futurity about them but only allegations, true or false, of a certain existing state of facts. They again are really terms in the contract and cannot in any case raise the questions we are considering.

In an ordinary contract under a true condition precedent or suspensive, not amounting to a promise, for instance, when a student engages lodgings in a university town conditionally upon passing his entrance examination, it seems that in our law (though authority on such things is extraordinarily scanty) the chief, if not the only, effect of the existence of the condition is to hold up any possibility of enforcement of the contract until the condition is satisfied. Thus when an insurance policy provided that upon the occurrence of a loss the person insured must 'procure a certificate of the minister churchwardens and some reputable householders of the parish, importing that they knew the character, etc., of the assured', which he failed to do, that was a condition precedent to his right to recover upon the policy and his action failed.[3]

---

[1] But the seller could by inserting a *lex commissoria* bargain for the right to treat the sale as discharged for failure to pay the price. D. 18. 3.

[2] (1861), 10 C.B.N.S. 84.

[3] *Worsley* v. *Wood* (1796), 6 T.R. 710.

Roman law dealt with, or created, some problems in connexion with conditional obligations which do not appear, at least obviously, in our law. Obligation was originally conceived of as a personal subjection. But a person who is to be in a state of subjection if some event happens is not as yet so, and cannot be said to be, in the old sense, *obligatus*, and though the notion of subjection is gone in classical law it has left certain traces. Thus though it was clear that one who had promised under condition had no right to withdraw, there is evidence of doubt whether it could strictly be said to be an obligation so long as the condition was outstanding. In the beginning a *persona obligata* was analogous to a *res obligata*, a thing pledged, with the obvious corollary that the relation was intensely personal, so that, at one time, it is not impossible that it died with the person bound. As a general principle this rule, if indeed it ever existed, is gone long before classical times, but it may have left a surviving trace in the doctrine that it was inadmissible for an obligation to begin in the *heres*—'inelegans esse visum est ab heredis persona incipere obligationem'.[1] A *heres* cannot inherit an obligation which could not have affected his ancestor. We are told this in relation to promises expressed to bind or benefit the *heres* alone, but it is equally applicable to conditional obligations if these are not perfected obligations. It is well known that conditional *institutiones* and legacies failed if the beneficiary died before the condition was satisfied, and there is some evidence that in classical law this may have been true of contract under condition.[2] But the notion is obsolete before Justinian. Similarly there are signs of dispute on the question, in classical law, whether there could be conditions on a consensual contract,[3] i.e. whether there could be said to be any effective consent at

---

[1] G. 3. 100.
[2] For references to the literature on this question see Buckland, *Textbook*, p. 425, n. 1.　　　[3] G. 3. 146; C. 4. 37. 6.

all where it was given conditionally. Further, it was certainly true at civil law that an attempt to novate an unconditional obligation arising out of a *stipulatio* by a conditional *stipulatio* operated only if the condition was fulfilled, the theory being that there was no obligation under the second *stipulatio* until that time; though any attempt to sue on the original *stipulatio* would be paralysed by an *exceptio doli* or *pacti conventi*.[1] There is conflict in the texts on the question whether a conditional creditor could claim in bankruptcy, i.e. could get *missio in possessionem* with the other creditors,[2] and on the question whether, if an action had been brought on the contract while a condition was pending and therefore lost, it could be brought again when the condition was satisfied, on the ground that there was now a new obligation, or whether it was barred on the principle of *res iudicata*.[3] Notwithstanding these traces of conflict it is fairly clear that under Justinian the actual law was that it was one and the same obligation all through. Clearly this would follow if the operation of fulfilment of the condition was retrospective, but it is questionable how far this consideration was present in the actual determinations of the questions.[4] Our law does not seem to have found any difficulty on this point; the previous judgement would not bar a new action brought after the satisfaction of the condition.[5] But, in general, on these matters it is difficult to find authority in our books. Either with the Romans these questions were mostly speculative school questions with little practical importance (which in the case of some of them at least is quite probable), or they were much more given to making commercial contracts under suspensive conditions than our merchants have been.

[1] G. 3. 179.   [2] D. 42. 4. 6. *pr.*, 7. 14, 14. 2.
[3] D. 20. 1. 13. 5; 21. 1. 43. 9; Inst. 4. 6. 33.
[4] As to this see Buckland, *Text-book*, p. 424 and references.
[5] *Heming* v. *Wilton* (1832), 5 C. and P. 54; *Hall* v. *Levy* (1875), L.R. 10 C.P. 154.

4. DUTY OF THIRD PARTIES NOT TO INTERFERE WITH CONTRACT

We have already seen[1] that Roman law, like our own, recognised the principle that a third person could not have rights or liabilities under a contract, and that, like our own, it succeeded in evading this in pressing cases. It should be added that in both systems, though a third party could not be bound, the contract does in fact, to use 'jurisprudential' language, generate a *ius in rem*, in the sense that there are remedies if a third person interferes in the performance of the contract, though the Roman law does not go so far in that direction as does ours. In Roman law such interference with a contract as made it impossible for one party to perform it and so released him gave to the other party an *actio doli* against the person interfering.[2] This is a very narrow protection. In our law the existence of a contract (at any rate of certain kinds of contract) imposes upon everyone a duty not knowingly to cause damage by interfering with the performance of it. Apart from the somewhat special rules affecting trade disputes, it is an actionable wrong, knowingly and without just excuse, to cause damage by inducing a party to a contract to break it. To what classes of contract this principle applies, and what are just excuses, are questions still in process of solution; but the typical class of contract affected by the doctrine is the contract of employment.[3] There seems to be no authority in our law upon the actual case above cited from Roman law, but the tort of interference with contractual relations is in a plastic condition, and a recent case[4] shows that it extends beyond the inducement of *A* to break a contract with *B* and reaches an act by the

---

[1] Pp. 214 *sqq.*, *ante.*   [2] D. 4. 3. 18. 5.
[3] See Jenks, *Digest of English Civil Law*, Sect. 939 and cases there cited.
[4] *G.W.K. Limited and Another* v. *Dunlop Rubber Co.* (1926), 42 T.L.R. 376, 593.

defendant himself (in this case the unauthorised substitution of tyres on a motor-car) which interfered with
the performance of a contract between A and B. There is
no doubt that I have an action for deprivation of services
against one who wilfully or negligently injures my servant
and makes it impossible for him to do his work, but the relation of master and servant introduces other considerations.

5. LIABILITY FOR NON-PERFORMANCE

In contract there are in most systems of law many circumstances in which a man is liable without any question of
fault, except on the rather circular reasoning that he is at
fault for having promised to do what in fact he cannot or
will not do. If I promise money I must pay it. There may
be defences, but inability to pay is not one of them. So if
I undertake to deliver a thing, or to do a piece of work, and
do not deliver it or do the work, or deliver something or
do something which is not within the description of what
I promised, there is a liability, apart from positive grounds
of excuse, with no question of fault but only of default. But
I may deliver the thing in a damaged state or do the work
badly. In this and a number of other cases the liability will
commonly arise only on some wilful or negligent failure to
take due care. Here there are two notable differences between the Roman and our way of looking at the matter.
Justinian's treatment of contract in Digest, Institutes and
Code is full of references to liability for carelessness: it is
the main factor in his treatment of the duties of parties
under a contract. But in our books we see nothing of the
kind. It is impossible to prove by citations a negative proposition of this sort, but it may be permissible to 'hold the
eel of science by the tail' and resort to index-learning. The
word negligence does not occur in the index to, e.g.,
Pollock on Partnership, Benjamin on Sale, Chalmers on Sale
of Goods. It occurs in the indexes of some treatises on
contract, but the few references are usually not concerned

with the ordinary law of contract, but with, e.g., a principal's liability for his agent's negligent tort and other outside matters of that kind. This is not to say that there is no discussion of negligence in any contract cases—it does occur, but it is far more prominent in cases of bailment than elsewhere, precisely because our law of bailment has dealt a good deal with Roman law and took its rise long before the modern remedy on contract came into being. The difference is puzzling because the law is very much the same. It may perhaps be due to the fact that in our modern law negligence can be either a substantive tort or an element in tort, and who thinks negligence instinctively thinks tort. In Roman law this is not so. There was no general principle that negligence causing damage was a tort, but only a specialised principle that negligence causing physical damage to property was a delict, and that is of course not nearly wide enough to cover the field of *culpa*, negligence. The necessary extensions by analogy seem to have come more easily, and therefore earlier, in contract than in delict. Or it may be that in England the contracts in which it is usual to make an absolute promise to do something, e.g. to let a house, to sell a horse, to build a ship according to specification, are commoner or come more into the courts than those in which it is usual to make a promise limited to the exercise of the promisor's due care and skill, for instance, to carry carefully passengers or goods, to use due surgical skill, etc. The limited promise is more likely to occur in cases of bailment but is not confined to them.

The other difference is that the two systems when they do talk of negligence do not state the matter in quite the same way. They agree that failure to show the necessary skill for work undertaken is equivalent to negligence, however carefully the work is done. 'Imperitia culpae adnumeratur' says the Digest.[1] 'Spondet peritiam artis',

---

[1] D. 50. 17. 132.

says Story on Bailments (Sect. 431). But with us, in general, differing circumstances call for different degrees of carefulness—a man carrying a delicate instrument must show more care than need be shown by one who is carrying a brick. Unintentional failure to show the care needed in the circumstances is negligence. Thus we do not in our law of contract or tort usually speak of degrees of negligence except to a limited extent in the law of bailments, which, as is well known, shows the impact of Sir John Holt's attempt to carry over a certain amount of the Roman law *via* Bracton so far as this matter is concerned. If we speak of degrees at all we speak of degrees of care, or at any rate we ought to. That this is the correct point of view for the common law is clearly laid down by Beven, who states[1] that 'the learning concerning degrees of negligence is scholastic, for the division of negligence into the three degrees of "ordinary", "slight", and "gross", although well known to the Roman law, does not exist in English law.... The positive quality is care according to the circumstances...'; it is the degree of care that varies with the circumstances, and lack of the required degree constitutes negligence. That appears to be the true doctrine; more epigrammatically it has been said judicially that gross negligence is the same thing as negligence 'with the addition of a vituperative epithet'.[2] But the temptation to speak of degrees is not always resisted. On the other hand, in the law of the *Corpus Juris* the matter is otherwise put. The texts speak not of degrees of care, but of degrees of carelessness, and in stating these degrees they do not take account of the kind of thing which is to be done: they do not say that it is less permissible to do one sort of thing

---

[1] *Negligence*, 4th ed. p. 15.

[2] Rolfe B. in *Wilson* v. *Brett* (1843), 11 M. and W. 113, 116; see also Willes J. in *Grill* v. *General Iron Screw Collier Co.* (1866), L.R. 1 C.P. 600, 612: 'Confusion has arisen from regarding negligence as a positive instead of a negative word. It is really the absence of such care as it was the duty of the defendant to use.'

carelessly than another. This is taken for granted: of course one who is winding a watch needs to act more cautiously than one who is winding a bucket out of a well. They distinguish on other lines. Putting the matter roughly, we may say that their position is that in certain transactions involving confidence and wherever one is beneficially interested under the contract one is liable for *culpa levis*, defined as failing to show exact care, such as a *bonus paterfamilias* would show. In other cases, e.g. deposit, a gratuitous service, one is liable only for *dolus* and for *culpa lata*, i.e. for gross negligence: 'non intellegere quod omnes intellegunt'.[1] Further complication is introduced by the cases in which one is bound to show the care which one habitually shows in one's own affairs, but this we need not consider. This distinction is not ancient in the law and its genesis and indeed the genesis of the whole conception of *culpa* is one of the most vexed questions in the history of the Roman law, into which we cannot enter.[2]

The curious way in which *culpa lata* is defined—'non intellegere quod omnes intellegunt'—and the crude proposition in the Digest—'magna culpa dolus est'[3]—led Mitteis to the view[4] that since it is not easy to tell whether a course of conduct was actually intended or not, the facts are allowed to speak for themselves: you may say that your gross disregard of the other party's interest was merely carelessness, but you must have known better than to do what you did: your conduct is indistinguishable from *dolus*, so that you are responsible. The result is that, even starting as the law clearly did in earlier classical times from the view that only *dolus* entailed liability in

[1] See, e.g., 18. 6. 3; 13. 6. 18. *pr.*; 50. 16. 213. 2; 50. 16. 223. *pr.*; 50. 17. 23; Coll. 10. 2. 1.

[2] For a general account of the matter see Buckland, *Main Institutions of the Roman Law*, pp. 299 *sqq.*

[3] D. 50. 16. 226.

[4] *Röm. Privatrecht*, pp. 325 *sq.*, 327, n. 42. See also Arangio Ruiz, *Resp. Contratt.* 2nd ed. p. 255.

a great many cases, the lawyers reached much the same result as was reached in later times. What later times called *magna* or *lata culpa*, they were prepared to treat as *dolus*. German law seems to retain the distinction and there are traces of it in the French Code Civil, but if we may judge by the commentaries it is of little use.[1]

'Non intellegere quod omnes intellegunt' expresses on the face of it an impossibility, but it seems designed to bring out just the relation between *culpa lata* and *dolus* above stated: whatever you say, you must have known what you were doing. In fact it is not negligence, but the state of mind called by Austin recklessness, consciousness of the possible results but no desire that they should occur.[2] And there is a close similarity between Austin's classification of recklessness under the head of intention and the Roman, at least the late Roman, *culpa lata dolus est*. Thus this conduct or habit of mind, recklessness, stands in both systems between *dolus* and *culpa*, between intention and negligence, and has a foot in both camps.

It may be noted that in our law of manslaughter this habit of mind appears again, though under a disguise. Mr Turner has shown[3] that the 'culpable negligence' which is necessary to a conviction for 'involuntary manslaughter' is in fact recklessness as defined above. 'Culpable negligence' seems a curiously chosen expression; for in telling us that the 'negligence' which creates liability for homicide must be 'culpable' negligence the proposition tells us nothing, for culpable means creating liability. The expression seems to be a creation of text-books and judges, not statutory, any more than is the almost equally unhappy expression 'involuntary manslaughter'. But the

---

[1] But French law allows one to insure oneself against responsibility for 'faute lourde', though not for 'dol'.

[2] On this, see Turner, '*Mens Rea* and Motorists', *Cambridge Law Journal*, v. (1933), pp. 61–76.

[3] *Loc. cit.*

statute book does even worse, for it speaks, in a different connexion, of 'wilful neglect',[1] which seems very like a contradiction in terms.

6. NEED AND NUMBER OF WITNESSES

If it is desired to prove a transaction it is necessary to submit some evidence of it, which may be documents signed by a party or certified in some way or the evidence of witnesses who testify to the occurrence of the transaction. But neither the old common law nor the earlier Roman law required the presence of witnesses as a requisite to the validity of transactions in many cases. No contract of the classical or later law normally required witnesses as matter of law. The normal contract of *stipulatio* never required them, nor did the formal *dictio dotis*. *Cretio*, the formal acceptance of a *hereditas*, did not require witnesses, though they were commonly used and testators often required them. Some writers indeed, in view of the nature of the act, assume that witnesses were required, but entirely without evidence. *Traditio* of property required no witnesses in classical law or under Justinian. Similarly with us a deed requires no witness at common law though attestation is a usual precaution and statutes have now required witnesses in many cases. But there is one notable difference. With the Romans ordinary transactions *inter vivos* rarely needed witnesses, but they were required in all acts involving a ritual which went beyond formal words. *Mancipatio* and its derivatives needed witnesses. The ritual search for stolen goods did.[2] *Confarreatio*, marriage with an elaborate ritual, needed witnesses. It is noteworthy that when Constantine surrounded *traditio* of land with ritual

---

[1] See, e.g., Offences against the Person Act, 1861, ss. 26, 35; *Words and Phrases judicially defined*, pp. 493–495. The condemnation in the text is perhaps a little too strong, for 'neglect' means no more than 'omission', which can of course be wilful.

[2] At least the simpler form of search into which it was modified did; G. 3. 186, 193.

observances, to secure publicity he required the presence of the neighbours.[1] Our own older law did not impose this requirement. Neither the speaking of the words of a feoffment nor the ensuing livery of seisin, a ritual delivery of land with the object of securing publicity, seems to have required the presence of anyone except the parties, though in its German home (if that be the origin) witnesses appear to have been necessary;[2] when later it became customary to record the feoffment in a charter, witnesses became usual. The transfer of copyholds, a ritual act 'by the rod', never required the presence of witnesses. But where the Roman law did require witnesses it seems to have called for what look to us inordinate numbers. *Confarreatio*, the ancient ritual marriage, required ten witnesses;[3] *mancipatio*, formal conveyance, required five witnesses.[4] Wills, not unnaturally in view of the postponed operation of the instrument, have required attestation in the developed law of both systems. But while our law has contented itself with three or more and now requires two, Roman law required a number varying historically, but normally five or seven.[5] These seven witnesses appear elsewhere. The formal notice of divorce under the *lex Iulia* required seven witnesses.[6] When it became usual to have written notes of transactions these were often attested, though that this was not legally necessary appears from the fact that many which have survived are not attested, and the number of witnesses is very often seven. Constantine required for certain *donationes 'conventus plurimorum'*.[7] In some cases we know only that witnesses were needed, not their number, e.g. in the search for stolen goods *'testibus praesentibus'*[8] and in the attestation of proceedings of the Senate.[9]

---

[1] *'Vicinis praesentibus'*, *'testibus significantibus'*, Vat. Fr. 35. 4, 6; C. Theod. 3. 1. 2. 1.   [2] P. and M. ii. p. 85.

[3] G. 1. 112.   [4] G. 1. 119.

[5] Buckland, *Text-book*, p. 286.   [6] D. 24. 1. 1; 24. 2. 35.

[7] Vat. Fr. 249. 6.   [8] G. 3. 186.

[9] Mommsen, *Staatsr.* iii. p. 1005.

7. THE RELATION BETWEEN THE GENERAL LAW OF CONTRACT AND THE LAW OF THE PARTICULAR CONTRACTS

A favourite subject of comparison has always been found in the Roman and English views of the relation between the general law of contract and the law of the particular contracts; but it may be doubted whether attention has been directed to the most interesting points of difference. It is true that in Roman law a general law of contract, so far as it existed, has had to be collected and brought to the surface in modern times. It is at best latent in the ancient books. The jurists dealt almost exclusively with the particular contracts, though in developing each contract they regularly made use of analogies from other contracts. With this procedure is usually contrasted that of the common lawyer, for in English law *assumpsit* seems to have given a general remedy for simple contracts. No doubt the law of the particular contracts is as voluminous in England as at Rome, but it seems to be a supplement to the general law of contract, and not a quarry from which that general law of contract must be hewed.

Two questions suggest themselves here. The first is whether this description of the English method is strictly accurate. The second is, what is the reason for the marked difference between the English and Roman methods, if it really exists.

(i) A little reflexion will show that the priority of the general law of contracts in English law has been somewhat exaggerated, and a fair amount of what is now brought under the general umbrella of contract was originally thought of as autonomous and distinct from contract. Thus the law of landlord and tenant was and still is thought of much more in terms of real property than of contract; and as often as not any action brought on the contracts in the lease would have been brought in covenant, not in *assumpsit*. Again, much that is now regularly considered contract was at one time only bailment; and indeed the incorporation of bailment in contract, never complete, has caused difficulties and some distortion in the law of contract, especially as regards the doctrine of consideration. The law of master and servant, too, is thought of much more in terms of status than of contract. It is to be found in Blackstone's first volume, which deals with public and personal rights, rather than in the second and third volumes, where he deals with property and civil wrongs. In all these cases we get excellent examples of a tendency which Pound has made much of in his various books, a tendency to think in terms not of the 'legal transaction, an act intended to create legal results to which the law carrying out the will of the actor gives the intended effect',[1] but of relations, the relation of landlord and tenant, of principal and agent, of vendor and purchaser, of partnership. If we leave on one side those which have just been discussed, and if we also disregard, as not yet forming part of the developed common law, such contracts as belong to the law merchant, what have we left? There is nothing very important except sale, and sale seems to have become, even more than in Roman law, the typical contract. From sale was developed the notion of consideration, which was generalised so as to be the one requirement in all simple contracts, and, for purposes of actionability, all those other relations came to be regarded as sales. But it is quite clear that they all existed before *assumpsit*. Thus it is not quite correct to say that English law first developed a general law of contracts, and then elaborated, under its aegis, the various particular contracts. In fact the parallelism between the Roman and English developments is much closer than has usually been thought.

(ii) There still remains, of course, a marked difference

[1] *Spirit of the Common Law*, p. 21.

in that Roman law never attained to a general principle of actionability. We can only conjecture the reasons for that difference, but I suggest that, apart altogether from reasons connected with conflicts of jurisdiction in fifteenth and sixteenth century England, much can be put down to different ways of looking at contract. Authors at any rate have concentrated their attention very much on problems connected with the formation and the discharge of contract, and the assignment of contractual rights and duties, all of them matters which can be dealt with generally for all classes of contracts, whereas in Roman law it is obvious that the jurists paid far more attention to the terms of contracts, and very little of this can be dealt with on a general level. One cannot ask in general what a contracting party naturally intends by his contract, but one can ask what is implied in a sale or in some other particular contract. Why the Romans concentrated on the terms, rather than on the problems more closely connected with the general law of contract, we shall probably never know— their habits of thought became settled during the latter half of the republican period, the most obscure period of all during the history of Roman private law—but one fact is clear: the central point of their thought is the difference between a contractual figure with a well-defined shape manifested in terms which can be implied from the nature of the transaction, and the unilateral promise, every term of which must be expressed. In dealing with the former they had the dexterity and tactical sense to establish those contractual figures which were most essential and which covered nearly all the transactions which naturally fell into well recognised types, and the rest they left to be dealt with by the unilateral promise, the *stipulatio*, or by combinations of such promises. A little reflexion will show how many transactions fell within the recognised figures of the consensual contracts. First there is sale, the great master contract to which, as Professor

Gutteridge has said,[1] so many other contracts such as 'carriage, insurance and finance are after all only ancillary'; then *locatio conductio*, which covered the ground now covered not only by landlord and tenant, but also carriage of passengers and of goods by sea or land, master and servant, work and labour, and, in certain cases, even such topics as insurance; partnership, which for the Romans meant any exploitation in common; and mandate, which, as it meant merely the undertaking of a task on the instructions of another, was made to cover not only all the relations of principal and agent *inter se*, but also assignment, certain types of suretyship, gratuitous services of various kinds, and even professional services. The proper choice and construction of these figures, so as to reconcile the firm outline of a specific shape with the inclusion of as many transactions as possible, was one of the most remarkable performances of the Roman mind.[2] It is a task which English lawyers never attempted; and the reason, I am convinced, does not lie in different views of actionability. The Romans did not prefer to have four or eight or ten actions to one because they preferred a multiplicity of actions—we have more actions in tort than the Romans had in delict—but they were more concerned than we have been with the implied terms of the various contracts. Perhaps their habits of mind were formed at a time when commerce was more stable than at the corresponding period of English legal history. On the whole the period of the late Republic and of the Empire was not a period of expanding commerce or of developing commercial methods. On the other hand there has never been a time since the fifteenth century when commerce and industry have been in anything like equilibrium. It is always necessary for business men to think out new terms for their contracts. In other words, express terms are

---

[1] *British Year Book of International Law*, Vol. xiv. p. 77.
[2] Engels, *Ludwig Feuerbach* (1935, Eng. tr.), pp. 63–64.

much more important than implied terms in English law, and indeed the most familiar of all decisions to the commercial lawyer is *The Moorcock*,[1] in which it was stated that the law will imply only such terms as are necessary to give business efficacy to the contract. Even where the law has, as in the Sale of Goods Act, built up a complete apparatus of implied terms, whole classes of merchants systematically exclude the Act and write out their contracts afresh. This was of course possible, and no doubt it happened, at Rome, for one of the great fields of usefulness of the *stipulatio* was in making contracts every term of which was express. But everything seems to show that the *stipulatio* was regarded as a supplementary way of contracting to be used in the rare cases where the particular contracts such as sale could not be used. Moreover, it was only with considerable difficulty, and, as it were, by an afterthought, that the Romans accepted the notion that one could vary the terms of these contractual figures by express pacts. Such a law of contract could never have suited us at any time after the end of the Middle Ages. Our contracts do not fall so easily into typical figures.

It follows that contracts such as those which modern civilians call innominate contracts have never presented any difficulty to the English lawyer; and that the problem for the Roman jurist was not quite that which usually appears in the books. It is usually thought that the main difficulty was to make such contracts, which do not fall within the well-known particular contracts, actionable. But it is probable that at any time after the beginning of the Empire the Praetor would have allowed an action on any such contract which seemed to call for it: we underestimate the number of stray actions given by the Praetor in particular cases without any antecedent promise in the edict. However, it seems to be agreed that it was only in the time of Justinian that any general principle of action-

[1] (1889), 14 P.D. 64.

ability was established in connexion with innominate contracts. In truth the classical jurists were not greatly concerned with that particular problem. It was enough for them that the plaintiff could get his action if he really needed it. What interested them far more was not whether a transaction which did not fall under the recognised particular contracts had an action, and was therefore to be considered a contract, but rather what contract it was, what was its shape, what were its implied terms.[1] That is a problem which can never be got rid of, because, however one adds to the number of particular contracts, there are always bound to be some gaps in the scheme. One certainly does not get rid of the question by formulating some general test of actionability.

It seems, therefore, clear that by the time of Justinian the point of view had shifted. Certainly if the classical jurists had been deeply concerned with the problem whether the innominate contracts should not be actionable, they could have invented an action for the purpose. That they did not do so shows that they were interested in a quite different point, namely, the terms of the particular transaction in question, and it seems almost certain that the technique by which they approached this problem was to tack each of these transactions, so far as was possible, on to the known particular contracts, so as to give to them the advantages of such implied terms as could be extended to them.

---

[1] Thus Zeno, when constituting *emphyteusis* a separate contract, was forced to lay down its implied terms. See J. 3. 4. 3.

CHAPTER VIII. PARTICULAR CONTRACTS

1. UNILATERAL CONTRACTS IN GENERAL

It has been noted that the Roman contracts break into two groups, those *stricti iuris* (so called only in later law) and those which gave *bonae fidei* remedies and may be called *bonae fidei* contracts, the former group and those alone being purely unilateral.

Unilateral contracts in this sense can hardly be said to exist with us. It is true that a man can make a gratuitous binding promise under seal, but such a thing is unusual and its commonest form, a deed of gift, is normally a transfer and not a contract creating an obligation. But it is not to be supposed that the Romans promised something for nothing more readily than we do, and though a number of their contracts were unilateral, it does not follow that the transaction of which they were the expression was also unilateral. Thus *mutuum* (loan of money and the like) is unilateral; but this is only because till the money is lent there is no contract at all. The most general contract of all, *stipulatio*, is unilateral, but such a *stipulatio* will not be a solitary act: in most cases it will be part of a dealing. It may of course be a promise by way of gift. But more usually it will be a promise to pay for some service already rendered (which with us would normally not be binding unless under seal), or given in return for a counter-promise. In this last case there will be an *exceptio doli* if the other party refuses to fulfil his counter-promise, and if, when the promisor has performed, the other party refuses to do his part, there will be remedies varying with the circumstances. Similarly the contract *literis, expensilatio*,[1]

---

[1] G. 3. 128 *sqq.*

though in form a unilateral transaction—it is so unlike anything in our law that we need not say much of it—is, at least usually, a novation of some pre-existing dealing. It may be remarked that this contract, a statement of indebtedness entered by the creditor in his account-book with the debtor's consent in the fictitious form of a loan to him, seems to be dispositive in the sense that it was the contract itself and not mere evidence of it.[1] It was, however, obsolete so early and so little is known of it that we cannot be very certain of anything about it. The rule of later law that a written acknowledgement of indebtedness or a written promise to repay a loan was, after a certain lapse of time, indisputable except on grounds of fraud or duress, seems to be, like our estoppel by deed, rather a rule of evidence than of substantive law. But there is reason to think that in Justinian's time the Greek notion of the writing in any transaction as being the contract and not mere evidence of it was in course of being absorbed. It may be that in all systems the difference between dispositive and merely evidentiary documents is not a sharp distinction, but a question of degree.

The description of the contract *literis* suggests a rather puzzling phenomenon. In the ancient formal acts of Roman private law, *inter vivos*, it is the person who is to benefit who goes through the formal act.[2] In this contract the entry of indebtedness is made by the creditor in his own book. In *mancipatio* it is the person who is acquiring who makes the formal declaration.[3] The same is of course true of the derivative forms of *mancipatio*, that is to say,

---

[1] It is perhaps relevant to mention the distinction between our Account Stated as a substantive cause of action and an I.O.U. which is purely evidentiary. Perhaps an even clearer instance of a dispositive act is a grant of land by deed, which does not merely evidence the intention of the grantor to pass the property but actually passes it.

[2] In the procedure of *legis actio* we get a similar state of things. Ritual words are prescribed for the person who is claiming, not for the defendant.

[3] See p. 111, *ante*.

coemptio, the *familiae mancipatio* by which wills were made in the classical period and *nexum*. In *cessio in iure* it is the person who is to acquire who utters the formal words, as in the variants, *manumissio vindicta*, the process of adoption, etc. In manumission *censu* it is the slave who enters his name, *consentiente domino*. In formal release *per aes et libram* it is the debtor who declares himself formally released. In *stipulatio* it is the promisee who formulates the promise. *Dictio dotis*, in which the *pater* or *avus* or the woman herself formally declares a *dos*,[1] is only in appearance an exception, for the persons who can promise in this way are precisely those to whom the *dos* so declared will revert on the termination of the marriage, so that their declaration that the property is to be *dos* establishes a reversionary right in themselves. *Votum*, a unilateral undertaking to a god,[2] does not seem to have had ritual words, and indeed it would be difficult to get a formal declaration of acquisition from the god. Even in *traditio*, which was entirely informal, it was the acquirer who acted, though the point is only to be inferred from the much greater difficulty the Romans found in admitting representation of the acquirer than of the transferor. The latter only needed to consent, and his consent could be expressed in whatever way he wished, even through an intermediary; whereas the acquirer had to do the taking himself, or through one in his power, and exeptions to this rule were admitted only piecemeal. With us it is the donor who makes the deed of gift; it was the feoffor who, in a feoffment, spoke the formal words. A conveyance is a declaration by the transferor and if effected, as is usual, by an indenture needs only execution by the transferor; indeed it can be done effectively by deed poll. It is not necessary that the grantee or donee or promisee under a deed should execute it, though of course it cannot impose any obligation upon him unless he does so; it takes effect as soon as the active party,

---

[1] Buckland, *Text-book*, p. 457.   [2] Buckland, *Text-book*, p. 458.

grantor or donor or promisor, has executed it (that is, sealed and delivered and, since 1925, signed it) and before the passive party is aware of it or has expressed his assent to it; but the latter may disclaim the benefit of the deed when it comes to his notice; he cannot acquire against his will but he can acquire passively; here the active part is taken by the grantor or donor or promisor. What the cause of the Roman rule may be is uncertain. In *mancipatio* it is perhaps, as Jhering says,[1] due to the intensity of their conception of property and of the truly 'quiritarian' mode of acquisition as being by seizure.[2]

In the conception of contract in both systems, both form and agreement played a part. But their history has not been the same in the two systems, and in each system their respective spheres have varied with the lapse of time. These factors make comparison difficult. A further difficulty is that with us the early law of contract is the law of certain actions, such as Debt, Covenant and Account, rather than the law of obligation, and in two of these, Debt and Account, the basis of the action is recuperatory, not consensual, while the early history of Covenant is almost entirely confined to transactions affecting land.[3] Nevertheless it seems true that with us, agreement, undertaking, became, apart from delict, the essential element in obligation at a relatively early date, whereas the Roman

---

[1] E.g. *Geist des röm. Rechts*, Erster Th. Sect. 10.

[2] G. 4. 16. Dr D. Daube has suggested to us in view of the existence of the same thing in some other systems that Jhering's solution may be inadequate. A primitive people might see in such a thing a beginning of enjoyment, a sort of *quasi-traditio*. But surely Jhering's point is a good one. Where a title is derived from a grant by another person, there may well be a suggestion that it is revocable by the grantor. Many examples of this can be found in political life. A nation may not feel safe in the enjoyment of its liberties unless it has won them for itself. While the original of the English practice of conferring, rather than acquiring, titles may be obscure, it fitted admirably the feudal system, under which all titles were ultimately derived from the king and, as it were, coursed from that root through the trunk and branches of the feudal tree.

[3] P. and M. ii. pp. 203–222.

law continued for much longer to consider the form gone through as more important than agreement. 'If a man said he was bound, he was bound', says Holmes[1] of a written acknowledgement of indebtedness in the early common law. It would seem that in the earlier period of Roman legal history the *stipulatio* played a much greater part than covenant did with us; but the general position was not very different. The great change came with the introduction, probably at much the same stage of legal development, of the Roman consensual contracts and of the English parol contract enforced by *assumpsit*. For whereas *assumpsit* could be used to enforce any lawful agreement, whatever its terms, so long as it satisfied the not very arduous requirements set by the doctrine of consideration, the consensual contracts had each a range which, though wide, was bounded by definite limits and—what was much more important—had each a set of standard implied terms which could at first, in most cases, not be easily varied by the parties. Hence the *stipulatio* had a very wide field of usefulness. Not only had it to be used to give validity to agreements which fell outside or between the various real and consensual contracts, but it must always have been the usual way of making a contract which, even though it belonged to one of the types furnished with their own particular actions, contained a number of terms specially agreed on between the parties. Moreover, the *stipulatio*, though not less strict than the covenant, was much less cumbrous in form. Indeed, if the parties were face to face with each other, it was as easy to make as any other contract. As no general doctrine of consideration ever appeared[2] it is not surprising that the formal unilateral contract is more prominent than it is with us.

---

[1] *Common Law*, p. 262.
[2] The Romans were not without the notion of consideration: the most important commercial contracts, those of sale, hire and partnership, all required it.

Holmes[1] says: 'In one sense, everything is form which the law requires to make a promise binding over and above the mere expression of the promisor's will. Consideration is a form as much as a seal. ...' That is true, but form has two different meanings and effects. In the earlier stages of legal development form is the factor which makes the transaction binding whether or not there was in fact real consent; for instance, the ritual act in *mancipatio*, the oral question and answer of *stipulatio* in its earlier days and the seal at that time in our history when 'a man was bound by his seal, although it was affixed without his consent'[2] and before he could plead 'non est factum'.[3] In this sense there is little difference between Roman and English legal history. Roman law, it is clear, even if we do not adopt the extreme views sometimes maintained, was slow in admitting the reliefs associated with 'reality of consent' and the like, for persons who had made formal promises. Even in England fraud could not be pleaded in defence to a deed at common law until Lord Mansfield. But in a second and later sense form denotes some factor required by the law, such as the 'memorandum or note... in writing', as evidence that the affair is seriously meant. This kind of form does not make the transaction binding if there is in fact no consent. It is in this sense that consideration can be called 'form'; to use Anson's phrase it is a 'test of actionability' of promises, evidence that the promise is one which the law ought to enforce. Of form in this (Holmes') sense the two systems have, apart from the *stipulatio* and consideration, singularly little. In particular, in neither system is writing a general requirement (for both peoples exhibit a strong tendency to regard a man's spoken word as being 'as good as his bond') and much important business is done without it.

[1] *Common Law*, p. 273.
[2] Holmes, *cit.* p. 272; P. and M. ii. p. 536; i. p. 508.
[3] See *Thoroughgood's Case* (1582), 2 Co. Rep. 9a.

2. LOAN FOR USE, DEPOSIT AND PLEDGE

The contracts of *commodatum* (loan for use), *depositum* (deposit for safe-keeping) and, apart from its 'real' effect, *pignus* (pledge), offer little material for comparison or at least for contrast, since our law is in this matter very largely derived from the Roman law. It may be noted, however, that the first two are essentially gratuitous bailments (like our loan of goods but not necessarily our deposit) and no contract at all exists until the thing has been handed over. If any hire is agreed on or any reward for the care it becomes an entirely different contract, namely *locatio rei* or *operis*, consensual contracts in which the mere agreement creates obligations. But none of them, whether gratuitous or paid, resembles bailment in one important respect. They do not give legal possession, but only detention or custody. Thus, on the one hand, they give no occasion for the rubric of larceny by a bailee, for the holder differed in position in no way from any third person who stole the thing, though this is not the place in which to discuss what amounted to a theft by such a holder; on the other hand, if these persons had, as the borrower had, but the depositee had not, an action for theft if the thing was stolen, this was not by virtue of any right or interest in the thing, but by virtue of what is sometimes called a 'negative *interesse*', i.e. the fact that they are responsible to the owner if the thing is stolen. The borrower is so responsible—the depositee, as such, i.e. the gratuitous depositee, is not, and has therefore no *actio furti*. The pledgee is in a different position. He has possessory rights and indeed more than possessory rights. He has normally certain powers of alienation and he has an action for recovery of the thing wherever it may be, which is a good deal more effective than the possessory interdict, the remedy of the possessor as such when he is deprived of possession. He has therefore an *actio furti* in respect of his positive interest, though it must be admitted that the texts are very far from clear as to the basis of his action and the measure of damages.[1] Our law too recognises the greater interest of the pledgee in the chattel pledged than that of other bailees, and, though he has possession only, his interest is often judicially referred to as being a 'special property' in the goods.[2]

It should be noted that, though these contracts of loan and deposit were binding only when the thing had been handed over, like *mutuum*, loan of money, they were not in the result unilateral, as that is. There were possible liabilities on both sides. Those of the depositee and borrower were obvious, but the other party had his obligations. The lender must, for instance, pay all unusual expenses of maintenance[3] and the depositor must pay all incidental expenses. The depositor was liable if the thing did damage through some noxious characteristic of which he knew or ought to have known; and even the lender was liable if actual knowledge could be imputed to him.[4] There is not a great deal of English authority upon the liabilities of the bailor in these two cases, but the lender at any rate is liable to the borrower for the consequences of any defects of which he was aware and which he did not communicate to the borrower; and, speaking generally, our law upon loan and deposit is very like the Roman law which is the source of so much of it.

It is curious that our law, like our language, seems to have experienced more difficulty than the Roman system did in grasping the notion of fungibility. The Roman law distinguished clearly between *mutuum*, loan not for use but for consumption, the debtor being bound to return not the same thing, e.g. the same money, corn or wine, but the same quantity of things of that kind and quality, and loan for use, the thing being returned, which later was recog-

---

[1] Buckland, *Text-book*, p. 580.
[2] *Attenborough* v. *Solomon*, [1913] A.C. 76, 84.
[3] D. 13. 6. 18. 2, 4.   [4] D. 13. 6. 18. 3; 47. 2. 62. 5.

nised as a 'real' contract and called *commodatum*. There is no sign that the two were ever confused. But in our law the remedy for the recovery of all things other than land was at first the same, the writ of debt, which closely resembled the writ of right for land. The defendant was ordered to render to the plaintiff so many marks or shillings 'whereof he unjustly deforces him' and it is not until after the time of Glanvill that debt is reserved for money and throws off detinue as the appropriate remedy for other chattels.[1] Even to this day 'we *lend* books and half-crowns to *borrowers*' and speak of having 'money in the bank'. Pollock and Maitland[2] attribute this confusion to the fact that 'time was when oxen served as money' and 'one ox must be regarded for the purposes of the law as exactly as good as another ox' (which is equally true of the history of Rome), and find the consequences of this 'pecuniary character of chattels' in the inadequacy of our remedies for the recovery of moveables. We distinguish clearly between loan of money and gratuitous loan of specific goods, but where a fungible article, such as corn, is handed over on the terms that an equal quantity of like quality in its original or in an altered form shall be restored, we appear to regard the transaction as sale (or at any rate as a transfer of property for value) and not bailment.[3]

3. CONSENSUAL CONTRACTS: GENERAL

In Roman law, apart from certain praetorian and later pacts, of relatively small importance, there were only four contracts which were binding by mere consent, and these

---

[1] P. and M. ii. p. 173.   [2] ii. p. 151.

[3] The evidence is scanty and unsatisfactory and is not easy to reconcile with the requirement of 'price' in Section 1 of the Sale of Goods Act, 1893: see *South Australian Insurance* v. *Randell* (1869), L.R. 3 P.C. 101; Jones on Bailments, 1st ed. sects. 47, 228, 283, 439; Hailsham, i. sect. 1227. There is not the same difficulty in the United States, where the Uniform Sales Act, s. 9(2), says that 'The price may be made payable in any personal property'.

were, naturally, those most important in everyday commerce, sale, hire, *societas* (partnership) and the contract of *mandatum*, which may be described as agency shorn of its main effects between the principal and the third party, with the exceptions which have already been noted. Of these contracts sale was of course the most important.

4. SALE

Sale was, as with us, purely consensual. There was no rule requiring writing in any case; indeed writing is very rarely required by law in Rome, in strong contrast with the attitude of Greek laws, which seem to have required a writing for most transactions. It is the contrast between *Romana fides* and *Graeca fides*: no Greek trusted another unless he had the matter set down in writing. And though in the cosmopolitan society of the Empire, steadily growing more and more Hellenistic, it was inevitable that the practice of putting transactions into writing should prevail—there was little of the old *Romana fides* left—there was never any general rule of law on the matter. In other respects the Roman rules of sale were very different from ours. We have already noted that the contract of sale never had a 'real' effect. The contract never passed ownership, with the practical result that if I had contracted to sell the same thing to two different people, the first to whom I made delivery became the owner, though his contract might have been the later.[1] But there are many other differences.

As with us there must be a money price, though there might be other elements in the price as well.[2] But there is the great difference that in Roman law the price must be fixed by the agreement: there must be a *certum pretium*,[3]

---

[1] The same result is achieved in English law in a roundabout way by the operation of S. 25(1) of the Sale of Goods Act, 1893; see also p. 292, *post*.

[2] Inst. 3. 23. 2; D. 18. 1. 79; Sale of Goods Act, 1893, sect. 1; *Aldridge* v. *Johnson* (1857), 26 L.J.Q.B. 296. The English authority as to a price which does not consist wholly of money is somewhat indirect: see Hailsham, xxix. p. 6 note (c).   [3] Inst. 3. 23. 1.

while, with us, when once it is clear that the transaction is a sale of goods the absence of a fixed price will not prevent the contract from being valid. There was in Roman law no such thing as a sale at a 'reasonable price', though, if there was a *certum pretium*, there might be other, uncertain, elements as well. An agreement to sell at a reasonable price was no more than a stage in the negotiations and bound neither party. Thus a sale 'at such a price as Titius shall fix' was, in Justinian's law, a contract only if and when Titius did fix a price;[1] it appears to be in the meantime a conditional contract. This is an unsatisfactory solution, for both parties may be held up indefinitely by Titius; the better view seems to be that of some older lawyers that there was as yet no contract at all. In English law an executory contract of sale at a price to be fixed by a third party is regarded as a valid contract subject to a condition subsequent and is avoided if the third party does not fix the price; but in so far as the contract has been executed by delivery of the goods to, and appropriation of them by, the buyer he must pay a reasonable price therefor.[2] A sale for 'all the money in that box' was on the accepted view a sale for a *certum pretium*[3] and it might have been argued, and probably was, for there were great disputes, that 'at whatever price Titius may fix' was on the same footing, and there was an immediate sale, or agreement for sale.[4] But this view was not accepted. In fact, the principle 'id certum est quod certum reddi potest' had a very narrow application and was not used to liberalise the law.

There was on the texts another remarkable difference. There might be, as with us, a valid agreement to sell a future thing, next year's crop or a thing to be made.[5] The

---

[1] Inst. *cit.* [2] Sale of Goods Act, 1893, Sect. 9. [3] D. 18. 1. 7. 1.

[4] The absence of any 'real' effect prevents the appearance in Roman law of the distinction between a sale and an agreement to sell which appears in our law. All Roman sales were 'agreements to sell'.

[5] D. 18. 1. 8. *pr.*, 39. 1; *Lee* v. *Griffin* (1861), 30 L.J.Q.B. 252.

sale need not be of a specific thing: it might be of a thing of a certain kind, but with an important limitation. So far as the texts go the thing of a kind must be from some specified mass. No text treats as a valid sale such a bargain as '100 quarters of best quality wheat'. Such bargains were made but they seem to have been carried into effect by *stipulatio*, not by the contract of sale.[1] To come under the head of sale it must be from some specified mass 'of the wheat in your barn' or, for that matter, in anybody's barn. There is indeed no text which expressly denies the validity of such a sale, and it is accordingly contended that the absence of references to such sales is merely an accident. Indeed some who reject the rule profess to find texts which recognise such sales, but none of them is convincing.[2] In fact there is nothing exceptional in such a rule. In all ancient laws sale is essentially a market transaction. The goods are thought of as on the spot and a number of ancient systems of law certainly had the same rule. It is found in Hindu law, in ancient Babylonian law, in the Talmud, in Mohammedan law and in the Graeco-Roman law of the early Middle Ages.[3] It is true that few if any of these systems had reached the notion of a purely consensual contract of sale, apart from borrowing from Roman law, but it is not in the least inevitable that the Romans in making this advance should have made the other also. There are indeed difficulties in applying the ordinary rules of *emptio venditio* to such sales, which would usually be 'bulk sales'. To take only one example, the problem of the seller's obligation to pass title takes on an entirely different form, for very commonly the point of the transaction is that he should acquire the ownership of someone else's goods and pass it on to the buyer.[4] But English experience in

---

[1] D. 45. 1. 54, 75. 2.

[2] Haymann, *Haftung des Verkäufers*, i. pp. 71 *sqq.* For the opposite view see Monier, *Manuel Elémentaire de Droit romain*, ii. no. 109.

[3] See the references in Buckland, *Text-book*, p. 484, n. 13.

[4] P. 283, *post*.

connexion with bulk sales, which are usually governed, not by the Sale of Goods Act, but by standard contracts, seems to show that instead of merely varying the terms of the ordinary law of sale, parties prefer to set out all the terms afresh. The *stipulatio* was peculiarly fitted for this purpose.[1]

Another rule, rather curious in view of the clearness with which the Romans handled the notion of ownership, is that the vendor is not bound to make the buyer owner. He must indeed do all in his power to make the buyer owner; he must, for instance, mancipate the thing if it is a *res mancipi*,[2] but his obligation is to give the buyer undisturbed possession and to guarantee him against eviction by superior title. One text is frequently cited to show that if the contract was definitely to transfer ownership, it would not be sale, but it does not really bear this interpretation.[3] The reason why the rule is put in this way is much disputed: the most probable explanation seems to be that proof of title may be costly and difficult, and the rule has the advantageous result that the vendor is not called on to prove his title till it is effectively disputed.

Turning to English law, it seems that transfer of ownership was not till recently an essential ingredient in the contract of sale of goods. In 1849 Baron Parke said:[4] 'the result of the older authorities is that there is by the law of England no warranty of title in the actual contract of sale' of goods 'any more than there is of quality. The rule of *caveat emptor* applies to both.' Later this rule was modified, and either a condition or a warranty was implied in the absence of rebutting circumstances. Then section 12 of the Sale of Goods Act, 1893, removing some uncertainty, implied, as regards transactions falling within the

---

[1] P. 275, *ante*.   [2] G. 4. 131a.

[3] D. 12. 4. 16. Discussion and references Buckland, *Text-book*, p. 488. For different views see De Zulueta, *Roman Law of Sale*, pp. 36–37; Lawson, 65 *L.Q.R.* pp. 364–366.

[4] *Morley* v. *Attenborough* (1849), 3 Exch. 500, at p. 512.

Act, a condition on the part of the seller that he has a right to sell. Apart from this section, while section 27 of the Act imposes on the seller a duty to deliver the goods, and while the Act contains rules for deciding when the 'property' passes, it nowhere imposes on the seller a duty to transfer ownership. 'Property' here seems to mean no more than the seller's full right and interest in the goods, though normally it amounts to complete ownership: the definition clause (section 62) does not help much.

These provisions of our law are not surprising, for the common law, in regard to moveables, has always dealt much more with possession than with ownership: it may almost be said that, so far as concerns remedies for its protection, the common law does not recognise such a thing as ownership of moveables, but the Roman law, in other fields, dealt so clearly and directly with ownership that the actual rule, convenient as it is, seems rather to jar with the rest of the system.

The rules as to liability for defects, as stated by Justinian, differ from ours in some important respects. The most obvious point is that in Roman law the seller was bound to disclose any material defects of which he was aware, even if he had expressly excluded all warranties.[1] This rule, which makes the non-disclosure of defects known to the seller fraud, is adopted by many foreign systems, and our own law (of which the case of the sale of typhoid-infected pigs 'with all faults' is a good example)[2] has been sharply criticised for not having it. Indeed the Roman law went further. Dealers in slaves and live-stock, we are bluntly told, were usually rascals[3] and the Edict of the aediles made them liable for any serious defects not disclosed whether they were aware of them or not[4]—a rather arbitrary way of disposing of the difficulty that

---

[1] D. 18. 1. 35. 8; 18. 1. 43. 2; 19. 1. 4.
[2] *Ward* v. *Hobbs* (1878), 4 App. Cas. 13.
[3] D. 21. 1. 44. 1.   [4] E.g. D. 21. 1. 1. 2.

although the vendor, a dealer in such matters, usually would be aware of the defect, it was almost impossible to obtain proof of his knowledge. The texts contain propositions to the effect that this rule of the Edict was extended to all commodities,[1] but it is very difficult to say how far this actually went. The original provision speaks of *morbus* or *vitium* of the slave or beast sold and there is much learning as to what is *morbus* or *vitium*. It would be difficult to apply this learning to sales of other things: probably it went little if at all beyond defects which made the thing unmerchantable. In the modern systems it certainly extends to fitness for general purposes,[2] but there are usually special rules for animals.[3]

Neither sales by description nor sales by sample could have any meaning for Roman law in the sense in which they were originally incorporated in the Sale of Goods Act. Since sales of wholly unascertained goods did not, apparently, fall under *emptio venditio*, neither description nor samples could be used for the purpose of defining the subject-matter of the sale, which was of course sufficiently defined otherwise. Hence we do not find in the text any clear references to sales by description or sales by sample. However, it has been held that the conditions and warranties implied by the Sale of Goods Act in sales by description or sample apply even where the goods are specific, and where, accordingly, the purpose of the description or the sample is, not to identify the goods, but only to imply the necessary conditions or warranties. Roman law would regard such descriptions or assertions that the bulk would correspond to the sample as *dicta*. The general rule is clear: the thing could be rejected if it did not answer the description by which it was sold or was such that it did not serve the purposes to which such things were ordinarily put, subject, of course, to agreement, and not where the

[1] D. 21. 1. 1. *pr.*; h.t. 63.   [2] E.g., French C.C., art. 1641.
[3] Colin et Capitant, *Cours élémentaire de Droit civil français*, ii. no. 921.

defect was patent or known to the buyer.[1] This comes near to our law (subject to the difference that in Roman law a breach of contract, however fundamental, did not discharge the contract, though it gave the other party a defence if he was sued and a claim for refund),[2] but the Sale of Goods Act embodies what looks like an unreasonable distinction. Apart from what may be called patent defects, if the sale is by sample the thing must be of merchantable quality, but if the sale is by description alone this rule applies only when the vendor is a dealer in such things, whether the manufacturer or not. That seems to be the effect of sections 14(2) and 15. There does not appear to be in the Roman texts any rule corresponding to section 14(1), which tells us (it is not a new doctrine) that 'where the buyer... makes known to the seller the particular purpose for which the goods are required, so as to show that the buyer relies on the seller's skill or judgment', the things being such as it is in the course of the seller's business to supply, there is an implied warranty that the things are reasonably fit for that purpose. To make that rule workable a limitation is necessary which is not stated in the section, though it seems to be implied in the cases, namely that the 'particular purpose' indicated must either be one to which such things are normally put, that is, their general purpose, or it must be a special purpose disclosed to the seller expressly or by implication. In that sense the Roman law gives much the same result as to the first case and probably as to the second.

In one respect our law seems to be more reasonable. In Roman law, if land sold proved to be subject to a servitude, an easement or the like, which was not disclosed, this gave the buyer no claim, unless the vendor knew of its existence, in which case his silence was *dolus*, or warranted that there was none, in which case there was a breach of contract.[3]

---

[1] D. 19. 1. 6. 4; h.t. 11. 3; h.t. 7; h.t. 27; h.t. 44. 1.
[2] P. 254, *ante*.   [3] D. 18. 1. 59, 66.

Of course such a thing is not likely to happen apart from
fraud, but in our law it seems that when the incumbrance,
e.g. a right of way, is latent, but not when it is patent, the
buyer would have his remedy.[1] The Roman law is usually
explained as resulting from the view that a servitude is not
so much a burden on the land as a quality or characteristic
of it, like unusual fertility, or liability to be flooded, of
which the buyer must take his chance. However this may
be, the rule can hardly be called satisfactory. It persisted
in the Gemeines Recht, but it has disappeared from the
Bürgerliches Gesetzbuch. And the French Code Civil
gives a remedy where the servitude was not apparent,
provided it was important enough to have determined the
buyer against the purchase.[2] Indeed both French and
German law impose liability for any defects seriously
affecting value, except such as were apparent, and subject
to contract. But it is curious to note that both these
systems have modified this in respect of animals, i.e. precisely in the field in which the Roman law itself was most
severe.[3]

We have already noted that, in Roman law, the contract
did not transfer ownership—a separate act of conveyance
was needed and was no doubt often contemporaneous.[4]
Notwithstanding this the Roman law of the texts places
the risk of accidental destruction on the buyer even before
delivery, an exception to the general rule—*res perit domino*.
This looks so odd that the view has been maintained that
the rule is not really Roman but was adopted only in the
later Empire, having been borrowed from Greek practice,
in which it was perfectly logical, since there the contract

---

[1] *Yandle* v. *Sutton*, [1922] 2 Ch. 199.   [2] Art. 1638.

[3] For France, see, e.g., the law of August 2, 1884. For Germany, see
Schuster, *Principles of German Civil Law*, p. 213.

[4] The French law had abandoned the Roman doctrine long before the
enactment of the Code Civil, but it was preserved in the German Gemeines
Recht, and has been maintained even in the modern Bürgerliches Gesetzbuch.

and the conveyance were the same thing: there was no consensual contract of sale, and the contract was completed only by delivery. This opinion is to say the least extremely doubtful; the better view is that it is ancient, but this is not the place in which to speculate on its origin. Whatever this may be, the rule survived because, it seems, it was commercially convenient.[1] French law adopted the rule but made it logical, as it is in our law, by making the contract pass the property, and this is the law of the Code Civil. The Gemeines Recht preserved the Roman rules unaltered, but the new Bürgerliches Gesetzbuch has reached a solution the opposite of that in France and England, but equally logical. It preserves the Roman rule that the contract does not pass the property but makes the risk pass only on delivery.[2] It would be interesting to know which was thought by commercial men the more convenient rule.

The rule that the risk passed to the buyer even before delivery, though ownership did not, was less severe than it looks. It did not apply so long as the sale was subject to a condition or so long as the goods were not in a deliverable state: so long as there was anything to be done to the goods, such as severance from the mass or even measurement of the mass sold to determine the price, the risk was not on the buyer and he would not have to pay the price if the goods were destroyed without his fault. The sale was *perfecta*, and the risk passed, only 'si id quod venierit appareat quid, quale, quantum sit, sit et pretium et pure venit'.[3] This is substantially the same as the effect of sections 18 and 20 of the Sale of Goods Act, that is to say the circumstances in which the risk passes in Roman law

[1] Buckland, *Text-book*, pp. 486 *sq*. and references; Lawson, 65 *L.Q.R.* pp. 361–364.

[2] Schuster, *Principles of German Civil Law*, pp. 209, 215. Though the effect of the postponement is mitigated by the possibility of constructive delivery.

[3] D. 18. 1. 35. 5 and 7; D. 18. 6. 8. *pr.*

are much the same as those in which the property passes
and with it the risk under our law. The practical difference
is not very great, but the fact that in Rome the risk passes
without the property is notable. As we have seen, in
French law the Roman rule as to risk is maintained, but
property passes much as with us, so that it is only in the
rare case of a postponement of transfer of property, though
the contract is *perfectus*, that the Roman anomaly can
arise.[1]

The rule that the contract of sale did not transfer ownership in Roman law, while with us it commonly does, under
the rules already stated, gives a distinction, which is one of
principle rather than of practical effect. It also illustrates
the fact that in contrasting two systems much depends on
the stages of historical development selected for the contrast. The Roman rule calling for separate conveyance
existed so far back as the history can be traced. That cannot
be said of our rule. There is evidence that up to Bracton's
time and later what mattered in determining where property lay was seisin, a term which then applied equally to
chattels and to land. 'That the ownership of the purchased
goods did not pass to the buyer until they were delivered
to him seems plain.'[2] Fry and Bowen L.JJ. in *Cochrane* v.
Moore[3] also point out how the rule stood in early law and
attribute the change to the introduction of the action of
assumpsit, which gave much increased importance to merely
consensual contracts. In consequence of the increased
importance of consent in contract the questions whether
and when property passed came to depend, in cases where
there was a *quid pro quo*, on the consent and intent of the
parties, with the result that a new exception was made to
the necessity of delivery.[4] That the same increased importance of consent did not produce the same effect in

---

[1] Amos and Walton, *Introduction to French Law*, p. 353.
[2] P. and M. ii. pp. 209–210.   [3] (1890), 25 Q.B.D. 57, 65.
[4] *Ibid.* at p. 70.

Rome is not surprising in view of the clearness with which they distinguished *iura in rem* and *in personam*.

It therefore appears that the Romans and the founders of our common law were at one in refusing to treat the contract as alienatory *per se* and in requiring delivery to pass the property. In the Roman case the reason is probably that sale was essentially a market transaction and that it accorded with common sense that so important a matter as the transfer of the ownership should be accompanied by, and depend upon, a visible act such as handing over. In our case the reason was probably the same, but the rule is doubtless reinforced by the fact that in our medieval law possession was very much more important than ownership and it was difficult to conceive of ownership unaccompanied by possession. 'Indeed we may be left doubting whether there was any right in movable goods that deserved the name of ownership.'[1] It is this fact which, as already mentioned, probably explains why it has been impossible to say —at any rate until recently—that the modern contract of sale of goods imposes an obligation to transfer ownership.

As the Romans made no great distinction between land and moveables and the distinction between *res mancipi* and *nec mancipi*, obsolete under Justinian, had no importance in the law of contract, the rules which have been compared with our law of sale of goods are those of sale generally. But there is one point in which a distinction seems material. Both systems agree in holding that, apart from fraud, the sale is void if the thing has ceased to exist before the agreement was made. Land does not, in these latitudes, commonly cease to exist, as goods may, but its characteristics may completely alter in a way which does not commonly happen with goods. One who bought a house, as with us, bought land with a house on it. One who bought an olive grove bought the land with what was on it. The burning down of the house or the grove does not really destroy

[1] P. and M. ii. p. 153.

what was sold, but it was in fact treated as destruction of the thing.¹ If this happened before the agreement was made, this was void, as there can be no sale without a *res vendita*.² Our law attains a similar result by a different route. When the house has been really destroyed, not merely damaged, before the date of the contract and without the knowledge of the parties, there is no contract, by reason of the common fundamental mistake.³ Roman law might have reached the same result on the ground of fundamental error, but the texts cited go on to discuss the effect of partial destruction and of knowledge in either party or both, in a way which is somewhat irrational (the conclusions can hardly be classical), but which suggests that this is not the actual point of view. The rule that if not more than half the house is burnt the contract stands, subject to allowance for lessened value, seems absurd and is modified by the Code Civil into a rule that in case of partial destruction the vendee may choose either to repudiate the contract or to maintain it subject to compensation.⁴ The Courts however have limited the right of repudiation to cases in which the destruction has been such that the party would not have bought if he had known of it.

EXCURSUS: THE PASSING OF PROPERTY AND RISK IN SALE

This topic can now, I believe, be handled more clearly than in the text; and it seems that the English, and still more the American, law approaches with extraordinary closeness to the Roman law.⁵ Both the Sale of Goods Act and the Uniform Sales Act contain headings⁶ which make

¹ D. 18. 1. 57, 58. ² D. 18. 1. 15. *pr.*
³ *Hitchcock* v. *Giddings* (1817), 4 Price, 135, 141; Williams, *Vendor and Purchaser*, 4th ed. pp. 771, 772, which is in accord with general principles; *Scott* v. *Coulson*, [1903] 1 Ch. 453; 2 Ch. 249.
⁴ Art. 1601. ⁵ See 65 *L.Q.R.* pp. 352–372.
⁶ Before S.G.A. sect. 16 and before U.S.A. sect. 17.

it clear that mere agreement to buy and sell the goods transfers the ownership only as between the parties and, although the point is not specifically taken up in the operative words of the Acts, the effect of the transfer is seriously cut down by later sections,[1] which are expressed to deal with transfer of title. Thus under both Acts a seller who remains in possession of the goods after sale has full power to pass them outright or by way of pledge to a *bona fide* holder for value who has no notice of the sale, with the result that they take exactly the same view as Roman law of the case where a seller sells the same thing successively to two *bona fide* purchasers. The first purchaser to acquire possession acquires the title.

Thus the mere fact that the property passes with the contract does not make it pass as against third parties. This rule was accepted at common law in Massachusetts as early as 1821.[2] It has been accepted in England only by a fairly long process of legislation.[3]

French law, which also has long made the property pass with the contract, has come to the same conclusion on this point, but it has done so by applying one of its most characteristic doctrines, the overriding rule that any possessor of goods, with very few exceptions, can give a good title to a *bona fide* purchaser for value. It is important to note that neither English nor American law has any such general doctrine, and in neither law has any far-reaching application been given to the doctrine of estoppel. In fact it looks as though both have made inroads on the doctrine that the property passes with the contract only to the extent of restoring the Roman solutions.

The question arises whether the passing of property as between the parties has any other effect than to pass the risk. At first sight it would seem that the buyer could

---

[1] S.G.A., sects. 21–26; U.S.A. sects. 23–40.
[2] *Lanfear* v. *Sumner* (1821), 17 Mass. 110.
[3] See the Factors Acts.

claim the property in the goods as against the seller instead
of merely bringing an action for damages for non-delivery.
That is undoubtedly true where he has paid the price, but
he is really in no better position than if he merely sued for
specific performance of the contract. For if he sues in
detinue or trover he will have to tender the price and it
will be in the judge's discretion whether to order specific
delivery or not: he will exercise his discretion in precisely
the same way as if the action were one for specific performance. Moreover, although the property has passed even
if he has not been paid, the seller has a lien for the price,
even against a sub-purchaser who has paid the price to the
original buyer. Indeed the only serious question is whether
the buyer will be preferred to the seller's creditors if the
goods are still in the seller's hands when he becomes insolvent. As owner, the buyer would certainly seem to be
in the better position. But the balance is redressed to a
considerable extent by the doctrine of reputed ownership,
in accordance with which a trustee in bankruptcy is entitled to retain goods which the buyer has allowed the
seller to retain, and which have been used for the seller's
trade or business. Doubtless there are occasions when
this doctrine does not operate—the most serious exception
is where a company is wound up—and to that extent the
buyer who has not taken possession of his goods may be in
a better position than he would have been at Roman law.
But it looks as though on the whole there would be little
change if we substituted Roman for English law.

The rule that the risk passes with the contract has really
nothing to do with the passing of property. It is a rule of
pure obligation, and merely says that if the goods have
deteriorated or have been destroyed without the seller's
fault between sale and delivery, the buyer will still have to
pay the price in full. However, it seems that it is habitually associated with the passing of property. Not only
do French, English and American law associate them, but

the Roman classical jurists themselves noted that their rule was an exception to the general principle that the risk lies upon the owner. No explanation hitherto put forward for the Roman rule has won universal acceptance, but I suggest that just as the passing of the risk is regarded in English and American law as a natural consequence of the passing of property as between the parties, so also in Roman law the ordinary buyer and seller may well have thought that the property passed as between them with the contract. However, Roman law was extremely intolerant of such half-way houses as a relative passing of property. Either the property passed, as against all the world, or it did not pass at all; and not only were the jurists able to express risk in terms of pure obligation, but it accorded excellently with their habits of thought, and with what they regarded as the claims of justice and convenience, that they should insist on an actual conveyance for the passing of property.

5. LEASE OF LAND AND HOUSES: LETTING OUT OF CONTRACTS AND SERVICES

The contract of hire also presented a number of somewhat remarkable differences. In Roman law the lessor of a house guaranteed that there should be a house, not in the sense that he was responsible if the house ceased to exist, but that he could claim no rent in that event. In the same sense the lessor of land guaranteed the exploitability of the land: he could claim no rent for a period in which the land was unavailable, through no fault of the lessee, and he must refund any rent already received in respect of such a period. And a farm tenant could claim abatement, as of right, if a season proved disastrous.[1] With us there is no such right to abatement. A landlord does not guarantee the existence of the house in any way, and, if it is destroyed by accidental fire the tenant, apart from express covenant, must still go on paying rent. This remarkable difference seems to ex-

---

[1] References in Buckland, *Text-book*, p. 501.

press the fact that our law contemplates the parties to such a contract as dealing on level terms so that they can protect themselves by express stipulations, while Roman conditions were such that the capitalist who owned the *insula* or the estate had, and was recognised by law as having, very much the whip hand.[1] As a consequence their common law made the adjustments which in our system are in the first instance left to the parties and only when the inequality has become obvious have been effected by express legislation, by Housing Acts,[2] Rent Restriction Acts, Tenant Right Acts, limitations on the power of distraint, and so forth.

There were, however, some exorbitant-looking rules under Justinian which cannot be reconciled with principle. Thus a text in the Code[3] allows the landlord to eject the tenant holding for a term if he wants the house himself, or if it needs repair, suffering no penalty but loss of rent. This last rule existed equally in classical law, but the first is surprising. The enactment is ascribed to Caracalla, but this provision is in an appended *nisi* clause, and though it is sometimes explained away as expressing only a local custom, it seems more probable that it is a hasty Byzantine addition.

Hire, like sale, is pure contract: it gives no *ius in rem*. The hirer of land or a house had no possessory right, any more than the hirer of a moveable had. There was therefore nothing corresponding to the action of ejectment against third parties. If a third party interfered with the

---

[1] But some place must doubtless be found for the fact that the actions on *locatio conductio* were *bonae fidei*.

[2] The Housing of the Working Classes Act, 1885, sect. 12 (now repealed), implied in every contract of letting of a house to the 'working classes' a condition that it should at the commencement of the holding be 'reasonably fit for human habitation', and this condition has been applied by later legislation, now the Housing Act, 1936, sect. 2, to the letting, at certain low rents, of houses generally, and has been extended to cover not merely the commencement but the whole duration of the tenancy.

[3] C. 4. 65. 3.

tenant's enjoyment, unless his act could be shown to be an insult giving the *actio iniuriarum*, the tenant's only remedy was against his lessor for not providing him with the enjoyment of the land; though by this means he could indirectly compel his lessor to take the necessary action.[1] This absence of rights against third parties, coupled with the fact that contracts by *A* could impose no duty on *B*, had the effect that if the lessor sold the property the buyer could eject the tenant with impunity; the tenant had his contractual remedy but none against the buyer, and no right to be put back on the land. Hence it was usual in sales for the vendor to stipulate that tenants should not be disturbed, but even if this was done the remedies were extremely circuitous. Inconvenient as this rule must have been, it remained in modern German law ('Kauf bricht Miete') until the enactment of the Bürgerliches Gesetz-buch, which abolished it. As the sale itself did not transfer the ownership this state of the law led to the adoption of unedifying dodges, e.g. in those parts of Germany in which actual delivery was necessary, the tenants, by pre-venting access to the property, could prevent *traditio*. In France it was got rid of piecemeal, but it seems to have remained in existence for houses till the enactment of the Code Civil.[2] In our law the tenant has been protected against ejectment since just before the fifteenth century.[3]

It has already been noted that hirers had no *possessio* and therefore no possessory remedies against the lessor or third persons. The owner still possessed. The curious con-

---

[1] D. 9. 2. 11. 9; 19. 2. 60. 5.

[2] However, the lessee's right has remained for all other purposes pure obligation. It cannot be hypothecated and it is treated as a moveable. See Colin et Capitant, *Cours élémentaire du droit civil français*, ii. nos. 1001–1005 *ter*.

[3] Plucknett, *Concise History of the Common Law*, 4th ed. p. 354, note 3. This refers to actual recovery of his term of years. He had been entitled to sue any ejector for damages since the reign of Edward II, *ibid*. p. 540.

sequence seems to have followed that in classical law (the difficulty was disregarded under Justinian) the owner, though he had a claim for damages under the contract, could not bring a real action against the hirer for the recovery of the property: he cannot sue anyone but an adverse possessor, and he himself possesses. However, for reasons into which we need not go, the resulting inconvenience was not great. The point cannot arise in our law, which nowadays has no real actions.

We saw that the landlord was bound to provide the land, and that if he failed to do so the tenant could treat himself as released from liability. On the other hand it is to be noted that the landlord had a corresponding right if the tenant failed to cultivate or to pay his rent. Here the rule at least of later law was that two years' failure entitled the lessor to treat the contract as at an end, i.e. to take possession of the land without liability.[1] It is probable that this is the origin of our old writ of *cessavit per biennium*.[2]

Leases of houses or land seem to have been usually for five years, a term borrowed from the ancient practice in State contracts. But for lodgings, *habitatio*, in a block of flats, no term at all seems to have been usual; it was a tenancy at will, and either could end it without notice; at least that seems to be the most probable interpretation of an obscure text,[3] where however the words 'prout quisque habitaverit' have been very variously interpreted by modern critics. If the tenant of land (it is not absolutely clear that this applied to houses) stayed on after the term had expired, to the knowledge of the lessor, but with nothing said, one text, the principal one, tells us that there was a new tenancy from year to year,[4] much as in our law, except that there was no requirement of notice on either

---

[1] D. 19. 2. 54. 1, 56.
[2] P. and M. i. p. 353; Holdsworth, iii. p. 16.
[3] D. 19. 2. 13. 11. *fin.*   [4] D. 19. 2. 13. 11.

side to put an end to the arrangement at the end of any year.[1] There was no such conception as tenancy on sufferance: a tenant who remained in possession without any consent, express or tacit, of the lessor was simply a person who had broken his contract, against whom an action would lie.

In comparing the rules of the two systems governing the letting of land and houses the privileged position of the English landlord seems to stand out. The tenant takes the land 'for better for worse'; if harvests are bad, he must nevertheless pay the stipulated rent, though in practice the good landlord habitually grants abatements. The English rule is logical, for it seems probable that in our early terms of years the element of speculation or investment was prominent.[2] The beneficial lease was granted in return for a premium or as a means of securing a loan, and in the case of 'husbandry leases' (which are not the earliest type) it is not unreasonable to suppose that the tenant originates in the servant or bailiff who, instead of accounting annually to his master, agrees to pay a *firma* and take the risk.[3] Similarly the tenant of a house takes it for what it may become, though recent legislation to some extent redresses the balance.[4]

The contract of *locatio operis faciendi*, letting out a contract, offers few points of contrast, for its methods have a very modern look: elaborate contract notes seem to have been usual, with, e.g., provision for a penalty if the work is not completed by a fixed date,[5] provisions probably as difficult to make effective as they are with us, or for a power to determine the contract and transfer it to someone

---

[1] Other texts, D. 19. 2. 14 and C. 4. 65. 16, seem to make the new term tacitly created identical in all respects as between the parties with the old one, including the period, but it may be that the words '*ex integro*', '*eandem locationem renovare*' are meant to refer only to the incidental terms of the lease.

[2] P. and M. ii. pp. 110–117.

[3] See Blackstone, ii. p. 141.

[4] See note 2 on p. 295 above.

[5] D. 19. 2. 58. 1.

else if it was not done within the time.¹ It was also usual
to provide that the work must be subject to approval,
which might be by the employer or his nominee, and, if
the job was extensive, to agree that approval, involving
liability for the cost and transfer of risk to the employer,
should be given by stages as the work progressed.² Sub-
contracting was also usual.³

Hire of services, *locatio operarum*, as opposed to *locatio
operis faciendi*, is simply hiring a man's services for a wage
or stipend. It had a curious arbitrary limit. Not every
service could be the subject of this contract but only those
'*quae locari solent*', i.e. *munera sordida* as opposed to liberal
arts. We are not explicitly told what were *munera sordida*,
but the constantly recurring cases are those of handicraft
and what may be called menial service. The line is not
drawn exactly where we might draw it: we learn for instance that the painting of pictures is not a liberal art.⁴
Practitioners of liberal arts were employed by *mandatum*,
which was formally gratuitous but, at least in the Empire,
admitted of *honoraria*, not recoverable under the contract
of mandate itself, but by a special process. For some higher
forms of service, such as those of professors of philosophy
or law, no fees were recoverable at all, the position being
much the same as that of barristers under our law. It is
clear, however, that very considerable fees were paid, and
it is believed that the services of barristers are not in fact
wholly gratuitous.

The texts really tell us very little about *locatio operarum*.
This is due to the constitution of Roman society. At the
time when the jurists were writing, most work of this kind
was done by slaves, and between a man and his slaves
there could be no question of legally enforceable rights and
liabilities. It is probable that this was no longer true under
Justinian, but the Digest is made up of texts from the

¹ D. 19. 2. 13. 10.   ² D. 19. 2. 24. *pr.*, 36, 37, etc.
³ D. 19. 2. 48 *pr.*   ⁴ D. 19. 5. 5. 2.

classical age, and so far as we can gather from the Code there was little legislation on the matter in later times: it was hardly a matter for legislation.

To the English lawyer, the idea that services are a thing that can be hired is unfamiliar. What we hire is the servant. At the now almost obsolete hiring fairs the hind or maid lets himself, or herself, rather than his or her services. We find no difficulty in thinking of a man as hiring himself out. And in Rome if one hired another man's slave or beasts, such as a team of mules, what was hired was not services, but a thing—one hired the slaves or mules. But language of that sort was not admissible where a freeman was concerned. He could not be treated as the subject-matter of the contract: he let out not himself but his services.[1]

6. PARTNERSHIP

Societas corresponds roughly to our partnership but differs from it in many important ways. Partnership is a commercial contract. Sir Frederick Pollock[2] defines it as: 'the relation which subsists between persons who have agreed to share the profits of a business carried on by all or any of them . . .'. But in Rome it had nothing necessarily commercial about it; any sort of continued joint exploitation, whether commercial or not, was a *societas*. If you and I rent a field for our common use as a lawn-tennis court, we are *socii*, and our relation is *societas*, as much as if we had bought it to lay out in building sites, and we are thus subject to obligations which differ from those which result from mere common ownership without use. Indeed it may be that in classical law any common ownership voluntarily created amounted to a *societas*.[3]

---

[1] The contrast appears in such texts as D. 19. 2. 19. 9; h.t. 26; h.t. 30. 2; h.t. 38; h.t. 43; h.t. 48, etc. For the extremely wide range of *locatio conductio*, see p. 268, *ante*.

[2] *Law of Partnership*, 14th ed. p. 4.

[3] Texts and literature, Buckland, *Text-book*, p. 507.

Another great difference results from the fact that it was merely a contract between the partners. Moreover, Roman law had no theory of agency, by which a partner could automatically have authority to bind his partners. If a *socius* made a contract on firm business it was, so far as the third party was concerned, a contract with the partner who made it, and there would be no action against other members of the firm. The *socii* would have claims against each other for account, but the third party had nothing to do with this. To some extent, indeed, this is more apparent than real. If, as would often happen, the *socii* or some of them had authorised one of the *socii* to contract, e.g. had put him in charge of the business carried on, those who had given the authority would be liable on his contracts (though not entitled under them, unless made *procuratores in rem suam*) by the *actio institoria* or *quasi institoria*, on principles already mentioned.[1] But this would be a result not of the *societas* but of the mandate they had given. On the one hand it would not necessarily affect all the *socii* but only those who had given the mandate; on the other hand these would be equally liable if there was no *societas* in the matter at all. One result of this fundamental difference is that while our Partnership Act and Sir Frederick Pollock's treatise on the subject are mainly concerned with the relations between the 'firm' and third parties, the title *Pro socio*[2] in the Digest deals almost entirely with the relations between the *socii inter se*.[3]

Societas was a consideration contract in the plain sense that it required a *quid pro quo*. Every *socius* must contribute something, capital or service. In general there was no such thing as the 'limited partnership' which seems to exist in most systems and has lately been introduced into

---

[1] P. 219, *ante*.   [2] D. 17. 2.

[3] There is in fact no text in the whole, fairly long, title, *Pro socio* (D. 17. 2), which clearly deals with remedies of third parties, though some of them have been made to do so by modern pandectists. See Monro, *Pro socio*, Appendix 2.

our own.[1] We do learn, however, that there might be an agreement that if the firm's transactions resulted in a loss on the whole, a particular partner should not be liable to contribute. We are told that a partner's qualities might be so valuable as to be worth having even on these terms.[2] Moreover, since the relation between *socii* was purely one of contract, there was nothing to prevent an agreement limiting the amount of any partner's liabilities to the others, though there seem to be few traces of such an agreement. It is true that there are traces of contributories to firms farming the taxes or public mines whose liability was limited to their *partes*, i.e. sums they had agreed to contribute,[3] or so it seems; but these were very early obsolete and very little is known of them. It is true also that it was usual to contribute agreed *quanta* to the capital of the concern, and that the shares of profit and loss were not necessarily the same and were arranged with elaborate rules in relation, normally, to these contributions; but this, though it would determine the proportion in which loss would fall on the individual *socii*, had nothing to do with limitation of liability. If a *socius* made, on firm business and with no negligence or breach of duty making him liable to the other *socii*, a contract which in the result absolutely ruined him, he would be the only person directly liable under the contract, but all the *socii* would be liable to him to contribute to the damages he had to pay, in proportion to their shares, but with no limit as to the actual amount. As there was in Roman law no system of bankruptcy putting an end to liabilities, so that a man owed his debts till he had paid them, the rules gave a result not unlike our own rule, which makes each partner liable to third parties for his fellow-partners' partnership debts, though the result was reached in a very roundabout way.

---

[1] Limited Partnership Act, 1907. It seems that little use is made of it.
[2] D. 17. 2. 29. 1.
[3] See Deloume, *Les manieurs d'argent à Rome,* 2nd ed. pp. 119 *sqq.*

Apart from State contracts, above mentioned, limited liability seems to figure in Rome only in a form which has nothing to do with *societas*, namely, in connexion with the *peculium* managed by a *filiusfamilias* or slave.[1]

It may be worth while to add that, as was said by Page Wood V.C. in *Reade* v. *Bentley*,[2] in neither system is any 'community of risk', by which he appears to mean equality of liability, necessary. It is clear that in Roman law the shares of the partners might differ and a partner's share in the losses might differ from his share in the profits, so fully so indeed that, as has been said above, a partner might be wholly excluded from loss, though not from profits.[3] The texts say that the share of the profits must be proportionate to the contribution, but since skill is a contribution, as the texts show, this calculation must have been difficult. The partnership would not presumably be void if this requirement was not satisfied, but the unfair advantage would be a *donatio* and subject to the restrictions on gifts. Section 24 of our Partnership Act provides, subject to any contrary agreement, express or implied, that 'all the partners are entitled to share equally in the capital and profits of the business, and must contribute equally to the losses whether of capital or otherwise sustained by the firm'. Equality is thus, as in Roman law,[4] not essential, but is merely a presumption, whether, as Lindley says,[5] 'the partners have contributed money equally or unequally, whether they are or are not on a par as regards skill, connection, or character, whether they have or have not laboured equally for the benefit of the firm...'.

The later Roman law had a classification of *societates*, elaborate and yet very imperfect.[6] There were indeed one

[1] See Buckland, *Text-book*, pp. 533 *sq.*; and pp. 28–29, *ante*.

[2] (1858), 4 K. and J. at p. 663.

[3] D. 17. 2. 29. 1, 29. 2, 30. In the English law of ordinary partnerships no such arrangement would prevent strangers from suing him.

[4] D. 17. 2. 29. *pr.*   [5] *Partnership*, 11th ed. p. 435.

[6] Buckland, *Text-book*, p. 507.

or two cases in which special rules were applied, in details,
e.g. *societas vectigalis* for State contracts and *societates argen-*
tariorum, but the really important distinction is between
ordinary partnership and *societas universorum bonorum*. This
is an odd institution, to which our law affords no exact
parallel. It is true that, apart from the rare limited partnership, a man may find his whole property swallowed up by
the liabilities of a partnership. That is a different matter.
The Roman *societas universorum bonorum* was communism
on a small scale. In its extreme form, which seems to have
been rare, all present possessions and later acquisitions as
they came in were thrown into the common stock. It seems
to be an imitation or extension of the ancient system of
consortium under which, upon the death of the *paterfamilias*,
his children, instead of dividing up the inheritance, continued to enjoy it in common.[1] How it worked is not fully
known. There must have been distributions of income, for
the texts contemplate property in the control of individual
socii. But it cannot have been important in practice.

It had, however, certain characteristics which ultimately extended to all *societates*.[2] It was said to involve a
certain *fraternitas* which had its effect on the rules. Thus on
the creation of a *societas* it was possible to agree that the
shares might be fixed by one of the *socii*, subject to correction if unfair, which is much as if one of the parties to a sale
were to have the right to fix the price, a thing which was
inadmissible.[3] And, as litigation and fraternity do not go
well together, any action on the *societas* (*actio pro socio*)
normally ended the concern.[4] And just as any *heres* in a
consortium could in historical times at any moment claim

---

[1] Light has been thrown on it by the recently discovered fragments
of Gaius (see De Zulueta, *Journal of Roman Studies*, 1934, p. 168; 1935,
p. 19), which show that it could be created artificially between persons not
actually brothers and sisters, a system which forms a connecting link with
the *societas universorum bonorum* of the texts.

[2] There is dispute as to the time at which these transfers happened.

[3] D. 17. 2. 6; 18. 1. 35. 1.   [4] D. 17. 2. 65. *pr.*

his share and put an end to the *consortium*, so in all *societas* there was a right of renunciation at any time, even though a term had been agreed upon. If this was done *intempestive*, at a time which made it unfair or disastrous to the concern, there would be an *actio pro socio*, but the *societas* was at an end,[1] a rule expressed in the maxim that one who so renounces 'liberat socios a se, sed non se a sociis'.[2] In our law there is a similar right of withdrawal at any moment, if there is no term, but no such right, apart from agreement, if there is such a term,[3] or if the partnership is for a single undertaking. The Roman *socius* can retire at any moment, though he may incur liabilities by so doing, but he ends the *societas*. In our law this right is qualified.[4] In both systems the death of a partner normally ends the partnership for all the members, but there is one fundamental difference; in our law it is possible to agree that this shall not be so and even that a retiring or deceased partner shall be replaced in the partnership by someone else, e.g. his son. But in Roman law this was not possible. What ended the *societas* for one ended it necessarily for all, and it was not possible to agree *ab initio* that, e.g., the *heres* of the deceased *socius* should replace him.[5] It is said in Inst. 3. 25. 5 that the death of a *socius* need not end the *societas* if a contrary agreement had been made *in coeunda societate*.[6] This proviso is probably due to Justinian, but in fact it means less than appears. It means only that though the original *societas* is ended by the death, the business does not necessarily stop: it may well go on, and usually will, but it will be a new *societas* among the survivors.

Both systems have the rule that if a partner agrees with someone not a partner to share his interest with him, this creates a subpartnership, but does not make the person so introduced a member of the principal partnership: 'socii

---

[1] D. 17. 2. 4. 1, 65. 10, 66.   [2] D. 17. 2. 65. 3.
[3] Partnership Act, 1890, sect. 26.   [4] Partnership Act, *cit.* sect. 32.
[5] D. 17. 2. 35 and 59.   [6] See also D. 17. 2. 65. 9.

mei socius meus socius non est'.[1] If he intermeddles in
the administration of what is firm business he makes the
actual *socius* responsible for what he does.[2] This would
probably be true in our law, though there seems to be no
authority.

In both Roman and common law the rule applies that
the partners must show the utmost good faith in their
dealing with the firm's affairs. Thus both systems have the
rule that the partner must bring into account profits made
by him in private dealings in matters in which the *societas*
deals, but not those obtained in non-competing businesses.[3]
It does not seem clear that a contract of partnership in our
law is a contract *uberrimae fidei* in the technical sense in
which that term is applied to the *formation* of certain contracts, and it is difficult to compare Roman law because the
treatment of non-fraudulent misrepresentation was quite
different. But the notion of *fraternitas* and the fact that
condemnation of any *socius* in the *actio pro socio* involved
infamia, with serious resulting civil disabilities, indicate
that, if there had been a scheme of contracts in order of
their confidential character, *societas* would have been near
the top of the list.

It will be noticed that in the absence of any doctrine of
mutual agency it was still more true in Roman law than it
is in our law that there is 'no such thing as a firm known
to the law'.[4] There could be no such thing as an action
against the *societas*, as such, and therefore no question of
being paid first out of firm assets, so far as they would go,[5]
before attacking the private property of individual partners.
The creditor could look only to the *socius* with whom he
had contracted, and those who had authorised him to con-

---

[1] D. 17. 2. 20; *Ex parte Barrow* (1815), 2 Rose, 252.

[2] D. 17. 2. 21.

[3] D. 17. 2. 52. 5; *Trimble* v. *Goldberg*, [1906] A.C. 494.

[4] Though under the Rules of the Supreme Court partners may sue and
be sued in the firm-name.

[5] As in Scots law.

tract, and on the other hand he could look to the whole of their assets whether they had been placed at the disposal of the *societas* or not. Even under our modern law it seems that a firm is not an entity such that it can be sued by one of its members. Lindley says that a partner cannot be a debtor or creditor of his firm.[1] It is surprising that Scots law, though usually based on Roman law, long ago recognised the firm as an entity, so that a member of the firm could sue the firm as such.[2] This was a recognition in Scotland, as elsewhere, that the Roman conception of *societas* was unsuited to modern conditions. In Germany the Roman principle had been abandoned long before the enactment of the Bürgerliches Gesetzbuch, which distinguishes between mercantile and non-mercantile partnerships, and with the Handelsgesetzbuch[3] gives to the latter almost complete legal personality. The French Code Civil contains much of Roman law on the point. It admits, like Roman and German law, non-mercantile partnerships. It is at pains to forbid an absolute *societas omnium bonorum* except between husband and wife.[4] But the rules of the Code de Commerce dealing with mercantile partnerships are in general very like our present law, with limited partnerships and limited companies, and while the Code Civil rejects for non-commercial partnerships the principle of mutual agency,[5] the Code de Commerce, for commercial partnerships, has rules very like our own.[6]

7. MANDATUM

Mandatum is one of the most interesting and important figures in the Roman law. Its original principle is simple enough. If *A* asks *B* to render him some service and *B*

[1] *Op. cit.* p. 151; *Meyer and Co. v. Faber* (No. 2), [1923] 2 Ch. 421.
[2] Bell, *Principles of the Law of Scotland*, Sect. 370.
[3] Commercial Code, a new version of which, drafted to keep company with the Civil Code (B.G.B.), was enacted in 1897.
[4] C.C., art. 1837.   [5] C.C., arts. 1860, 1862.
[6] C. Com., arts. 18–64.

undertakes to do it, then, subject to certain rights of revocation and renunciation in both parties, *A* has an action
against *B* if he fails to carry out the service properly and,
on the other hand, *B* has against *A* an action for reimbursement of expenses and indemnification. It was originally nothing more than a friendly service, but out of it
grew a very flexible and all-pervading institution. We
have already noted that it was in connexion with mandate
that Roman law got nearest to the conception, or at least,
the practice, of agency; though the provision of remedies
to the third party against the principal was not due to any
development or application of ideas inherent in *mandatum*,
but to express praetorian legislation, introducing the *actio
institoria*, and the juristic construction of the *actio quasi
institoria*, which gives the third party an action against the
mandator. But the rules of mandate itself made it useful in
all manner of fields. In the formal manumission of a slave,
per vindictam, the necessary *adsertor libertatis* acted under
mandate. In the adoption or emancipation of a child, the
person to whom the child was collusively sold[1] was in fact a
mandatary, though, since an action for damages would not
serve the purpose where the intent was to create or destroy
a *patria potestas*, other and more effectual remedies were
devised.[2] If a man at my request became surety for me,
his means of recovery of money he was compelled to pay
was an *actio mandati*. An *adstipulator* acted under mandate.
Representatives in litigation acted under mandate.[3] But
there were more ingenious applications. If I asked *A* to
lend money to *B* and he did so, and *B* failed to repay him,
A could call on me to make good his loss, since a mandator
is bound to reimburse his mandatary; thus I was in effect
surety for *B* to *A*, and this in fact became a usual form of

---

[1] Buckland, *Text-book*, pp. 121, 131.
[2] The Praetor used his power of *coercitio* to enforce the *fiducia* involved.
See Buckland, *Text-book*, p. 432.
[3] G. 4. 84.

suretyship, having some advantages over the more direct forms. Again, as in the common law, rights under contract were unassignable and the device was hit upon of appointing the intended assignee my representative (mandatary) to sue on my behalf, with exemption from any obligation to account, *procuratio in rem suam*.[1] It was an imperfect method, for a mandate could be revoked and was *ipso facto* revoked by the death of either party, and further, since the debtor was no party to the transaction, there was nothing to prevent him from paying the original creditor and so discharging himself. All this was gradually amended, and, by the time of Justinian, if notice had been given to the debtor or if he had already made a part payment to the assignee, the assignment was thoroughly effective, though, to the end, as in our equitable assignments, the form still remained that of an authority to sue on behalf of the original creditor.

In our law the development has been similar, though retarded by scruples unknown to the Romans and arising from the rules against maintenance.[2] The common law would allow a creditor to give his assignee a power of attorney to sue the debtor in the creditor's name. Equity permits assignments, even when informal, and requires notice (not necessarily written) only in order to bind the debtor. Finally, the Judicature Act, 1873,[3] introduced in addition a direct written assignment, in which express written notice to the debtor is essential to the validity of the assignment itself.

Roman law never got so far as direct assignment, though it got very near it, for the *actio utilis* in his own name, which classical law gave to the assignee where the mandate had been revoked, was given in an increasing number of cases

---

[1] The expression 'for his own profit' in our early letters of attorney may be reminiscent of this: see Ames, *Lectures on Legal History*, p. 213, n. 2.

[2] Holdsworth, vii. pp. 535, 536.

[3] See now Law of Property Act, 1925, S. 136.

where there had been no mandate to sue but one might be claimed, beginning with the case of buyer of a *hereditas*, but never becoming a general rule.[1] While it is probable that equity has always required consideration for an assignment (at any rate unless there was a completed assignment and not a mere agreement to assign),[2] the Judicature Act, for the cases to which it applies, does not; and in the Roman system of procedural mandate there was no question of consideration. Even the *utilis* action in his own name given where an assignment could be claimed was given in later law in some cases where there was no consideration. But the Romans never reached the notion of negotiability. It is said that the *partes* in the State contracts passed by transfer from hand to hand with no form, but in reality very little is known of these. The *tesserae frumentariae*, which were in effect claims on the public stores, passed by delivery and were bought and sold.[3] We have also texts which seem to contemplate the passing of obligations affecting property to subsequent holders of the property,[4] but it is generally held that these refer only to 'universal successors'. In any case there is no negotiability in the modern sense: all rights would pass subject to equities: 'nemo dat quod non habet'.

8. INNOMINATE CONTRACTS

As we have noted, *stipulatio*, contract by demand and promise, question and answer, was in one sense the most important of contracts, since it could be applied to any sort of bargain. It is true that it was unilateral, but it was usually only a part of the whole transaction. It was also largely

---

[1] See Girard, *Manuel*, 8th ed. p. 780.
[2] The distinction has been recently brought out in *Holt* v. *Heatherfield Trust, Ltd.*, [1942] 2 K.B. 1.
[3] See, e.g., Cuq, *Manuel*, 2nd ed. p. 103, n. 7.
[4] E.g. D. 40. 12. 22. *pr.*; 8. 4. 13. *pr.*

used to supplement other contracts, e.g. on a loan of money it was usual to stipulate for its return—if there was to be interest a *stipulatio* was necessary. Many of the obligations which were implied in sale in later law had originally been imposed by express stipulations. But the greatest generalisation in the law of contract, and the nearest approach to modern ways, was provided by the so-called innominate contracts. These originated in the principle that if there had been an agreement for mutual service of any kind and one had done his part (though, if the agreement was informal, it could not be directly enforced), the party who had performed could, if the other refused to carry out his part, recover at least the enrichment of the other party by a *condictio* or an action of deceit (*actio doli*). This is not enforcement; it merely undoes, so far as possible, what has been done. But about the beginning of the Empire the Praetor gave in some cases an *actio in factum* for actual enforcement, i.e. for damages for non-performance, but only where one party had fully performed. At a later date, but by what steps, and when, are disputed questions, a civil action was introduced for such facts, an action which came to be called the *actio praescriptis verbis*. Here we have a perfectly general kind of contract, with no formalities, but with the important limitation that the action is available only where one has performed: it is essentially a contract on executed consideration. It is like *assumpsit* before it was extended to cover an executory consideration.

There is another development which is almost equally important. When it became usual to put all important transactions into writing and the rule had also developed that a writing purporting to record a stipulation was in effect a *stipulatio*, it became the practice to add an allegation of stipulation to all sorts of contract notes (and indeed elsewhere).[1] By these various devices a fairly workable general

---

[1] See, e.g., Mitteis, *Reichsrecht und Volksrecht*, p. 487.

system of contract was produced, though it did not prove adequate for the needs of modern times in the countries governed by Roman law.

9. JOINT, AND JOINT AND SEVERAL, OBLIGATIONS[1]

In Rome, as with us, it was possible for more than one person to be liable under a contract, but the distinction between joint and several obligation does not appear: the matter is differently conceived. With us, where the liability is joint all should be sued together and any debtor separately sued can normally require the others to be joined, subject to the discretion of the Court;[2] if he does not and the action proceeds against him a judgement even unsatisfied bars an action against the others.[3] And the liability of a joint debtor does not survive against his representatives.[4] But equity always looked askance at purely joint liability, and since the Judicature Acts it has been uncommon apart from trusts. In the common case of joint and several liability the creditor can sue any or all; an unsatisfied judgement against one does not bar action against the others and the obligation is not affected by death of the person liable. In Roman law, either the transaction, though made between several persons, could be analysed into separate contracts, when the question of joint liability does not arise, or it was what is commonly called 'correal' liability. This arose in contract only where the parties so intended, an intent shown in *stipulatio* by the peculiar form in which the contract was made.[5] In such cases it does not seem to have been impossible to sue the parties together, though in fact there is very little evidence that

---

[1] For English law see, generally, Glanville L. Williams, *Joint Obligations* (1949).

[2] *Wilson* v. *Balcarres*, [1893] 1 Q.B. 422.

[3] *King* v. *Hoare* (1844), 13 M. and W. 494.

[4] *Richardson* v. *Horton* (1843), 6 Beav. 185.

[5] Inst. 3. 16.

this was done, but the creditor had the right to sue any one of the debtors for the whole sum. In classical law, however, the mere joinder of issue in this action barred any action against any other debtor: there was but one obligation and the same matter could not be sued on twice.[1] Under Justinian this harsh rule no longer held and, so long as the claim was unsatisfied, any of the debtors could be sued. The resulting state of things was not unlike our joint and several liability. There is, however, a difference which is more apparent than real. With us any one of joint and several debtors who has paid can require contribution from the others. In Rome he had, as such, no such right. But this means little. Becoming correal debtors almost necessarily presupposes previous dealings between the persons rendering themselves so liable, and these will commonly have created an obligation to contribute. Thus, in the very wide conception of *societas*, *correi* will usually, or often, be *socii*, if only in that transaction (*societas unius rei*), and *socii*, as such, were under an obligation of contribution.

There may be joint creditors as well as debtors. Roman law admitted of *correi credendi* as well as *correi debendi*, and at least in classical law an action by one, reaching joinder of issue (*litis contestatio*), barred action by any other. But in fact very little indeed is said of this case; the other was obviously that which occurred in practice. The mutual agency of partners gives more room for it in our law, but even so it is not prominent; in practice the partnership sues as such.[2]

[1] Details, Buckland, *Text-book*, pp. 452 *sqq.*

[2] Nothing is here said of the exceptional cases in which not suing one but only full satisfaction released the others (simple solidarity)—such cases appear to be equitable relaxations of the rule—or of the cases of penal joint liability in which the obligation was cumulative, i.e., each debtor had to pay the whole even if the others had paid. Much confusion is caused by the use of the term 'solidarity' and the phrase 'in solidum' to designate both of these types of liability as well as that described above.

10. SECURITY

Roman law, like our own, recognised both real and personal security. Real security took three forms, *fiducia*, involving transfer of ownership, resembling our old legal mortgage;[1] *pignus*, involving transfer of possession but not ownership as in our pledge or pawn; and hypothec, involving no transfer of actual possession or ownership, but giving a right to take possession, and particularly appropriate to land.

Thus there was an evolution somewhat like our own, but the development was by the introduction of new institutions, functioning side by side, rather than by such gradual modification as has altered the character of our mortgage, at one time a conveyance defeasible upon condition, and now, by recent legislation, recognised as being no more than a charge. No doubt there was in earliest Rome a sort of pledge; a thing could be handed over as a guarantee that an undertaking would be carried out, to be forfeited if it was not, but this was rather a conditional transfer than anything else. The real security of earlier Rome was *fiducia*, a conveyance of property with an agreement for reconveyance if money was paid by a certain time. This was much like Littleton's *mortuum vadium*.[2] There was no equity of redemption, and the creditor, being owner, could at any time make a good title to a transferee, so that the debtor's only remedy would be against the creditor. *Fiducia* endured, with no material change, throughout the classical age, and, though something like an equity appears in later law, it is not very

---

[1] Under the recent property legislation the mortgagee of land, for conveyancing reasons, gets merely a term of three thousand years or, alternatively, a charge by way of legal mortgage having substantially the same effect. But in either case his powers do not greatly differ from those of the old legal mortgagee to whom the borrower transferred his whole interest.

[2] See Co. Lit. 205 a.

clear how far *fiducia* still existed. It is obsolete under Justinian.[1]

When in the Republic the Praetor introduced purely possessory remedies, a new form of security appeared, *pignus*, pledge, which gives the creditor possessory rights, enabling him to keep and recover possession of the thing but, of itself, giving no power of realising the security. It was customary to agree for a power of sale and, in course of time but not till rather late, this power came to be implied. So too it was usual to agree for a right of foreclosure. But both these agreed rights were superseded in later law by statutory rules on the matter of which something will be said hereafter.

About the beginning of the Empire hypothec appeared, in which the creditor, acquiring the same possessory rights as the pledgee, did not take actual possession. This rendered possible successive charges with resulting complications: apart from this there is no difference between *pignus* and hypothec—we are told that the difference is only in name.[2] The system of hypothec, as opposed to pledge, is alien to our common law and equity. It is a little difficult to explain in Roman law, which adhered in general so strictly to the rule that transfer of what we call *iura in rem* needed physical transfer. But in fact pledge, giving no right of exploitation or enjoyment, was not thought of as a *ius in rem*. Its whole content was conceived of as procedural: it is the right to take certain procedural steps. It does not seem that any text ever speaks of pledge or even of possession as a *res*.[3]

The change involved in the introduction of *pignus* and hypothec, though in appearance more fundamental, was in effect much the same as that which the Court of Chancery made in our law by creating the equity of redemption.

---

[1] For comparison of *fiducia* and mortgage, see Hazeltine, Introduction to R. W. Turner, *The Equity of Redemption*.   [2] D. 20. 1. 5. 1.

[3] See, for discussion, Buckland, *Text-book*, p. 203.

The Roman reform reduced the creditor's right to a mere security for the payment of a debt, and the equitable view of the position of a mortgagee, who is owner at law, was long ago expressed in the same terms. 'The principal right of the mortgagee is to the money, and his right to the land is only a security for the money.'[1] So, Justinian defines *pignus* as a transfer to the creditor for the better securing of his debt.[2] The further development of the two systems has followed similar lines; each system having looked after the debtor's interests to an extent which to some observers has seemed unfair to the creditor and in the long run disadvantageous to debtors too. It has been said that the mortgagee in possession is the most unenviable of creatures, so closely are his actions scrutinised. There was at least as great severity in Roman law. Unless there was an agreement that he might take proceeds in lieu of interest, the creditor might draw no benefit from the property, and any receipts from it were set off against the debt, so that if his debtor was solvent or the security was sufficient he had no inducement to see that the land was used to advantage. He had, however, to take the greatest care of the property, and was liable if it was stolen from him, even, it may be, where it was stolen without any fault of his,[3] and he was bound to account for any fruits, not only which he had received, but also which he would have received if he had been careful.[4] His power of sale, itself of gradual growth, was hedged round with increasing statutory restrictions.[5] The agreement for foreclosure (*lex commissoria*) was forbidden by Constantine, having already been largely superseded by legislation which, apart from agreement, allowed foreclosure, but only after attempted sale and considerable delay.[6] Under Justinian the protection of the debtor was

---

[1] *Thornborough* v. *Baker* (1675), 2 Freeman 143.   [2] Inst. 3. 14. 4.
[3] D. 13. 7. 13. 1.   [4] C. 4. 24. 3.
[5] Roby, *Rom. Pri. Law*, ii. p. 109; Moyle, *Inst. of Just.* Exc. 2 *fin.*
[6] C. 8. 33. 1 and 2.

carried still further: if the creditor wished to realise his security it would normally be several years before he could feel secure that the debtor was finally barred.[1]

Although we had at common law no such institution as hypothec,[2] the old mortgage by conveyance of the fee simple, and, still more, the modern mortgage by long term of years, had come to resemble it very closely. Not only does the mortgagee very seldom enter into possession of the land, but the conveyance or demise had become largely fictitious. In any case the charge by way of legal mortgage, which may exist since 1925—and seems to be much commoner in practice than the mortgage by long term of years—is in substance pure hypothec; though technically it is rather awkwardly tied up with the mortgage by long term. Hypothec also offers interesting analogies with our law of lien, especially as further developed in equity. An ordinary special hypothec corresponds closely to an equitable lien, though where it is created by express agreement there is nothing of the trust about it, so that there can be no question of its being defeated by sale to a buyer without notice. It is good against every one but a prior chargee, subject in later law to the requirement of registration. Hypothecs arising by act of law were numerous: though like equitable liens they did not depend on actual possession, they were in their range more akin to common law liens. But most of our common law liens not only rest on physical possession: they do not really give a possessory right. If the possession is lost, there is an end of the right, and there is in general, apart from statute, no power of sale. Even the landlord's right to distrain is lost if the goods leave the land, unless removed clandestinely, fraudulently, and after the rent became due, and even then if

[1] C. 8. 33. 3.
[2] For the letter of hypothecation used by bankers, and the doubtful security it affords, see Gutteridge, *Law of Bankers' Commercial Credits*, pp. 74–82.

they have been sold to a *bona fide* buyer. In Roman law, however, once the right had attached, the goods could be seized wherever they were.[1]

We do find hypothec, however, and precisely in that department of our law where we might expect to find it, the maritime law, largely influenced by Roman law. This maritime lien results from the express hypothecation contained in bottomry and *respondentia* bonds and also arises tacitly in respect of damage by collision, salvage, wages of seamen and some other cases.[2] Discussion of this lien is foreign to our purpose, but one or two remarks may be made. It involves no transfer of property or possession, and merely confers a right of action against the property subject to it which can be enforced in the Admiralty Court. Since in bottomry and *respondentia* the lender was repaid only if the voyage terminated successfully, they stood outside the old usury laws and a high rate of interest could be exacted (subject to reduction by the court in rare cases), as in the Graeco-Roman transaction known as *fenus nauticum*, which was not our bottomry or *respondentia*, though the same element of repayment conditional on safe arrival existed.[3] Though called a lien, maritime lien in its present form is in fact a hypothec: it avails even against a *bona fide* purchaser of the ship without notice,[4] though our Government has signed, but not yet ratified, an international convention which will make it necessary to get rid of this characteristic. Roman law did not, so far as appears, recognise a maritime lien similar to ours. The *privilegium* of shipbuilders and some others was hardly a lien: it was

---

[1] See Lenel, *Edictum Perpetuum*, 3rd ed. p. 493.

[2] As to the probable origin, Roman or other, of this lien, see Holdsworth, viii. pp. 270–273 and Marsden, *Collisions at Sea*, ch. iii.

[3] Holdsworth (viii. p. 262), citing Bensa, *Histoire du Contrat d'Assurance au Moyen Âge*, says that these originate not in classical Roman law but in the medieval development of it in the commercial cities of Italy.

[4] At any rate where reasonable diligence is employed: *The Bold Buccleugh* (1851), 7 Moo. P.C. 267.

a preferential claim in bankruptcy,[1] though an express hypothec had a special priority.[2]

There were, however, cases of true lien in the Roman law, cases of *ius retentionis*, with no right of sale, e.g. the right of a *bona fide* possessor to hold the property till certain expenses were made good to him,[3] which, as we have seen,[4] does not exist in our law. In early Roman law even a pledgee had no more than this right and the same was probably true till earlier classical law for a depositee or borrower, in respect of any claims they might have. The carrier and innkeeper do not seem to have had any such right. In fact the law was much more concerned with protecting the customer against them than with looking after their interests. But it is probable, indeed there is evidence, that, for services of these kinds, payment was commonly required in advance.[5]

The ordinary subject-matter of pledge or lien is, of course, a chattel, something the property of the debtor, but in both systems of law it is possible to pledge other things than what one 'owns'. Thus, in both systems there may be pledge of an interest less than ownership or of a debt.[6]

In both cases there may be sub-pledge or repledge, i.e. pledge of a pledge. In our law this seems clearly to be pledge of the creditor's interest:[7] in Rome it seems to be regarded as a second pledge of the thing itself under implied powers, but it is clear that such a pledge fails when the principal debt is satisfied.[8]

In both systems the pledge is a security for the debt, and must therefore end if the debt is in any way satisfied. But a debt has not necessarily ceased to exist because it has become irrecoverable. It is clear that in Roman law the

---

[1] D. 42. 5. 26 and 34. [2] D. 20. 4. 5.
[3] Inst. 2. 1. 30; D. 41. 1. 7. 1 etc. [4] P. 125, *ante.*
[5] D. 19. 2. 15. 6; cf. h.t. 19. 6. [6] D. 20. 1. 11. 2; h.t. 20.
[7] *Donald* v. *Suckling* (1866), L.R. 1 Q.B. 585.
[8] D. 13. 7. 40. 2; 20. 1. 13. 2.

pledge was not affected by the mere fact that the debt was time-barred: the pledgee retained all his rights as pledgee,[1] and it is probable that the same rule applied whenever some technical rule barred recovery of the debt by action, without actual satisfaction or an equivalent, and there were several of such cases. An action for the debt or an unsatisfied judgement for it did not affect the pledge, nor did loss of the action by reason of *plus petitio*.[2] Most of these cases of destruction without satisfaction are gone under Justinian and late legislation enacted a time-bar for the enforcement of hypothecs.[3] In our law, so far as liens are concerned, it is equally true that the fact that a debt is time-barred does not destroy the lien: it is the remedy, not the debt, which is destroyed, and accordingly the lien remains.[4] But it is still only a lien, a *ius retentionis*, giving no power of sale or other realisation. In actual pledge there seems to be no direct authority, but it is probable that the creditor would continue to hold the article, though perhaps he would have only a lien.[5]

In Roman law the rule 'nemo dat quod non habet' governed pledges: a pledgor could give no rights greater than he had, so that the pledgee's right was always subject to defeasance by superior title. This is true not only of charges voluntarily created, but of those established by law. Thus the lessor of a house had a hypothec over goods brought on to the property, but this did not cover goods brought in by guests or by subtenants.[6] In our law the same principle applies in general, but is subject to considerable exceptions. As to pledges voluntarily created the Factors Acts and the Sale of Goods Act, 1893, protect pledgees in good faith in many cases in which the pledgor

---

[1] C. 8. 30. 2.   [2] D. 20. 1. 27.
[3] C. 7. 39. 7. 1.   [4] *Spears* v. *Hartley* (1800), 3 Esp. 81.
[5] See *Kemp* v. *Westbrook* (1749), 1 Ves. Sen. 278 and *Carter* v. *White* (1883), 25 Ch.D. 666, where, however, the point is somewhat different.
[6] D. 19. 2. 24. 1; 20. 2. 5. *pr.*

had an apparent right to pledge. As to charges created by law there are also exceptions. The explanation usually given of the common innkeeper's lien upon goods brought to his inn by a guest as his own is that he cannot ordinarily refuse to accept goods tendered to him in the course of his calling. The position of the common carrier is similar.[1]

Many points are common to both the Roman law and ours. 'Once a mortgage, always a mortgage.' If the agreement is essentially for security, no collateral terms can destroy the debtor's right of redemption. Moreover, where a mortgagee put up a nominee to buy the thing for him, this was no sale and the right to redeem still existed.[2] And there was the same difficulty, to be decided on the facts, in determining whether the transaction was intended to create a security, or was essentially nothing more than a sale with special conditions.[3]

The creditor has the power, under certain conditions, of selling the pledged property. What was his position if the title proved defective? This was the subject of dispute and legislation. The rule laid down by Ulpian is that apart from fraud, which covered knowledge of the defect, the creditor selling under his powers was not liable for any defect in title.[4] This was the solution reached by the common law, at any rate in the case of sale by a pawnbroker,[5] whatever the position may be since the Sale of Goods Act.

Exception was taken by Roman law to penal stipulations raising the rate of interest if the money was not punctually paid, but the rule laid down was that such a stipulation might be valid as to interest accruing after the default, but not for the earlier time.[6] The evasion which has satisfied our Courts does not seem to have occurred to the Romans.[7]

---

[1] Hailsham, iv. sect. 8.   [2] P. Sent. 2. 13. 4 and see C. 8. 34. 1.
[3] D. 18. 1. 81. *pr.*   [4] D. 19. 1. 11. 16.
[5] *Morley* v. *Attenborough* (1849), 3 Exch. 500.
[6] D. 22. 1. 17. *pr.*   [7] Hailsham, xiii. sect. 179.

Both systems admit of a floating charge, a charge on the property of the concern present or future, subject to the right of the debtor to go on dealing with it, even to the extent of disposing of it in the ordinary way of business as if the charge did not exist. English equity recognises this right, but almost entirely in a very narrow field, i.e. in the case of the property of limited companies, but in Roman law, though not commercially more important, it was operative in a wider field. A charge on after-acquired assets might be created between any persons for any debt,[1] or might arise by operation of law without express agreement in the case of certain privileged creditors, e.g. the Fiscus.[2] There was, however, nothing floating about this: when the goods were acquired it was an ordinary hypothec. But there was a rule, stated as it seems only by Scaevola, and thus possibly rather late, that if a man pledged his business this included his stock-in-trade (*merx*) and that the pledge did not follow what was sold but covered what was added, so long as it was part of the *merx*.[3] This is similar to our floating charge.[4]

The intention to include future acquisitions in a general contractual hypothec needed express statement, till Justinian, who provided that this term was to be understood in all such future conventions.[5] This is, in fact, treating the *merx* as a *universitas*, just as *grex* and *peculium* are so treated for some purposes,[6] but it carries the conception further than do the texts referring to these. The institution seems to have worked badly in France, since the Code Civil adopts a rule established during the Revolution

---

[1] D. 20. 4. 11. *pr.*; D. 20. 4. 11. 3, etc.

[2] D. 49. 14. 28; C. 4. 46. 1; 10. 1. 1, etc. Such tacit general hypothecs played a great part in family law, e.g., a wife had one over her husband's property for return of her *dos*.   [3] D. 20. 1. 34. *pr.*

[4] Within certain limits substituted chattels may be comprised within a security bill of sale (Bills of Sale Act (1878) Amendment Act, 1882, 6 (2) and Schedule; *Seed* v. *Bradley*, [1894] 1 Q.B. 319), but it is not a floating charge.   [5] C. 8. 16. 9. 1.   [6] D. 6. 1. 3. *pr.*; D. 31. 65. *pr.*

forbidding agreements for the hypothecation of future acquisitions,[1] though more recent legislation has authorised them in a narrow field.[2] The institution does not appear in the modern German law.

As to the circumstances of the sale of the property by the creditor, the debtor was rather better treated than he is in our law. The creditor's position was somewhat more like that of the tenant for life selling under the Settled Land Act, 1925. He must give notice to the debtor, and in selling must have regard to his interests, rules resulting naturally from the *bonae fidei* nature of the contract of *pignus*, under which the sale takes place.[3] He must pay over any surplus, with interest, if he had used it, or failed to pay it on demand,[4] and, as the sale was in his own interest, he was personally liable to the debtor for this surplus, and therefore could not put him off by assigning his rights against the buyer.[5] Moreover, as the creditor was not the legal owner, the buyer was not absolutely secure. If the sale was made when, e.g., the debt was not yet due, it was simply void, and in any case if the buyer was party to any circumstances of the sale unfair to the debtor, damages could be got from him if the creditor's estate was insufficient.[6]

Property cannot be pledged to two people independently, but so soon as hypothec appeared it became possible to create second charges, and these appear fairly early. Till rather late in the classical age the second charge seems to have been conditional on discharge of the first, but from the middle of the second century a later chargee had nominally all the powers of a pledgee, subject to the rights of earlier chargees.[7] This meant in practice that he could not sell with a clear title. This led to a system under which,

[1] C.C. art. 2129.
[2] Amos and Walton, *Introduction to French Law*, p. 111.
[3] C. 8. 27. 4, 7; D. 13. 7. 22. 4.   [4] D. 13. 7. 6. 1, 7.
[5] D. 13. 7. 42.   [6] C. 8. 29, *passim*.
[7] Herzen, *Mél. Gérardin*, p. 299.

by advancing the money to pay off the first chargee (*successio in locum*) or actually paying him (*ius offerendae pecuniae*), a later chargee could stand in the shoes of the earlier. He could thus acquire the means of giving a clear title to a buyer. But it did not improve the position of any earlier advance of his as against a mesne incumbrancer: there was no question of tacking. Difficult questions of priority arose, which we need not discuss beyond pointing out that in the fifth century Leo established a system of registration giving priority (apart from some privileged hypothecs) to that first registered, but, unfortunately, spoilt the rule by giving the same priority to a hypothec made before three witnesses.

It may be said in conclusion that the rule 'redeem up and foreclose down' is represented in Roman law fairly closely by the rule that any incumbrancer could sell and thereby destroy all rights of a later incumbrancer except in any surplus in the price, subject to certain statutory delays.[1] A subsequent incumbrancer could prevent this only by redeeming the earlier, and conversely he could not himself take any steps toward foreclosure so long as there were prior incumbrancers unredeemed.[2]

11. SURETYSHIP

It is a remarkable but unmistakable fact that the Romans preferred personal security, surety, to real security, pledge. In later law this is not surprising for, owing to the existence of many tacit hypothecs with artificial priority, pledge was rather uncertain. As has been said, a man with a first charge might wake up in the morning to find that it had become a second charge.[3] But this does not explain the fact; the preference is much older than these artificial priorities; it is especially marked in early law.[4] It is prim-

---

[1] C. 8. 18. 1, 3; D. 20. 4. 12. 7.   [2] D. 20. 5. 1, 5. *pr.*
[3] Sohm-Mitteis-Wenger, *Institutionen des römischen Rechts*, p. 352.
[4] Cuq, *Manuel*, 2nd ed. p. 642.

arily an expression of the solidarity of social groups: the *gentilis* was under a duty to come to the support of a member of the same *gens*. But even when this is gone the preference remains. It seems to have been regarded as less oppressive, a fact reflected in the rule of later law that a creditor who had both forms of security must enforce all his personal rights before realising the hypothec, if the thing was in a third person's hands.[1] And there seems to have been no difficulty about getting sureties.

The preference is all the more remarkable in that, though in general the rules of suretyship were somewhat like our own, subject however to a mass of complicated legislation, they differed from ours in ways which must have prejudiced the creditor.

An initial difficulty presents itself in making comparisons on this topic. Our law recognises only one kind of suretyship or guarantee, having much the same effects in all cases, except that when under seal there need be no consideration to support it and the period of limitation is longer (the Statute of Frauds requires writing in all cases, which Roman law did not). Roman law, on the other hand, had no such general conception and therefore no term by which to express it; *adpromissio*, a term of later law, covers suretyship by *stipulatio*, which had itself three types differing essentially in their forms and effects, but did not cover either *mandatum credendae pecuniae* (above mentioned), which also had very special rules, or *constitutum debiti alieni*, an informal praetorian guarantee which also had in classical law very special rules. In Justinian's law some of them have disappeared and those which survive tend to be assimilated in their effects. But it is impossible here to go into these differences.

In classical law, action against the principal debtor released the surety, the old obligation having been extinguished by joinder of issue, and, on the view generally

[1] Nov. Just. 4. 2.

held but at least more doubtful, *vice versa*.[1] Under Justinian
suing one of these parties no longer had any effect on the
liability of any other, though of course satisfaction had. It
is indeed very widely held that since, if there is no debtor,
there can be no debt, and the surety is liable only for a
debt, the 'deportation', involving civil extinction, of the
debtor, or his death without successors, released the surety.
As it is usually an insolvent man who dies without successors and it is only in insolvency that suretyship is really
important, this rule is startling, if it existed. But it rests
only on a far from irresistible logic and is contrary to the
texts. It is alleged that these have been altered; in any case
the alleged doctrine is not true for Justinian's law.[2]

In classical law, as with us, a creditor might proceed
against the surety even though he had not sued the defaulting debtor;[3] indeed, it was only in that event that in
classical law he could sue the surety at all. But there was
an important practical restriction on this: to sue the surety
when the principal debtor was ready to pay was an actionable *iniuria*.[4] Under Justinian, however, after the Digest
was published, elaborate rules were laid down under which
in general no action could be brought against the surety
until the debtor had been sued.[5] As with us, a contract of
indemnity was distinct from one of suretyship,[6] though
under Justinian they tend to become confused.

In our law the fact that the principal debt is time-barred
does not release the surety.[7] In Rome the point was less
important since most contractual actions could not be
time-barred in classical law (the actions were *perpetuae*),
and when in the fifth century a time limit was imposed this
was very long, normally thirty years; so far, however, as
can be made out the rule there was the same.[8]

---

[1] See hereon Buckland, *Text-book*, p. 451 and references.

[2] Buckland, *Text-book*, p. 446 and references, and *Rev. Hist. de Droit*,
1933, pp. 116 *sqq.*   [3] Hailsham, xvi. sect. 59.   [4] D. 47. 10. 19.

[5] Nov. Just. 4.   [6] Buckland, *Text-book*, p. 451.

[7] *Carter* v. *White*, above.   [8] Arg. D. 46. 3. 38. 4.

There was frequently more than one guarantee, and, as they were not necessarily taken at the same time or with each other, there was no privity between the sureties. The result was that while one surety who had paid the debt had his claim under mandate against the principal debtor, this would commonly be illusory against him, for he was probably not able to pay, and the surety had in principle no claim at all against his co-sureties. This was early remedied as to the most ancient forms of *adpromissio* by legislation which in effect limited his liability to his proportion of the debt. The rule did not apply to what became the most usual form of *adpromissio*, i.e. *fideiussio*; but this defect was later remedied first by entitling the surety, as in our law, to claim a transfer from the creditor of all securities he held,[1] and secondly, under Hadrian, by limiting the liability of the *fideiussor* to his proportion in a way analogous to, but differing in detail from, the protection given by the earlier legislation (*beneficium divisionis*). In particular the debt was divided only by the number of solvent sureties. In our law the sureties, whether they had contracted the obligation together, in any way, or not, seem always to have had the right to call on the others for contribution and even to have them joined in the action, if any. And under the Judicature Act, 1873, the division is on the lines of Hadrian's *beneficium divisionis*: only the solvent sureties are counted, as had been the previous rule in equity, though not at common law.[2]

Under our law, so soon as an ascertained sum is due from the debtor to the creditor, a surety for the debtor can obtain an order directing the debtor to pay, whether demand has yet been made on the surety or not.[3] The Roman law had no such machinery. On the other hand,

[1] *Beneficium cedendarum actionum*, D. 46. 1. 17, etc.; Mercantile Law Amendment Act, 19 and 20 Vict. c. 97, sect. 5.

[2] See now Judicature Act, 1925, sect. 44.

[3] Rowlatt, *Law of Principal and Surety*, 3rd ed. p. 188 and the cases there cited, n. *u*.

with minor exceptions which do not affect the principle, all types of surety known to the later Roman law were released by any act of the creditor which absolutely destroyed the principal debt, the doctrine being that a surety could not owe where there was no principal debt.[1] Thus a formal release, an *acceptilatio*, absolutely released the sureties.[2] But an informal release by a pact not to sue the debtor, though enforceable, did not necessarily release sureties, since the debt still existed, though it could not be enforced against the debtor. It did so, however, if it was expressed *in rem*, i.e. not limited to the debtor; this is an exception to the rule that an agreement cannot bind or benefit third persons, justified on the ground that apart from this effect the pact would be useless, since the surety if called on to pay could then sue the principal debtor. The corollary followed from this reasoning that if from any cause the surety was barred from claiming from the principal debtor, the pact with the latter did not release the surety.[3] In our law it is possible to reserve rights against the surety where the transaction with the principal debtor is anything short of an absolute release. The normal surety, the *fideiussor*, was not released by concessions made to the debtor, such as giving him time, which left the debt intact, though these release him in our law.[4] But where the suretyship took the indirect form of a mandate to lend money to a third party, so that the lender was a mandatary, and owed duties to his surety, the mandator, it was a breach of these duties for him to do anything which lessened his rights against the debtor, and any such conduct released the mandator.[5]

---

[1] This was the reasoning in *Coutts and Co.* v. *Browne-Lecky*, [1947] K.B. 104, where a guarantee of an infant's overdraft was declared void. But, as Cheshire and Fifoot say, *Law of Contract*, 2nd ed. p. 301, note 2: 'It would seem that rightly construed the contract was one of indemnity, not of guarantee.'

[2] D. 46. 4. 16.

[3] D. 2. 14. 32.

[4] Rowlatt, *cit*. pp. 247 *sqq*.

[5] D. 46. 3. 95. 11.

CHAPTER IX. QUASI-CONTRACT AND
NEGOTIORUM GESTIO

At some time in the Empire, probably rather late, an apparently heterogeneous group of civil obligations, themselves much older, acquired the name of *obligatio quasi ex contractu*. This name we have borrowed, though rather in treatises on law than in actual practice, and applied to a similar but far from identical group. No one has succeeded in isolating a positive common element of all these cases to serve for a definition, either for the Roman law or for ours. The latest definition, that of Sir Percy Winfield,[1] is negative: it denotes 'liability, not exclusively referable to any other head of the law, imposed upon a particular person to pay money to another particular person on the ground of unjust benefit'. As he shows, the name is unsuitable. The implied promise which plays so great a part in our rules, and may historically account for the name, is often in flagrant contradiction with the facts; any real analogy with what we ordinarily call contract, an obligation essentially based on consent, is often not to be found. In Roman law the association of these cases with the notion of contract is perhaps historically better justified. We are accustomed to think of contract as actionable agreement, but there is evidence that for some at least of the lawyers of the early Empire it was not so limited. The word was not then common, but it was sometimes applied to anything which could be called a *negotium*, at least a civil *negotium*. Thus Gaius places the action to recover money paid by mistake under the head of contract and apologises for doing this, not because there is no agreement, but because it is not

---

[1] *The Province of the Law of Tort*, p. 119; adopted in R. M. Jackson, *History of Quasi-Contract*, p. xxiii.

exactly a *negotium*.[1] Elsewhere, however, we are told by Julian that one who pays money when it is not due 'hoc ipso aliquid negotii gerit', and the same text[2] refuses the action in a case where justice obviously requires it, on the ground that 'nullum negotium inter eos contraheretur'. With them, however, as with us, the verb is used more widely than the noun: a man can contract an obligation in many ways besides contract. It is true that *condictio furtiva*, the action to recover the value of things stolen, apart from the penalty, which is quasi-contractual, does not rest on any sort of *negotium*, but *condictio furtiva* is an exception to all rules. The great classical lawyers of the second century always limit the noun *contractus* to an agreement with a civil action. It is only after this has become settled practice that the name quasi-contract comes to be applied to those relations which do not rest on agreement or presuppose any wrongdoing. It may be noted, however, that under Justinian the wider signification of the word *contractus* recurs. Thus he calls legacy and *donatio* contracts.[3] The notion of contract (in the sense of agreement) implied in the law, which according to Holdsworth[4] underlies the common law of quasi-contract and according to Winfield[5] has at least played a large part in it, has thus no place in the Roman law of the matter: the texts repeatedly emphasise the fact that there is no agreement.[6] It seems in our law no more than a survival of the notion to be found in our older books that there was no conceivable source of obligation in the common law, except tort or agreement, so that if there was clearly no tort the thing had to be linked with agreement;[7] though what the holders of this view would do about obligations arising from status it is not easy to see.

When we compare Winfield's list with those in books

[1] G. 3. 91.   [2] D. 12. 6. 33.
[3] C. Just. 4. 11. 1; 7. 39. 8. *pr.*; cf. D. 5. 1. 20.
[4] viii. pp. 96–98.   [5] *Cit.* ch. vii.   [6] E.g. Inst. 3. 27 *passim*.
[7] 'The fact is the covenant or agreement, or the offence, which two are the only way [of] making obligations': West's *Symboleographie*, pt. i, sect. 3.

on Roman law, or the list given by Justinian, we find that though they have much in common they are far from coinciding. The action for money had and received covers largely the same ground as the Roman *condictiones* for recovery of unlawful enrichment (we need not here consider whether enrichment is exactly the right word), but not exactly. And *quantum meruit* on discharge by breach could not occur, since breach is never of itself a ground of discharge in Roman law.[1] *Quantum meruit* 'as a mode of redress on a new contract which has replaced an earlier one'[2] was always treated in Roman law as substituted contract. *Quantum valebat*[3] could not arise, for there was no such thing as sale at a reasonable price. The case of the stakeholder is represented in Roman law by the *sequester*, who receives a thing from more than one party, to be given to the winner of the dispute; and this is always treated as contract. Though, so far as the texts go, no one but the parties to the deposit has an action, there seems no reason why, if the agreement was that it was to be given in a certain event to a third party, the case put by Winfield,[4] the *actio utilis* which we saw[5] to be given to the third party, should not apply here. But it would be *pro tanto* contract for a third party: such a thing is not contemplated as quasi-contract. Reimbursement of money paid on request is in Roman law pure contract; there is no doctrine of consideration, and the case is one of *mandatum* giving a claim to reimbursement. The same would be true of recovery of unauthorised gains made by an agent. Very few of Winfield's cases of compulsory payment[6] could arise in Roman law. If *A* made a nuisance on *B*'s land to the detriment of *C* without *B*'s privity, *B* was bound only to allow *C* to abate the nuisance and to cede any action he had against *A*.[7] It was never thought of as quasi-contract; it is in fact

---

[1] See p. 254, *ante*. [2] Winfield, *cit.* p. 159. [3] Winfield, *loc. cit.*
[4] *Op. cit.* p. 160. [5] P. 216, *ante*. [6] *Op. cit.* pp. 161 *sqq.*
[7] See, e.g., D. 39. 3. 6. 7; 43. 24. 16. 2; h.t. 15. 1, etc.

praetorian and quasi-contract is civil. For convenience modern writers sometimes treat it as quasi-contractual, but this is rather bold. The fact that some unauthorised person had enabled a third person to acquire a lien over property was no answer in Roman law to the claim of the true owner, as we have seen.[1] Account stated was always contract. The conception of delict was, as we shall shortly see, so different from that of tort that there was no such thing as waiver of tort. The surety's right to recoupment will almost always be contractual, since authorisation to pay was a mandate and that is a contract. An unauthorised person who voluntarily pays my debt has in general no claim in either system, but at least in Roman law he might have such a right under the rules of *negotiorum gestio*, if his intervention was beneficial to the principal and reasonable in the circumstances. There seems to be no corresponding right in our law except when the payment was made under threat or pressure of legal proceedings or legal restraint of goods.[2]

But another difference is more striking: it is in the conception of the relation. With the possible exception of the stakeholder, all Winfield's cases are of what Austin calls 'sanctioning' rights. They are all cases in which the relation arises only when there is a right of action, when there exists, not perhaps a wrong done, but a financial maladjustment which needs correction. And they all seem to be cases of unilateral obligation. The Roman attitude was different. Having in their minds a *negotium* as the basis of the matter they include in their list a number of relations which set up obligations, in some cases reciprocal, where there is as yet no right of action.[3] Thus it is that the *condictiones*, which correspond to the action for money had and received to my use, and the like, are not the most

---

[1] P. 320, *ante*.

[2] See Jenks, *Digest of English Civil Law*, 4th ed., Sect. 684.

[3] We need not discuss the analytical question whether these 'primary' rights are really rights at all—for the Romans they certainly were, though they do not speak in terms of right and duty.

important, are indeed the last to be mentioned by Justinian, while it seems clear that this action, with that for money paid, dominates the English view of the matter. *Negotiorum gestio*, of which we shall have more to say, may perhaps come within the English notion, for the relation does not exist till money is due, but not exactly, for it sets up reciprocal obligations. The obligations between *tutor* and ward, between common owners, between *heres* and legatee, are all cases in which there is a standing 'quasi-contractual' relation, but not necessarily any immediate right of action. It may be mere historical accident which leads to the difference of conception. The relations of guardian and ward in modern English law are matter for equity: of common owners *inter se* the obligations seem to have attracted very little attention in our system. The relation of executor and beneficiary, first established in ecclesiastical Courts, is now matter for equity.

If the cases in the Institutes and Digest[1] are examined, it will be seen that the writer is much put to it to explain why the obligation is *quasi ex contractu*. It is repeatedly said that there is no contract[2] or no *negotium*, sometimes treated as the same thing,[3] and the passage often winds up with the absurd proposition that because there is no contract and no delict, the liability is *quasi ex contractu*.[4] The truth appears here and there in the proposition that the action is given *utilitatis causa*, i.e. the schematic basis is renounced.[5] But there is in all of them except *negotiorum gestio* a property relation arising by act of party which can reasonably be called a *negotium*.[6] It is probable on the form of the texts that Gaius, who is the chief authority, nowhere called these obligations *quasi ex contractu*, but, in his *Liber Aureorum*, the source of the passages in the

---

[1] Inst. 3. 27; D. 44. 7. 5. [2] E.g. Inst. 3. 27. 1; D. 44. 7. 5. *pr.*
[3] Inst. 3. 27. 2. [4] Inst. 3. 27. *pr.*, 2; D. 44. 7. 5. 1.
[5] Inst. 3. 27. 1, middle; D. 44. 7. 5. *pr.*
[6] The anomalous *condictio furtiva* does not appear in these lists.

Institutes and Digest, called them *obligationes ex variis causarum figuris*, renouncing any scientific general basis. But it is always possible that this name too is post-classical.

Negotiorum gestio is an institution which is not recognised in our law with the generality it had under Justinian.[1] The principle was that if *A* interfered in the affairs of *B*, without his authority, he must compensate for harm done, and account for profits received. On the other hand he could claim recoupment of any proper expenditure, and indemnification from liabilities, but only if, in the circumstances, his intervention was reasonable, i.e. the thing done was reasonable and it was, in the circumstances of urgency, reasonable for him to step in and do it. In the early Empire it was certainly much more limited, and it is generally held that only absence of the principal so justified his intervention as to give him a claim, though the counterclaim against him was of course not subject to this limitation. What was recoverable was the amount of the benefit or the cost, whichever was the less, and if the act was beneficial when it was done the fact that afterwards it came to nothing did not bar the claim.[2] It was also essential, at least under Justinian, that the intervention be in the interest of the principal, i.e. not an act equally necessary for the protection of the doer's own interests, and that it should have been done in the expectation of recoupment and not *donandi animo*. But the history of these requirements is much controverted.

Our law contains no general rubric of this character.[3] The governing principle is that no voluntary service can of itself give either a lien or a right of action for reimbursement.[4] There is indeed very little trace of even sporadic cases.

---

[1] Its earlier history is much disputed; see Buckland, *Text-book*, p. 537 and references.   [2] D. 3. 5. 9. 1.

[3] It is a recognised part of Scots law. See *Kolbin* v. *United Shipping Co.* (1931), S.C. (H.L.) 128.

[4] *Falcke* v. *Scottish Imperial Insurance Co.* (1886), 34 Ch.D. 234, 241, 248; *Sorrell* v. *Paget*, [1949] 2 All E.R. 609. If a person has, *under*

It appears that a husband, being bound to bury his wife, is liable to anyone, even a pure volunteer, who, in reasonable circumstances, has arranged for the burial;[1] whether there is any wider liability under this head is not clear, and it is not insignificant that there was in Rome an *actio funeraria* for funeral expenses long before the *actio negotiorum gestorum* reached its wide development.[2] Salvage is also a case in which purely voluntary service gives a claim, but this is not a common law notion: it is a matter of admiralty law, though common law seems to have recognised a possessory lien in such a case, giving a right to refuse the goods till compensation for service was given.[3] It will be noticed that the rule is not the same. Roman law in its wider field gave no claim to reward but only to reimbursement and indemnity. The lien gave a claim in respect of the service rendered and the modern law of salvage gives also a reward, which may be as much as half the value of the goods salved, or even more.[4]

While the common law was unable to comprise the principle of *negotiorum gestio* within the limits of the enforceability of undertakings express or implied,[5] the readiness of the Roman law to accept it was certainly partly due to the existence from very early times of *condictiones* for the recovery of what had been unfairly or unjustly received. But though our law rejects the principle of *negotiorum gestio* it is able, by its doctrine of agency by necessity, to give relief in some cases which present a certain analogy to it. Thus a shipmaster may, in case of urgency, pledge his principal's credit; a carrier who is carrying perishable

constraint, paid money which another person was liable to pay, he can sue that other person for money paid to his use; see *Brooks Wharf* v. *Goodman Brothers,* [1937] 1 K.B. 534.

[1] *Bradshaw* v. *Beard* (1862), 12 C.B.N.S. 344.

[2] As to the somewhat different conditions of this action, Girard, *Manuel,* 8th ed. p. 665, n. 4.   [3] *Hartfort* v. *Jones* (1699), 1 Ld. Raym. 393.

[4] See the cases collected in Kennedy, *Civil Salvage* (2nd ed.), pp. 127 *sqq.*

[5] The facts in *Hunt* v. *Bate* (1568), 3 Dyer 272a present a typical case of *negotiorum gestio.*

goods and is unable to communicate with the owner may in certain circumstances sell them; a person who supplies necessaries to a wife who is deserted by her husband may have a claim to reimbursement. These cases have been compared with the Roman *negotiorum gestio*, but it is to be noted that the case is not so much one of a service rendered as of a contract made: the party dealing with the agent of necessity recovers from the principal not the value of the service when it was rendered, but what is due under the contract; and in the third case the supply of necessaries can hardly be said to be done for the benefit of the husband, as at least the later Roman law required.

The *condictiones* for the recovery of unjust enrichment are closely analogous to our action for money had and received, and it may be said that in both systems the scheme is not exhaustive: in both there are cases in which money may be retained which morally ought not to be. Each system provides a rather haphazard list of cases in which recovery is possible. And while, as we have seen, there are many cases in which our law brings the matter under this head, while Roman law dealt with it otherwise, so it may be that there are cases treated under the *condictio* in Roman law which are not dealt with in our law by the action for money had and received. Thus *condictio furtiva* was quasi-contractual in Roman law, while with us the action would be in tort, trespass, but that is not a very good example since this particular *condictio* is an anomaly even in Roman law. The efforts of our system to evolve an adequate remedy for unjust enrichment have recently been described by Sir Percy Winfield[1] and by Professor Gutteridge.[2] From time to time the need of it has been felt, but the difficulties of finding a place for it within the categories of contract or of tort or of *indebitatus assumpsit*

---

[1] *Op. cit.* ch. vii.
[2] Gutteridge and David, 'The Doctrine of Unjustified Enrichment', *Cambridge Law Journal*, v (1934), pp. 204–229.

have hitherto been fatal to more than sporadic instances of recognition: amongst these it seems to be right to include *Phillips* v. *Homfray*,[1] where the value of minerals wrongfully abstracted from under the plaintiff's land by a deceased trespasser and added to his estate was allowed to be recovered from the estate, thus constituting yet another exception to the maxim 'actio personalis moritur cum persona', which would have defeated an action in tort.[2] Whether, after the discussion in the House of Lords in *Sinclair* v. *Brougham*,[3] it will be possible to incorporate the doctrine of unjust enrichment into our law without the aid of legislation remains to be seen.[4] Its more successful career in France is described by Professor David in the article cited above.

It is observable that the action for recovery of money paid over for an unlawful purpose differs in one important way from the corresponding *condictio ob turpem causam*. Where the wrongful purpose was common to both in equal degree the Roman law did not allow recovery.[5] In our law there is a *locus poenitentiae*; the money can be recovered before the unlawful purpose is substantially carried out.[6]

In Roman law, quasi-contract, like contract itself, is a civil conception. Modern writers tend, for convenience, to ignore this limitation and to expand the Roman law list by adding to it some of the almost innumerable praetorian rights and liabilities, the list varying in different books, but in practice covering what the individual writer thinks the more important. In many of them, e.g. those protecting the rights of adjoining owners, there is no shadow of a *negotium*.

---

[1] (1883), 24 Ch.D. 439.   [2] Winfield, *cit.* p. 145, n. 4.
[3] [1914] A.C. 398.
[4] The most recent general discussion is to be found in Cheshire and Fifoot, *Law of Contract*, 2nd ed. Part IX, pp. 472–495.
[5] D. 12. 5. 3. 4. 1.
[6] *Taylor* v. *Bowers* (1876), 1 Q.B.D. 291 and the cases cited, Winfield, *cit.* p. 160, n. 5. Cheshire and Fifoot, *Law of Contract*, 2nd ed. p. 263.

CHAPTER X. DELICT AND TORT

1. GENERAL

As a first step in the comparison of the English tort and the Roman delict it is reasonable to describe the two institutions, i.e. to provide answers to the questions: What is a tort? What is a delict? But this is a difficult business. Common lawyers are not yet clear on the question whether there is a general conception of tort and still endeavour to frame their definition after examining all the phenomena known to be torts and searching for a quality common to these and not found elsewhere. The result is not as yet very satisfying. That it is a breach of a duty primarily fixed by law, that it is a breach of a *ius in rem*, that it is a wrong which can be brought within the purview of certain ancient writs, all these have been maintained and rejected.

The procedural difficulty in defining tort, namely, the fact that there are certain wrongs remediable elsewhere than in common law jurisdictions and otherwise than by an action in tort, need not detain us, for it did not arise in Roman law. But there is a difficulty or apparent difficulty of substance which requires a few words. Sir Percy Winfield tells us[1] that he has reluctantly abandoned the definition of a tort as 'a civil wrong which infringes a right *in rem* and is remediable by an action for damages', and that his substantial reasons for doing so are that there are some torts which are not breaches of *iura in rem*, and that the definition 'will not include some wrongs which are, or ought to be, reckoned as torts, but which are breaches of rights *in personam*'. He then instances the refusal of an innkeeper to receive a guest or of a common carrier to accept goods for carriage, and describes the rights against these persons as rights *in personam*. But is this view correct?

[1] *Province of Tort*, pp. 237, 238.

Surely a right which exists only against all persons who place themselves in a certain category such as common innkeepers, common carriers, users of the highway, prosecutors, occupants of premises, writers and printers, etc., does not on that account cease to be a right *in rem*.[1] The point is that the innocuous traveller has a right of reception against any person who sets up as a common innkeeper in England and has room in his inn, just as I have a right against any person who institutes a prosecution against me that he shall do so without malice and with reasonable and probable cause. Conversely, the common innkeeper's duty of reception is none the less *in rem* because it is only owed to those who are travellers, nor the prosecutor's duty because it is only owed to his victims. It is of course true that the breach of a duty *in rem* gives rise to a secondary, sanctioning right *in personam*. It is also true that in the case of the common innkeeper or the common carrier the reception of the guest or the acceptance of the goods for carriage creates rights *in personam* between the parties. Those rights are enforced sometimes by an action in contract, sometimes by an action in tort, like the passenger's action against a negligent railway company. But the *original* right of the traveller against the common innkeeper to be received as a guest and the latter's *original* duty to the traveller to receive him—and it is these which trouble Winfield—are *in rem*.

In Roman law the special liabilities which rested on carriers and innkeepers all seem to be based on a previous undertaking: there was no 'common calling'. They were essentially penal liabilities reinforcing the law of contract. Wanton refusal of an innkeeper to accept a guest or his goods might have been an *iniuria*, but this outrage on personality is a breach of an ordinary *ius in rem*: the relation of the parties merely gave the occasion for it.

It may, however, be possible to define delict, as Winfield

[1] For a discussion of rights *in rem* see p. 89, *ante*.

does tortious liability,[1] as 'breach of a duty primarily fixed by the law...towards persons generally and...redressible by an action for unliquidated damages'.[2] Even if this description be correct, it is necessary to point out that there are great differences between the conceptions of tort and delict. Our law of tort is essentially common law, what is called the general custom of the realm, though it has been considerably modified by statute and perhaps owes much of its flexibility to the enabling provisions of the Statute of Westminster II, 1285.[3] The Roman law of delict is essentially statutory; all the civil law delicts, the only wrongs expressly called delicts, are based on statute, and even the numerous praetorian wrongs are all created by express enactment in the Edict. Conversely, as was bound to happen, the lawyers created most of the law of the matter. The statutes were very brief propositions which needed and received a vast amount of amplification by juristic interpretation. This origin is the more remarkable as, on the whole, statute played a less important part in the private law of Rome than with us. Moreover, in Roman law, each of the delicts has a distinct origin, separate provisions in the XII Tables, the *lex Aquilia*, and the Edict, while with us the major part of the law of tort rests on the gradual extension and expansion of one original writ, the writ of trespass, Maitland's 'fertile mother of actions'.

If we exclude the action of detinue, much older than trespass and recuperatory in origin, which remedied certain wrongs to-day usually regarded as torts, there are very

---

[1] *Op. cit.* p. 32.

[2] See also Holdsworth, *Jour. Soc. Public Teachers of Law*, 1932, 41, who regards it as the breach of a duty arising from 'neither consent nor relationship'. Relationship is indeed a vague term, but what is meant seems to be what the Romans called *negotium*, as in D. 12. 6. 33.

[3] For the most recent views on this very controversial topic see Fifoot, *History and Sources of the Common Law: Tort and Contract*, pp. 66 *sqq.* and, for the literature, p. 66, note 4.

few torts which cannot be traced back to the writ of trespass or to the development of that writ and one or two others, with the help, say some authors, of the powers given by the Statute of Westminster II. Defamation had an independent origin, but, once adopted by the common law Courts, it found a seat, eventually two, in the Case omnibus;[1] similarly, the old writ of deceit, which lay for trickery in connexion with legal proceedings, gave rise to deceit on the case and the modern tort of deceit,[2] and the old writ of conspiracy produced an action on the case in the nature of conspiracy.[3]

Since it is to the Statute of Westminster II that some still attribute a large share of this activity, it is perhaps possible to say that nearly all these writs and the torts which they created had in a sense a statutory origin, though not in any reasonable sense created by the statute.[4] The history of these writs is perhaps not well known, but as the statute provided for consultation of Parliament where the clerks were uncertain, some of them had, if not a statutory, at least a parliamentary basis. But it seems clear that they were only extensions of common law notions: the legislature did not create them: at most it made them possible. Here a certain perhaps remote parallelism may be found in Roman law. The field of the action for *iniuria* underwent an extension very like that of the action for trespass. We shall deal with it later;[5] here it is enough to say that, beginning as a remedy for minor unjustified assaults, it ultimately became the remedy for a great variety of wrongs. The extension of Aquilian liability to new forms of damage followed only a slightly different technique.

Delictum strictly is a conception of civil, as opposed to praetorian law, and, apart from certain ancient actions which were almost completely absorbed into the wider

---

[1] Holdsworth, v. p. 205.   [2] Holdsworth, iii. p. 408.
[3] Holdsworth, iii. p. 405.
[4] See Fifoot, *cit.* on this controversy.   [5] Pp. 378 *sqq.*, *post*.

delicts of classical law,[1] there were but three: theft, including robbery, damage to property, and *iniuria*, outrage on personality. But it is customary to treat under the same head a number of praetorian wrongs, and it is almost inevitable to think of these as in some way analogous to equitable wrongs. But the resemblance or analogy is very superficial. They were not created by the action of a court, but by express legislation in the Praetor's Edict. They were not adjudicated on by a separate tribunal, but by the ordinary court, in the ordinary way, giving rise to a judgement for a penalty, like a true delict. Some of them have special rules, not those of ordinary delict, especially where several persons are involved, but essentially they are the same thing, differing only in that they were created by a different mode of legislation. And the most important of them, that giving the *actio doli*, is closely similar to the case of the action for deceit: we shall therefore take them into account.

An interesting difference between Roman and English law is brought out by Professor R. W. Lee, in the following passage:

A man must see that he does not wilfully invade another's right, or, in breach of a duty, wilfully or carelessly cause him pecuniary loss,[2]

and again:

In the modern law the Roman terminology serves as a general touchstone of liability. The underlying principles of injuria and damnum injuria datum are applicable to all kinds of delict. To-day all delictual liabilities (with few exceptions) are referable to one or other of these two heads. I am answerable for wilful aggression on another's right (*injuria*), though it may not cause him pecuniary loss. I am answerable for wilful or careless aggression on another's right which causes pecuniary loss (*damnum injuria datum*).[3]

The liability for negligently causing damage is therefore roughly the same in the two systems, but the place of

---

[1] Not altogether: some still existed in later times, e.g. the *actio aquae pluviae arcendae*.

[2] *An Introduction to Roman-Dutch Law*, 4th ed. p. 320.

[3] *Ibid.* p. 323.

iniuria, in which liability exists only for *dolus*, is in English law taken, not only by certain torts in which malice is a necessary ingredient, but also by various torts which are actionable on a basis of strict liability, that is to say, where the defendant is liable not merely if he acts without wrongful intent, but also if he acts without negligence. Such torts are trespass and defamation.

However, the matter is not so simple as that. The treatment of defamation is certainly strikingly different in the two systems, for in English law the plaintiff may recover substantial and even vindictive damages for a publication which was quite innocent on the part of the defendant. On the other hand, the more recent developments of trespass make that action normally available for the assertion of a right, and substantial damages are hardly ever given unless the trespass was wilful. Indeed, according to the better view, the actions for trespass to the person and trespass to goods[1] will not lie at all unless the defendant has been guilty of either wrongful intent or negligence. Trespass to land is still in form a tort of strict liability; however, the Limitation Act allows the defendant to tender amends and to disclaim any exercise of a right, and in such cases the plaintiff will not even win his action. Moreover, the action of trover, which still enforces strict liability, really puts in issue the right to possess the goods. It is obvious that the true Roman analogues of trespass and trover are to be found in the various real actions, the *rei vindicatio*, the *actio confessoria* and the *actio negatoria*.

Thus the comparison between delict and tort—if we leave out of consideration negligence—takes on a new form. *Iniuria* is seen to correspond not to all other torts, but to the malicious torts and to trespass when accompanied by wilful intent or aggravating circumstances, the place of simple trespass and conversion being taken, for all practical purposes, not by anything in the Roman law of delict, but

[1] *National Coal Board* v. *Evans*, [1951] 2 All E.R. 310.

by real actions of one kind or another. Viewed in this light
the differences are not very great except in the one case
already mentioned of defamation. It is perhaps significant
that defamation is one of the few torts where the need for
reform is usually considered urgent.

2. COMPENSATION OR PENALTY

There is a further difference. Various as are the many
suggested definitions of tort,[1] a frequently recurring
element is the statement that the remedy for a tort is an
action for unliquidated damages. Here the important
word for us is 'damages'. In the law of tort it is the
primary aim of the action to give the aggrieved party compensation for damage wrongfully inflicted on him. It is
true that in some cases there may be vindictive or exemplary damages, i.e. that in some cases the action has a
definitely penal aspect, e.g. in cases of aggravated trespass
to property,[2] and in defamation, where the damages
awarded by the jury are often obviously penal, but in
principle an action in tort is an action for compensation,
an action, to use Roman language, *ad rem persequendam*.
For the Roman actions on delict we must reverse these
propositions. Delict is imbued with the idea of vengeance,
and the action is primarily not for damages but for a
penalty, though this is usually unliquidated; the primary
aim is not compensation. It is true that in some cases,
indeed in many cases, there is a compensatory element,
e.g. in the *actio e lege Aquilia*, for damage to property, but,
in principle, even here the action is not *ad rem persequendam*, but *ad poenam persequendam*. The distinction is fundamental. It allies the law of delict with that of crime rather
than with that of other civil obligation, so much so that
Mommsen in his *Strafrecht*, somewhat to the confusion of

---

[1] The most important can be seen in Winfield's *Province of Tort*, chs. iii
and xii.   [2] *Emblen* v. *Myers* (1860), 6 H. and N. 54.

his readers, hardly distinguishes between delict and crime except in matters of procedure. And while *delictum* and *maleficium* are the appropriate names for a delict and *crimen* is used mainly in connexion with crime, the distinction is not maintained at all clearly in Justinian's books and not entirely in the surviving classical texts.[1] A similar blurring of the line between tort and crime, a line which can easily enough be drawn for practical purposes, but is very hard to fix scientifically,[2] is found in our law. The old appeals of felony straddled across the line, and the writ of trespass, which arose out of them about the middle of the thirteenth century, bore for many centuries more the mark of its criminal ancestry in the words 'vi et armis...et contra pacem nostram'. Indeed, until 1694, the unsuccessful defendant in trespass paid his fine to the Crown for his offence in addition to the damages recovered by the plaintiff.[3] But although the criminal origin of our conception of tort or torts has left its mark, we seem to have had less difficulty than the Romans in differentiating between the two conceptions. The Roman law of delict has far more affinity to the criminal law than to the law of tort; the penalty is indeed paid to the injured party, not to the State, but still it is a penalty and not damages.

Since the action *ex delicto* is penal it dies in principle with the wrongdoer, without necessarily doing any injustice, since this does not affect the *actio ad rem persequendam* which frequently coexists with it. The same rule in our law may have had a Roman origin,[4] but with us it worked more unfairly since the action in tort was normally the only remedy. It must however be admitted that in relation to damage to property, negligent or wilful, the

[1] Albertario, *Maleficium*, Studi Perozzi, pp. 221 *sqq.*; *Delictum e Crimen*, 1924.
[2] Kenny, *Outlines of Criminal Law* (1933), ch. i; Winfield, *Province of Tort*, ch. viii.
[3] Maitland, *Forms of Action*, p. 361.
[4] Pollock, *Law of Torts*, 13th ed. pp. 62–66.

Roman law was no better, for unless, as often occurred, the facts arose in connexion with a contractual or quasi-contractual relation, the action *ex delicto* was the only remedy, and it died in principle with the wrongdoer.[1] The rule that any enrichment to the *heres* resulting from the delict could be recovered from him is only a small corrective.[2] On the other hand an action *ex delicto* was not in general affected in classical or later law by the death of the aggrieved party: the only important exception is the *actio iniuriarum* for personal outrage,[3] and this exceptional treatment is presumably due to the fact that it is essentially, more than others, *vindictam spirans*.[4] But it is also to be noted that the rule applied only to actions not yet begun: if the action had reached the stage of joinder of issue (*litis contestatio*) it was not affected by the death of a party, except that certain procedural modifications were necessary: it did not abate.[5] It is indeed possible that in very early law all delictal actions died with the plaintiff, as they did in our law; with us, though very wide exceptions had been made by statute and in very early times, the rule still existed until 1934, when, subject to certain conditions and exceptions, it was abolished.

This fundamental difference, i.e. that the action on delict is penal, not compensatory, had important practical results. Thus, subject to some limitations which we shall not consider, if several were engaged in a delict, each was liable for the full penalty, as indeed he is with us. But, as it is for a penalty and not for damages, even where, as in some cases, it really includes a compensatory element, the fact that one of them has paid, either under suit or otherwise, in no way releases the others: they are still liable to the penalty, a rule which may be referable to the difficulty

---

[1] Inst. 4. 12. 1.
[2] As to this, see Buckland, *Text-book*, p. 692, note 1.
[3] D. 47. 10. 13. *pr.*   [4] Buckland, *Text-book*, p. 591.
[5] See Pollock, *loc. cit.* as to modern English law, and Buckland, *loc. cit.*

of subdividing vengeance.[1] As to damage to property, we are told[2] that what one has paid does not release the others, precisely for this reason, *cum sit poena*. This is a very strong case, since here the compensatory element was very prominent: as we saw, unless there was a contract or the like, there was no means of recovery but this action, which, in favourable conditions, where there were several wrong-doers, might be extremely profitable. With us, on the contrary, judgement against one wrongdoer, even if unsatisfied, released the others,[3] and (it is believed) satisfaction by one of a judgement against several wrongdoers barred any execution against the others. These were the common law rules; now, under the Law Reform (Married Women and Tort-feasors) Act, 1935, if the judgement against the joint tort-feasor is wholly or partially unsatisfied, the plaintiff can sue any other joint tort-feasor, but only for the residue.[4] Moreover, at common law, anyone who fully satisfies judgement in an action for conversion acquires title to the goods converted. Another consequence of the penal aspect of delict is that liability was not destroyed by *capitis deminutio* of the wrongdoer, since although his legal personality was changed he remained the same man. It will be remembered that in our law there are certain morally reprehensible wrongs liability for which survives even bankruptcy.

Penalty and compensation being distinct things, there was no question of action on contract or on delict as being, on given facts, alternative ways of recovering the same thing, and thus no question, in principle, of 'waiving a tort'. But while this is reasonable in *furtum* where the penalty and the compensation are distinct things and recoverable by different actions, it might lead to injustice

---

[1] D. 47. 4. 1. 19; C. 4. 8. 1.   [2] D. 9. 2. 11. 2.
[3] *Brinsmead* v. *Harrison* (1872), L.R. 7 C.P. 547.
[4] The Act also introduces the principle of contribution between joint tort-feasors.

where, as in actions under the *lex Aquilia* for damage to property, the penalty included the compensation. If there was also a contract, in careless performance of which the damage was done, there would be both actions and one would not formally bar the other. But to allow both actions was to allow double recovery in effect, and accordingly there was machinery, which we need not discuss, by which this was in fact prevented.[1]

3. PERSONAL CAPACITY

Another practical consequence of the fact that in Roman law an action on delict was one for a penalty for wrong-doing, was the rule that there was no liability in delict if the person who did the act was, as we say, 'not responsible' for his acts. Thus a lunatic or an *infans* was not liable to an action *ex delicto* for, e.g., damage to property, because his acts were not properly imputable to him: 'quae enim in eo culpa sit cum suae mentis non sit?'.[2] The fact that an action lay for damage which had been done by an animal and that there was an alternative of surrender (*noxae deditio*) in this action (*actio de pauperie*)[3] just as where a delict was committed by a slave, so that it is apparently contemplated as a delict, may seem to throw doubt on this conception. But the *actio de pauperie* is extremely ancient[4] and existed no doubt in a time when, as in the Middle Ages, no one saw any difficulty in imputing guilt to an animal, or perhaps it would be better to say, when the notion of guilt as an element in imputability was not clearly grasped—who breaks, pays. The contrast with our law is at first sight sharp. The common law principle seems to be that a lunatic is liable for his tort, which does not look very logical, since tort seems to imply wrongful conduct and it is difficult to attribute that to a lunatic. It is, no doubt, in conformity

---

[1] See, e.g., D. 19. 2. 25. 5: h.t. 43.
[2] D. 9. 2. 5. 2. The same is true for *furtum* or any other delict, D. 47. 2. 23.   [3] D. 9. 1.   [4] D. 9. 1. *pr.*

with our rules of trespass to property, also ancient, under which a man is liable for trespass even though he does not know and has no means of knowing that he is trespassing. The test question would be: Is a lunatic liable for infringement of an absolute right? But in fact there is little authority on the subject of liability of lunatics for tort, and it is said[1] that nowadays a lunatic would probably not be held liable if the evidence showed that, from disease of mind, he did not know what he was doing. In any case the old rule is more intelligible in a system in which the action is for compensation than in one in which it is for a penalty. It is, however, worthy of notice that in France, where there is strict liability for damage done by things which one has under one's care, the Courts have recently held that a lunatic is not responsible for killing a man with a revolver, the irresponsibility of the lunatic bringing the case within the exceptions of *cas fortuit* and *force majeure*.[2]

As to infants there is plenty of authority, ancient and modern, for the rule that in our law infants are liable for tort. All the cases, however, seem to deal with infants of a larger growth, persons who are infants in our technical sense, i.e. are under twenty-one, persons who are old enough to know what they are about, not with infants in the Roman sense, that is, children too young to have *intellectus*, to understand the nature of the act done, let alone to appreciate its wrongfulness or its consequences. From the language of the older books[3] and modern textbooks[4] it seems that it is generally held that on this matter

[1] Hailsham, xxi. p. 288.

[2] In many of the continental codes the solution is on the following lines: (1) the lunatic is not liable for tort; (2) if someone responsible for his care could have prevented the wrongful act, that person is liable; (3) otherwise the judge takes into account all the circumstances, including the relative economic positions of the lunatic and his victim, and orders payment of such sum as he considers equitable out of the lunatic's estate. See Winfield, *Text-book of the Law of Tort*, s. 27, and notes.

[3] E.g. Bacon's *Abridgement*, s.v. *Infancy*.

[4] E.g. Pollock, *Law of Torts*, 14th ed. p. 48.

our law is in practice much the same as the Roman. When there is no mental element in the tort, such as malice or want of care, an infant, however young, is probably liable, provided he is old enough to 'act', that is, is capable of volition; when there is a mental element he is probably liable only if he is 'old enough to know better'.[1] If we applied the analogy of crime and said that a child under seven would be held not liable in tort, and that above that age it would be matter of evidence, that would be in fact the rule under Justinian, but we cannot be so precise.

4. BORDER-LINE BETWEEN CONTRACT AND TORT

In Roman law, as in ours to-day, there was a difficult piece of country on the boundary between contract and delict, and many relationships existed which gave rise to an action on delict or in contract or to both. In addition, in both systems, cases arise in which there is a delictual remedy for the wrong, though, but for a contract, the defendant would not have had the opportunity of committing the wrong. If I employ a piano-tuner to tune my piano and he does it badly, in fact does not really tune it, I have a claim for recovery of what I may have paid, and for damages for breach of contract, and I can resist action on the contract if I have not paid. But there is no question of tort: the duty broken was created by the contract. If, however, he not only fails to tune the piano, but in the course of his operations breaks some of the hammers, the case is altered. If he breaks the hammers negligently, I can sue him for the damage either in contract or in tort; if intentionally, then I can sue him in tort or (probably) in contract. A glance at our books will show that many actions of negligence, and most actions of deceit, are based on acts connected with a contract between the parties.

---

[1] *Hodsman* v. *Grissel* (1608), Noy 129; *Johnson* v. *Pie* (or *Pye*) (1665), 1 Keble 905, 913; 1 Sid. 258. Cf. D. 47. 2. 23.

Roman law shows a similar concurrence of remedies in contract and in delict. Thus, in addition to an action on the contract, an Aquilian action lay for the delict of damage to property where a workman, hired to do a piece of work, damaged the property entrusted to him.[1] If we do not find the same in the *actio doli*, this is because that action was subsidiary, subordinate, and was in general not allowed if there was any other remedy.[2]

One of the most difficult questions in Roman law arises where an act is such as would normally give rise to an action under the *lex Aquilia* on the ground that the doer has been guilty of *culpa*, but has actually been done in connexion with the performance of a contract, e.g., deposit, when the doer is liable contractually only for *dolus*. On the whole it seems that if the act is actually done as part of the performance of the contract, the Aquilian action does not lie, but only that on the contract; but that if the act is really independent of the contract, though it might not have occurred had the contract not been made, the Aquilian action will lie. However, good authorities have differed on the point, which must be considered unsettled. In English law, a similar question might arise where a person lends gratuitously or makes a gift of a chattel which he did not know but ought to have known was dangerous, and the chattel does damage to the recipient. However, in English law the tendency has been hitherto not to differentiate contract and tort, but to say that the liability in tort is mitigated to the extent that liability in contract was mitigated in such cases in Roman law.[3]

[1] D. 9. 2. 27. 29: 19. 2. 13. *pr.*: 19. 2. 25. 7, etc.

[2] D. 4. 3. 1. 1. A similar notion seems to have existed with regard to the action of Case. Thus in *Slade's Case* (1604), 4 Co. Rep. 92 b one of the defendant's arguments, though unsuccessful, was that Case was an 'extraordinary action' and would not lie because Debt lay, and he added *nullus debet actionem agere de dolo, ubi alia actio subest.*

[3] For an attack on what is here described as the English rule, see N. S. Marsh, 66 *L.Q.R.* p. 39.

CHAPTER XI. PARTICULAR DELICTS AND TORTS

1. THEFT

It is odd to our eyes to see Theft constantly treated in the Roman texts as a *delictum*, i.e. a tort, though it would not seem so odd to an English lawyer of some centuries ago who was familiar with the Appeal of Larceny and the restitution of property which could be obtained upon a conviction.[1] But *furtum* was also a crime and even the texts tell us that it was usually so handled,[2] and theft in our law is also a trespass, though we hear much more of it as a crime. But as theft has requirements which trespass has not, closely resembling the requirements of *furtum*, it seems more convenient and useful to compare *furtum* with larceny than with trespass to property. The law of *furtum* underwent great historical changes tending to greater definiteness and fixity of rule. The Digest contains texts representing the different stages in this development; this is convenient for the historical study of the subject, but, it must be supposed, it was rather inconvenient to those who had to use the book as a code of law and therefore is not very convenient when we desire to see just what the law was in the time of Justinian. The first point to note is that the Roman law, so far as we know it, never had our highly technical rule of asportation:[3] the thing need not have been moved. But it had an almost equally technical requirement, that of *contrectatio*: the thing must actually have been handled, *furandi animo*.[4] As the penalty was based on the value of what was stolen, it is easy to see that difficult questions would arise as to what has been actually

---

[1] Holdsworth, ii. p. 361.   [2] D. 47. 2. 93.
[3] Kenny, *Outlines of Criminal Law* (1933), p. 189.
[4] Inst. 4. 1. 1.

handled. If I drew wine from a cask, had I 'contrected' all the wine in it?[1] If I handled a box, had I handled its contents?[2] If I took one thing from a heap, had I handled the whole heap?[3] Further, at least for Justinian there must have been intent to gain dishonestly some economic advantage out of the thing—*animus lucrandi*.[4] This *animus lucrandi* is not at all an easy conception to handle, but it has one important effect: wanton making away with a thing was not *furtum*. If I threw your money into the sea, the remedy at least under Justinian was an action (*utilis*) under the *lex Aquilia* for *damnum*.[5] What our law on this point is is not quite clear, for the cases commonly cited to show that wanton throwing away is larceny[6] are both cases in which there was a purpose to be gained which might possibly have brought the cases within the very wide conception of *lucrum* in the Roman texts.[7]

More striking is the fact that there was no need of intent to deprive the owner of his whole interest in the thing. Indeed here the rule was extraordinarily severe, in view of the fact that condemnation in an *actio furti* involved *infamia*, with great resulting disabilities. If a depositee used the thing, or a borrower used it in unauthorised ways, without any *bona fide* belief that the owner would have consented if he had been asked, this was *furtum*.[8] This is what Justinian calls *furtum usus*. It is true that most of the specific applications of the principle are to cases in which the wrongdoer had already the lawful physical possession (not necessarily the legal *possessio*) of the thing; thus they do not actually decide the point which gave difficulty, and led to our legislation, in the so-called 'joy-riding' cases, of

[1] D. 47. 2. 21. 5.
[2] D. 47. 2. 21. 8.   [3] *Ibid.*
[4] D. 47. 2. 1. 3.   [5] D. 9. 2. 27. 21.
[6] *R. v. Cabbage* (1815), R. and R. 292; *R. v. Jones* (1846), 1 Den. 188.
[7] Kenny, *cit.* (1933), p. 215, gives the case of one who in spite throws a thing into the river, but he cites no decision.
[8] G. 3. 196, 197; Inst. 4. 1. 6, 7.

persons who took and later abandoned motor-cars in such a way that the owner would probably recover them, so that there was no proof of intent to deprive him of his whole interest. But there are texts which go beyond this, and others say in general terms that it was *furtum* to make a profit out of the illicit use of another's goods.[1] In D. 47. 2. 40 the words show that the borrower using in an unauthorised way is given only as an illustration of the wider rule that any unauthorised use may be *furtum*.

In principle, as with us, a theft must be of the property of some other person, but also, as with us, it was possible in various ways for the owner to be a thief. The results in the two systems are much the same, but they are reached by different roads. In Roman law, where the owner took the thing from one who had a right to possession of it as against him, he was said, under Justinian, to have stolen, not the thing, but the possession of it, e.g. where he took the thing from a pledgee.[2] But though this conception fits the case of a pledge it does not fit others. A borrower had not in Roman law, as in ours, the possession of the thing, i.e. he had no possessory remedies, but only detention or what is sometimes called custody, such as that of a servant. But if he had a right of retention against the owner, e.g. for unusual expenses, and the owner took the thing, he had an *actio furti*.[3] And where a thing belongs to *A* but *B* has a life interest (*ususfructus*), *A* is *dominus* and has technical *possessio*. As we have seen,[4] the life interest, limited in time, was not thought of as ownership, but as an 'incorporeal hereditament' not susceptible therefore of possession.[5] But if *A* takes the thing from *B* he commits *furtum*.[6] This is not *furtum possessionis*, for the owner *A* already had *possessio*, but *B* had a right to hold the thing, as against *A*,

---

[1] D. 47. 2. 52. 20; h.t. 66; G. 3. 195, 198; Inst. 4. 1. 6, 8.
[2] Inst. 4. 1. 1; 4. 1. 10.
[3] D. 47. 2. 15. 2.   [4] *Ante*, p. 93.
[5] Inst. 2. 2. 2; D. 41. 2. 3. *pr.*   [6] D. 47. 2. 15. 1.

as in the case of a borrower with a *ius retinendi*. It is in fact a stronger case, for though *B*, as the result of a highly technical conception of *possessio*, was not thought of as possessing, he had similar protection against third parties and was said to have *quasi-possessio* or *possessio iuris*.[1] The Roman law is therefore more correctly stated by saying that the owner could steal from one who had the right to retain the thing, as against him, leaving the technical question of *possessio* out of account. In our law we say, rather oddly, that the owner can steal from one who has a 'special property' in the thing, and though there are some cases in which this 'special property' has been created by statute, there does not appear to be any authoritative definition of it. The rule of our law seems however to be that any one with a right to hold the thing against the actual proprietor, whether he is technically a bailee or not, has the special property which makes wilful wrongful taking by the owner a theft. So far, with different terminology, the law is as in Rome. But there are old cases which make it larceny for the master to take a thing from his servant in such circumstances as will amount to a fraud against someone else, e.g. he disguises himself and robs his servant of the goods, intending under the (then) existing law to claim the value from the hundred. Mr Justice R.S. Wright[2] doubts whether this doctrine is still law, probably with reason. He seems inclined indeed, though without discussion, to reject nearly all cases of theft by the owner, apart from statutory rules, e.g. giving the Postmaster-General a special property in postal packets;[3] in any case, apart from this last type, the substantive law of the two systems seems to be much the same.

[1] As to this see Buckland, *Text-book*, p. 197 and references, and Frag. Vat. 90, 91.

[2] Pollock and Wright, *Possession in the Common Law*, pp. 139, 229.

[3] See now Larceny Act, 1916, sects. 1 (1) and also 1 (2) (iii), whereby 'owner' includes 'any part owner, or person having possession or control of, or a special property in, anything capable of being stolen'.

This use of the notions, *furtum possessionis*, and 'special property', is curious in view of the fact that our law habitually treats theft as an inroad on possession, while the Roman law regards it primarily as an inroad on ownership. Mr Justice R.S. Wright[1] observes that while 'the ordinary conception of theft is that it is a violation of a person's ownership of a thing...the proper conception of it is that it is a violation of a person's possession of the thing accompanied with an intention to misappropriate the thing'. The difference is a natural, one may almost say a necessary, result of the difference in the architecture of the two systems of law. Our common law, at least in relation to moveables, has always thought in terms of possession rather than in those of ownership. As Sir Frederick Pollock says,[2] 'The Common Law never had any...process at all in the case of goods for the vindication of ownership pure and simple. So feeble and precarious was property without possession, or rather without possessory remedies, in the eyes of medieval lawyers, that Possession largely usurped not only the substance but the name of Property', a piece of history which explains the term 'special property' and the practice in indictments of 'laying the property' in someone. Roman law on the other hand had a well-marked scheme of proprietary remedies before possessory remedies were invented by the Praetor. It is, however, to be noted that in the second century there are signs of a conception of *furtum* as an inroad on possession very like our own. Scaevola says[3] that *furtum* is an inroad on possession, that where no one was in possession there can be no *furtum* and that this is why there can be no *furtum* of the goods of a *hereditas* on which no *heres* has as yet entered. There are other texts which apply the same notion to the same case. But it does not seem that this is the original view and it is not that which predominates in the

---

[1] *Op. cit.* p. 118.
[2] *Ibid.* p. 5.   [3] D. 47. 4. 1. 15.

sources: the reason was that no one owned the vacant *hereditas*.[1]

But neither our system, essentially based on possession, nor the Roman law, at any point applies the notion of possession with any strictness: the Roman law has many cases quite inconsistent with it, which we shall not discuss. The best illustration perhaps is that of the finder of lost goods. The Roman law made no attempt to apply the notion of possession to the case. It is clear that the possession was lost.[2] A finder was a thief if he took the thing in bad faith, i.e. not in the belief that it had been abandoned by the owner or belonged to no one,[3] and this attitude made it unnecessary to enquire where the possession was, an enquiry which has had such curious results in our law.[4] Our own law purports to apply the notion of taking out of possession to goods found in the street: it appears to hold that, for the purpose of the law of trespass and larceny, they are still in the possession of the owner. Actually they are not in anybody's possession, and to attribute possession to the owner is really only to say that for such cases the doctrine of taking out of possession is not to apply. It might be interesting to enquire how the law would deal with a case in which the owner drops a thing in the street, and a dishonest person picks it up, and so steals it, in fact takes the possession, and then fearing that he is observed, drops it again: is the possession restored to the owner, as against any new thief? If a bailee loses a thing in the street, does he still possess or has he restored the possession to the owner?

There is another difference in the matter of finding. As we have seen, a finder who took the thing in bad faith was, in Rome, a thief. In our modern law this is not so unless

---

[1] See, for discussion and texts, Buckland, 43 *L.Q.R.* (1927), pp. 338 *sqq.*
[2] D. 41. 2. 25. *pr.*   [3] D. 47. 2. 43. 5 *sqq.*
[4] Goodhart, *Essays in Jurisprudence and the Common Law*, pp. 75–90. See also *Hannah* v. *Peel*, [1945] K.B. 509; *Hibbert* v. *McKiernan*, [1948] 2 K.B. 142.

there was at the time of finding some reason to think the owner could be found,[1] probably a better rule but not easy to apply. In our law it does not seem to be quite clear whether a finder with a clue who takes intending to find the owner and restore the thing but afterwards changes his mind and applies it to his own purposes has committed theft or not. On the cases he has not: it is conversion after innocent taking and this cannot be theft, which involves a wrongful taking.[2] But it is said by Mr Justice R.S. Wright[3] that such a person should be treated like a bailee who breaks bulk and thereby determines the bailment. Such a rule would do no injustice, but it is extending a highly artificial doctrine, itself invented to get the law out of a difficulty, in a way which does not logically follow. For the possession under the bailment rested on the consent of the owner, which might well be regarded as destroyed by the act of breaking bulk, but there is nothing of this sort in the other case. We have to suppose a tacit consent of which neither party is in any way conscious. The point does not seem to be directly discussed in Roman texts, but since a pledgee could commit theft,[4] it does not seem that the jurists would have seen any difficulty in the fact that the first taking was innocent.

Since taking out of possession played a very small part in the Roman law, and, in particular, since most of those holders whom we call bailees, and endow with possession, had no possession in Roman law, but only detention (custody), e.g. borrower, depositee, carrier, the Roman lawyer escaped some of the difficulties which have arisen in our law. If a servant intercepted and made away with property he had received for his master, this was simply *furtum*.[5] There was no separate offence of embezzlement and no

---

[1] *Reg.* v. *Preston* (1851), 5 Cox C.C. 390.
[2] See Kenny, *cit.* (1933), p. 217.
[3] Pollock and Wright, *cit.* p. 185.
[4] D. 47. 2. 55. *pr.*, 74.   [5] D. 47. 2. 43. 1.

need for it. The depositee or borrower who makes away with the thing commits *furtum*, simply.[1] The only important practical case resembling our larceny by a bailee is that of the pledgee, who certainly has *possessio*. But the fact of his having possession is nowhere treated as creating a difficulty.

Modern writers say that the Roman owner, usufructuary, etc. had the *actio furti* by reason of their positive *interesse* in the thing stolen. Others, such as the *commodatarius*, had it by reason of a negative *interesse*; they were interested in the safety of the thing because they would be liable over to the bailor if the thing were stolen. A bailee such as a depositee, who was not so liable, had not the action.[2] In English law all bailees have possession and so can prosecute for theft; and *The Winkfield*,[3] which was decided in trover, held that the bailee's possession availed him even if he could not be liable over.

As with us, land could not be stolen,[4] though some of the earlier lawyers took a different view.[5] But they never found any difficulty about 'things savouring of the realty'.[6] Our own lawyers probably would not have experienced this and many other difficulties if the punishment for theft in older times had been less cruel. And, the notion of inroad on possession not being really part of Roman law, there was no question of the necessity of separation both in time and intent, i.e., an act 'not continuated but interpolated'.[7] If a man cut and immediately carried away crops, this was *furtum*.[8]

The normal theft in both systems is secret taking, called, by the Romans, *subreptio*. But there may be dishonest taking without *subreptio*, e.g. by taking advantage

---

[1] G. 3. 195 *sqq.*; Inst. 4. 1. 6 *sq.*; D. 47. 2. 40, 48. 4, etc. These texts deal with cases short of making away with the thing—*a fortiori* this is theft.

[2] See Jolowicz, *De Furtis*, pp. xxviii–lv.

[3] [1902] P. 42.

[4] D. 47. 2. 25.

[5] Aul. Gell. xi. 18. 13; D. 41. 3. 38.

[6] D. 47. 2. 25. 2, 52. 8, 58.

[7] Hale's *Pleas of the Crown*, ch. 43.

[8] D. 47. 2. 68. 5.

of a mistake. This kind of thing was often *furtum* and has been called by commentators *furtum improprium*. But the circumstances in which one may have applied to one's own purposes, fraudulently, what was the property of another are infinitely various and not all of them are theft or *furtum*. Both the Roman and the English systems ultimately reached what is at any rate a principle. If in our law the ownership passes as the result of the transaction the act is not larceny, though it may be the offence of obtaining by false pretences or possibly no more than an actionable fraud.[1] Similarly in the Roman law of the Digest if the ownership passes it is not *furtum*, though it may be the offence of *stellionatus* or perhaps only a ground for the *actio doli*.[2] But the earlier history of the two systems is very different. Our law, up to quite modern times, dealt so severely with theft[3] that the judges invented all sorts of artificial doctrines in order to exclude from the notion of larceny, involving liability as a felon, many acts of fraud which were normally at least on the same level. But the Roman law, at least in historic times, had no such severity: a penalty of twice, or in some cases four times, what was stolen, is in no way excessive. And, on the other hand, the earlier Roman conception of *furtum* seems to have been extraordinarily wide. Owing to the rather haphazard way in which the Digest was compiled, much evidence of this wide conception of *furtum* is contained in it, though it seems to be anachronistic. Thus we several times get the proposition that knowingly to receive money not due is *furtum*.[4] On such a general doctrine almost any fraudulent acquisition would be theft. But the actual rule of later law was more precise. A type of case prominent in the texts

---

[1] Kenny, *cit.* (1933), p. 246.

[2] D. 47. 2. 43. 3; D. 47. 20. 3. 1; cp. D. 47. 2. 43. *pr.*

[3] Sir J. Stephen, *General View of the Criminal Law*, pp. 71 *sq.*, speaks of 'extravagant severity', 'the horror of the old system'. See also Radzinowicz, *History of English Criminal Law*, vol. i. *passim.*

[4] D. 13. 1. 18; 47. 2. 43. 2.

affords a good illustration of it. I hand a thing to *B* to take to *C*, the intent being that he shall be no more than a messenger. If he converts it, this is *furtum*, whether or not he purported to be authorised to receive it for *C*, and whether he was in fact so authorised or not. The reason is not that he did not get *possessio*, though that is true, but that he did not acquire the ownership. *B* alleges that he is authorised to collect a debt due to *C*. I pay him, intending to vest the money in him subject to a duty to account to *C*. Here, if he converts this, there is no *furtum*, whatever else it may be, as the ownership vested in him. *B* says that he is *C*, who is, to my knowledge, authorised to receive money on behalf of *X*, and I give it to him as before. Here, if he converts, it is *furtum*, because there was no intent to transfer the property to him but to *C* and therefore ownership did not pass.[1] It is obvious that cases of this type might often produce *apices iuris*, which would give as much trouble as the points which arose in *Reg.* v. *Ashwell*[2] and in *Reg.* v. *Middleton*.[3] It is clear that there was much dispute, though most of it is suppressed in the texts as edited under Justinian. It is also clear, for Roman law, that in handling cases of this sort we are discussing not so much the law of theft as the law of transfer of ownership, i.e. what sort of error, however caused, will prevent the delivery from passing ownership.[4]

'The rule is settled in our modern law that a servant does not possess by virtue of his custody, except in one case, namely when he receives a thing from the possession of a third person to hold for the master';[5] but this distinction between possession and custody has recently received a severe jolt from the Court of Criminal

---

[1] D. 47. 2. 43. *pr.* –3; h.t. 44; h.t. 52. 21; h.t. 67. 3, 4; h.t. 76; h.t. 81. 5–7.

[2] (1885), 16 Q.B.D. 190; probably *furtum* in Roman law.

[3] (1873), 2 C.C.R. 38; certainly *furtum* in Roman law, D. 47. 2. 22. 1.

[4] As in *Cundy* v. *Lindsay* (1878), 3 App. Cas. 459.

[5] Pollock in Pollock and Wright, *Possession in the Common Law*, p. 60.

Appeal[1] in holding that a maid-servant in a house, her master being in the garden and within call, had a 'special property' in her master's coat, so that in an indictment for robbery it was correct to lay the property in the servant.

2. NEGLIGENCE
(a) GENERAL

It has long been matter of controversy whether our law has such a tort as negligence, or whether the law is not more accurately stated by the proposition that in some torts negligence is a minimal requirement. The better view seems to be that negligence is now an independent tort as well as an element in certain other torts.[2] The difficulty is increased by the ambiguities which hang about the word. Does it mean a state of mind or a course of conduct? Does it cover inadvertent omissions as well as inadvertent acts? Is the inadvertence as to the act or omission itself, or as to a given consequence?[3] To these questions it may perhaps be answered, notwithstanding the language of some of the books, (i) that we are concerned with conduct, not with states of mind; that, from this point of view, negligence means failure to observe the standard of conduct of a reasonable man in the circumstances as a commonly observant person would have seen them; (ii) that in our law (as in the Roman) failures to act do not as yet cause a liability for resulting damage unless there existed, *aliunde*, some duty to act; and (iii) that for practical purposes what is meant is inadvertence as to 'reasonably' probable consequences. But there is another question: Does negligence refer to the conduct alone or does it include its

[1] *R.* v. *Harding* (1929), 46 T.L.R. 105; 21 Cr. App.R. 166; 46 *L.Q.R.* (1930), p. 135.

[2] See Winfield, 42 *L.Q.R.* (1926), pp. 194 *sqq.*, and Salmond, *Law of Torts*, 10th ed. by Stallybrass (1945), pp. 29 and 428.

[3] See also, as to negligence and recklessness, Turner, *Cambridge Law Journal*, v (1933), pp. 61 *sqq.*

consequences? So stated, the question seems absurd. Negligence is what a man does or fails to do, not what happens as the result of his conduct. It would be more logical to call the tort 'damage' (as the Roman law did), though no doubt such names as negligence, deceit, etc., have convenience and tradition on their side. For the gist of the action is the damage: if the point were material, which it is not likely often to be, prescription would run from the time of the damage, at any rate where no breach of contract is involved, and not from that of the act.[1]

Our books and cases are full of a certain duty to take care, relative to a certain person. We are told that, to constitute the wrong, there must be (i) a duty to take care, as against the plaintiff, (ii) breach of that duty, and (iii) resulting damage.[2] It is clear that this 'duty to take care' is a part of our law, though it seems to be possible to state the law without it.[3] But it may be doubted whether it is very logical or useful. Since breach of it gives in itself no right of action, for there must be damage, it would seem better to speak of a duty not to damage by careless conduct, a duty owed to everyone, subject to questions of contributory negligence, remoteness, etc. Indeed the 'duty, relative to the person affected, to take care' seems to be little more than another name for a particular kind of remoteness.[4]

However this may be, it is clear, on the one hand, that the Roman law had not this conception of duty to take care, and, on the other, that there was no such general proposition as that damage negligently caused gave a right of action. What we do get is a liability based directly or indirectly on the *lex Aquilia* for damage to property,

[1] Salmond, *cit.* p. 170.

[2] See, e.g. (but it can be found everywhere), Salmond, *cit.* p. 430; on the history of the requirement, Winfield, 34 *Columbia Law Review* (1934), pp. 41 *sqq.* [3] E.g. Fraser, *Law of Tort* (1st ed.).

[4] See, for discussion, Buckland, 51 *L.Q.R.* (1935), pp. 637 *sqq.* For a different view see Excursus: Duty of Care (p. 367, *post*).

caused without justification, and it may be caused either wilfully or negligently. That is far from a general liability for the consequences of negligence, though it is not so narrow as it looks. On the one hand, where property was damaged, much consequential damage could come into account, compendiously described as '*damnum emergens*' and '*lucrum cessans*',[1] which we need not illustrate. On the other hand, the Praetor (or possibly only later authority) extended the liability to what was not exactly property, e.g. the body of a freeman; though here, too, the Roman law, like our own apart from statute, gave no remedy where the unfortunate man was killed.[2] This limitation is all the more remarkable as in a neighbouring region another line is taken. Where a thing is thrown from a house and a freeman is killed there is a penalty of 50 *aurei*, formally an *actio popularis*, parallel to our penal actions, but with certain preferences as to who might bring it.[3] But all this leaves it much narrower than our law of negligence. It is true that there are texts which say that there is an *actio in factum* for cases to which the *lex Aquilia* does not apply.[4] On the face of it this might extend the liability for negligent or wilful damage indefinitely, even where no physical thing was affected, but there is no text which suggests such a case. It probably refers to cases where the thing is not damaged but is rendered unavailable, e.g. money is thrown into the sea, in which there certainly was an action *in factum*.[5] On another point we must regard Roman law as more favourable to the plaintiff. A Roman master had

---

[1] G. 3. 212; Inst. 4. 3. 10; D. 9. 2. 22. 1, etc. The terms are not technical.

[2] At any rate the texts nowhere deal with any Aquilian liability where a freeman is killed. See D. 9. 1. 3; 9. 2. 7. *pr.*

[3] Buckland, *Text-book*, p. 598. The civilians of the seventeenth and eighteenth centuries merged this action with that on the *lex Aquilia* so as to justify the admission—in any case inevitable—of an action for negligent killing of a freeman. See 38 *H.L.R.* 499.

[4] D. 9. 2. 33. 1.

[5] Inst. 4. 3. 16 *in fin.*; D. 9. 2. 27. 21.

an action under the *lex Aquilia* not only if his slave was damaged but also if he was killed. English law gives no remedy for the death of a dependant.

It may be remarked incidentally that the Roman criminal law usually required wilfulness even in the Empire. It is true that there are texts which deal with punishment for negligent homicide,[1] but these seem rather to refer to the undefined magisterial power of *coercitio* than to the true criminal law. But in the Empire and specially in the later Empire there was a good deal of legislation making officials responsible for negligence in connexion with their office. Our own law does not seem to go much further.

Our standard for negligence is that of the reasonable man in the circumstances. The Roman is, at least in terms, more severe. What is necessary to avoid liability is extreme care: 'in lege Aquilia et levissima culpa venit'.[2] It is doubtful however whether there is any difference: this *culpa levissima* is the *culpa levis* of other texts, i.e. failure to show the care which a *bonus paterfamilias* would show, and that must mean much the same as the conduct of a reasonable man. On the other hand it was indifferent, so far as Aquilian liability was concerned, whether the act was wilful or negligent; the liability was the same. This seems more appropriate to our law, where the action is for compensation and not, as in Rome, for a penalty, and we have already seen[3] that where the act is wilful and wanton our law is willing to allow vindictive damages. But in fact the outcome in the two systems is the same. Any wilful infringement of another's rights (and intentional damage to his property is certainly this) was, or might be, an *iniuria*, and we are expressly told that for wilful damage there might be, over and above the Aquilian action, an *actio iniuriarum* for the insult,[4] so that the injured party gets his vindictive damages, though by a separate action.

---

[1] See Costa, *Crimini e Pene*, pp. 154 *sqq.*   [2] D. 9. 2. 44. *pr.*
[3] P. 344, *ante.*   [4] D. 9. 2. 5. 1.

The Aquilian action gave compensation and, it might be, more, for the plaintiff was entitled to value the thing at its highest value within a certain time before the act was done.[1] It is obvious, however, that often the thing will not have materially changed in value within the year (for destruction of slaves or cattle) or month (for any other damage), so that in effect the whole content of the claim is in many cases only compensation. And, by machinery which we need not consider, it barred in fact, though not formally, any action, contractual or quasi-contractual, for the same damage. Yet it was contemplated as a penal action and had all the characteristics of a penal action. It was cumulative where more than one were concerned.[2] It died with the wrongdoer.[3] This might cause injustice, as it did, till very recently, in the case of personal injuries in our law, since there was or might be no other remedy. There might of course be an alternative contractual or similar action and this would not ordinarily be affected by the death. The action was for double damages if the liability was denied, but that of itself does not make an action penal: it was equally true of the action to obtain conveyance of what had been left by legacy in a certain form in classical law and to certain favoured beneficiaries in later law.[4]

[1] D. 9. 2. 2. *pr.*; 9. 2. 27. 5. This was certainly always true of damage falling under cap. 1; Dr D. Daube, 52 *L.Q.R.* p. 253, thinks that cap. 3 awarded a penalty equal to the damage materialising within thirty days after the accident. This may well be true, but by the classical period the penalty was fixed on lines analogous to those laid down in cap. 1.

[2] D. 9. 2. 11. 2 *in fin.*

[3] G. 4. 112. Any enrichment of the *heres* out of the facts, a thing which might occur, was recoverable from him, and this, at least in later law, by the Aquilian action itself. D. 9. 2. 23. 8.

[4] Inst. 4. 6. 23; G. 4. 9.

EXCURSUS: DUTY OF CARE

Buckland took very seriously his attack on the Duty to take Care,[1] and so I could not without impiety exclude all reference to it from this edition. All the same, I consider it ill-founded. As my own defence of the concept is not very accessible,[2] I summarise it shortly here.

It is admitted on all hands that the actual technique of the duty to take care is not found in Roman law. What seems to take its place is a distinction, barely discernible in the classical texts, but sufficiently clear in the Institutes,[3] between physical damage caused negligently to the person or property of the victim, and mere pecuniary damage, that is to say, financial loss caused to him without any physical damage to the person or property. The example given of the latter is negligently to release a slave without injury to the slave, but with the result that his owner loses his value. It seems that by the time of Justinian at least and probably by the end of the classical period actions would be given almost as a matter of course for physical damage caused negligently. It seems also pretty clear that in the classical period actions for pecuniary damage caused negligently were given only sporadically, and probably in each case only if the Praetor was satisfied that the facts, if proved, ought to give rise to a cause of action. It looks as though liability for merely pecuniary damage was, by the time of Justinian, generalised, though there is a slight suggestion that it was limited to cases where although no specific object was damaged, yet the pecuniary damage to the plaintiff was in respect of some particular object.[4] Finally it seems pretty clear that there was no general liability for damage caused by a mere omission to act. Where there is liability it is because the

---

[1] See also his later attack in *Some Reflexions on Jurisprudence*, p. 111.

[2] See 22 *Tulane L.R.* (1947), pp. 111–130.   [3] J. 4. 3. 16.

[4] See Windscheid, *Lehrbuch des Pandektenrechts*, ii, §455.

defendant has created a danger which can only be averted by positive steps on his part, and he has failed to take those steps, or again where he has accepted the duty to take care of a potentially dangerous thing, and has failed to do so.[1]

The position in English law, since the decision in *Donoghue* v. *Stevenson*,[2] seems to be as follows: There are the same distinctions as in Roman law, between physical damage to persons and property and merely pecuniary damage, and between liability for positive acts and liability for mere omissions to act. As in Roman law one may almost certainly say that there is a general liability for physical damage caused to persons or property by a positive act, subject to one exception, namely, the much disliked line of cases which refuses to make an owner of property liable to third parties of whose existence he ought to be aware for the dangerous state of land or houses. There would seem to be good reason for thinking that even a careless misrepresentation would make a person liable for *physical* damage caused by it.[3] On the other hand, it may be that one ought to admit the possibility that the Courts may admit new exceptions to this general liability.[4] It is also clear, as in Roman law, that there is no general duty to take positive steps, however reasonable, to avert damage which threatens another person, and where, exceptionally, there may be liability in Roman law, there is probably liability in English law also. On the other hand the treatment of mere pecuniary damage caused by a positive act seems to differ from the Roman treatment. There are here three different schools of thought.

The first says that there is never any liability for carelessly causing merely pecuniary damage. Either liability is strict, as in trespass to land, conversion, and defamation, or it is dependent upon proof of intent to harm, or know-

---

[1] D. 9. 2. 27. 9.   [2] [1932] A.C. 562.
[3] See *Sharp* v. *Avery*, [1938] 4 All E.R. 85, especially the judgement of Slesser, L.J.   [4] As W. L. Morison suggests (11 *Modern L.R.* 20–22).

ledge of some kind. It must be conceded to the defenders
of this position that it is extremely hard to find cases
establishing such a liability, and almost all of them are
suspect on one ground or another. The second view, which
Buckland might have taken had his attention been drawn
to the specific point in issue, is that no real distinction can
be made between physical and pecuniary damage, and
that so long as the damage is not too remote and there is
no possibility of raising the defences of contributory negligence or *volenti non fit iniuria*, there is no more reason
why a careless person should escape liability for pecuniary
than for physical damage. If faced with the question why
in that case there is no liability for negligent interference
with trade relations, of the type which, if malicious, would
give rise to an action for conspiracy, the partisans of this
view would probably say that for good or bad reasons the
law has marked off certain territories occupied by well
known heads of liability into which the law of negligence
must not enter; though I find it not at all easy to understand this position if, with Sir Percy Winfield,[1] they assert
that it is possible to get rid of the effect of *Derry* v. *Peek*[2]
by saying that the case was decided, not in negligence,
but in deceit; for if you take that line, there is no reason
whatever why you should not get rid of the effect of all the
decisions on conspiracy, injurious falsehood, and malicious
prosecution, by reframing the action in each case as an
action of negligence. It is perhaps not unfair to say that
this position is far less defensible than the former.

The third school of thought, to which I belong, holds
that this particular type of damage, that is to say, merely
pecuniary damage caused carelessly, is, like damage caused
by mere omission to act, a field peculiarly appropriate to
the technique of the Duty of Care. In other words, one
is liable for negligently causing pecuniary damage if one
owed a duty to take care to avoid damage in one of a

[1] *Text-book of the Law of Tort*, s. 114.   [2] (1889), 14 App. Cas. 337.

number of particular types of situation. Those situations certainly cannot be generalised, and I admit that they are as yet very rare, just as the situations in which there is a duty to act positively are rare; but there are one or two cases where such a duty has been established,[1] and from certain hypotheses put forward in judgements[2] it seems that others may be added to them. In other words, in this field, as in that of pure omissions to act, it will be necessary, and it seems it will be possible, for the plaintiff to start proceedings by satisfying the judge *in limine*, as Sir Percy Winfield has it,[3] that there was a specific duty to take reasonable care to avoid the damage. Elsewhere I believe I have shown that, except in Germany, where the Civil Code rigorously excludes liability for merely pecuniary damage caused negligently,[4] all foreign systems utilise, overtly or in a disguised form, this Duty of Care.

(b) CONTRIBUTORY NEGLIGENCE[5]

The Romans had not exactly a law of contributory negligence, i.e. they did not think of the matter quite in that way. It is true that modern writers have invented and attributed to the Romans a theory of what they call '*culpa* compensation',[6] into which they have attempted to force the Roman texts. It is an unsuitable name in any case, since it suggests set off (*compensatio*), a quantitative estimate of the negligence on each side, or, at best, our Admiralty rule rather than the common law rule recently discarded. And it completely falsifies the Roman view. They seem to have applied here a theory of causation, no

---

[1] E.g. *Wilkinson* v. *Coverdale* (1793), 1 Esp. 75.

[2] E.g. by Lord Roche in *Morrison Steamship Co., Ltd.* v. *Greystoke Castle* (*Cargo-owners*), [1947] A.C. 265, at p. 280.

[3] *Textbook of the Law of Tort*, §123.

[4] This is the effect of §§ 823–826 of the B.G.B.

[5] For English law generally see Glanville L. Williams, *Joint Torts and Contributory Negligence* (1951).

[6] E.g. Pernice, *Sachbeschädigungen*, p. 62.

doubt a theory of causation which is not satisfactory, but that is not exceptional in theories of causation.[1] The Roman view was that the negligent or intending person was liable for the harm if he caused it but not if some intervening agency prevented his act from producing its effect. Many applications of this principle are recorded which have nothing to do with contributory negligence. I stab a slave with what is clearly a mortal wound, but, before he dies, *A* cuts his throat or an earthquake overwhelms him. These agencies have killed him; my attempt to kill has been frustrated: I have only wounded him, with resulting effects, not indeed very important, on the measure of damages.[2] The same is true if the intervening event is something done by the victim or by the plaintiff—not necessarily the same. If I injure a slave so that he will certainly die unless attended to and a doctor is called in who neglects the case or treats it wrongly so that the patient dies, it is the doctor who killed, not I.[3] This is the act of a third party. If his master undertook the treatment and neglected him, it is he who killed, not the wounder.[4] This is the act of the plaintiff, the master. If I mortally wound a slave and he destroys himself to avoid the agony, I have presumably only wounded him.

Contributory negligence is illustrated from another point of view. If a man crosses a field where people are lawfully practising javelin throwing and is hit and wounded, there is normally no action.[5] If I am cutting off a branch of a tree and shout a warning and you nevertheless pass under and are hurt, there is no liability.[6] Perhaps it may

---

[1] Pernice indeed treats *culpa* compensation, which for him leads to a cancellation of claims on both sides, as a consequence of the difficulty of deciding which party caused the damage.

[2] D. 9. 2. 11. 3; 9. 2. 15. 1. 9. 2. 51. *pr.* takes the opposite view, perhaps *per incuriam*, the wish to date the killing back to the infliction of the mortal wound prevailing over the need for an uninterrupted causation.

[3] D. 9. 2. 7. 8, 8. *pr.*; 9. 2. 52. *pr.*   [4] Arg. 9. 2. 30. 4.

[5] D. 9. 2. 9. 4.   [6] D. 9. 2. 31.

be said here that there was no negligence in me at all. There is, however, at least an apparent difficulty. The result ought logically to be the same whether my original act was intentional or merely negligent. If I did not cause the result in the one case I did not in the other. In the javelin case indeed we are told that if seeing the man crossing I intentionally throw at him, I am liable. But this would be true on any theory. I was the direct cause. I was the proximate cause. I had the last chance. His presence was the *causa sine qua non*: my act was the *causa causans*. But it would seem that neither Roman nor English law would allow the doctrine of contributory negligence to operate so as to relieve an intentional wrongdoer of liability.

It seems that the Romans reached a result very like our own without any conscious analysis. A text[1] states the case of a barber shaving a slave in a place where people were playing ball; a player hit a ball rather hard and it hit the barber's hand and the slave's throat was cut as a result; we are told that whichever party (the player or the barber) was negligent, to be determined on the facts, is liable *lege Aquilia*. The text ends with the remark that one who sits down to be shaved in such a place has himself to blame for what happens. This may be either contributory negligence or an application of the maxim 'volenti non fit iniuria'. There is perhaps the same fusion of the two notions in the maxim:[2] 'Quod quis ex culpa sua damnum sentit non intellegitur damnum sentire.' But the rule as to willingness to take the risk is more clearly illustrated in other texts, e.g. where a man engages in a contest he accepts the ordinary consequences,[3] a *filius* who permits himself to be treated as a slave has no action for the *iniuria*, though his father may have,[4] just as, in our law, in the case

---

[1] D. 9. 2. 11. *pr.*
[2] D. 50. 17. 203. The text is corrupt. As to contributory negligence in Roman law, see Pollock, *cit.* 13th ed. Appendix D.
[3] D. 9. 2. 7. 4.   [4] D. 47. 10. 1. 5.

of seduction of a woman, her consent debars her from recovering damages for the trespass, but does not preclude her employer's or parent's action for seduction.

Our expression 'contributory negligence', as applied to the law before 1945, was an unfortunate one—quite apart from the fact that the word 'contributory' was misleading because much more than a contribution was required of the plaintiff before he disentitled himself to recover. It was unfortunate because it accepted as the main basis of its operation the view that the plaintiff was being punished for his own negligence, whereas among many competing theories there is attractive authority for the view that an important, if not the important, ground was that the damage was not caused by the defendant, and therefore he could not be held liable.[1] The Roman texts have no expression corresponding to 'contributory negligence'. They do not indeed discuss the topic at all fully, but it is clear that breach of causal *nexus* between the *culpa* of the defendant and the damage done is the guiding principle in the matter.[2]

The Law Reform (Contributory Negligence) Act, 1945, has substituted for the old practice that of reducing the plaintiff's damages (and of course those of a counter-claiming defendant) 'to such an extent as the Court thinks just and equitable having regard to the claimant's share in the responsibility for the damage'. Our law is thus brought into line with that of most other countries.

(c) NECESSITY

Necessity appears in Roman texts as a defence in an action for damage, e.g. where a ship was driven without fault into a position in which the only hope of avoiding wreck was by cutting the cables of another ship,[3] or again, where it is

---

[1] See Salmond, *Law of Torts*, 10th ed. p. 452, and *British Columbia Electric Railway Co., Ltd.* v. *Loach*, [1916] 1 A.C. at p. 727.

[2] See the texts cited, Buckland, *Text-book*, p. 587.   [3] D. 9. 2. 29. 3.

necessary to pull down a building to prevent a fire from destroying one's own house.[1] How far this goes in our law is not quite clear, but it is settled that the same rule applies as to checking a fire.[2] It might be said that there is no *culpa* here: no more is done than a reasonable man would do, and the case is analogous to self-defence, recognised in both systems of law.[3] But in Roman law self-defence was no reply in itself to a third person who was damaged by my act,[4] and the English law seems not very clear on this point.[5] In Roman law it does not appear on the texts that there was any means of obtaining compensation for the harm thus lawfully caused, even where a house was pulled down. It is possible that in English law there may be a claim upon the public funds.[6] It should be added that these points have, properly speaking, nothing to do with negligence (though they have with damage to property), for the act is done with full advertence both to the act and to its consequences. Both in Roman law and in ours contributions (general average) are obtainable by the owner of maritime property sacrificed in the interests of the whole venture (*levandae navis causa*), but that is pure borrowing by way of the law maritime and therefore irrelevant to our purpose.

(d) ACTS AND OMISSIONS

In principle, liability under the *lex Aquilia*, for damage to property, required a positive act. There is nothing harsh or anomalous about that. In ordinary circumstances no one is under a legal obligation to act unless he has done something to put himself under an obligation to act. In Roman law a surgeon who had operated at once came

---

[1] D. 9. 2. 49. 1.   [2] Pollock, *cit.* p. 132.
[3] D. 9. 2. 4–5. *pr.*; h.t. 45. 4; Pollock, *cit.* pp. 134–137.
[4] D. 9. 2. 45. 4.   [5] Pollock, *loc. cit.*
[6] Pollock, *loc. cit.* For discussion see Winfield, *Textbook*, s. 18.

under an obligation to give or arrange for after-treatment.[1] If I lit a fire, I was under a duty to take precautions to see that it did not spread, to the damage of some other person.[2] The English law seems to be the same. A statute may impose an active duty, e.g. of fencing a danger spot, and, if this is for the protection of the public, one who is damaged by the results of neglect of this duty will have an action. But in general there is no duty to act.[3] Omission will not create a liability for negligence unless there was some relation, or earlier act, which imposed a duty to take active precautions. There is a clause in the Bürgerliches Gesetzbuch which can be understood so as to impose a duty to act wherever 'gute Sitte' requires it,[4] and is in fact so understood by some writers,[5] but not apparently in practice.

There are, however, cases which seem to create a certain difficulty in Roman law. *A* lights a fire lawfully and instructs *B* to watch it; *B* does not do so and it burns *C*'s house. The texts make *B* liable, though he has done nothing, but do not state any clear principle of liability.[6] It is possible to put the case on a basis of assumption of liability, but the texts do not do so.[7] Certainly, if a mere passer-by, noticing that the fire was approaching the boundary, watched it for a while and then went on his way, no one, except possibly those of Stammler's way of thinking, would hold him liable.[8] But suppose, not contenting himself

---

[1] D. 9. 2. 8. *pr.*   [2] D. 9. 2. 27. 9; h.t. 30. 3.

[3] See *Giles* v. *Walker* (1890), L.R. 24 Q.B.D. 656.

[4] Sect. 826. Schuster, *Principles of German Civil Law*, p. 338, confines the breach of the rule to acts, but the German hardly justifies this.

[5] E.g. Stammler, *Lehre von dem richtigen Rechte*, p. 302.

[6] D. 9. 2. 27. 9; Coll. 12. 7. 7.

[7] This is not surprising in view of the frequency with which the jurists omit to give reasons for their decisions. In fact *B* took upon himself a duty of care.

[8] But there is a strong tendency nowadays to make it a criminal offence to refuse assistance to persons in danger, provided that one could act without danger to oneself (cf. French Penal Code, art. 63). This automatically, in a law like the French, makes the defaulting party civilly liable also.

with watching, he had done something to the fire and it afterwards spread and did damage: it does not appear that he would be liable either in Roman law or in ours unless his intervention was in some way careless. A man who without any obligation takes some precautions in a proper way can hardly thereby bind himself to take further precautions. In the case mentioned he may have been under an obligation of some sort, or duty, e.g. as a slave or as a mandatary, but it is not easy to see how this should put him under an obligation to other people in the absence of a very wide conception of negligence. The only way to justify the decision seems to be on the ground of an assumption of responsibility already mentioned.

English criminal law presents a very similar case, *R. v. Smith*,[1] where a man had a tramline constructed under a private Act of Parliament authorising him to construct and use it. The line crossed a road. It was his practice to station a man at the crossing to give approaching traffic warning when a truck was about to cross the road. One day he set Smith on duty there accordingly. After a time Smith abandoned his post. An accident happened in which X was killed. Smith was indicted for manslaughter, but Lush J. declined to allow a conviction, concurring in the argument that 'the facts of the case disclosed no duty between the prisoner and the public' and holding that, since the owner's private Act of Parliament imposed no duty on him to place a watchman where the tramway crossed the road, therefore Smith was merely the owner's private servant and his negligence did not involve such a breach of duty as to make him guilty of manslaughter. The obvious implication is that, if the statute had imposed such a duty, Smith would have been liable. It has been doubted[2] whether the case is correctly reported, and it is certainly very meagrely reported. It is possible to wish, apart altogether from humanitarian grounds, that X had

---

[1] (1869) 11 Cox C.C. 210.   [2] Russell on Crimes, 10th ed. p. 466, n. 69.

been only injured, so that the civil issue could have been directly raised. In Roman law there is no doubt on the texts above cited that Smith would have been liable to·an *actio utilis* under the *lex Aquilia*, if *X* had been a slave or had been only injured.

The general result seems to be that while the Roman law was narrower than ours both in the proprietary interests protected (for it gave no protection to the interests of some classes of what we call 'bailees') and in the nature of the damage (for it dealt only with damage to physical property with some analogous extensions), it had, within that field, a rather wider conception of what amounted to negligence. Apart from negligence connected with contract there is in our books very little about negligent omissions. Beven[1] passes over them with a few not very helpful words.

When the fact of negligence in conduct has been established (and in our law, it seems, though not in the Roman law, a duty to take care has been shown), the question still remains whether the actual damage which was done can be said to have been 'caused' by the negligent conduct, so as to be imputable to the defendant. In the treatment of this matter our cases make a distinction. Where the plaintiff is one to whom there clearly was a pre-existing duty the question put assumes the form: Was the damage too remote? Where the plaintiff is less directly connected with the act of the defendant the question is put: Was there any duty to this person not to cause this damage? It will be gathered from what has been said above[2] that in the opinion of the writers these questions are one and the same, that when an English judge says the defendant owed no duty to the plaintiff, or an American judge says that the defendant was not negligent in regard to the plaintiff, they really mean

---

[1] *Negligence*, pp. 5, 6. Some, at least, of the cases where an occupier of premises is liable to an invitee are cases of negligent omission.

[2] P. 363, *ante*. The element of remoteness finds some recognition in *Grant* v. *Australian Knitting Mills Limited*, [1936] A.C. 85, 104.

what they say in the other case, i.e. that the damage was not so connected with the defendant's act as to be imputable to him. Was it 'too remote'? The answer is extremely difficult. It has been put in many ways. Was the act the proximate cause? Was the damage a 'direct' consequence? At the moment this seems the orthodox way in which to put the question. Was there a *nova causa interveniens*? As has been said above, this is the way in which the Romans seem to have looked at the matter. But difficult as the question is with us, difficult as it is to reconcile the various decisions and dicta on the matter, it must be admitted that the Roman authorities are still more unsatisfactory. It seems quite impossible to gather a conclusion of principle from the scanty texts. It seems true to say that apart from simple cases, such as those above mentioned where a man is mortally wounded but is actually killed by a second wound from another, or *vis maior*, or negligence of a surgeon, they never really faced the question of remoteness. It is a fair excuse to say that the difficult problems caused by modern industrial developments never arose, and were probably inconceivable to them.

3. *INIURIA*

The delict of *iniuria*, which primarily means outrage or insult, has the special interest that, like our trespass, it was originally a remedy of a rather narrow scope which ultimately became the remedy for a large number of wrongs of very varied character. It is less comprehensive than trespass and its derivatives, because, as we have seen, Roman law had more independent roots for the law of delict than our law had, but it still covered a very wide area. Originally limited to provisions in the XII Tables for fixed penalties for assaults, called *iniuriae*,[1] these being no doubt the only kind of insult to which a primitive people is sensible, it was first modified, though not extended, by the

---

[1] XII Tables, 8. 4.

Praetor, who substituted penalties assessed by the court for the ancient fixed penalties which had become derisory with the change in value of money.[1] This was followed by other edicts which were real extensions, i.e. they dealt with many other forms of contumelious conduct with which a less civilised age had not concerned itself.[2] By the beginning of the Empire, however, the Praetor's first general edict had come to be understood as covering also these other cases.[3] Thus the later edicts became unimportant, except that they tell us what was an *iniuria*, so that the term still covered only a limited group of cases. Then in the hands of the earlier classical lawyers the term *iniuria* was held to cover any contumelious conduct whether included in these edicts or not. Finally, and still in the classical age, the view was reached that any wanton infringement of anyone's rights was to be treated as contumelious and thus an *iniuria*, giving the *actio iniuriarum*.[4]

The extension gave no help in negligence, since there must be intent to insult, but it gave a remedy in many cases for which our law has provided in other ways. The difficulty felt and surmounted in *Ashby* v. *White*,[5] where a man was prevented from voting, would have been no difficulty for Ulpian: it was a clear case of *iniuria*. There was no action for simple trespass, *per se*, but trespass to land after prohibition, or even without prohibition on land which one knew to be barred, such as a private house or a preserve, was an *iniuria*.[6] Seduction of a daughter, or even an attempt to seduce, was an *iniuria* with no need to appeal to the notion of loss of service by which our law has provided a remedy.[7] Indeed *iniuriae* are innumerable.

---

[1] Lenel, *Ed. Perp.* 3rd ed. pp. 399 *sqq.*
[2] Lenel, *loc. cit.*   [3] See, e.g., D. 47. 10. 1. 1, 15. 3.
[4] See, on this evolution, Jhering, *Actio iniuriarum*; French translation, de Meulenaere.
[5] (1703), 2 Ld. Raym. 938.
[6] D. 47. 10. 15. 31, 23; p. 102, *ante*.
[7] D. 47. 10. 1. 2, 10, 15. 15; C. 9. 35. 2.

As the action was based on insult it had special rules, notably that intent to insult must appear and that anger must have been shown so soon as the facts were known.[1] It is clear, however, that so far as the final extension is concerned intent to insult was presumed: 'res ipsa loquitur'.

We have seen[2] that the Romans had no general conception of abuse of rights, and that the texts indicate no general rule that the exercise of a right without any economic purpose but solely with the view of insulting or annoying another person was an *iniuria*.[3]

One important case of *iniuria* is defamation. The question whether it was in writing or not appears to be indifferent in Roman law, so far as liability is concerned, though no doubt it might make a difference in the assessment of damages. But the basis of the liability is different. It rests not on loss of reputation but on outrage to the feelings, so that it was not necessary to liability that it should have been published to a third party. This at least seems to be the trend of the texts, though it does not seem to be explicitly laid down. An insulting letter to me would seem to be an *iniuria* even though no one else saw it.[4] There was a special Edict about *convicium*, or public insult.[5] A number of texts deal with *iniuriae* done *infamandi causa*. *Famosi libelli* are differentiated from other *iniuriae* in the rubric of D. 47. 10 and have a special title in the Code,[6] no doubt because there were special enactments about them. But here too publication does not seem to be necessary: to have anything to do with any such thing at any stage was an *iniuria*.[7] Indeed to see such a thing and not at once destroy it was a criminal offence in later law.[8] And no doubt the penalty in the *actio iniuriarum* would be

---

[1] Inst. 4. 4. 12; D. 47. 10. 3. 1; 47. 10. 11. 1.
[2] Pp. 96 *sq.*, *ante*.   [3] P. 98, *ante*.
[4] *Maledicere* was an *iniuria*, D. 47. 10. 15. 11.
[5] D. 47. 10. 15. 2 *sqq.*   [6] C. 9. 36.
[7] D. 47. 10. 5. 9.   [8] C. 9. 36. 2.

more severe where the matter was actually published. As with us, in civil actions, truth of the allegations made was a complete defence,[1] and there does not seem to have been any protection against raking up old stories. The need for intent to insult the person who was insulted prevented the questions which have arisen in our law, where a writing does in fact hold up a man to ridicule, but clearly was not so intended,[2] though if the intent·was to insult me it was no defence in Roman law to show that there was a misunderstanding as to my identity.[3] So too there could be no liability on a publisher or the like in respect of the content of a book, unless he actually knew of it.

There were cases which correspond to our absolute privilege. Thus no action could be brought against one's patron for an *iniuria*,[4] though there is a text which says it could be brought against a magistrate[5] even for what was said in his official capacity. But though this appears as a general proposition in the Digest, it is probable that it was of much more limited scope in earlier law. On the other hand there was nothing like qualified privilege and no need for it, since the 'malice' which would exclude our qualified privilege had to be shown in all cases; nor is there any trace of a defence on the lines of our 'fair comment'.

Some forms of *iniuria* were also criminal from early times, and it seems that in later law all forms of it were.[6] It does not appear that the principles were in any way different from those of the civil forms: in particular there is no sign, in the criminal treatment of the matter, of the

---

[1] D. 47. 10. 18. *pr.*; *McPherson* v. *Daniels* (1829), 10 B. and C. 263. 'For the law will not permit a man to recover damages in respect of an injury to a character which he either does not, or ought not to, possess', p. 272.

[2] *Hulton* v. *Jones*, [1910] A.C. 20.   [3] D. 47. 10. 18. 3.

[4] D. 47. 10. 11. 7.   [5] D. 47. 10. 32.

[6] D. 47. 10. 35, 45. As to the *lex Cornelia de iniuriis*, Buckland, *Textbook*, p. 590.

rule that it was necessary to prove in defence that the public interest was served by the publication or of the doctrine that 'the greater the truth the greater the libel'.

It is perhaps worth while to add that in some cases *iniuria* to be actionable had to be gross (*atrox*), for instance, where it was done to a slave, since only in that case did it reflect on the master,[1] and that naturally enough where it was *atrox* the damages were on a higher scale. This rule also brings out another point. Though the insult might on the face of it apply only to the person to whom it was addressed, it might, and in some cases necessarily would, have a reflex action on others. Thus an insult to a *filiusfamilias* was also one to his *paterfamilias*; an insult to a woman was also one to her husband, but not *vice versa*.[2] In Roman law it was no *iniuria* to defame the character of a deceased person, but insult to his body or to his funeral was *iniuria* for which the *heres* could sue.[3] Similarly with us, defamation of the deceased is not actionable in damages at the suit of his family, but criminal proceedings will lie if the libel amounts to a 'vilifying of the deceased with a view to injure his posterity'. That is our nearest approach to a remedy available to one person for an insult to another, except that a 'husband may sue for any special damage which has accrued to him through the defamation of his wife'.[4]

It should be noted in conclusion that though our law knows no such tort as outrage or *iniuria*, this does not mean so much as it seems at first sight to mean. There are a number of cases in our law in which 'exemplary' or 'vindictive' damages may be given, either because the actual money damage cannot be measured or because, though it can be measured, it would in no way correspond to the

---

[1] Inst. 4. 4. 3. This is the general rule. For exceptions, perhaps more apparent than real, see Buckland, *Text-book*, pp. 591–592.

[2] Inst. 4. 4. 2. [3] D. 47. 10. 1. 4, 1. 6.

[4] Odgers, *Libel and Slander*, 6th ed. p. 340.

heinousness of the wrong. If the cases are looked at it will
be seen, as Sir Frederick Pollock notes,[1] that they are all
cases which would come within the Roman notion of
iniuria. But there is an important difference: in all these
cases some other substantive tort must have been committed before this principle comes into play, so that the
fact that the act was outrageous does not of itself make it
a wrong. Wanton and wilful trespass on a man's property
is a case in point. The practical outcome may not be greatly
different, as our law of tort is more comprehensive than the
Roman law of delict, but it is not quite the same. To call
a man an offensive name when no one else hears it is not
in our law a tort, though in Roman law it would be an
iniuria, if it could be proved. But, even here, the artificial
principles of our law have provided a remedy, though not
a civil remedy. To call a man by an opprobrious name is
not *per se* a tort, but, on the one hand, if it can be construed
as a threat it may lead to proceedings to obtain recognisances to keep the peace or for good behaviour,[2] and, on
the other, it might be construed as an act directly pro-
voking a breach of the peace and so constitute a punishable
offence.[3]

4. *DOLUS*

Though an action of deceit has existed in our law from
very early times,[4] it was at first confined to 'trickery in
legal proceedings', and, till relatively modern times, to
what we now call contract, falsity of warranties and the
like. It was not, it seems, till 1789, that in *Pasley* v.
Freeman[5] the Court recognised a definite tort called deceit,
having no necessary relation to contract. The wrong was
equally unknown to the early Roman law, but it appeared

---

[1] Pollock, *cit.* 14th ed. p. 153.
[2] Stone's *Justice's Manual*, 81st ed. pp. 279–282.
[3] Stone, *cit.* p. 472.
[4] Jenks, *Short History of English Law* (1938), p. 139.
[5] 3 Term Rep. 51.

at a relatively much earlier date than with us when Aquilius Gallus introduced it in the time of Cicero, in what may fairly be called the infancy of scientific law. The general field of the action of deceit and the *actio doli* are, at any rate for the earlier classical period, much the same; the *actio doli* lies for deceitful and fraudulent manœuvres by which a person, contemplated specifically or generically, is damaged. But there are serious differences. One is perhaps only apparent. In our law the fraud must actually have induced the act causing the damage, while this is not laid down in the Roman law; but as it is laid down that it must have deceived and must have been serious it may perhaps be said that *res ipsa loquitur*.[1]

Another difference is more important. The *actio doli* had a much narrower field than the action of deceit. It was essentially a subsidiary action, aimed at restoration of the *status quo ante*, and, in principle, was not allowed where there was or ever had been any other way of recovering what was due.[2] Thus, while it is clear on our Reports that the action of deceit is very commonly brought where the facts arise under a contract and between the parties to it, this could not happen in Rome, since the contractual action would always be available and would exclude the *actio doli*.[3] It seems also to have been narrower in another sense. As with us, the false representation need not have been made actually to the person who suffered if it was intended that he should act on it, but this seems to be applied in the texts only to cases where the representation was made to my procurator or agent and I suffered.[4] The facts in

---

[1] D. 4. 3. 1. *pr.*, 7. 10, 9. 5. See also pp. 198, 284.

[2] D. 4. 3. 1. 4 *sqq.*; there were exceptions, which we need not consider.

[3] In D. 4. 3. 37 there is an apparent exception; words of commendation by a vendor not such as could be imported into the contract might give an *actio doli* if they were intended to and did deceive the buyer. Presumably they would have given a good defence in the action on sale. But the relevant passage is almost certainly either corrupt or interpolated.

[4] E.g., D. 4. 3. 7. 9.

Langridge v. *Levy*[1] would probably have given an *actio utilis* under the *lex Aquilia*, which would exclude the *actio doli*, but, even apart from this, it does not seem that an *actio doli* would have been available. There is no trace in the texts of liability for statements addressed to a wide class, like those in a prospectus of a company or a railway time-table, giving an action to anyone misled and damaged thereby, who can show that he is a member of the class to whom the fraudulent statement was addressed;[2] but this may mean no more than that such things did not occur in Roman life. The *actio doli* is also narrower in another important way. It seems clear that in the original conception of the action (and apparently it remained necessary throughout its history) there must have been a definitely dishonest intent, not necessarily an aim at personal profit, but intent to cause harm to the other party. Thus it does not seem that an *actio doli* would have lain on such facts as those in *Polhill* v. *Walter*,[3] where the assumption of authority though not made from a corrupt motive was certainly false to the knowledge of the maker, who, however, believed that it would be ratified and no harm would come to the person to whom the representation was made.

But *dolus* seems to have been wider in another sense. Its primary meaning is planned deception to the damage of another.[4] So far it is clear and its operation creates no difficulty. But it has wider senses. Thus it is commonly used to mean simply dishonesty, with no element of planned deceit, as indeed it was in our earlier law where attempts were made to treat wilful non-performance of a contract as a form of deceit and so found a remedy for non-feasance by way of *assumpsit*.[5] The innumerable texts

---

[1] (1837), 2 M. and W. 516; (1838), 4 M. and W. 337.

[2] *Peek* v. *Gurney* (1873), L.R. 6 H.L. 377.

[3] (1832), 3 B. and Ad. 114.

[4] See the definitions in D. 4. 3. 1. 2.

[5] Fifoot, *History and Sources of the Common Law: Tort and Contract*, pp. 332–334.

on *dolo desinere possidere* in the claim of a *hereditas,* in *vindicatio rei* (action to recover property) and in the *actio ad exhibendum* (for production) amply illustrate this meaning.[1] It is *dolus* for a mandatary not to hand over what he has received under the mandate.[2] It is *dolus* to take by force what is not yours.[3] It is *dolus* to drive your cattle on to my land so that they may feed on my *glans*.[4] The word is also used still more widely to denote wilful breach of duty, with no specific allegation of dishonest intent, e.g. in deposit,[5] *sepulchri violatio*,[6] under the *lex Aquilia,* where *dolus* is wilful damage, and in the law of *maiestas*.[7] Acts of a slave giving rise to noxal actions are generically described as *dolus*;[8] setting fire to crops is *dolus*.[9] It is *dolus* to pursue an action after a compromise,[10] or to obstruct *iudices* in their official business.[11] It is *dolus* to give a wrong judgement from *inimicitia, gratia* or *sordes*;[12] to incite a mob to do damage;[13] to commit wilful adultery,[14] etc. These wider and narrower meanings are well illustrated by texts on *vis* and *dolus.* In relation to *rapina* we are told that 'qui vim facit, dolo facit'.[15] Yet, for liability for carrying off one who has been summoned to court (*in ius vocatus*), we are told that it is enough that it is 'vi, quamvis dolus malus cesset'.[16]

All these texts, however, are concerned with the presence of *dolus* as creating ground for various specific legal liabilities: the question is how far they can be carried over to the *actio doli* where there is no other specific remedy. The extended meanings are clearly classical, and we are told on the one hand that the *actio doli* has the same *causa*

---

[1] See, e.g., D. 6. 1. 27. 3; 5. 3. 13. 14; 10. 4. 8.
[2] D. 17. 1. 8. 9.   [3] D. 47. 8. 2. 2.
[4] D. 10. 4. 9. 1.   [5] D. 16. 3. 1. 21.
[6] D. 47. 12. 3. *pr.,* 1.   [7] D. 48. 4 *passim.*
[8] D. 9. 4. 4. 2.   [9] P. Sent. 5. 20. 5.
[10] D. 12. 6. 23. 3.   [11] D. 48. 6. 10. *pr.*
[12] D. 5. 1. 15.   [13] D. 47. 8. 4. 6.
[14] D. 48. 5. 13.   [15] D. 47. 8. 2. 8.
[16] D. 2. 7. 3. 2.

as the *exceptio doli*,[1] and on the other, in a number of texts, that the *exceptio doli* is available in many cases where there is no element of concerted fraud or of deceit.[2] There are also many texts in which the *exceptio doli* is given in rebuttal of a formally valid, but in the circumstances inequitable, claim.[3] These applications are classical and have nothing to do with the so-called *exceptio doli generalis* which could be used in later law as a substitute for any other *exceptio* of which the availability was known to the plaintiff.[4] Since the *exceptio* was available, without obvious limits, to adjust such cases, it seems that the *actio doli* would be equally available to adjust inequitable gains and losses where no other remedy was available. *A* licenses me to dig chalk on his land, not by binding contract, and when I have incurred some expense he stops me from digging the chalk. I have an *actio doli*.[5] *A* promises land and before delivery imposes an easement on it. The promisee has an *actio doli* with, so far as the text goes, no need to allege fraud.[6] A man has promised the slave *A* or the slave *B*. Before delivery he kills *A*. This destroys the alternative and he must give *B*. Before delivery is due *B* dies. The promisor is released. There is no liability under the contract, but there is *actio doli*.[7] Under an informal agreement for mutual services, one having done his part, the other wilfully refused to do his; there was, before the development of the *actio praescriptis verbis*, no action in contract, but there was *actio doli*.[8] A slave agrees with *X* that *X* shall promise his master money to free him, the slave to take over the liability when freed. He is freed and then refuses. There is *actio doli*.[9] *A* promises *B* a slave.

---

[1] D. 44. 4. 2.
[2] E.g. D. 5. 3. 39. 1; 29. 7. 15; 35. 1. 89.
[3] E.g. G. 2. 76–78.   [4] D. 44. 4. 2. 5.
[5] D. 4. 3. 34; analogous case, D. 19. 5. 16. 1.
[6] D. 4. 3. 7. 3. The text gives analogous cases.
[7] D. 46. 3. 95. 1.   [8] D. 19. 5. 5. 3.
[9] D. 4. 3. 7. 8.

C kills the slave and so releases *A*. *B* has *actio doli* against *C*.[1] The depositee of a will obliterates it. *Heres* and legatees have *actio doli*.[2]

How far does this go? Some of the texts deal with inequitable gain, but many only with inequitable loss. Many of the texts are suspected of interpolation. Mitteis[3] thinks the cases are classical. Letter[4] thinks the classical texts always required planned *machinatio* for the *actio doli* and that the texts have suppressed this. For our purpose that is not material: the question is how far the rule went in the *Corpus Juris*. There is no difficulty about the original rule: preconcerted fraud causing damage is a cause of action. But the case is different when we come to mere unfairness of conduct. What is the principle? *Machinatio* is likely in some of the cases where it is not stated, but in others there is no hint or likelihood of it. It is not enough to say that the act must be wrongful. For since, by the hypothesis, there is no other remedy, it is not wrongful unless there is an *actio doli*, and to say that there is no *actio doli* unless the act is wrongful is thus circular. A rule that the action lay wherever one made a profit at another's expense or caused him a loss, wilfully and without justification, might not be unfair, but it would be somewhat unmanageable, and we should still have to determine what is a justification. Certainly the texts do not express any limit. In most of the cases the parties to the action are parties in some other relation, in the action appropriate to which the *dolus* cannot be dealt with, but sometimes, e.g. in D. 4. 3. 18. 5, the person liable for *dolus* has nothing to do with the transaction in connexion with which the liability arises; but it

---

[1] D. 4. 3. 18. 5; analogous case, D. 4. 3. 19.

[2] D. 4. 3. 35, but there are obvious difficulties of proof, and D. 9. 2. 41, 42 seem to give other remedies. Other cases expressing the same wide notion of *dolus* are D. 4. 3. 9. 3; 11. 6. 2. 1, 5. *pr.*; 11. 7. 14. 2; 39. 3. 14. *pr.*, which however is so altered and abridged as to be hardly intelligible.

[3] *Röm. Privatr.* pp. 316 *sqq.*

[4] *Festg. für Güterbock*, pp. 257 *sqq.*

may be noted that, in the case referred to, the act done (the killing of the slave) was certainly wrongful, though the duty broken was not to the plaintiff in the *actio doli* but to the owner of the slave killed.

The question arises how far this principle extended, that an *actio doli* would lie in respect of an act which, apart from this action, infringed no right. If it applied where there was no *negotium* in the matter, it would give a basis for a theory of abuse of right, since it is clear that for the *actio doli* there need be no intent to make profit. If I let my house to a tenant whom I know to be undesirable and noisy, in order to annoy my neighbour or to lessen the value of his property, is there an *actio doli*? The better answer seems to be that there is not. The very numerous texts like D. 50. 17. 55: 'nullus videtur dolo facere qui iure suo utitur',[1] seem conclusive, though it is possible to quibble as to what are the limits of one's right. Such evidence as we have about abuse of rights is never in any way connected with the *actio doli*, but either with abuse of process or with one of the various water rights between neighbours.[2] On the whole the better view seems to be, as is said above,[3] that there is no rule against abuse of right and that these applications of the *actio doli* which we have noted are no more than sporadic attempts to do justice and are partly, though certainly not entirely, post-classical. It is plain that in some of the Roman cases given there is no such 'inducement to an act' as seems to be necessary to the English action of deceit.[4] Where *A* makes an agreement with *B* on a condition within *B*'s power, and as things have turned out the contract would be highly profitable to *B*, and *C*, not connected with the matter, wilfully prevents *B* from satisfying the condition, no contract has arisen in either system, but in Roman law *B* will

---

[1] They are collected in Bonfante, *Corso di Dir. Rom.* ii. 1, p. 295.
[2] Bonfante, *cit.* ii. 1, pp. 289 *sqq.*   [3] P. 98, *ante.*
[4] See, e.g., Pollock, *cit.* p. 234.

have *actio doli* against *C*. Whatever remedy there may be in English law, it will certainly not be an action of deceit.

Dolus was not a delict in the strict sense: it was a praetorian, not a civil law, institution. And it has characteristics which bring it, at least superficially, nearer to the notion of tort than to that of delict. It is conceived indeed as a penal *actio*: it does not, e.g., survive against the *heres* except to the extent of his profit.[1] The fact that *condemnatio* in the action involves *infamia* does not make it a penal action: this occurs in many *actiones ad rem persequendam*.[2] But the substantial aim of the action is reparation—*rem servare*.[3] It follows that if the damage has been made good in any way the action does not lie. Thus while return of the property was no defence in theft, it was in the *actio doli*. From this it follows that if several were concerned the liability is not cumulative as it is in ordinary delict:[4] if one has made complete restitution the others are released from liability.[5] It is for our purpose indifferent whether this rule is classical, as it probably is, or the work of the compilers, as it is sometimes said to be.

The residuary character both of the *actio doli* and the *exceptio doli* is striking. The first has many resemblances to our Case, which, as Maitland said,[6] 'becomes a sort of general residuary action'; the second was employed for many purposes for which we should look to a Court of equity. Probably every legal system affords instances of this constant struggle to make law do justice by a gradual and often unavowed extension of existing remedies.

5. *METUS*

Metus is, as to the facts which give rise to the action, very like our duress or menaces or intimidation. But in Rome it was a well-recognised praetorian wrong, handled in general like *dolus*, except that it was not subsidiary (i.e. it

---

[1] D. 4. 3. 26.   [2] D. 3. 2. 1.   [3] D. 4. 3. 2–4, etc.
[4] P. 346, *ante*.   [5] D. 4. 3. 17.   [6] *Forms of Action*, p. 361.

lay even though there were other remedies), that it lay at least in later law against innocent third party acquirers to the extent of their benefit, and that, if it was allowed to proceed to *condemnatio*, the damages were fourfold, though this could always be avoided by restitution at any moment before *condemnatio*.[1] In our law, though it seems to be clear that it is a tort,[2] it seems usually to be treated, apart from the criminal law, as being quasi-contract, involving waiver of tort.[3] It is of course entirely outside the Roman notion of quasi-contract—indeed it seems to require a considerable sense of humour to appreciate the English way of looking at the matter. For it seems that in our courts a man who extorts money from me by threats of extreme violence is regarded as making an implied promise to pay it back again.

6. *CALUMNIA*

A praetorian wrong which can be called a delict is *calumnia*. This was the bringing of an action without reasonable grounds, i.e. in bad faith. It differed from our action for malicious prosecution in that it applied primarily to the bringing of a civil action,[4] while our action for malicious prosecution applies primarily to the bringing of criminal proceedings. But while it is only in very few cases that an action lies under our law for maliciously taking civil proceedings, e.g. bankruptcy proceedings,[5] *calumnia* seems also to have applied to criminal charges generally. It is true that we are told this only of a cognate form, bringing proceedings corruptly for reward,[6] but this may be due to the fact that under Justinian the ordinary *actio de calumnia* was obsolete; he substituted other machinery, so that we know but little of it.[7] As with us, it was normally essential

[1] D. 4. 2. 14. 1–4.
[2] See, e.g., Winfield, *The Province of the Law of Tort*, pp. 172 *sq*.
[3] Winfield, *loc. cit.*   [4] G. 4. 174, 178.
[5] See, e.g., Pollock, *cit.* p. 251.   [6] D. 3. 6. 1. *pr*.; h.t. 8.
[7] C. 3. 1. 14. 1; Inst. 4. 16. 1.

that judgement should have gone for the injured party. It
is curious to note that *calumnia* never seems to have been
regarded as an *iniuria* except where a man was claimed as
a slave.[1]

7. NUISANCE

A tort prominent in our books but having no direct parallel
in Roman law is nuisance. In fact, however, the Roman
law did provide a remedy in most of the cases which are
nuisances under our law. With us a public nuisance such
as digging a trench in a road or obstructing the use of a
road gives no action unless the plaintiff suffers some
damage other than that which falls equally on the public
generally.[2] On facts of this kind the Roman law gave a
remedy under the *lex Aquilia* for *damnum iniuria datum*, if
there was damage to limb or property.[3] But where there
was no actual damage of this kind it does not seem to have
provided for such cases as expense incurred by reason of
having to divert goods to another route owing to the obstruction.[4] It is, however, possible that in Justinian's law,
where the wrongful act was done in knowledge of its
wrongfulness, an *actio doli* might lie, though such a case
does not seem to be illustrated. So far as the normal type
of private nuisance is concerned, the protection given by
Roman law seems to be as effective as ours, though the
machinery is entirely different. Some nuisances, such as
overhanging trees, were dealt with by very early law.[5]
But the ordinary type of nuisance, consisting in unjusti-
fiable interference with my enjoyment of my property, was
not dealt with by an action on tort or delict. These nuisances
are normally inroads on ownership or some other real right
and the existence in Rome of 'real actions', actions as-

---

[1] D. 47. 10. 12, 22.
[2] *Winterbottom* v. *Lord Derby* (1867), L.R. 2 Ex. 316.
[3] D. 9. 2. 9. 4, 28. *pr.*, 29. *pr.*, etc.
[4] *Rose* v. *Miles* (1815), 4 M. and S. 101.
[5] XII Tables, 7. 9a; D. 43. 27. 1. 8, 2.

serting such a right, long since obsolete in our law,
enabled the aggrieved person in many cases to proceed
by an action asserting his right. Thus, if an excessive
intrusion of smoke caused actual damage, there would be
an action on delict, under the *lex Aquilia*, but, even apart
from this, there was an action claiming ownership free of
any such servitude as would be necessary to justify the
intrusion.[1] Similarly an interference with lights to which
one was entitled would be met not by an action on delict,
but by a real action asserting the right, called, under Justinian, *actio confessoria*.[2] But in addition to this there
existed an elaborate set of provisions against interference
with rights by neighbours, partly of ancient civil law,
partly praetorian. Thus there was an old *actio aquae pluviae
arcendae*, which more or less controlled a neighbour's
dealings with floodwater.[3] There was a machinery by
which security could be taken from a neighbour whose
premises, whether by his fault or not, were in such a state
that they threatened damage to my property,[4] a situation
which we should apparently deal with by an injunction in
a *quia timet* action. Again, if work was being done or about
to be done of a nature likely to injure neighbouring land,
there was available a speedy procedure of *operis novi nuntiatio*, the machinery of which was very elaborate; by
means of it I could, by notice on the spot, where it appeared
that the work would interfere with my rights, restrain the
continuance of the work, or rather, put the doer in the
position that he worked at the peril of having it all
destroyed if I proved to be in the right.[5] With us an
interim order or interlocutory injunction would be granted
pending the trial of the action, upon terms of an undertaking by the person claiming the injunction to abide by

---

[1] D. 9. 2. 49; 8. 5. 8. 5, which also allows an interdict for interference
with possession. As to the *actio negatoria*, Buckland, *Text-book*, pp. 675 *sq.*

[2] Buckland, *loc. cit.*   [3] D. 39. 3.

[4] *Satisdatio damni infecti*, D. 39. 2.   [5] D. 39. 1; 43. 25.

the order of the Court as to damages if eventually the injunction or order should be discharged.

Where work was done secretly or against prohibition which interfered with my rights or seemed to do so, I could obtain an *interdictum quod vi aut clam*, a process resembling a mandatory injunction, giving me the right if I proved my case to have the work destroyed and to claim damages.[1] And as we have seen, many of such things amounting to interference with my possession might be met by the ordinary possessory remedies, *interdictum uti possidetis, utrubi, unde vi*. The remedies overlap to some extent; they underwent historical changes and there is much controversy about some points; but their prominence in the texts testifies to their importance throughout the history of the law.[2] Between them they must have fairly well covered the ground of what we call private nuisance.

The rules of abatement of nuisance, which enable the injured person in many cases to put the matter right without legal process, had very little development in Roman law. The tendency in our law seems to be to reduce its field: in Rome there is little trace of it. It seems to be confined to nuisance involving actual trespass to the soil of the injured person's property. If a man made a watercourse across my land, I might dig it up, but where he made a projection from his wall over my land I might not cut it off but must proceed by legal process.[3] So too I might drive out trespassing cattle, taking due care not to harm them.[4] Even the rule of the XII Tables requiring overhanging trees to be cut back gives no power to the landowner affected to cut them. He must call on the owner of the tree to do it and sue him if he does not.[5]

---

[1] D. 43. 24.
[2] The best account of them is in Bonfante, *Corso di Dir. Rom.* ii. 1, chs. xv–xix. [3] D. 9. 2. 29. 1.
[4] D. 9. 2. 39. [5] P. Sent. 5. 6. 13.

Self-help was in fact discouraged at all historical times. Our law, on the other hand, appears to have no objection in principle to the redress of injuries by the act of the party injured and contents itself with safeguards against abuses, of which the Distress for Rent Acts afford an example. Blackstone includes in his *Commentaries* a chapter (iii. 1) on self-help and makes no apology for doing so.

8. QUASI-DELICT

Justinian in the Institutes gives us a fourth variety of obligation, which he calls *quasi ex delicto*. They are all, either in fact or in form, cases of vicarious liability. But they do not exhaust the cases of this: noxal liability, the liability for delicts of a *filius* or slave, limited by the right to surrender them to the aggrieved person, would also belong here. They are all praetorian, which might be held to exclude noxal liability, for that has its roots in the civil law, though it was extended by the Praetor.[1] But they are far from exhausting praetorian liabilities. When we remember that Justinian arranges his heads and sub-heads and further subdivisions in the law of obligation in fours, and that he gives four quasi-delicts, it seems unnecessary to see more in the classification than an attempt to complete his scheme of fours. It is therefore unnecessary to attempt to compare them with the various applications of the notion of quasi-delict which have been made in our law.[2] But the topic suggests that of liability without fault. This, or liability apart from fault, seems to be a better expression than 'irrefutable presumption of fault', since in some of the cases this presumption is entirely untruth-like. The liability existed in some cases in Roman law and does in ours, but some of the cases are not really significant. There are of course many cases in contract in which a man is liable without fault: inability to pay is no answer

[1] G. 4. 75, 76.
[2] As to these see Winfield, *Province of Tort*, pp. 208 *sqq.*

to a claim of a debt. This consideration removes from the
field some apparent cases. In Roman law live-stock dealers
were responsible for all serious defects whether they knew
of them or not. It is true that historically, by reason of the
methods and powers of the aediles who created the
liability, the action was penal in character, but essentially
it is a case of implied warranty, since it was possible to
contract out where the defects were unknown.[1] The special
liabilities of innkeepers and carriers which exist in both
systems can be analysed in the same way, though in both
systems there is an action in tort or delict.[2] The liability
for refusing to carry or receive, the conception of a common
calling, did not exist in Roman law, and is not in point, for
the liability is for refusal without excuse. The liability to
custodia in some contracts[3] is of the same type, but is regarded as contractual.

Justinian's first head of liability *quasi ex delicto*, that of
the *iudex qui litem suam facit*, can be thought of as vicarious
in the sense that the judge, by his wrongful conduct, took
upon himself the liability of one of the parties; but it is not
liability without fault. However, with this exception, the
various cases of vicarious liability in both systems are
essentially liabilities without fault. This is shown clearly
in the Roman law of noxal liability by the rule that the
liability is limited by the right of noxal surrender: if there
is actual fault in the employer he is liable in full, with no
option of surrender.[4] It is also shown by the history of the
matter: originally the wrongdoer alone was liable, but his
master had a right to ransom him by paying the penalty.[5]
But in all these cases, noxal liability and the quasi-delicts
and those coming under our principle of *respondeat superior*,
though the defendant may have committed no wrong, a

---

[1] Buckland, *Text-book*, pp. 491 *sqq.*
[2] Buckland, *cit.* pp. 580 *sq.*, 599; Winfield, *cit.* p. 151.
[3] Buckland, *cit.* pp. 560 *sq.*; p. 339, *ante.*
[4] D. 9. 4. 2. *pr.*   [5] Buckland, *cit.* p. 600, n. 9 and references.

wrong has been committed. It is true that the same rule applied in Roman law to damage by animals, *actio de pauperie*,[1] and the texts are clear that wrong cannot be imputed to animals; but the rules date from primitive times, when, on the one hand, this was by no means clear, and, on the other, the notion of guilt as an element in liability had hardly developed.

More interesting are the cases in which, so far as appears, there is no fault at all. They are difficult to find in Roman law. Where a liability for *damnum infectum* arises[2] it is not necessarily anyone's fault that the neighbouring property has got into a dangerous state. In the possessory interdicts a defendant possessing in good faith may find himself bound to pay for the fruits twice over, a penalty without fault.[3] This appears to be a historical survival, into the source of which we need not go. In our law the best illustrations of it are perhaps the rule commonly based on *Rylands* v. *Fletcher*,[4] of strict or 'absolute liability',[5] and the policy of the Workmen's Compensation Acts. It is observed by Dean Pound,[6] speaking however rather of American tendencies than of those of English law, that while the nineteenth century aimed at getting rid of liability without fault, the modern tendency is to increase its scope. To some extent the existence of liability without fault is a confession of practical inability to get evidence of fault; but this applies especially to cases where the safety of premises, plant, etc., is deemed to be warranted. The liability of the master is justified partly by the need to get a better defendant, for the workman in charge of dangerous things is not likely to be able to compensate for the damage he does, and partly by the fact that the employer who for his own purposes equips the servant may reasonably be

---

[1] D. 9. 1. [2] P. 393, *ante.*
[3] G. 4. 167. [4] (1868), L.R. 3 H.L. 330.
[5] As to the inadmissibility of this expression, Winfield, 42 *L.Q.R.* (1926), pp. 37 *sqq.* [6] *The Spirit of the Common Law*, pp. 188 *sq.*

required to take the risks attendant on the undertaking. The policy of the Workmen's Compensation Acts, where there is no fault at all, or need not be, is no doubt, as Dean Pound says,[1] due to 'a strong and growing tendency, where there is no blame on either side, to ask in view of the exigencies of social justice, who can best bear the loss'. But it may be suggested that the rule would not comply with the 'exigencies of social justice' if it were not for the great development of insurance, which in fact in the great majority of cases now spreads each individual loss over the whole body of employers. Indeed, one may hazard the guess that if the principle of the National Insurance Act, 1911, had been accepted two decades earlier, it would have been extended to cover the risks of injuries to workmen. This from the point of view of a coherent legal system would have been preferable to creating a new kind of liability without fault.[2]

---

[1] *Loc. cit.*

[2] This development has now taken place. See National Insurance (Industrial Injuries) Act, 1946 (9 and 10 Geo. VI, c. 62).

CHAPTER XII. PROCEDURE

1. SUBSTANTIVE AND PROCEDURAL LAW

To many persons, especially to those theorists who maintain that there are no rights but rights of action, the law of procedure, or, rather, the law of actions, is the most important part of the system. It is not easy to think of it as merely the machinery by which the real law, the substantive law, is put into operation. Thus it comes about that our earliest legal text-book of any importance, Glanvill's, though called a *Treatise on the Laws and Customs of England*, is mainly concerned with procedure. In modern times J. D. Mayne states a great part of the substantive law in a treatise on damages, i.e. he regards a man's right as, essentially, what can be recovered by litigation. So too Henry Roscoe in the same way states a great mass of substantive criminal law in a work entitled *The Law of Evidence and Practice in Criminal Cases*. There is nothing new in this: it is indeed the primitive way of looking at law. Chapter xi of Maine's *Early Law and Custom* is a demonstration of the fact that in all early communities the procedure dominates the law and that (p. 389) 'substantive law has at first the look of being gradually secreted in the interstices of procedure'; the XII Tables begin with, and appear to deal most fully with, procedure. The Edict and Digest follow this plan. It is only in the institutional books that procedure takes its place as an instrumental or adjective law. In Justinian's law the old forms of action are gone: the plaintiff states his case in the way which seems most convenient to him. Nevertheless the Byzantine lawyers still think in terms of actions: with them, as with us, though the forms of action are dead, 'they still rule us from their graves'.

2. CONSENT OF THE PARTIES. ARBITRAL ORIGIN OF ROMAN PROCEDURE

In both systems of law there was a great reluctance, more than a reluctance, to give judgement against a defendant who had not appeared. But the underlying principles do not seem to be the same. In our law this reluctance does not rest on need for consent of the parties:[1] the basis is that 'the law wants to be exceedingly fair, but is irritated by contumacy',[2] though the practical result is much the same, and all sorts of inconveniences are inflicted on the defendant who fails to defend the action. There does not seem to be here any underlying idea that the Court could not have proceeded to judgement if it had thought fit to do so, but only that it was not fair play. But in the older Roman law the rule was based on the principle that all jurisdiction depended on the consent of the parties.[3] This in turn rests on the notion that litigation is essentially a private arbitration established under the approval of the State, as a substitute for self-help, the business of the State officials being only to see that this arbitration is conducted in proper form. This character the procedure retains in form, and to some extent actually, throughout the classical age. But in fact ways were found of putting pressure on a recalcitrant defendant, ways based on the *imperium* of the magistrate. If a defendant would not take the proper procedural steps after he had been summoned, or if he evaded summons by hiding, the Praetor would order seizure of his goods, *missio in possessionem*.[4] The arbitrator (*iudex*), a private citizen, must be one chosen by the parties

---

[1] Though cases have occurred in which consent to a particular mode of trial might be essential, as is shown by the *peine forte et dure*; so too in certain cases a person's consent is needed before he can be tried summarily.

[2] P. and M. ii. p. 595.

[3] The parallel in the law of nations is striking, whether the reason be the same or not.

[4] Buckland, *Text-book*, p. 631.

in agreement. But if a defendant persisted in rejecting names, without reason, he was probably treated as *indefensus*, liable to *missio in possessionem*. In some cases security was required for various purposes. A defendant who refused this was *indefensus*. These securities were in form contracts, like our recognisances, and, like them, they were contracts only in name, for they could be compelled and their content was fixed by the magistrate.[1] Thus in classical law the consent, though nominally necessary, was very unreal, and in the procedure of later law, when cases were tried by a *iudex* who was a public official, or a person deputed by him, it had disappeared altogether.

It is a result of the fact that the *iudex* was a mere private person, chosen as a sort of arbitrator with the sanction of the Court, that the initiation of proceedings was entirely informal, and was done by a summons delivered by the plaintiff himself *mero motu*, known as *in ius vocatio*. This seems to have been the Anglo-Saxon method,[2] which also like the Roman required the plaintiff at the time of the summons to state generally the ground of complaint. But while private summons soon disappeared from our ordinary procedure, it was the normal method in Rome as long as the formulary system lasted, i.e. till the middle of the third century. Indeed it lasted longer, for though one would not expect a citizen to set in motion an administrative enquiry like the later procedure by his own volition, it seems that the *litis denuntiatio* which had superseded the *in ius vocatio* remained an entirely private act till early in the fourth century. Even then it continued so far private that the summons was served by the party himself, though he had to have previous authority from the magistrate. But in the fifth century there was a change. *Litis denuntiatio* was gradually superseded by what is called the libellary process, in which the first step was a statement of claim submitted to the court, which then itself issued a

---

[1] D. 45. 1. 52; 46. 5. 1. 10.   [2] Holdsworth, ii. p. 103.

summons to the defendant accompanying it by a copy of the statement of claim—*libellus conventionis*. The writ was returnable in a very short time, but this high rate of speed was abandoned for the later steps; very long delays were permissible to the parties, but there is still some obscurity as to the law under Justinian on these matters. There seems to have been the same speediness of beginning and slow progress afterwards in the matter of appeals.

From its origin in arbitration comes the most marked characteristic of Roman classical procedure. The trial was in two stages. The issues were formulated before the magistrate and agreed on by the parties, approved by him, and then sent for trial to the *iudex* accepted by them. This *iudex* must not be thought of as a kind of single juryman who had to try the facts, with guidance from the court as to the law; he decided the issue as stated in the pleadings with no authority over him, though he commonly had his own legal advisers. But he had nothing to do with execution: for this it was necessary to go back to the magistrate.[1] The unofficial position of the *iudex* had other results which look odd to modern eyes. No witnesses could be compelled to attend. There were very few rules of evidence. Hearsay was freely admitted. Written statements might be put in from persons unsworn and not present. Indeed there hardly could have been rules of evidence, for there was no obvious way of making them effective, since, the *iudex* being a private citizen, not an officer in a hierarchy, there was no appeal from his judgement. Perhaps such rules were not so necessary as they are thought to be in a modern jury case, for the common juryman is not usually a well educated or highly intelligent man, while the *iudices* were selected by the parties from a list consisting of men in the upper ranks of society. Practically the only check on the *iudex* was that if he acted with clear unfairness or obvious

---

[1] As in England to enforce the award of an arbitrator it is necessary to resort to the Court.

negligence he might himself be liable to an action by the sufferer ('iudex qui litem suam facit').[1] Execution might be resisted, but only on the ground of some formal defect in the proceedings, not for error. In default of this it might be possible to get some magistrate to exercise his power of veto upon any proceedings under the judgement, but this procedure must often have been a matter of influence.

In later law all this was changed. The judge was an official, usually, or often, a lawyer. There was an elaborate system of appeals. All the proceedings were in the hands of officials. Thus, the original summons, which had been by the party himself, on his own authority, was now done under the authority of the magistrate. Witnesses were officially summoned, and punished if they did not appear. Consent being no longer necessary, there was now no need for the indirect means of compelling co-operation which had been employed, and judgement could be given against an absent defendant, though only after long delays. More rules of evidence appeared. Hearsay was in general excluded and there was much legislation as to minimum of evidence and exclusion of certain persons from giving evidence. The rule developed (there are earlier traces of it): 'testis unus testis nullus'. In fact it is clear that in the age of Justinian oral testimony was discredited, and the main material, in civil suits, was documentary evidence, a practice borrowed from the Greeks, and rendered possible in commercial matters by the fact that, again a borrowing from the Greeks, commercial transactions were now almost invariably written.

Another fundamental change, also a part of the growing officialism of the process, was the abandonment of the old division into two parts. The magistrate or his deputy now heard the whole case from start to finish. The procedure has become (it had been from the third century) 'administrative', an enquiry conducted by administrative officers; thus, under Justinian, it does not seem, though the matter is

---

[1] D. 44. 7. 5. 4; Inst. 4. 5. *pr.*

disputed, that the public had any right to be present at the hearing, which was now in a court-house, a state of things very different from that in classical law when the *iudex* sat in the open *forum*. The mode of execution also reflects the changed conception of the proceeding. In classical law this was not for the Court but for the plaintiff, under supervision by the Court. There still survived in classical times an old crude system under which the defendant could be seized, under authority of the magistrate, and detained till he saw reason, but the more usual method was to obtain the leave of the magistrate to seize his whole estate and sell it *en bloc*, a stage which would not commonly be reached except in full insolvency, where there were many creditors. In later law execution was carried out by the magistrate by compelling the actual handing over of the thing in dispute where that was possible. If this was not applicable, as where the judgement was an order for payment of money, the court either took pledges or seized and sold so much as was necessary to satisfy the judgement, on modern lines.

3. OATHS

The mere oath, as a form of proof, played a much greater part throughout the history of Roman law than it has in our system, except in our very early days. The Roman proceeding looks very archaic. In some actions, especially claims for certain sums of money, the classical law allowed the plaintiff in the opening stage of the process to offer the defendant an oath, i.e. challenge him to swear to the truth of his defence, i.e. not to his good faith, of which something more is to be said, but to the absolute validity of his defence. If he took the oath the action was lost. If he refused it he was condemned. He was however entitled to take a third course, i.e. to offer the oath back to the plaintiff (*relatio*), who thereupon had the same two alternatives with analogous results, but had no right again to offer it back. The odd result was that if the plaintiff had once initiated this proceeding (the defendant could not do so) the matter could never get to an actual hearing. In later law the scope of the proceeding was extended. It could be done in any action and, under Justinian, at any stage in the proceedings. It no doubt served to shorten proceedings where there was no real defence and, in the case of claims for certain sums of money, the effect is not unlike that of our procedure under Order XIV. As the defendant had yet another possible course when the oath was offered, i.e. to require an oath of good faith from the plaintiff, with refusal of the action as the penalty for refusing to take it, the whole thing looks rather like *compurgatio*, but the resemblance is only superficial.

4. DISCOVERY OF FACTS AND DOCUMENTS

The Roman classical procedure admitted Interrogatories. In both systems they are a means of discovery of facts. In Roman law they occupied a much narrower field than in ours, but in that narrow field they were of great importance. In actions for wrongs committed by a man's slaves he could be interrogated on the ownership and actual possession of the slave, with serious consequences if the answer was false or was refused. So in actions against the *heres* of a debtor the defendant could be asked whether he was in fact *heres* and, if so, for what share (since he was liable only *pro rata*), with analogous penalties for falsity or refusal. And there were a few other cases. In later law this system had disappeared, but on the other hand any party could be interrogated on any point at any stage, but his answer, or refusal to answer, only provided evidence. It will be noticed that in the *actiones interrogatoriae* of classical law the machinery is open only to the plaintiff. But perhaps it is unnecessary to pursue this topic further, because it seems probable that our system of interrogatories, which was the creation of the Court of Chancery, is thus only a borrowing from a Roman source.

There were also rules more analogous to our discovery of documents. In our law the rule seems to be, roughly, that *either party* may call on the other to specify on oath all the documents which are or have been in his possession or power relating to any matter in question in the action; thereupon, he will, subject to a claim of privilege in certain cases upon the validity of which the Court will decide, be ordered to produce any or all of these documents for inspection by his opponent. In Roman law the Edict *de edendo* gave the defendant the right to call for all documents on which the plaintiff proposed to rely and, as it seems, for his accounts, though these were not going to be put in. This is entirely in the interest of the defendant; there was no corresponding provision for the plaintiff. As Gaius says in another connexion: 'facilius enim reis praetor succurrit quam actoribus'.[1] And the Praetor went still further; owing to the way in which business affairs were conducted in Rome, bankers were closely concerned with their clients' affairs, and in fact kept their books for them. Consequently the Edict provided, with certain safeguards, that *argentarii* and *nummularii* might be compelled to produce their accounts (but only it seems by their clients), even though they were not parties to the litigation.[2] But the plaintiff could not compel the defendant to produce any documents. There does not seem to be any direct equivalent, even in the later Roman law, for our 'subpoena duces tecum', under which persons not parties can be compelled to appear as witnesses and to produce any material documents in their possession. In the later law, however, witnesses could be compelled to appear and to give evidence of what they knew or to swear that they knew nothing about the matter,[3] and it seems likely that in practice this would involve production of any material documents in their possession.

---

[1] G. 4. 57.   [2] D. 2. 13; C. Just. 2. 1.
[3] C. 4. 20. 16, restored from *Basilica*.

5. REPRESENTATION IN LITIGATION

The Roman civil procedure admitted of a form of representation in litigation in which the representative occupied something like the position at one time occupied in our law by the attorney. It seems probable that most legal systems in their early stages look upon litigation as essentially personal and find difficulty in accepting the principle and practice of representation for that purpose.[1] So Herman Cohen,[2] commenting on a passage in Glanvill, says that 'the principle is that representation normally depends on reasonable absence, and the tribunal ought to have formal authority for the representative'; and under the Statute of Westminster II (1285) every litigant had to appear in person and be present throughout the hearing unless he had leave to appear by attorney. Similarly in Roman law all parties had to be present. Under the old *legis actio* system no representation was allowed, with some exceptions, somewhat obscure, but not such as to affect the principle.[3] But after the introduction of the formulary system it was possible to appoint *cognitores* and, a little later and less formally, *procuratores*, to act as representatives. There was, however, a very great difference between these persons and a modern attorney. The requirement of actual co-operation of the party remained, and the only way in which to reconcile this with the appointment of a representative was to make the representative the actual party to the suit. Thus, where such a person was engaged, the *formula* was so framed as to direct the *iudex* to give judgement, not for or against the real party interested, but for or against the representative;[4] with the obvious consequence that only the representative could get execution and only the representative's property could be taken in execution. And, since *res iudicata* is of force

[1] Holdsworth, viii. pp. 115–117.   [2] *History of the English Bar*, p. 85.
[3] G. 4. 82.   [4] See G. 4. 86.

only between the parties to the suit, the person really interested was not formally barred from bringing his action again. This last result was not, however, applied where the representative was a *cognitor*: he was always regarded as bringing his principal's case into issue, and the other inconvenient result was gradually whittled away, but not completely till near the end of the classical age, when the effect became exactly the same as if the real principal had been the actual party. It had of course been necessary to guard against the old inconveniences by an elaborate system of guarantee and some of this remained in use, out of sheer conservatism, long after it had ceased to serve any purpose.

Thus the *cognitor* or *procurator* had a function very unlike that of the modern barrister or solicitor. There is another great difference. Though the party (be he principal or representative) must be present, he normally took no part in the proceedings: he could not even give evidence, apart from the interrogations already mentioned; the actual conduct of the case was in the hands of advocates (*advocati*, *patroni*). These, however, were not lawyers: they were *oratores*. The skilled lawyers, the jurists, were in the background, advising, but they took no official part in the proceedings. There was no Bar in the modern sense of the word. Hence it is that for the period before the legal treatises which we possess were written, much of our knowledge is derived from the speeches of *oratores*, especially Cicero. And these have to be taken with caution, partly because they are at best speeches of counsel on behalf of a party, and are thus evidence only of what it was desired that the court should believe, and partly because neither the speaker nor the *iudex* whom he addressed was a lawyer. As might have been expected, the difference between the *orator* and the *iurisprudens* tended to disappear in later law, and the men who argued before the official judges of the later Empire were very like our modern barristers.

6. FORMS OF ACTION

The historical course in the matter of forms of action was very much as with us. The Praetor's Edict, as revised in the second century by Julian, was a sort of *Registrum Brevium*.[1] No action could be brought unless the claim could be expressed in the terms of one of the *formulae* set out in the Edict, except indeed that the Praetor could and did allow *formulae* not quite covered by existing writs by allowing *formulae* which may be described as *in consimili casu*. The gradual accretions to the Edict in the end of the Republic, and to some extent later, till the crystallisation of the Edict by Julian, correspond to the steady enlargement of the *Registrum*. The Praetor, however, seems to have had a freer hand than the Clerks of the Chancery. If he wished he could definitely introduce what was in fact a new rule of law by creating a *formula*. He was not confined to extending existing actions (though he did a great deal of this) as our trespass was extended, so as to make the same notion cover both the absolute right independent of damage which trespass looks after and the many wrongs consisting in damage which have been brought within it. But the story is much like ours. Just as with us the abolition of forms of action in the nineteenth century, enabling the parties to state their case in any convenient form, did not release them from the obligation of showing that they would have had a claim under the old system, so too it does not appear that the abolition of the *formula* (also at a late stage in legal history) had any direct effect on the substantive law. The plaintiff must still show that he would have had a claim under the older law, though the new system led the way to a fusion of the praetorian and the civil law, very much as the Common Law Procedure Acts led the way to the Judicature Acts.

There was a further curious development. The *formula*

[1] But see, for a distinction, Holdsworth, ii. p. 519.

had used precise words the implications of which were well known. That precision was now gone, but the names of the old actions were still preserved as they are with us, and the post-classical lawyers developed rules as to what they called the *natura actionis*. Every action had its *natura*, in practice the rules of substantive law which governed it except so far as they were excluded by agreement, at least in the region of contract and the like. The Byzantines added *essentialia*, i.e. rules of substantive law which could not be excluded, e.g. in sale, that there must be a money price: if there was none, there was no action on sale whatever other protection there might be: it was *contra naturam actionis*. And there were also *accidentalia*, matters not 'natural' to the action, but which could be imported by agreement.[1] There is not much about this in the *Corpus Juris*, but it appears often in the Basilican commentary, and it seems to be at least as old as Justinian's time. What if any connexion there may be between this and the un-official collections of writs which are known in our history as the *Natura Brevium* and the Old *Natura Brevium*[2] we do not know.

7. CONTRACTS OF RECORD

As has already been noted, Roman law had what may be called contracts of record, somewhat like our own. The magistrate or the *iudex* might for various purposes in con-nexion with a litigation require a party to give an under-taking or to offer personal security. The form of the promise, whether by a party or by a surety, was a *stipulatio*, but we are told that it was not left to the parties to frame it: the terms of it were prescribed by the Praetor and could not be varied except by him. But there is a difference with regard to another form of contract of record. With us a judgement is a contract of record and can be sued on as

---

[1] They also speak of *natura contractus*, thus transferring the notion from adjective to substantive law. See Rotondi, *Scr. Giur.* 2. 211.

[2] Holdsworth, ii. p. 522.

such. In Rome also it could be sued on. In fact in classical law (it is not very clear how far this survived into Justinian's law) an action on the judgement, an *actio iudicati*, was a necessary preliminary to proceedings in execution. But the judgement was not itself thought of as a contract. According to the doctrine first suggested by Wlassak and now almost universally accepted, the contract was made at the joinder of issue, *litis contestatio*, a contract to submit to judgement, i.e. possibly, condemnation.[1] The judgement and the condemnation were thus only proceedings under the contract made at *litis contestatio*. We do not know how the action on the judgement was actually formulated: there have been various attempts to reconstruct it, but Lenel holds[2] that we have not sufficient material.

Superficially our 'closing of the pleadings' might appear to have some resemblance to *litis contestatio*: it is when the pleadings are closed that, to quote Odgers,[3] 'the issues are clear, and the case is ready for trial'; but there is no trace of any contractual element in closing the pleadings. A closer analogy is our submission precedent to arbitration. 'A submission is merely a contract between the parties of which some of the terms are to be left to be supplied by the award. The submission and award together constitute a complete contract.'[4] But this is perhaps more like the Roman *compromissum* in which no question of *litis contestatio* arises.[5]

8. APPEALS

We have noted that under the *formula* there was no appeal. Later, there were appeals from every one but the Emperor himself or persons acting as his delegates. These became in fact, as they have with us, a possible agency of injustice;

---

[1] Wlassak, *Anklage und Streitbefestigung*; Wenger, *Pauly-Wissowa*, s.v. *Editio*.   [2] *Ed. Perp.* 3rd ed. p. 443.

[3] *Pleading and Practice* (13th ed. 1946), p. 205.

[4] Redman, *Law of Arbitrations and Awards*, 5th ed. pp. 4, 5; Lord Eldon in *Wood* v. *Griffith* (1818), 1 Swanston 44.

[5] Buckland, *Text-book*, p. 532.

for they were expensive and the rich man could appeal all the way up from the municipal magistrate to the Emperor himself, who, however, commonly delegated judges. And most of us have heard of cases in which wealthy corporations in modern times have defeated justice in the same way. Something has been done by us to limit the number of possible appeals; in Rome a great deal was done. There was legislation drastically cutting down the number of appeals in any case and, in particular, in Justinian's law, forbidding altogether appeals on interlocutory points. These had to be reserved to the general appeal, if any.

9. JUDGEMENT

Judgement in the classical procedure was always for money. Hence there could never be, technically, judgement for specific performance,[1] except indeed where it was the same thing. In fact over the main field of obligations there was nothing of the kind. But in actions *in rem*, i.e. actions to enforce rights *in rem*, and a few others, there was a device, the *arbitrium* clause, which gave a somewhat similar result. When the *iudex* had made up his mind in favour of the plaintiff, he made a *pronuntiatio* to that effect, but before proceeding to give judgement he could, if he thought fit, direct the defendant to make restitution *in specie*. If the order was disobeyed there would be a money *condemnatio*, and if the disobedience was wilful, the *condemnatio* might be based on a valuation by the plaintiff,[2] under oath, and we are told that in such a case the plaintiff's veracity was not severely scrutinised, so that the valuation

---

[1] The classical law, like our common law, aimed, not at making a party carry out his contract, but at making him pay for not doing so.

[2] It is just possible that this may be the source of the corresponding incident in our action of detinue, in which the plaintiff had to value the chattel he claimed. If that is so, then Roman law is responsible for one of the most momentous of all the principles of our law, namely, the division of property into real and personal; for it is by reason of the presence of this option available to the defendant to pay the value of the chattel (as estimated

would usually be high, operating as a penalty on the recalcitrant defendant.[1] There is a text of Paul[2] which might mean that actual delivery might in classical law be compelled under a sale, but this would conflict with all the other evidence, and it probably means no more than that non-delivery or non-*mancipatio*, as the case might be, would be ground for an action, with no reference to the method of enforcement. In the later *cognitio* system when the *iudex* was an official, things were altered, and he had power in any action to condemn *in ipsam rem*, and the magistrate would see that the order was obeyed, *manu militari* if necessary. This goes further than our law, for there is no suggestion that he is not to do this if damages would be an adequate remedy: there is nothing subordinate about this specific performance. Texts in the Code suggest that condemnation *in ipsam rem* was then the usual course, but there is very little sign of actual operation of the rule in ordinary contractual cases. In the Digest it is usually assumed that the *condemnatio* will be for money. The explanation may be that in the Digest the language of the jurists is reproduced without reference to the actual change of practice. The Digest has many survivals of this kind, a fact which is helpful to legal historians, though they must have been stumbling blocks to contemporaries who had to administer the law as it stood in the *Corpus Juris*.

10. PRESCRIPTION: LIMITATION AND ABATEMENT OF ACTIONS

Prescription, the exclusion of an action by a lapse of time from the occurrence of the facts on which the claim is based, is not handled alike in the two systems. In classical

---

by the plaintiff), instead of restoring to him the chattel itself, that Bracton bangs, bolts and bars the door against the inclusion of the action of detinue amongst actions *in rem*, thus marking off personal from real property: see *Bracton and Azo*, Selden Society, vol. viii, ed. by Maitland, pp. 172, 173, and P. and M. ii. pp. 174, 175.

[1] D. 12. 3. 11.   [2] Sent. 1. 13a. 4.

law, with a few exceptions of no great importance, civil law actions were not subject to any such limitation: they were *perpetuae*, not barred by any lapse of time. Thus *vindicatio* of property was perpetual. It is true that it might be met by a defence that the claim was no longer true, since the defendant had acquired the thing by *usucapio*, which, it must be remembered, had several requirements other than mere lapse of time.

The Romans kept quite distinct the notions of barring an action and of acquisition of property by long enjoyment. Our law has failed to grasp this distinction and deals with these two different matters in an empirical and frequently puzzling manner. It seems that neither our legislature nor our judges have ever faced squarely the relevant questions of principle, and the result is that any writer who seeks to discover an underlying theory, and does not merely state the law as he believes it to be, finds himself in difficulty. In the first place, it is believed to be true to say that our only *direct* recognition that lapse of time can be a means of acquiring property occurs in connexion with easements and profits, and we usually reserve the term 'prescription' for this case. Here we have something approaching *usucapio*. In minor respects the conditions of the two systems differ, but the effect is the same; both are positive means of acquiring title, and the Act of 1832 tells us that after an enjoyment of so many years, 'the *right*...shall be deemed absolute and indefeasible'. Accordingly, our prescription of easements and profits is sometimes called acquisitive prescription.[1]

On passing from easements and profits to land and moveables, we enter the sphere of limitation of actions, and all we find is that a new possessor's defeasible title has become indefeasible by the extinction of the former title, a consequence now normally attached to the limitation of the action.

[1] See further pp. 132 *sqq.*, *ante*.

Since the statutory provisions create the bar of a claim, not a mode of acquisition, the period runs only from the time when there was an adverse possessor: there can be no claim if there is no wrong. It has, however, been construed to require more than this. In *Trustees, Executors and Agency Co.* v. *Short*,[1] in which the Judicial Committee were applying an Australian statute in the same terms as those of the Act of 1833, it was held that not only must there have been an adverse possession to ground the action, but that this adverse possession must have continued throughout the twenty years (the period required by the Act of 1833); to quote Lord Macnaghten,

if a person enters upon the land of another and holds possession for a time, and then, without having acquired title under the statute, abandons possession, the rightful owner, on the abandonment, is in the same position in all respects as he was before the intrusion took place.[2]

This view is now confirmed by Sect. 10 (2) of the Limitation Act, 1939:

Where a right of action to recover land has accrued and thereafter, before the right is barred, the land ceases to be in adverse possession, the right of action shall no longer be deemed to have accrued, and no fresh right of action shall be deemed to accrue unless and until the land is again taken into adverse possession.

It follows therefore that we have in fact no statute of limitations, properly so-called, for real property. What we have is a rule that no lapse of time out of possession *ipso facto* bars the owner, but that it is possible for a holder to have acquired a possessory title, so that not only is the old owner barred, but a new title is created in the sense that what was formerly defeasible is now indefeasible. The result is substantially that of the classical Roman law, where the action to recover the property was perpetual, but might be defeated by adverse *usucapio*.

When we turn to such remedies as are available for the protection or recovery of personal chattels, we find that

---

[1] (1888), 13 App. Cas. 793. For a criticism of this decision see Clerk and Lindsell on Torts, 8th ed. pp. 332, 333.　　　　[2] At p. 798.

if more than one conversion or detention takes place, then time runs from the original conversion or detention, unless possession has been retaken in the meantime. Thus there is a true statute of limitations for personal chattels.

In the later Roman law all actions were limited to thirty years, in general, so that while an adverse possession for the period of acquisition (then longer than in classical law) would, if the other requirements for acquisition existed, of necessity bar the claim, a period of thirty years barred the claim whether the other person had acquired a right or not. The two notions were quite distinct.

Personal actions at civil law were also not normally barred by lapse of time though they might be barred by many other facts, e.g. an action on delict was barred by the death of the wrongdoer. The maxim 'actio personalis moritur cum persona' is not Roman, though there were rules in Roman law which may have suggested it. So far as contract is concerned, and speaking broadly, it may be said[1] that the common law and probably the Roman law had a very early phase in which rights of action on contract were determined by the death of either party; but that was primitive. In the developed systems the maxim does not in general apply to actions on contract at all.[2] But, in the region of tort or delict the rule seems to have been much more severe in our system than in the Roman. With us, at common law, it seems that any right of action in tort was destroyed by the death of either party—a rule which has been much modified by statute and has been almost abolished by an Act of 1934. It is possible that a similar

---

[1] See Goudy, 'Two Ancient Brocards', *Essays in Legal History*, ed. Vinogradoff, 1913, pp. 215 *sqq.*

[2] Personal representatives were formerly unable to recover on contract mere damages for personal injuries sustained by their deceased (see now, however, the Law Reform (Miscellaneous Provisions) Act, 1934, and decisions thereon); but damage to the personal estate, such as medical expenses and loss caused by inability to attend to business, was and is recoverable (*Bradshaw* v. *L. and Y. Railway Co.* (1875), L.R. 10 C.P. 189).

rule was applied in very early Roman law, but in historical times the general rule, with very few exceptions, was that the death of the injured party had no effect on the right, which passed to his *heres*. On the other hand, actions on delicts being penal, the death of the defendant put an end to the liability (except that in later law and to some extent in classical law the *heres* could be sued for any enrichment).[1] This rule remained under the law of Justinian, and there was no such modification as that made in our similar rule by the statute 3 and 4 Will. IV, c. 42, permitting actions against personal representatives for certain torts of the deceased, subject to certain limits of time.

Turning to praetorian actions we get a very different state of things. Most of these, except in so far as they were merely amendments and extensions of civil remedies, were subject to an extraordinarily short period of limitation, usually one year. It was an artificial year, being in fact a year of days available for litigation, so that it might be a great deal more than a calendar year, but it is extremely short. Why the Praetors took this line is not clear. It may be because most of these actions were originally thought of as penal, though many of them had lost this character in the Empire, and the Praetor's authority being itself temporary, a similar limit was placed on the actions, though the *annus utilis* had in fact no relation to the Praetor's year of office. These short periods still remained under Justinian's law.

One principle which greatly modified the working of the rule does not appear in our law. If an action had reached the stage of joinder of issue, *litis contestatio*, it was no longer affected by a limit of time or by death of a party, though in the case of death there had to be formal steps to substitute a new party, *translatio iudicii*.[2] Here, it may be said, the action technically abated, but practically it did

---

[1] Compare our cases, of which *Phillips* v. *Homfray* (1883), 24 Ch.D. 439 is a type: see p. 346, *ante*.   [2] Buckland, *Text-book*, p. 713.

not. In our law the fact that the action has been begun does not prevent its abatement by death if the cause of action is one which is terminated by death, though it does stop the running of time. Where the action was one which survived to or against the personal representative it was formerly necessary to reconstitute it by a process something like the *translatio iudicii* of Roman law, but nowadays the action simply proceeds with the addition of any necessary party to it. But whether the action is one which survives the death or not, it is in no way affected by a death occurring after verdict but before judgement.

A question wholly distinct from the foregoing is that of the possibility of basing an action on the death of a human being. Apart from an edict which gave an action for a fixed penalty where a man was killed by something thrown from a house,[1] an exception which does not affect the principle, the Roman law allowed no action for the killing of a freeman, and it is a probable conjecture that this is due to the impossibility of valuing a freeman.[2] The evidence is essentially negative: it consists in the existence of many texts giving action for wounding while there is none which gives one for killing.[3] It seems clear that a man's representatives had no action if he was killed and that a *paterfamilias* had no action if his son was killed.

The common law rule known as the 'Rule in *Baker* v. *Bolton*'[4] was stated by Lord Ellenborough C.J. in that case as follows: 'in a civil court, the death of a human being could not be complained of as an injury.' It operates to prevent a person from recovering damages for the permanent loss of the services of a wife (including the loss of her society) or of a child or of a servant, caused by death. In all these cases it is cheaper for the negligent

---

[1] Inst. 4. 5. 1; 9. 3. 1. *pr.*, 5. 5.   [2] See D. 9. 3. 1. 5; 9. 3. 7.

[3] The most significant is D. 9. 2. 5. 3. For discussion and references to the principal texts, see Grueber, *Lex Aquilia*, p. 17. See also p. 364, *ante*.   [4] (1808), 1 Camp. 493.

railway company or motorist to kill the victim outright. The rule, which, in origin, is probably due to confused thinking,[1] has now been upheld by the House of Lords[2] and can be removed only by legislation. This course was recommended by the Law Revision Committee in 1934, but their recommendation was not adopted.[3]

11. DELAY IN SECURING JUDGEMENT

Prescription is distinct from another set of rules which do not seem to have any equivalent in our law. Our judges have a power, regulated by the Rules of the Supreme Court,[4] to dismiss a case or strike it out for want of due prosecution; but there does not appear to be, in ordinary cases, any rule requiring that an action once begun shall reach judgement within a certain limited time. In Roman classical law some actions (*iudicia legitima*) became extinct by the expiration of eighteen months from *litis contestatio*, i.e. from joinder of issue, and others (*iudicia imperio continentia*) by the expiry of the term of office of the magistrate by whom the formula was approved, i.e. in less than a year. We need not discuss the basis of the distinction between the two groups, which does not correspond with that between civil and praetorian actions. The rule was important, since an action which had once reached the stage of *litis contestatio* could never be brought again, unless the facts brought the matter within the rather narrow range of cases in which a man could get *restitutio in integrum*. It is clear that all that is left is a *naturalis obligatio*, which is not directly enforceable.[5] These rules, and the division of the

---

[1] See Holdsworth in 32 *L.Q.R.* (1916) pp. 431–437; 33 *L.Q.R.* (1917) pp. 107–109.

[2] *Admiralty Commissioners* v. *Owners of SS. Amerika*, [1917] A.C. 38.

[3] Interim Report, Cmd. 4540; Law Reform (Miscellaneous Provisions) Act, 1934. The rule does not apply to actions in contract: *Jackson* v. *Watson and Sons*, [1909] 2 K.B. 193.

[4] See *Annual Practice, sub tit.* 'Dismissal of Action'.

[5] D. 46. 8. 8. 1.

actions into these two types, belong to the formulary system. What the rule was in the fourth century is not clear. But, early in the fifth century, Theodosius enacted[1] that actions must be determined within thirty years from joinder of issue, an astonishingly long period, almost long enough for Lord Eldon. This has nothing to do in itself with the rule that all actions must normally be brought within thirty years, though, characteristically, Theodosius mixes the matters up and provides that the beginning of the action shall not stop the running of the normal thirty years' prescription. Justinian, though he preserves some enactments which retain this system, seems to have cut down the duration of the action to three years.[2] But it was now less important, since the rule destroyed nothing but the action: joinder of issue no longer consumed the right, so that there was nothing to prevent the bringing of another action.

12. INTERDICTS AND INJUNCTIONS

The interdict was in point of form very similar to the injunction of our law, and it is probable that the suggestion for the latter came from the former.[3] But, in practice, the differences are more notable than the resemblances. There was of course no such struggle between jurisdictions as has enlivened the history of the injunction. The Praetor, by virtue of his *imperium*, could issue commands and see that they were obeyed, and the earliest interdicts, which were probably mainly concerned with protection of public rights, were issued only after investigation, so that the issue of the interdict was in effect a decision. In historic times they have a different character. They were issued without enquiry on application and as a matter of course. In some respects they resemble interlocutory injunctions (which are sometimes issued *ex parte*); these, however, do

[1] C.Th. 4. 14. 1. A.D. 424.   [2] C. 3. 1. 13. 1.
[3] Spence, *Equitable Jurisdiction*, i. pp. 669, 670.

not go as of course, but only where harm is imminent and normally with some kind of undertaking from the person claiming the injunction that damage to the other party shall be made good if it proves that the injunction ought not to have been issued. The protection to the other party in Roman law was on different lines. The interdict states the conditions in which its command becomes operative. 'Produce that freeman whom you unjustly detain'; 'Restore to the plaintiff the land from which you have ejected him by force and arms.'[1] If the facts were not so the order could be safely disregarded, while with us the order must be carried out subject to a right of compensation if it proves to have been wrongly issued. The fields of application are different. Interdicts were not used as a way of enforcing contracts, or in delict. There is no sign of an interdict forbidding defamation. They are essentially for the protection of public rights or of property in a wide sense. In this field they often, even usually, deal with what we should call torts, e.g. interference with a right of way, but it must be remembered that such things in Rome were not dealt with by delictal actions.

Possessory interdicts are the best known. Through the possessory actions of Justinian and the *actio spolii* of the canonists, they are remote ancestors of our possessory assizes,[2] which, however, they do not much resemble. They are like interlocutory injunctions (which, however, have nothing especially to do with possession), in that they presuppose an outstanding question of right, not disposed of in the interdictal procedure. As we have seen,[3] the question of right could not be raised in possessory proceedings. Thus they were provisional, but this is due not to a characteristic of interdicts, but to the provisional nature of possession. Many of the interdicts are final, especially, but not exclusively, those protecting public rights.

[1] D. 43. 29. 1. *pr.*; Lenel, *Ed. Perp.* p. 467.
[2] Maitland, *Forms of Action*, p. 321.   [3] P. 70, *ante*.

Restitutory interdicts in certain of their aspects resemble our mandatory injunctions, but, narrow as their field was, it was wider than that of the mandatory injunction, which is used to compel a defendant to remove an obstruction or to restore something to its condition at the time of the plaintiff's complaint. The restitutory interdicts were used mainly for the restitution of property or for the putting right of interferences with public rights or easements and the like. They never prescribe a course of conduct, but only order a specific thing to be done, and the point to which we have already adverted, the exact statement in the order itself of the conditions on which it is to be operative, prevents it from doing injustice. Thus part of the work of these interdicts is done, with us, by means of actions for the recovery of land or chattels.

The interdict is essentially the initiation of a piece of litigation, so clearly so that in later law it was replaced by an action, a change which might well have been made centuries earlier. The injunction, interlocutory injunctions apart, is the last stage in the process: it is the result of a decision. Hence comes a great difference in the effect of the issue of the order. To disobey the injunction is a contempt of court, likely to lead to sequestration, imprisonment or fine. There was nothing of this under the interdict. Indeed, nothing is more remarkable than the contrast between the strenuous language of the interdict and the comparatively feeble way in which it was enforced. The words of the order are imperative and uncompromising: 'vim fieri veto'; 'exhibeas'; 'restituas'. But if it is disregarded the result is only an ordinary litigation, in rather complicated form, in which the question thrashed out was whether the conditions making the order operative actually existed, and which resulted, if this proved to be so, in an ordinary condemnation for money. It is true that in the procedure under the interdict pressure might be put on the defendant to make actual restitution by means of the *arbitrium* clause already considered.[1] If the defendant, however, was recalcitrant and preferred to pay the high valuation rather than to restore, the plaintiff had to put up with this: there was no question of anything like a mandatory injunction. There is however a text which gives another possibility. Where the wrong continued the *iudex* might allow a new interdict so that the defendant might be repeatedly penalised,[2] a process somewhat like the repeated fining inflicted by the Court of Chancery in *Awbrey* v. *George*.[3] But this was exceptional: we find it only in a case of detention of a freeman, where damages obviously did not suffice. It would not avail where as in questions of property or possession payment of the damages vested the right in the defendant, so that the wrong was ended, or where the wrong was done once for all, e.g. by building or destroying in defiance of an order. Such an order was discharged on satisfaction and no new order would be of any use, since there would be no new disobedience.

In later law under the new procedure the orders of the Court might be directly enforced by its officers.[4] But an order to rebuild or to pull down could not be enforced in this way; the old indirect methods alone were possible in the absence of powers of coercion, such as that of commitment exercised by the Court of Chancery. It was only in connexion with the production or delivery of things in dispute that the Roman methods, even of the later law, could have been very effective.

---

[1] P. 412, *ante*.   [2] D. 43. 29. 3. 13.

[3] (1600), Monro 757, as cited by Ashburner, *Equity*, 2nd ed. p. 31. See also Amos and Walton, *Introduction to French Law*, p. 186, for the practice of enforcing a judgement specifically by *astreintes*.

[4] P. 413, *ante*.

INDEX